MAYA EXPLORER

John Lloyd Stephens *and the Lost Cities of Central America and Yucatán*

Maya EXPLORER

John Lloyd Stephens *and the Lost Cities of Central America and Yucatán*

by VICTOR WOLFGANG VON HAGEN

CHRONICLE BOOKS • SAN FRANCISCO

First paperback edition published 1990 by Chronicle Books
by arrangement with the University of Oklahoma Press.

Cover illustration redrawn from THE ANCIENT
MAYA, Fourth Edition, by Sylvanus G. Morley and
George Brainerd; revised by Robert J. Sharer, with the
permission of the publishers, Stanford University Press,
copyright © 1946, 1947, 1956, 1983 by the Board of
Trustees of the Leland Stanford Junior University.

Printed in the United States.

Library of Congress Cataloging in Publication Data

von Hagen, Victor Wolfgang, 1908-1985
Maya explorer: John Lloyd Stephens and the lost cities
of Central America and the Yucatán/by Victor
Wolfgang von Hagen.
p. cm.
Reprint. Originally published: Norman: University
of Oklahoma Press, 1947.
Includes bibliographical references.
ISBN 0-87701-703-4
1. Stephens, John Lloyd, 1805-1852. 2. Mayas−
Antiquities. 3. Explorers−Mexico−Biography. 4.
Explorers−Central America−Biography. 5. Yucatán
Peninsula−Antiquities. 6. Central America−Antiquities.
I. Title.
F1435.S86V6   1990
972.81′016−dc20   89-48101
                                                              CIP

Distributed in Canada by Raincoast Books
112 East Third Avenue, Vancouver, B.C., V5T 1C8

10 9 8 7 6 5 4 3 2 1

Chronicle Books
275 Fifth Street
San Francisco, CA 94103

For VAN WYCK BROOKS
who delivered John Lloyd Stephens out of
a literary limbo and rediscovered him in
The World of Washington Irving, and who
encouraged me to write this book on the
discoverer of the Mayas.

Contents

Which Briefly Introduces Mr. Stephens

"In his own way, John Lloyd Stephens, like so many other artists and writers, was one of the discoverers, in the forties, of the American scene. He revealed, at least in part, the visible past of a Pan-America that was scarcely as yet aware of its own existence. . . . For in style, in the quality of his imagination, in his sombre sense of the flight of time, Stephens was one of the few great writers of travels. . . ."—Van Wyck Brooks, *The World of Washington Irving.*

In the humid silence of the jungle, a young man, bearded in a reddish frenzy of Dundreary-like whiskers, stood unwontedly mute before the cyclopean walls of ancient Copán. The effect of his discovery on him was rhapsodic—something like the feeling that the poet Keats expressed upon seeing Greek sculpture for the first time. Yet, for this young American, it was utterly different, for in the discovery of time-mythed Copán—which still exhibited its bizarre sculpture despite the enveloping embrace of jungle—he was actually beginning the discovery of a new world within a new world. This was not an isolated ruined city, but a city of an entire culture, then without name, without history. Copán was a lost city of the Mayas, and its rediscoverer was John Lloyd Stephens, a New York lawyer. On that November 17, 1839, a new world, a new science—American archaeology—came into existence.

Even this science might have been delayed had it not been for Stephens, the writer, for these archaeological discoveries—told, as they have never been told since, in a delightful style overflowing with anecdote and salacious adventures—went streaming through ten editions in three months, establishing Stephens as a discerning archaeological dilletante and a gifted writer, laying the foundation (so excellent his judgments) on which Maya archaeology has since rested. And not alone this. For from that day forward, the whole American continent from Alaska to Patagonia became one vast laboratory for men who pursued the broken shadows of Archaeos, searching for the broken fragments of man's protohistory on the American continent. Stephens was the immediate cause of all this. Moreover, as is seldom the case in first discoveries, his judgments have withstood the test of time and a century of investigation; so much so that an archaeological scientist, Dr. S. G. Morley, author of *The Ancient Maya* and not given to unearned compliments, has said of him: "Stephens enriched Maya archaeology with an interest and romance and charm which have never been equalled."

By this time John Lloyd Stephens has taken his place among that handful of men of kindred horoscope who were the discoverers of lost civilizations: Heinrich Schliemann, the little German gold seeker, who, taking Homer at his word, dug out high-walled Troy in the Turkish hills of Hissarlik; Paul Émile Botta, who escaped the French Consular Service to unearth the Assyrian civilization in the hills of Mesopotamia; and Sir Arthur Evans, who discovered in Crete the Palace of Minos, "where Daedalus wrought in broad Cnossos for fair-haired Ariadne." Yet Stephens, in a sense, is even greater than these, for he was an American discovering an American civilization, with scarcely a published history and little tradition, a fact fully recognized by Latin American scholars who unhesitatingly call Stephens "*el padre del Mayismo*," "the father of Mayaism."

Yet he was no dry-as-dust scholar; he was not one of those inwardly consumed, half-remembered writers who had to wait until a later century for recognition. In his own time—the generation of Poe, Prescott, Bancroft, and Humboldt—he was fully appreciated, and his contemporaries wrote significant encomiums. As the pace and pattern of his life were those of a man of action, he was more, to them, than the man who rediscovered a lost culture. He was a *littérateur* who wrote four excellent books, an empire builder who gave substance to a fabulous dream—the bridging of the Panama isthmus—a lawyer, a diplomat, a businessman, a world traveler, an admirer of the ladies in Casanovese fashion; in short, a remarkable man of a remarkable era.

This, then, is Stephens' portrait—the zestful vertebrate, John Lloyd Stephens, along with vignettes of his contemporaries who, like himself, were cast in the alembic of "Manifest Destiny." Here will be Frederick Catherwood, the English artist who traveled with him, and William Hickling Prescott writing his "Conquests"; Fanny Calderón de la Barca with sharp tongue and agile brain; and Albert Gallatin, Andrew Jackson, Martin Van Buren, Baron Humboldt, Philip Hone, the incredible Count Waldeck and the whole concourse of the Knickerbockers; and all those other half-remembered, half-forgotten names of men who laid the basis of America's intellectual life before Manifest Destiny gave check to its *rinascimento*. But this Stephens portrait, it must be owned, will not have a Boswellian distinctness, for most of his journals, letters, and papers are lost, and the intimate details are in many places a complete blank. But out of the dust of a century, John Lloyd Stephens will here appear mostly as he drew himself, and as against the background of his time.

It has been a long, extensive literary expedition to dig out "Mr. Stephens," to piece together the broken potsherds of his life, as much the work of an archaeologist as a biographer. This has not alone been the unhelped industry of the author. So many people have aided in the cleansing of these Augean stables, so long the list of gracious and generous people who have assisted, that a separate chapter is given to these acknowledgments.

Now—Mr. Stephens and his New Jersey genesis.

V. W. v. H.

Westport, Connecticut,
February, 1947

Acknowledgments John Lloyd Stephens has been restored to something of his zestful living self only by the unselfish aid of many persons and institutions. Foremost is Mr. Van Wyck Brooks, who not only urged me to complete the Life of Stephens when I emerged from the army, but graciously permitted me the use of his Westport, Connecticut, home during the winter of 1945–46. In his library most of this book was written.

The librarians of the University of California (Los Angeles) and the Huntington Library at San Marino, California, were very helpful; and Mr. James T. Babb, librarian of the Sterling Library at Yale University, allowed me the full use of the extensive collections there. The Library of Congress searched for obscure titles, photostating many items unobtainable elsewhere. Mr. Roscoe R. Hill, archivist of the National Archives, aided greatly in the search for Stephens' diplomatic correspondence. In New York, I had the invaluable aid of Miss Dorothy C. Barck, librarian of the New York Historical Society; the staff of the New York Public Library; Mr. Milton Halsey Thomas, curator of Columbiana, within Columbia University; Miss Bartlett Cowdrey, of the Old Print Shop; and a very charming lady, Mrs. Sarah C. W. Hoppin, of Oyster Bay, who spared neither expense nor time to help me find the loose ends of Mr. Stephens.

In New Jersey, I had the good fortune to meet Miss Louise Hartshorne of Middletown, the granddaughter of Charles Hendrickson (cousin to John L. Stephens). She searched for and found the Hendrickson correspondence used in this biography. At the Monmouth County Historical Society, I enjoyed the hospitality of Mr. and Mrs. W. S. Holmes, who allowed me to browse in their collections which gave background to Stephens' life; from New Jersey, Miss Virginia Stiles Burnett, curator of special collections of the Rutgers University Library, made researches for me on the Stephens family which were truly encyclopedic.

In Boston, where my researches naturally carried me because of the relation of Stephens and Prescott, I had the excellent assistance of Mr. Allyn B. Forbes of the Massachusetts Historical Society, far, far beyond the "call of duty." And there, in Boston, I had the pleasure of meeting Dr. Godfrey L. Cabot (the son of Dr. Samuel Cabot who traveled with Stephens in Yucatán in 1842), who prepared for me a brief memoir of his father that it might be used in *Maya Explorer*.

Mr. Albert Williams of New Haven, who, himself, began a life of Stephens for his doctorate but then abandoned it when there was not sufficient autobiographical material, generously allowed me to use that which he had collected.

And there are many others—Dr. A. M. Tozzer of Harvard, Dr. A. V. Kidder of Carnegie, Dr. S. G. Morley, who gave me great aid from Yucatán, Mr. Hans Lenz of San Angel, Mexico, D. F., who copied numerous obscure papers for me, Mr. J. Eric Thompson, Mrs. Ruth Lapham Butler of the Ayer Collection of Newberry Library, Mr. Samuel T. Fisher of Litchfield, and Miss Frances L. Hepburn of Boston—to name but a few.

To all these gracious, helpful hands who made John Lloyd Stephens live again, the author expresses his deepest gratitude.

MAYA EXPLORER

John Lloyd Stephens *and the Lost Cities of Central America and Yucatán*

Chapter 1   The innkeeper of Shrewsbury Towne, Josiah Halstead, dispensing his week-gathered gossip, some old, some new, along with his hot buttered rums, had two items to relate to the Monmouth County farmers of New Jersey who gathered in his tavern: the destruction of the French fleet at Trafalgar by Lord Nelson, and the birth of a son to Clemence Stephens on November 28, 1805.

This Shrewsbury, where every personal event was warp and woof of the social fabric, had more than superficial interest in the matter of its latest addition, for this new "Stephens" was, on his mother's side, a Lloyd, and the Lloyds had been associated with New Jersey ever since settlers had come to Monmouth. In 1743 John Lloyd, who was to provide name and ancestry to his famous grandson, was born in Imlaystown. When the Revolutionary War came, he quickly espoused the rebel cause and, exhibiting superior attainments, was commissioned a captain in Waddell's Company. At first these Loyalists, led by Governor William Franklin, the affable, engaging bastard son of Benjamin Franklin, had the uppermost hand, until the leader was arrested in the name of the Continental Congress and packed off, amidst insult, to imprisonment. All imperial authority now dissolved, and local revolutionary committees took over. Then, in July, 1776, General Howe arrived with a hundred sail, dropped anchor off Sandy Hook, landed his troops on Staten Island, and not long after occupied the best lands of Sussex and Monmouth counties. Washington appeared to oppose the British, but with his raw troops he was able to offer only guerrilla warfare, and was forced to retreat deeper into Jersey.

For two years Captain John Lloyd fought the discouraging guerrilla fights of George Washington's strategy. Then when the rebels took the offensive in January, 1777, he resigned his commission and began supplying Washington's troops. An excellent mixture, one part patriotism, two parts profit, John Lloyd made a palatable dish out of his *olla podrida*—and a sizable fortune from his army contracts.

While war still convulsed the Jersey land, John Lloyd married Sarah Couvenhoven, by whom, before she died, he had two children. After the death of his first wife, he married, in 1776, Anna Longstreet and, on her demise, a widow, Mrs. Elizabeth Brown. Finally, when he was a patrician, Judge John Lloyd of the Inferior Court of Common Pleas, he married, for the fourth and last time, his cousin, Elizabeth. Out of these plural marriages—although conducted one at a time—he sired what he felt a malediction and an affront to his masculinity—five daughters. All of them married gentlemen of Monmouth. The last to marry, and Judge Lloyd's favorite, was Clemence, the youngest. A delicate child, whose features were endowed with the generous Lloyd nose and brilliantly high-lighted eyes, she was of a romantic turn of mind. At the age of fourteen,[1] Clemence Lloyd was married to Benjamin Stephens, house carpenter and merchant of Shrewsbury Towne.

Benjamin Stephens, twice the age of his young bride, was, by the time of his marriage, a man of some substance in the township. Of middling height, strong-featured and stern-willed, his dress reflected his simplicity—coarse homespun knee-breeches of the Jerseyman, cotton stockings, and buckled shoes—no outward ornaments to make him look like a popinjay. A prototype of Thomas Jefferson's *American*, farmer and house carpenter, Benjamin Stephens was, like the other men of the province, grim and strict, one of those Jerseymen who "counted their pennies and held their tongues." He was a member of the petit bourgeois; a strait-laced monitor not given to speculations either in business or in morals. Born on June 11, 1771—an issue of the "Stevenson affair"—he was baptized at Christ Church, Shrewsbury. The circumstances surrounding his birth brought him very close to that colonial church with its tall, white spire decorated with an English crown on its

---

[1] The records are not clear. Clemence was married either on May 31, 1798, or October 17, 1802. If the latter date is accepted, she would have been eighteen—which seems the more correct as her first child was born in 1803.

weather vane; for not long after the vestrymen met to decide in what direction "the corner of the new church be fixed," his future mother, Amelia Shepherd, was exposed to the "Trouble." The "Trouble" it hardly need be mentioned, was that devil "sex," which, when he appeared in the little hamlet, eyes aflame with desire, metamorphosed into Shore Stevenson, a young resolute buck of infinite tongue who followed young Amelia to the home of her father. When later it became known that Amelia was with child, great was the consternation in the Shrewsbury township; for while America then enjoyed extramarital relations when there was "anticipated marriage," it was socially unforgivable to sire a bastard. Shore Stevenson made no offer of marriage; he kept beyond the law, appearing at home only on the Sabbath, at which time he was immune from arrest. His mother, in an attempt to mitigate the problems arising from the "Trouble," wrote Amelia's father, and Thomas Shepherd in Jovian wrath replied to her, April 27, 1771:

". . . I do not imagine you would attempt to vindicate your son's conduct in this unhappy affair . . . we may justly conclude that a person so devoid of all honour as to carry on such an affair intirely upon dishonourable designs and with no other view but the accomplishing his end with the ruin of the person & family is such an one whose word or assertions can be but verry little relyed upon. . . . You blame me for permitting the use of my house to yr son without being informed of his designs   if every scoundrel could be known at first sight we might be always guarded against them. . . . I took him for a person of probity and honour and concluded the son of such a father could not possibly be gilty of such mean and base conduct. If [I] understand your letter you in comparing the character of the two persons give the preference greatly in your sons favour for to press him to joyn the other person you seem to conclude would be ill done and not agreeable to the mind of a candid person but notwithstanding all this and all his schemes and . . . must think her much preferable to his for the great & only blot in hers is the misfortune of haveing kept company with the ungenerous and unjust Shore Stevenson. . . ."

On June 11, 1771, Amelia gave birth to a son. As prescribed by custom and law, she had her thrashing and her father paid a heavy fine to the community. Shore Stevenson was banished. Amelia appeared alone at the parish to have her son baptized. She named him, for reasons now fully obvious, Benoni ("Son-of-my-sorrow") Stevenson.[2]

By the time the world had spun into the new century, Shrewsbury had almost forgotten that Benjamin Stephens had once been Benoni Stevenson. He was a vestryman of Christ Church, a propertied man (all the result of his own industry), and a merchant owning his own sloop, moored at the Shrewsbury estuary, in which, twice monthly, he took the produce of his farms to New York. Benjamin Stephens was no longer a house carpenter but a rising merchant of Jersey, with a store on Greenwich Street in New York City. In 1803 he bought a house on the Four Corners in Shrewsbury, across from Christ Church, and there he brought his girl-wife, Clemence. It was a small, unpretending, gambrel-roofed house which had been erected in 1746 (in the chimney of the room that was kitchen, sitting room, and part bedroom they found an inscribed brick of the original builder. *"Michael White, his brick, 1746").*

As for Shrewsbury, it was one of the oldest settlements in New Jersey, and the *American Gazeteer* of 1805 listed it as a place where "much genteel company from Philadelphia and N. York resort during the summer months for health and pleasure." Historically it was a village of importance. It was listed by Dr. Samuel Breese as a post town "12 miles east from Freehold, 50 southeast from Trenton . . . containing 12 or 15 dwellings, an Episcopalian and Presbyterian church, 1 tavern and 2 stores." This simple detailing gave small idea of its influence. Ever since New Jersey had been settled under the Monmouth patent, Shrewsbury had been a religious center. As early as 1672 the Quakers erected their first meetinghouse, and to it, three years later, came George Fox, its founder. It drew other sects, too, Episcopalians, and stern-faced, strait-laced Presbyterians, all of whom built parish houses within a prayer book's throw of each other. Those who settled in the

---

[2] On the foxed, water-stained pages of the records of Christ Church, Shrewsbury, there is the name of "Benoni Stevenson," baptized in that church on December 18, 1770 (surely an error for 1771). The name is scratched out and under it, in pencil, "now Benjamin Stephens of New York."

6

glebe about Shrewsbury found it rich soiled, easy to farm, and, as it was well watered by the estuaries, a good land for cattle. In addition, the Shrewsbury River offered a haven for small ships, from which, once clearing "Sandy point under the Main," the farmers could sail their earth produce to New York City within three hours. It is little wonder that an English traveler who journeyed to the New Jerseys in 1708 "rechon'd Shrewsbury the chief town of the Shire," and its inhabitants generally industrious, "shunning the public vices which beget Idleness and Want." Shrewsbury, one of the "Two Towns of the Nevysink," with its well-tilled fields, peaceful and idyllic, was enthusiastically recommended to the prospective English emigrant as the "Garden of America . . . the best country I have seen," said Andrew Burnaby, "for men of middling fortunes and for people who have to live by the sweat of their brows."[3]

In this little old Shrewsbury, Clemence Stephens began, at once, her long list of accouchements. First a daughter, who was named Amelia Ann, then a son, called Benjamin after him who sired him. The third child, also a son, conceived during the terribly contested presidential campaign of Thomas Jefferson, was born on November 28, 1805. To honor the old Judge, her father, she named him John Lloyd Stephens.

[3] Being closely questioned by Londoners desiring to emigrate, a traveler was asked "if there were no lawyers in the Jersies." No! "And are there any Physicians?" No, nor parsons, added the gentleman. "Upon which they cr'd What a happy place it must be and Worthy of the Name of Paradise."

Chapter II At the age of thirteen months John Lloyd Stephens by force of circumstance became a New Yorker. Ever since the year of his marriage in 1802, his father had maintained offices at 185 Greenwich Street, a narrow cobblestone street which paralleled the Hudson River. There, in the year 1806, memorable for the inclemency of its weather, Benjamin Stephens brought the whole of his family and installed them in the Dutch-gabled second floor of his Greenwich offices.

New York City was then "only fourteen miles around," a little, overgrown Dutch village with crooked and winding streets lined with trees, so many trees in truth, sighed the city fathers, that it was injurious "for the health," and a fine of £5 was posted for tree-planting south of Catherine Street, "except in front of churches." Houses, mostly in the Dutch fashion, high-peaked with gabled ends and weathercocks, lined the unpaved New York streets, where dogs and scavenger pigs scrambled for refuse tossed there by housewives. Despite the "drowsy ruminant Dutch," New York was cosmopolitan enough, with a sprinkling of French, Swedes, Germans, and Irish to swell its population to 60,000 freemen and 3,456 slaves, and quaint enough to please the Knickerbockers with its "Kissing Bridge," "Maiden Lane," and "Canal Street." Three banks were deemed sufficient to handle all of New York's finances, while the postmaster—with ample time for daylight tenpins—kept his office in the basement of his home. The Battery—since City Hall Park was not yet a reality—was the place of promenade and the center of elegance, lined with the residences of the aristocracy, and Bowling Green, the center of popular riots and popular sports, as Stephens remembered, associating the "Green" with his earliest recollections. "It had been my playground when a boy, hundreds of times I had climbed over the fence to get my ball. I was one of the boys who held it long after the corporation of New York invaded our rights." It was the dreamy, casual New York of the Knickerbockers; Brooklyn was a small village, Greenwich Village a potter's field, Hoboken a verdant expanse of Elysian fields where New Yorkers went abroad to enjoy the rural solitude, conveyed by one of the four ferries—the *Firefly*, the *Jersey*, the *York*, and the *Nassau*—that bridged the Hudson. It was the New York of the youthful Washington Irving who was then wandering through its picturesque streets gathering the impressions that would become the immortal *Knickerbocker History*.

America still looked to Europe for its standard in manners and taste; and its society was, quite naturally, a microcosm of England, New York itself being a "little London." Men dressed as they did there, albeit two seasons behind, in powdered queue, white-topped boots, silk stockings, and breeches with buckles; the cloth of their frock coats made from bat's wing, mouse's ear, or drake's head. Cocked hats complemented the revolutionary manners and the formal speech. The dress of women was "Empire," made from materials offered as dordurets, durants, dowlas, fearnaughts, honeycomb, tammies, and tichlenburgs, draped so that the waist was high, and a long sweep of material hid all but the points of their prunella slippers. Their bodies were corseted in things called "shapes," exposing their pallid breasts in disquieting deshabille.

But neither New York nor America was an Arcadia. Below the surface of the land there were deep, ominous rumblings in the body politic. New Yorkers were still on edge from the presidential campaign of 1804 that had sent Thomas Jefferson to the White House for his second term and Hamilton to his grave. The campaign had been one of unbridled bitterness, reaching its climax on the heights of Weehawken, for not only had Alexander Hamilton died at the hand of Aaron Burr, but with him had died Federalism, and as a corollary in its demise the dream of Jefferson that America be a land of husbandmen and "free from the corruptions of industrialism." Pressure from abroad, actuated by the centuries-old struggle for Continental dominance between Great Britain and France, had lapped up to America's very shores; impressments of sailors at sea and seizures of the American vessels created hostilities that produced the Embargo Act of 1807. This was the serpent of Jefferson's "Eden," for manufactures began to spring up everywhere in America to fill the void of the Continental blockade.

Young John Stephens grew up with this America. He was learning to walk when the Expedition of Lewis and Clark was examining the real estate America had acquired with the Louisiana Purchase; he was a bright-eyed, mischievous boy when Pike placed his standard in the Rocky Mountains and when the Burr Conspiracy convulsed the land. He had learned to babble his first sentences when Fulton's steamboat *Clermont* anchored directly in front of his Greenwich Street home, before steaming to Albany. As John Stephens matured, so did his country, and this left a deep impression on him.

Not long after James Madison became the fourth president of the United States, little Clemence died. The Stephens' fifth child, resembling her mother with her great dark eyes and delicate body, had been a favorite in the household. The last of Mrs. Stephens' many accouchements, little Clemence lived only to her first year. After the child's interment, the mother's health, severely undermined by the birth and death, declined rapidly; she ceased to give lessons to her youngest son, John, and he, having reached six years, was sent packing six days the week to the public school of Mr. Boyle.

At school John had his first taste of learning. Reading and making sums were taught by driving them in, and John got so vigorously and incessantly birched on that part of the anatomy which was considered in his day, as he remembered, "the channel of knowledge into a boy's brain," that he outdistanced his fellow pupils. All those years, while he struggled with the mechanics of numbers and the mysteries of the alphabet, America dragged itself through the War of 1812—a meaningless date since war was still being waged in 1815. Stephens was one of the hundreds of small boys in nankeen pantaloons who stood wide-eyed as Commodore Decatur prepared the Battery's defenses for the anticipated attacks of the British. And his was one of the small voices that cheered Captain David Porter when he sailed on the U.S.S. *Essex* with a banner fixed to his masthead: "Free Trade and Sailors Rights."

But Porter's victories in the Pacific, in and about the Galá-
pagos Islands, did not prevent the almost total destruction of
American commerce. The war dragged along inconclusively until
Napoleon, at last pinned down by the Grand Alliance in Paris,
surrendered his throne and with the empty title of Emperor sailed
to exile on the Isle of Elba. With France defeated, England put
vigor into her war with America. Fourteen thousand veterans who
had fought with Wellington were sent to Canada, while General
Ross, with a body of 3,500 men spirited by their victories over
Napoleon, landed in Chesapeake Bay and, joining there with Admiral Cockburn's marines, marched to Washington. President
Madison, accompanied by General Armstrong, marched out to
give battle, but a mere whiff of grapeshot at the bridge of Bladensburg was sufficient to send the Americans in retreat; Madison and
his cabinet took to the woods; "The Race of Bladensburg," Mr.
Boyle contemptuously called it. At last it ended. Young Stephens
was in class the day that the news came of the signing of the peace
at Ghent between Britain and America, and the students were
given a half-holiday, in itself a great event, to help the celebration.

Jacob Radcliffe was His Honor, the Mayor, when in 1815
Benjamin Stephens, still wearing knee breeches and tricornered
hat, took his son John to the Classical School, the gate to Columbia
College. It was conducted by Mr. Joseph Nelson, a Dublin-born
Irishman, well recommended to Stephens, Sr., as one who "was
wonderously good at drill and flogging." Joseph Nelson—a tall,
spare man with mutton-chop whiskers—was an able Latinist, a
Columbia graduate, who very tragically had gone blind in his
senior year. His sisters, like the daughters of Milton, read to him,
in Latin and Greek, and through these assists he developed into
a classicist. Blindness gave him an almost uncanny sense of direction. When a student was asked to recite his lessons, Mr. Nelson
would turn his fixed Oedipus eyes on him, snap open the case of
his large-sized watch, place his left thumb on the minute hand,
and impatiently drum out the seconds. A false translation, a slip
in meter, and in one movement Nelson would snap shut the watch-
case, spring at the student, collar him, and flog him, "making no

11

errors of his own in the matter of quantity." So characteristic was this stance—left thumb on an open-faced watch—that he was portraited thus by an unknown artist.[1]

Stephens' school term was composed of four quarters of twelve weeks each, with holidays of two weeks in the spring and autumn to enable boys who did not live at home to procure changes of clothing suitable for New York's seasons; Fourth of July, Evacuation Day (November 25), Christmas, and New Year's were the only other holidays. This gave young John and the other students quite a good deal of Joseph Nelson. Training was classical, with brief excursions into analytical arithmetic, history, some mechanics, chemistry that savored of the alchemist—the rest was the classics. "While your son remains here," the blind Mr. Nelson said to Benjamin Stephens, fingering his watch, "he will be exercised in Latin and Greek composition; the higher he gets the more he will have of it." And so he did. John remained at the Classical School for three years.

Then in 1817 Clemence Stephens died.

The family had gone to Imlaystown, in New Jersey, just six months before to bury old Judge John Lloyd, and had remained there while the will of the patriarch, dividing his ample estate among his daughters, had been probated. On the way back to New York Clemence took cold, developed pneumonia, and perished six months later in the arms of her husband. Again there was the long trip to Imlaystown and then the interment of Clemence Stephens beside her father. The sensitive nature of young John, who was very close to his mother and from whom he inherited his dark, lustrous eyes, was deeply affected by her death; and it saddened his happiest hour, the escape from Mr. Nelson.

At the age of thirteen—there being then no intermediate school—John Stephens moved on to Columbia College.

Columbia's five faculty members arranged the admissions into college. For boys of thirteen the examinations were formidable:

"No student shall be admitted into the lowest class unless he be

[1] Joseph Nelson still stares with his sightless eyes upon the students of Rutgers University at Kirkpatrick Chapel (for he had been a professor there until his death in 1829).

accurately acquainted with the grammar of both the Greek and Latin tongues, including such rules of prosody as may be applicable to such of the Poets as he is to be examined upon; be master of Caesar's *Commentaries* . . . of the *Orations* of Cicero against Catiline, the Oration for the Poet Archias, and the Oration for *Marcus Marcellus;* of the first eight books of Virgil's *Aeneid;* of the first five books of Livy; of the Gospel according to Luke and St. John and the Acts of the Apostles [for Columbia was intensely Episcopalian]; of Dalzel's *Collectanea Graeca Minora;* of the first three books of Xenophon's *Cyropaedia* and the first three books of Homer's *Iliad.* He shall also be able to translate English into grammatical Latin, and shall be versed in the first four rules of arithmetic, the rule of three direct and inverse, decimal and vulgar fractions, with Algebra as far as the end of simple equations; and with modern geography. The classical examination to be *ad aperturam libri.*"

Young John, nervously twisting his nankeen pantaloons, vaulted over Caesar and Cicero; he did well to bless the memory of that Cerberus of the Classical School; he passed the examination with flying colors and entered Columbia in March, 1818.

The faculty which taught this formidable curriculum was composed of men sufficiently extraordinary for their time: James Renwick, easily the best known, was professor of natural and experimental philosophy appearing in the student's junior year; Henry James Anderson tried to guide the students through analytic geometry and fluxions; while the Reverend John McVickar, known for his moral inflexibility, expatiated on moral and intellectual philosophy, rhetoric, belles-lettres, and political economy. Nathaniel Moore and Charles Anthon taught the classics. The year of Stephens' admission had seen a struggle between the trustees and Professor Moore over the teaching of the classics; they thought that the ". . . seventh book of Caesar ought to be omitted since its heavy tediousness would bring disgust to the students; they recommended that Ovid might cover the chasm between Caesar and Virgil. . . . Students might range with the velocity of Pegasus through the delightful and various scenes of Sallust and Livy, but he would drag his way through the pages of Cicero like a lazy nag under the pressure of its burden."

13

It was Professor Charles Anthon who gave the background to Stephens' life. He was—for a full professor—relatively young, at most only eight years the senior of his students. Rich in learning, exact in his execution of it, he, too, was a Columbia alumnus. He went far beyond the bare requirements of the curriculum and introduced his students to Goethe, Schiller, Herder, and Wieland as a sort of intellectual equipoise to Shelley, Byron, Keats, and Henry Hallam. Although he was America's most famous classicist (he published fifty textbooks), he was also a champion of American letters and one of the earlier admirers of Edgar Allan Poe. Later, much later, when his favorite pupil John Lloyd Stephens wrote his first book and Poe was given his first New York assignment to review it, he was helped by Charles Anthon. Anthon was Stephens' first real influence. To the boy's imagination, spirit, and quickness of perception, Anthon added a dimensional depth; he planted the first germs of humanism. Under his guidance young Stephens developed into a young man of endless curiosity and boundless tolerance, that sort of tolerance which derives from satisfied curiosity.

There were other character-molding influences at Columbia which helped to create the latter-day Mr. Stephens: there were the two pre-fraternal bodies, the Philolexian and Peithologican societies—"established for mutual improvement, oratory and composition." Stephens belonged to both of them, an unusual occurrence, for the societies were rivals. Throughout the college term the societies met to encourage oratory, forensic discussion in programs consisting, in the main, of orations and debates on the questions of the day. "Would it be expedient to extend the benefits of a liberal education to the Female sex?" is the title of one resolution that appears in the ancient, foxed pages of the minutes of the Philolexian Society; another: "That it is theoretically consistent with morality and right that a widower should marry his wife's sister." Young Stephens early exhibited his gifts as a speaker; throughout the minutes one often finds that "The duty of speaking was performed by Mr. Stephens."

After four years of Columbia, in August, 1822, at the stout age of seventeen, Stephens was graduated. Commencement, usually in

John Lloyd Stephens about 1840
From an unpublished portrait by an unknown artist

Contemporary view of Shrewsbury. *Christ Church, erected in 1769, is at the right. Allen House, built in 1667, is at the opposite side of four corners. The Stephens house, slightly obscured by the building in the foreground, is on Sycamore Avenue.*

Columbia College as it appeared in 1820.

From a drawing by Andrew J. Davis

June, had been delayed because of an epidemic of yellow fever. In June a few cases appeared in the neighborhood of Old Slip, then spread through Rector Street, Wall Street, and up Broadway into Columbia. The college closed its doors, business came to a standstill, people poured out of New York into the village of Greenwich, a way "uptown," as far as Fourteenth Street. All streets leading to the infected area—there had been four hundred deaths—were fenced off; at night the city was peopled only by the city watch and sneak thieves.

When at last the epidemic ended, the traditional parade of Columbia graduates, capped and gowned according to custom, marched from the College Green down Broadway to Trinity Church. The janitor of the college, in coarse homespun, led the procession, followed by the students of arts, the candidates for the degree of Bachelor of Arts, former graduates, the band, the faculty, the president, the trustees, the corporation of the city, judges, clergy, "Strangers of Distinction," the regents, and the governor of the state; graduation was then a momentous affair. John Lloyd Stephens, by virtue of his marks, held fourth position in a graduating class of twenty-two. A not overly distinguished class, most of them were destined for either law or clergy. Only one, Edward M. Willett, son of the famous General Marinus Willett, enters our history. A close friend of Stephens, he later married Stephens' sister, Amelia Ann.

Commencement was a day filled with orations, prayers, and music, a tedious ordeal, for the audience was "requested to abstain from everything which does not comport with the solemnity which ought to be observed on such occasions." In midday, as one of the "young Gentlemen of the Senior Class," Stephens delivered an oration. It was no moment for gaiety, and Stephens suppressed his usual exuberance. He had to. His oration, suggesting something of his later interests, was a formidable one: "On the Oriental and Classical Superstitions as affecting the Imagination and Feelings."

It was now time for young Stephens to review all the possible occupations open to him. It was not necessary for him to plan an immediately lucrative profession, for Benjamin Stephens was now one of New York's leading merchants (Stephens and Cowles, 211 Pearl Street), a man of reasonable wealth, residing in widower-hood with his children in fashionable Dey Street. Young Stephens thought of a military career and imagined his slim, trim figure accentuated by an elegant military pelisse going off to battle. He even joined the 197th Regiment of the New York State Militia,[2] but after serving a whole term without once being promoted, he resigned. The clergy, an outlet for men of family, did not appeal to Stephens, for while he was an Episcopalian—held strictly in line by his father—his sense of humor was too much developed for him to become one of those strait-laced monitors. Since he was not at the moment seriously concerned about his future, he allowed himself to dream, to visualize the most enticing and picturesque possibilities of various professions. Finally he elected law. Now there was a profession to fit his talents. He was a good speaker, he had quickness of perception, an agile mind, his social connections were excellent, and business, thanks to father Benjamin, could be easily attained. Therefore, he went to read Blackstone in the office of Mr. Daniel Lord. An able lawyer, this Daniel Lord ("strictly professional, no politics") had gone to Yale and then had read law at Tapping Reeve's Law School at Litchfield. He was, in 1817, already famous for the Supreme Court case involving the seizure of the prize ship *Hiawatha*. Daniel Lord believed that Stephens would make a good lawyer; hence he urged him to attend his old law school at Litchfield. At first Stephens did not like the idea of leaving New York with its theaters, its clubs, and its balls, to go—at least for a year—into "exile" in Connecticut. Then he learned that there was in the same town Miss Sally Pierce's Female Academy. He needed no further incentive. In the last days of September, 1822, John Lloyd Stephens left for Connecticut.

Litchfield, a stately, isolated Connecticut town (although in

2 "I served out my whole term without being once promoted. Men came in below and went out above me; ensigns became colonels and lieutenants generals, but I remained the same; it was hard work to escape promotion, but I was resolute. Associated with me was a friend as quartermaster, with as little spirit of the soldier in him as myself, for which we were rather looked down upon by the warriors of our day."

1823 it ranked fourth in population in the state), lay on a high plateau above the Naugatuck Valley, just east of the Housatonic, and on the main line of post coaches. In 1722 it had been an outpost for the northwest frontier and in 1776 a concentration for arms and supplies, for after the capture of New York City by the British it was on the principal military artery to Boston. Here was born Ethan Allen, the hero of Ticonderoga; here Aaron Burr left the law classes of his brother-in-law Tapping Reeve to enlist, as a private, in Benedict Arnold's expedition to Quebec; here the leaden statue of George III, which once ornamented Bowling Green, had been torn down by the revolutionists and sent to be converted into 42,088 Continental bullets; and here in the autumn of 1823 came John Lloyd Stephens, law student.

He arrived in one of the great creaking four-horse coaches which made connection with the Hudson sloops at Poughkeepsie. Into Litchfield the red coach careened, whips cracking, horns blowing, rattling down the main street past the dignified colonial houses overhung by giant elms. Litchfield was wondrously cosmopolitan despite its minuscule six thousand population. Painted signs overhanging the red-bricked sidewalks announced an importer, a hatter, a bookbinder; and the *Gazeteer* listed the town as having "4 forges, 1 slitting mill, one nail factory . . . 1 paper mill, comb factories, hatters and grain." But it was not its modest commerciality that made Litchfield cosmopolitan but the students it drew from all America to its schools.

Tapping Reeve's Law School, which lived for fifty years after its founding in 1782, managed to turn out, in the course of a half-century, two vice presidents, sixteen senators, fifty members of Congress, two Supreme Court justices, ten governors, five cabinet members, and countless judges, lawyers, businessmen, artists, and writers with the stamp of New England upon them. Miss Sally Pierce maintained the Female Academy, the first finishing school in America, where young ladies of good family learned drawing, music, dancing, reciting, and "other accomplishments very well adapted both to taste and delicacy of their sex." Every state of the Union, every territory of the United States was represented at Litchfield. Even as Stephens stepped out at Grove Catlin's Tavern

17

on the "Green," two coaches pushing up from Danbury brought students from Georgia, Maryland, Virginia, North Carolina, and Delaware. Stephens knew that he would find the law interesting, for one of the first objects that met his eyes was a procession of girls from the Female Academy mincing down North Street, walking under the lofty elms to the rhythm of flute and flageolet.

The Law School was held in a small frame building adjacent to the home of Tapping Reeve. At first, in 1784, Tapping Reeve had given the classes in his home; but as his fame spread and more students arrived, he built America's first law building. Tapping Reeve taught there until he was appointed to the Superior Court and his place taken by James Gould. A former pupil and a remarkably handsome man—his portrait painted on glass still hangs in the American Wing of the Metropolitan Museum—Gould became on the death of Tapping Reeve in 1823 the full proprietor of the school. As the classes grew in size, he employed two former students to assist him in expounding the law, Jabez Huntington, "a bachelor rather above forty who studies, thinks, and talks *law* sleeping and walking," and Origan Seymour, a native of Litchfield. Seymour was only twenty-seven, but much admired by his students for a "sterling mind and manners" and for his brain, "completely identified with the study of *Law*." These were the mentors of Stephens and the other forty-three students of the Class of 1823.

The law, as taught at Litchfield, was most thorough, as its catalog suggested: "... every ancient and modern opinion whether over-ruled, doubted, or in any way qualified, is here systematically digested." Lectures were given in the mornings, six days a week, for an hour and a half while the students took voluminous notes[3]; the rest of the day was spent consulting the authorities. On Saturday afternoon the students were examined on the week's lectures, and on Monday—usually in the evening—occurred the high point of the week: the students held—with Stephens much in the spot-

[3] The curriculum was arranged to cover the whole field of law and was divided, with no set sequence, into forty-eight subjects. Stephens learned of Municipal Law, Baron and Femme, Master and Servant, Contracts, Bailments, Sheriff and Gaoler, Evidence, Writs of Error, Highways, Stoppage in Transit—in fact, all the legal abracadabra that one could learn in the required fourteen months.

light—their moot court, in which they argued hypothetical cases before a court of their own peers.

All this was well worth the yearly one-hundred-dollar tuition, for not only was law propounded in spirited lectures but the student had access to one of the finest law libraries in the country; there one could consult Blackstone's *Commentaries*, Powell's *Elementary Treatises*, Epinasse's *Nisi Prius*, Kyd on *Awards*, Jones on *Bailments, Doctor & Student*, Loveless on *Wills*, Gilbert's *Law of Evidence*, Gilbert on *Devises*, Cunningham on *Bills of Exchange*, and all the other titles that would make an acute legal mind; textual aids to turning out members of a profession whom Philip II of Spain denied entrance to the Americas "since they make disputes where none existed before."

Life in Litchfield was not all Blackstone. The students were quartered with different families in town—Stephens stayed at the Widow Lord's—at a cost of $45.00 the year (board cost $2.75 the week and fireplace wood $4.00 the cord), where he roomed with two students from Georgia, one of whom, Eugenius Aristides Nesbit, became a famous Georgian judge and drafted—beginning the Civil War—the Ordinance of Secession. The Southerners were gay blades wearing pink gingham frock coats, adept at pretty speeches which the young ladies of Miss Pierce's school accepted with violent bosom-heavings. In the winter there were sleigh rides to Goshen and Farrington, with late suppers at the tavern—turkey, oysters, pickles, and cake—and dancing to the tunes of Black Caesar on his cracked fiddle. There were dances at the big ballroom at the United States Hotel given by Miss Pierce for her pupils. In the summer the students played wickets, a form of cricket, and there were picnics with the young ladies. Since the young women were too many to board at Miss Pierce's, they also lived in the homes of Litchfield residents, sometimes in the same spacious colonial houses as the law students, "which allowed," said one Litchfield historian with becoming naïveté, ". . . occasions for companionable intercourse."

John Stephens steered a good course between law and love; he managed, in the fourteen months of his Litchfield sojourn, to finish his law course without, as many of the other students, having himself tied in anticipatory marriage to one of the young ladies of the Female Academy. In September, 1824, in company with many New Yorkers who had courted both the law and the ladies in Litchfield, he returned in one of the high-wheeled red coaches to New York City.

John Stephens did not, like the other Litchfield graduates, hurry to Albany to have himself sworn in as "counselor at law"; instead, to the great surprise of his family he announced—subject, of course, to his father's approval—that he was going to take a trip, a long trip, far out west into the Illinois Territory. Cousin Charles Hendrickson of Middletown, who had come to New York to work with the firm of Stephens and Cowles, had brought one of the latest letters received from Aunt Helena.[4] It was filled with details of life in the West: Indians, prairies, buffaloes, log cabins, floating arks in the then Wild West about Carmi, Illinois, the heart of the Shawnee country. All this aroused John Stephens' latent instincts for travel. Aunt Helena, one of the five daughters of the late Judge John Lloyd, had married a New Jersey Quaker, Caleb Ridgway, and they, in 1819, migrated to Carmi, Illinois Territory, on the banks of the Little Wabash.

Closing her narrative of travel, she asked "that they do not forget they have an Aunt in a far distant land." This John Stephens proposed not to forget. This was to be his *wanderjahre*, his first trip and the genesis of Stephens, the traveler. He and his cousin received the benediction of Benjamin Stephens; then each bought a brace of brass pistols and new boots and homespuns for the long journey. As they left for the West, they passed through New Brunswick, as Charles Hendrickson wanted to say good-bye to his mother, a fearful, tearful ceremony, for Mary Hendrickson was a young widow dearly attached to her children. After they had gone, she wrote them a long letter, dated from Middletown, September 20, 1824:

[4] Charles Hendrickson letters from the collection of his granddaughter, Miss Louise Hartshorne of Middletown, New Jersey, who graciously allowed me to use these letters which she discovered in the effects of her grandfather.

My Dear Son,

This is the eighth day since you and your Cousin John left New Brunswick and I think it has been the longest Eight Days that I had ever experienced. . . . I hope my Son you will not Stay longer than you can possibly help. . . . Tell your cousin John that his Aunt says he must think of her and not make his visit long . . . do not expose yourself to bad weather or travel dangerous roads. . . . O! My Son if you and your cousin John have the good luck to arrive Safe to your Uncle Ridgways I flatter Myself you will be a welcome guest."

Over the national turnpike the adventuring cousins rode, bounding along on one of the blue, fourteen-foot-long Conestoga wagons to the tune of the barbaric jingle of the bells attached to its six horses. By the twenty-sixth of September they had reached Pittsburgh, and Charles Hendrickson instantly wrote his mother that "John and myself are well and eat everything that is put before us. . . . After a plesant ride over the Allegany mountains we arrived safe in this place last Sunday. . . . the reason of our staying at Pittsburgh is to have company down the river. We have been much pleased since we came here in visiting the different factories which this place abounds with, they burn nothing but coal here which makes it a very dirty place. We visited one of the coal pitts which is certainly a very great curiosity you go 100 yards in the ground then their are branches which extend as much farther each way and large Rooms to make the air circulate through, it puts you in mind of another country. . . .

"There was a dreadful time here last Monday Evening between some of the lower class of Citizens and the Circus men, the mob was trying to clear the circus men out of the place and as soon as the performance had commenced for the Evening the mob commenced throwing stones at the house which soon made the audience leave, and as soon as the audience was out they began to tear of[f] the weather boards and the Circus Men fired upon them and *killed* one man dead on the spot and wounded several others."

All of this must have confirmed in Mary Hendrickson's mind that son Charles and cousin John would never reach Illinois alive, but Charles was quick to assure her of the respectability of their company: "Dear Mama we expect to leave hear tomorrow in a keel boat in company with some merchants of Kentucky and Mr. Ramsey a son of Doct. Ramsey of Cincinnati *who all appear to be very respectable men*. The Steam Boats do not run at this season of the year the water being to low they Run from Cincinnati we shall take the Keel to that place and then take the Steam boat to Shawneytown. *P.S.* I forgot to mention . . . we put up at the Pittsburg Hotel in the midst of the Lawyers who are attending the supream Court, John and myself had the honour of being introduced to the late Governor of this State Mr. Finley . . . so Mama you see we are not among wild men yet."

"Fabulous as this West was," Mr. Van Wyck Brooks has written in an inimitable picture, "there were untold thousands of people who knew it. Indeed, in 1800 almost half a million of them already lived west of the Alleghenies, Pittsburgh was a largish town, Kentucky swarmed with pioneers, and Cincinnati, Marietta, and Chillicothe in Ohio were rapidly growing outposts of civilization. Covered wagons crawled along the highways, heading for Wabash or the Scioto, with their furniture, family Bibles, and Watt's hymn-books; and the settlers sent back lumber, wheat and potash in exchange for molasses, hoes, axes, pots and clothes. The Yankee pedlars followed, with clocks, knives, latches, ribbons, essences and books, and, while the ubiquitous log-cabin was the typical dwelling everywhere, one could never tell what a year might produce in the way of an architectural wonder. . . . for Northern emigrants Pittsburgh was the most popular gate of the West, for thence the Ohio followed to the Mississippi. The shores of the Monongahela and the Allegheny that formed the Belle Rivière were lined with keelboats, flatboats, broadhorns and arks, and there one heard already the clang of hammers and the winter snow mingled with the soft-coal smoke that rose from forge and furnace. There, as in other frontier towns, all manner of human beings gathered, trappers, Indian hunters, traders, boatmen, together with the German professors, French nobles in exile and the families of American officers of the Revolution. Beyond the great sycamore groves and the chimneys and coal-hills lay the unbroken forests of the Indian country."[5] And into that West went John

Stephens on his first hegira, the beginning of a lifetime of adventures.

By October 13, 1824 the two young men had reached Cincinnati. Unfortunately Stephens' account of the journey is lost—if it ever existed—but Cousin Charles Hendrickson kept up a running commentary for his mother: "After starting in a keel boat [from Pittsburgh] . . . with 5 passengers besides John and myself we were one week going to Wheeling [West Virginia] which is one hundred miles, you must know that is slow traveling when we arrived at Wheeling we concluded to take the stage direct for this place which we did with Mr. Ramsey one of our fellow passengers in the boat . . . passing through all the principal towns in the State of Ohio." In Cincinnati they hired horses and journeyed out to Colerain Township "to see cousin Lydia Lloyd"; for a branch of the Lloyds had settled there in the eighteen twenties near the holdings of Giles Richards [a merchant who had made a sizable fortune in Boston]. "They do not live quite as comfortable here as the Folks do in Middletown but very good for this part of the world they live in a log house one room and a kitchen on the floor which is something uncommon. . . . Cousin Lydia is very much pleased with this part of the country and says she would not go back for anything I don't admire her taste much. I can tell you, of all the places I have seen Middletown is the place for me."

John Stephens had different sentiments. He had already extended the itinerary beyond Illinois to the Mississippi, and apparently had suggested a trip to Natchez. This thoroughly alarmed Charles' mother: "O! my Son I long to get a Letter after you get to Illinois and hear you begin to talk about coming home. I hope you and your cousin John will have too much prudence to go to Natches, for it is very Sickley there the Yellow Fevour rages very much, if you examin the papers you will see for yourselves I whould not have you both run the risk on any account, I think you both Ought to be satisfied after going so long a jaunt and come home contented. . . . P.S. . . . tell your Cousin John that George Taylor came from New York yesterday left them all well at Uncle Stephens save Benjamin's eye is more troublesome."

[5] Van Wyck Brooks, *The World of Washington Irving*, 91–92.

They were now on the edge of the frontier. It had not been many years before that John James Audubon had kept a store in Louisville, using his off hours from flour and calico to hunt egrets, bitterns, herons, and warblers that enlivened the sparsely settled countryside so that he might paint them for his *Birds of America*. Legends of Daniel Boone—who had died in 1820—still abounded in the village-becoming-a-city called Louisville. The cousins had reached Louisville by steamer from Cincinnati, where they "found water so low [they] could proceed no farther in a steam boat and we did not much like the Idea of going in a keel boat for we had a trial of this before, so we concluded to go no farther until the water [was] high enough to go by steam." Therefore, they went to Lexington to see the races. Charles Hendrickson sought to allay his mother's anxiety: "Dear Mama I suppose you would want to know what kind of company we have fell in with we started from Cincinnati in company with Two Mr Andersons from New York . . . one a merchant . . . the other practising law in Albany and is traveling for his health, they have been very polite to us. we also at this place fell in company with a Mr. Lewis one of our stage passengers from Wheeling to Chillicothe. . . . he introduced us to the family of Mr Martins *who are very respectable people* they are going down to Natches, to spend the winter, they gave us an invitation to wate and go down with them, we however decline[d] excepting it. . . . we intend starting tomorrow from [Louisville] . . . and take passage to Shawneetown . . . so in the course of 10 or 12 days we will be at Uncle Ridgways. . . . Traveling is very pleasant business but it takes the money out of your pocket very fast. I have no time to write more. John is dressing now and keeps all the time hurrying me to do the same."

On November 23, 1824, after "a very tegious passage" from Louisville, John Stephens and Charles Hendrickson arrived in Shawneetown. There they made inquiries about the direction to the matted wilderness of Carmi and Uncle Ridgway. Caleb Ridgway everyone knew, for he was a man of consequence. The Ridgways were a Quaker family and had been merchants in Philadelphia; first came David Ridgway to Illinois Territory, in 1817, then followed his brother Caleb. The first appearance of Caleb Ridgway was in the first Illinois census in 1820 where he was listed as head of a family of "five white males under twenty-one, three white females under twenty-one, and two white females over twenty-one"; eventually he became judge probate of Clay County.

Twenty miles from the mouth of the Little Wabash was Carmi, where the Ridgways lived; and the adventuring cousins, mounted on horses and on the lookout for Indians, were guided to it by a friend from Shawneetown. The land was sparsely settled; they rode for hours without seeing a single house, only an occasional Indian, who silently watched them ride by. Carmi, when they found it, was a post town with less than a square dozen of houses, although it lay, as the *Gazeteer* said, "in lands of good quality."

"It was about dusk when we arrived," Charles Hendrickson wrote to his mother, "and we decided not [to] let ourselves be known. Weed [the guide] went in and asked if we could stay there all night they informed us we could. . . . Uncle Ridgway came home . . . we talked with him some time, none of them knew us, after keeping them in suspence for about an hour we made ourselves known to the great joy of all the family. Aunt Helena said she had not spent such a pleasant Evening since she had been in Illinois, yesterday she was delivered of a fine son and I expect they will call him Benjamin. . . . I will attempt to tell you a little how they have to get along, in the first place Aunt Helena and Elizabeth have to do all the cooking and work of the house. Uncle Caleb and the boys do all the work on the farm. Uncle makes all their shoes himself, this winter he is going to keep school he has commenced and has got about Twenty scholars. You know it must be pretty hard times to drive Uncle Caleb to that. Aunt Helena has went out and worked by the days work herself for the purpose of getting a little necessaries for the family which is what I never expected she would come to."

After a few days with the Ridgways John Stephens set their new goal; they were to go to New Orleans. Charles, completely dominated by his travel-loving cousin, now had to explain the matter to his mother, and it takes no philologist to see the logic of John speaking through Charles' quill: "Dear Mama you write that

I must not go to New Orleans on account of the sickness I can assure you I shall not be in any danger if I can avoid it, but it has got so late in the season that there is no kind of danger. It seems to be a pitty after coming so far not to go there. We have concluded to go and I hope it will meet your approbation. . . . we will go to St. Louis and from there take a steamboat to New Orleans."

St. Louis they reached by December 4, after a long cross-country journey through Illinois, which was thinly settled. There were few houses, and many the night they had to spend in the woods, sleeping around a roaring fire which they had ignited with their pistols. In St. Louis they found a place upon a steamboat that was sailing directly to New Orleans. And the cousins announced to their families that they could be expected home in January, for Charles admitted that he began to "want New Jersey very much. I can tell you there is no place I can find to hold a candle to it. I want to see all I can this time, for I do not think I shall be for takin' another jaunt very soon." The journey had the opposite effect on John Stephens; he wanted to continue to travel and would have gone out West with one of Captain William Becknell's wagon trains had he not been restrained by his promise to his Aunt Mary that he would bring Charles home as soon as possible.

The raw country was then only beginning to feel its strength. It had not been many years before that Schoolcraft had followed the upper sources of the Mississippi and had written his *Journal of a Tour into the Interior of Missouri and Arkansas*, "performed in the years 1818–1819." In that year 1824, land-hungry Americans were gathering in all the frontier cities ready to make the test of the wilderness. On one of the steamboats carrying emigrants (in their fur caps and bearing rifles), the cousins descended to New Orleans. By February, 1825, after doubling back to Gotham in a steam packet from New Orleans, John Stephens was again back in New York City.

John Lloyd Stephens, by the grace of the passage of time, had come of age. Now his face, complying with the beau monde, was festooned in a magnificent set of reddish-colored Dundreary whiskers; his clothes were the extravagant dress of the Knicker-bockers—and he smoked, to the amazement of the urchins and the horror of the ladies, long black cheroots, a habit that he had de-veloped on his western tour. After putting off for three years his admission to the bar, he at last journeyed to Albany in 1827 and was admitted as a lawyer. The same year he appeared, for the first time, in the New York City Directory, listed as "Merchant, 52 Front Street." Young Stephens was not too pleased, one gathers, with this role, but everything had quickened about New York and business was so brisk that Stephens and Cowles had need of the agile-minded younger son of Benjamin Stephens.

New York State had become, with the opening of the Erie Canal—"Clinton's Ditch," the wits called it—an empire state, and the products of the Northeastern states were pouring through the canal, down the Hudson to Manhattan, where quaint old Knicker-bocker New York was suddenly changed. Overnight, it seemed, small businessmen became merchant princes and the middle class became the dominant element, cultural and economic, in Ameri-can life. To keep pace with its financial position New York con-stantly changed its face: "the city is now undergoing its annual metamorphosis," wrote Philip Hone[6] in his diary; "houses are be-ing pulled down, others altered. Pearl Street and Broadway in par-ticular are almost impassable by the quantities of rubbish with

[6] The Philip Hone who will appear often in these pages is an inexhaustible source of information for the period. In the New York Historical Society are twenty-eight quarto volumes of Philip Hone's manuscript diary covering the period between spring, 1821, and spring, 1851. In these two millions of words there is a detailed history of the American scene.

Hone, descendant of a German immigrant named Horne, was born in New York City, on October 25, 1780. At sixteen he entered his brother's business at Pearl Street, near the firm of Benjamin Stephens (whom he knew intimately). He became a cultured man with excellent taste in books, pictures, and music. Every-one soon knew Philip Hone, the tall, handsome gentleman with curling hair, keen blue eyes, and full cheeks. "He looked the man of fashion," writes Allan Nevins, "and his equipage showed him to be a person of means." He was elected mayor of New York in 1825, and after that date, with a generous competence, he gave less time to business and more to the arts and to Whig politics. His diary has been the best source material of the period for details on the personal history of John Lloyd Stephens. There were two extracts made of the diary: one edited by Bayard Tucker (2 vols., 1889), the other by Alan Nevins (2 vols., 1927). There is a crying need for a detailed index of the whole twenty volumes of the diary.

which they are obstructed." The "Greek Revival" relieved only somewhat the uniform solid red brick of the houses, which was the reigning style. Gaslight, under the impulse of commerce, was being introduced; and bathtubs, never mentioned in polite society, were being installed within the houses, commonly enough for the Council of Philadelphia to ordinance against them on sanitary grounds! Under the influence of these *nouveaux riches*, New York exhibited a changing culture, even though the scavenger pigs still ran through the streets.

Politics was the lifeblood of New Yorkers, and the presidential election of 1828 that ushered Andrew Jackson into the White House found no more fervent partisan than John Lloyd Stephens. A copious, clever talker, Stephens fought throughout the campaign for Jackson and continued to do so as long as Jackson occupied the White House. There was discontent in the land, especially with the rise of the new industrialism and the spiraling prices, and with what many believed was "the betrayal of the Jeffersonian promise of equal rights" and the control of capital by a limited few. This brought a new political philosophy into America—and Andrew Jackson was its god. His whole first term in office was hardly more than a prolonged electoral campaign, and as the Nullification controversy convulsed the land, followed by the fight over protective tariff—and the classic struggle of Jackson against Nicholas Biddle and the Bank of the United States—there was, for the ordinary citizen, no middle ground. One was either pro-Jackson or anti-Jackson.

When the government withdrew funds from the Bank of the United States, plunging New York into a financial panic, the Knickerbockers were a house divided. Said Philip Hone, elbowing his way through a mob that surrounded a closed bank: "public opinion means something more than the drilled voices of certain political friends of General Jackson who are pledged, body and soul, to support him at all events." But this was precisely what Stephens was doing. Law, which Stephens practiced from his offices on Wall Street, did not very much hold him; "he never felt," a friend remembered, "much ardour or zeal in the practise of law." Instead, his enthusiasm was directed toward politics.[7]

Throughout the years following Jackson's second election to office, Stephens kept up his political speaking. His weekly appearance at Tammany Hall, the organization founded by William Mooney in 1789 "for the smile of charity, the chain of friendship, and the flame of liberty," was looked upon as an event, for Stephens was, as Rev. Francis Lister Hawks wrote, Tammany's "pet speaker."

New York City as usual held the balance of power for the state, and New York, then as now, was the most potent factor in national politics. Both parties, Whig and Democratic, were jockeying for power in the coming presidential elections. The control of New York City was vital. The Whigs nominated Gulian C. Verplanck ("an able writer on subjects connected with *belles lettres* but he knows little of mankind"); and the Democrats, Cornelius W. Lawrence. It was one of the most riotous elections that New York—a city of riots—had ever seen. Stephens was in the midst of it, much to the consternation of his father, who sided with the merchants against Lawrence. In Stephens' ward—"the Sixth"—there were riots throughout April; "respectable persons were beaten and trampled in the mud," says Philip Hone. The riots increased throughout the day, with many clashes between Whig and Democrat, until at last the mayor had to order out Colonel Sanford's regiment and a troop of horse. To what extent Stephens was mixed up with the rioting is not known, but his law partner, George D. Strong, was specifically accused.[8]

Lawrence was elected by the thinnest majority of 181 votes. But this was only the prelude to the October campaign to elect the governor of New York. William H. Seward was nominated by the Whigs and opposed by William L. Marcy, who had left the Senate to be elected New York's governor to take Van Buren's place when he became Jackson's vice president. It was a violent and hard-fought campaign into which Stephens threw himself with accustomed vigor. Fortunately for Stephens, and for science,

[7] And Philip Hone: ". . . politics occupy all my time."

[8] "This outrage [the attack on the Whigs] has been instigated by a few men in the Sixth Ward—George D. Strong, Abraham Le Roy, Dr. Rhinelander, Preserved Fish, and a few like him. Let them answer for it!"—Philip Hone, *Diary,* April 10, 1834.

his speaking led to a throat infection, and in the midst of the gubernatorial campaign, Stephens was laid low by a streptococcic throat infection, which ended, for the time being, "his politicking."

Let us pay homage to that ogre Politics and to General Jackson, for if it had not been for these, Stephens might have disappeared in life's stream instead of rediscovering the Maya civilization and enriching American literature with the most fascinating of archaeological books. Let us pay homage to those anonymous microscopic bacteria of the family *Coccaceae*, for their hold upon Mr. Stephens' throat was so firm that the family doctor, baffled by their persistence, suggested a trip to Europe for his patient's health.

In autumn of 1834, while the newsboys shouted themselves hoarse over the re-election of William L. Marcy, John Lloyd Stephens embarked for Europe on the packet *Charlemagne*.

Chapter III   Rome, which Stephens reached after Paris, was full of Americans—travelers, artists, writers, and diplomats—most of whom he seemed to avoid. He did make the usual tour of Salerno, Paestum, Beneventum, and even climbed Vesuvius, forgetting in the enthusiasm of his travels that he was sent to Europe for rest. In Naples Stephens met Dr. Marinus Willett, brother of the Willett who had married his sister, and when he heard that he was bound for Greece, he altered his itinerary and, in a leaking tub, sailed with him.

Their first landfall was Missolonghi, famous as the spot where Lord Byron, dressed in a scarlet uniform borrowed from an obliging colonel, landed in January, 1824—and died. At Missolonghi, to remind him of the Greek Revolution, was the widow of Marco Bozzaris, the Greek hero who had been killed at midnight when he attempted the guarded tent of Omar Pasha at Carpensinia. The name of Marco Bozzaris, thanks to the poem written by Stephens' friend Fitz-Greene Halleck, was as well known in America as in Greece. Madame Bozzaris was a tall, stately woman dressed in black, animated by burning black eyes set in a face as white as alabaster; she deeply impressed Stephens. He was also enamored of her daughters, especially sixteen-year-old Constantine, the darkly complected one with dark hair set off by a red embroidered cap "and large black eyes," Stephens said, "expressing a melancholy quiet, but which might be excited to shoot forth glances of fire." Thinking her a "mere child," he had "fully made up his mind to take her on his knee and kiss her; but the appearance of the stately mother recalled him to the grave of Marco Bozzaris."

After that Stephens and Willett sailed through the Gulf of Lepanto, passed the promontory of Actium where Cleopatra, with her fleet, had abandoned Anthony, leaving to Augustus the empire of the world. In those historic waters Don Juan of Austria had humbled the Turkish galleys, and there Miguel de Cervantes had had his hand mangled in battle. Stephens went through Greece, trying to recall his classical history until his head was humming with Homer and Herodotus. At Athens he left Dr. Marinus Willett in the heterogeneous colony of Frenchmen, Bavarians, Americans, and Danes, with a major sprinkling of Greeks, and moved on to the plains of Argos. He traveled lightly—with only a carpet bag—accoutered in stiff coat, grey pantaloons, and black hat. He was followed only by his servant, a fierce-mustachioed Greek. He entered Mycenae, saw the mute remains of its cyclopean walls, and passed under the Gate of Lions where Agamemnon had led out his forces for the siege of Troy. The bare bones of history stood before him, begging to be fleshed with engaging details, and now, for the first time, Stephens excoriated himself for not listening more carefully to his mentor Joseph Nelson when he tried to drive in the classical tales of Greece. But he took notes, filling his journal with impressions of war-torn Greece, for every step from Missolonghi to Argos was marked by the ravages of war.

In 1821 Greece under an awakened nationalism had risen in revolt against its Turkish masters. It was a cannibal war, hostages were slaughtered by both Greek and Turk, and it was to go on for years, eight years of *lèse-humanité*. At first the Greeks held the vantage since they controlled the seas. Then the Pasha of Egypt, called to the aid of the Porte, took Crete and made it a base of operations against the Greeks. It was only a matter of weeks before the Pasha sent home a bagful of maggot-infested ears torn from Greek heads, as evidence of his triumphs, to be nailed to the Great Gate of the Seraglio. Poets raised their voices, volunteers under the generic name of "Philhellenes" flocked to Greece—Napoleonic veterans, Jena students, Russian mystics, Englishmen, a sprinkling of Americans, and disappointed Italian carbonari. The world could no longer maintain a policy of Olympian detachment; and the great powers, as usual, sang the praises of liberty but jockeyed the while for power in the Mediterranean. Metternich of Austria was in constant fear of a *conflagration général*, while Lord Canning, showing himself indisposed to romantic policies, at first remained aloof. Then the Russians, appealed to by their Greek Orthodox blood brothers, made shift to enter the war. A cacophony of diplomatic voices met the maneuver: "Russia," England declared, "was only using the Greek war to gain control of the Bosphorus and find a way into the Mediterranean." The Tsar denied it: "I have no ambition," he shouted, "my Empire is already too big for me."

While Hellas lay torn and bleeding, the Powers haggled over the conference table trying to find a way out of the impasse. They arranged an armistice between Greek and Turk; then maintained, as they had in the latest Spanish revolution, a joint naval patrol—British and French fleets supplemented by Russian ships of the line. Then the sequel. The fleet of the Pasha of Egypt collided with the armistice control, and this became in history the Battle of Navarino; on October 20, 1827, the fleet of the Pasha was totally destroyed. An answer came swiftly enough; the Sultan proclaimed a Holy War against the Christians; Russia declared war against the Turks; and England, fearing that Russia would dictate the peace, had no other choice than to send an expeditionary force to Greece, which ousted the Turk and freed Hellas from its centuries of domination by the Porte.

No struggle, except its own, had aroused America as much as Greece's war of liberation, and huge sums, for the times, were raised in the United States. As a Columbia undergraduate John Stephens had solicited funds for Greece, as a debating student he had orated on Greece, and he knew, it seemed, every campaign by heart. It was only when he stood on the island of Scio that the war's destruction fell full upon him—"women were ripped open, children dashed against the walls, the heads of families stuck on pikes out of the windows of their houses." Then the city was gutted by the Turk. Stephens walked through Scio: "an awful solitude, a stillness that struck a cold upon the heart. . . . We saw nobody and our own voices and the trampling of our horses upon the deserted pavements of Scio sounded hollow and sepulchral in our ears."

His career, although he was then unaware of it, began in the oriental city of Smyrna, in the Levant. This was the birthplace of Stephens the author. There, under the blood-red flag of the Mussulmans, pages of fairy scenes walked before his eyes: caravans led by turbaned Turks, camels walking down the narrow aisles of sun-splashed streets, veiled women of the harems dressed in white, their covered faces effectually concealing every feature and bringing to "bear only the artillery of their eyes," and Tartars, Greeks, Turks, and Franks—it was like the Scheherazade. When he arrived in Smyrna on April 16, 1835, he wrote to Charles Fenno Hoffman: "I have just arrived at this place and I live to tell it," and he proceeded to write in a delightful letter his adventures from Athens to Smyrna. It was a letter rich in detail. He wrote of Greece, Homer, and Scio, he painted verbal pictures of the land, and although at points he damned the Turks, he admitted they had "exceedingly good points: chibouks, coffee and as many wives as they please." He confessed to Fenno Hoffman that the ladies gave him no rest: "I never saw so much beauty . . . such eyes large dark and rolling. And they walk too, as if conscious of their high pretensions . . . under that enchanting turban charged with the whole artillery of their charms. It is a perfectly unmasked battery; nothing can stand against it. I wonder the Sultan allows it." Fenno Hoffman, the editor of the *American Monthly Magazine*, printed the whole of the letter in successive issues of the *Monthly*, even though Stephens told him: "you who have a tender regard for my character, will not publish me." The letter, published under the title of "Scenes of the Levant," anonymously of course, with a liberal sprinkling of asterisks, was widely reprinted, and even as Stephens moved on his journey his literary career, unbeknown to him, was being born.[1]

Stephens proceeded to Constantinople "in less time," as he said,

[1] "An account of my journey from Athens to Smyrna, given in a letter to friends at home, was published during my absence and without my knowledge in successive numbers of the American Monthly Magazine, and perhaps the favourable notice taken of it had some influence in inducing me to write a book."

These articles, entitled "Scenes in the Levant," appeared in the *American Monthly Magazine* as follows: Vol. I, No. 2 (October, 1835), 88–99; Vol. I, No. 3 (November, 1835), 174–83; Vol. I, No. 4 (December, 1835), 262–68; and Vol. II, No. 3 (November, 1836), 480–89.

"than swift-footed Achilles could have travelled it"; he went by
steamboat. "Join me now in this race," he wrote to Fenno Hoffman, "if your heart does not break at going by at the rate of eight
to ten miles an hour, I will whip you over a piece of the most
classic ground . . . in history." He sailed past the Isles of Greece,
Lemmos, shadowed by Mount Olympus, past Sigaeum, where
Homeric battles were fought, into the Hellespont—"where Le-
ander swam for the love of Hero, and Lord Byron and Mr. Eken-
head for fun," all the while conversing with two Americans returning from a tour of Egypt. They spoke with enthusiasm about
the ruins. Stephens was sorely tempted to try the Nile, but at that
moment cholera was raging in Alexandria, and he gave up the idea.

Constantinople was, like most of the Levantine cities, relatively new ground for an American. In 1800 Commodore William
Bainbridge, bearing the annual tribute to the Dey of Algiers, had
put into Constantinople, bringing for the first time the American
flag into this Saracen world. Two years later a consul was appointed in the Levant, whence Turkish opium and Smyrna figs were ex-
ported to Boston. In 1831, only three years before Stephens' arrival, Commodore David Porter had been transferred from the
consulate at Algiers, raised to the rank of chargé d'affaires, and
sent to Constantinople. Meeting Commodore Porter was to Stephens like coming face to face with a hero out of the *Iliad*, for
every school boy knew of the exploits of Porter and the U.S.S.
Essex in the War of 1812; how he had annihilated British shipping
in the Pacific until he was set upon by British men-o'-war in the
port of Valparaiso. Stephens was one of the thousands of boys
who had cheered the *Essex* when it left the Battery to sail against
England.

Porter, forty-five years of age, was waging a losing battle with
angina pectoris. He exhibited little of his famous quarter-deck personality—small, dark, weather beaten, his flashing eyes were his
best features. There had been a strong bond of sympathy between
Andrew Jackson and the Commodore, and Porter gave Stephens
an interesting account of his interview with Jackson on his recall
from South America, the aftermath of the "Foxardo affair." He
spoke of it with intense bitterness. Congress had adopted so mili-

tant an opposition to him that Jackson was unable to find a position for him which did not demand Congressional approval.

"I want an office," Porter wrote to Jackson, "of honour and trust and a salary not dependent upon any contingency.... Whatever the salary shall be I shall contrive to live upon it." So Jackson first named him consul general at Algiers, then later, in 1831, chargé d'affaires in Turkey. The Sultan he found a friendly monarch, interested in ship construction and willing to listen to an old sea dog. Porter liked the Sultan, but he grumbled at the salaams as well as at the devil-around-the-stump business of having to go through a triple cascade of translations, English to Armenian to Arabic, before he brought his threadbare, biting words to the Porte. Eventually Commodore Porter was confirmed as minister to Turkey in 1839. There he remained until his death in 1843. Stephens and Porter became fast friends and later saw more of each other when bound-for-Arabia Stephens stopped off at the Porter's *lazaretto* in Malta.

Stephens had made arrangements for an ill-smelling Tartar to ride with him through the Balkans to France, but at the very moment of departure a Russian government vessel, a miserable benighted *pyroscaphe*, announced its departure for the Black Sea and Odessa. So Stephens chucked the stinking Tartar and went to Russia.

At Odessa, Stephens was struck immediately "with the military aspect of things." In front of the examining officers the passengers paraded, one at a time, for examination—Turks, Christians, Jews, Germans, Russians, Poles, Greeks, Illyrians, Moldavians, Wallachians, Bulgarians, and one American: John Lloyd Stephens, New Yorker. They were stripped of their clothes, fumigated, and then examined by the port doctor;[2] forced to pass through

2 "We were obliged to strip naked [but] the bodily examination was as delicate as the nature of the case would admit; for the doctor merely opened the door, looked in, and went out without taking his hand from the knob. It was none of my business, I know, and may be thought impertinent, but as he closed the door, I could not help calling him back to ask him whether he held the same inquisition upon the fair sex; to which he replied with a melancholy upturning of the eyes, that in the good old days of Russian barbarism this had been part of his duties, but that the march of improvements had invaded his rights and given this portion of his professional duties to a *sage femme*."

an involved *pratique*, including the declaration at customs of all books banned by the censors. Stephens did not declare his Byron. The author of *Childe Harold* had long been on the Russian list, for in an outburst he had lampooned "that coxcomb Tsar, that autocrat of waltzes and war." But Stephens was loath to part with his Byron, for it had been, as he said, "my companion in Italy and Greece . . . so I put the book under my arm, threw my cloak over me and walked out."

Odessa—which had been a swamp until Empress Catherine decreed a city to be built in 1796—was a regal city by 1835; there was a promenade a mile in length, a palace for the governor, a casino, a theater—where Stephens witnessed a performance of the *Barber of Seville.* "I should," confessed Stephens, "as soon thought of an opera-house at Chicago as here; but I already found what impressed itself more forcibly upon me at every step, that Russia is a country of anomalies. . . . There is no country where cities have sprung up so fast and increased so rapidly as in ours: and altogether perhaps nothing in the world can be compared with our Buffalo, Rochester, Cincinnati, etc. But Odessa has nothing of the appearance of our cities."

With the sagacity of some latter-day Tocqueville, Stephens compared Russia with his own country. "We are both young, and both marching with gigantic strides to greatness, yet we move by different roads; and the whole face of the country, from the new city, Odessa, on the borders of the Black Sea, to the steppes of Siberia, shows a different order of government and a different constitution of Society. With us a few individuals cut down the trees of the forest, or settle themselves by the banks of a stream, where they happen to find some local advantages, and build houses suited to their necessities; others come and join them, and, by degrees, the little settlement becomes a large city. But here a gigantic government, endowed almost with creative powers, says '*Let there be a city!*' "

A few days later Stephens was bound for that never-never land, the Russian interior, bouncing across the steppes, facing without undue anxiety two thousand miles of travel in a springless *podorshni*. Henri, the driver he had procured in Odessa, was a wild-looking Frenchman with a scar across his mouth where a saber had knocked out most of his teeth, causing him to shovel out his words from the side of his mouth. When Stephens asked him on his hire if he were French, Henri drew himself up with great dignity, smoothed out his coat, and replied with great hauteur: *"Monsieur, je suis Parisien."*

Henri mounted the driver's box, and they bounded across Russia, dashing past miserable villages whose unwashed people ran out at their appearance to give obeisance to what they believed to be a grand seigneur. They came to Kiev (Stephens was the first American ever to pass through it) and then followed the river Dnieper on the way to Moscow. Stephens was horrified by the abject misery of the serf. "I found in Russia many interesting subjects of comparison between that country and my own, but it was with deep humiliation I felt that the most odious feature of that despotic government found a parallel in ours. . . . I do not hesitate to say that, abroad, slavery stands as a dark blot upon our national character . . . it will not admit of any palliation . . . I was forcibly struck with a parallel between the white serfs of Russia and the African bondsmen at home."

At the opening of the nineteenth century Russia was still a semi-Asiatic power. The waves of Tartar hordes had left behind a residuum of barbarism, which (despite the Westernization of Peter the Great) had arrested what would have been the normal development of the Russian people in the European concert of nations; of Russia's fifty millions, more than one-third, in Stephens' time, were serfs bound as vassals to the aristocracy, the Church, and the Crown. Nicholas I, who succeeded Alexander, was, like his prototype Philip II of Spain, the incarnation of the absolute; and he sought, most successfully it must be owned, to protect his analphabetic subjects from any contact with European influences. "God has placed me over Russia, and you must bow down before me, for my throne is His altar. . . . My watchful eyes detect internal evils and the machinations of foreign enemies. . . . I have no need of counsel."

There were neither inns, taverns, or restaurants; and Stephens had to "trust," like Napoleon when he invaded Russia, "to make up the rest . . . of their food . . . by foraging." The only succor they received was offered by Jews who were the postmasters on the road.

Moscow presented a magnificent vista. Six hundred churches—multiple-domed with gilded crosses, spires, and steeples—towering above the buildings, gave it an extraordinary appearance. The dwellings were tastefully planted with gardens, a vivid contrast to the walled monasteries. Even the Kremlin, cold and forbidding, had the appearance of a convent. After a Turkish bath and installed in the Hotel Germania, Stephens toured Moscow. He was constantly amazed by the paradox of Asiatic Moscow: it was an inextricable mixture of barbarism and Parisian elegance. In his hotel, Stephens talked to a French marquis, dressed in threadbare elegance, who had remained in Moscow after his capture in Napoleon's invasion. The marquis insisted, between sips of brandy, that the only difference between Russian seigneurs and serfs was that one wore his shirt inside his trousers and the other outside; "but my friend," Stephens wrote, "spoke with the prejudice of twenty years exile." The Frenchman earned his rubles by acting as a spy against foreigners. He confided to the American that he must watch not only his language but the content of his speech. Wrote Stephens: "It is almost impossible for an American to believe that even in Russia he incurs any risk in speaking what he thinks; he is apt to regard the stories of summary punishment for freedom of speech as bugbears or bygone things. In my own case, even when men looked cautiously around the room and then spoke in whispers I could not believe there was any danger. Still I had become prudent enough not to talk with any unnecessary indiscretion of the constituted authorities."

The road from Moscow to St. Petersburgh—macadamized the whole way—was Europe's best. Inns were operated by the government and regulated by tariffs. Stephens very much liked St. Petersburgh, the window that Peter had built so that the Russians might look upon Europe. St. Petersburgh was splendidly conceived with its palaces, its Hermitage, its memories of Peter, Catherine, and her lover Potemkin, and its regiments of gaily uniformed soldiers. He spent several days at the capital and celebrated the Fourth of

July at the American Embassy with the American minister, William Wilkins.[3]

Leaving St. Petersburgh was more difficult than entering it. At first, on arrival, he had obtained a *carte de séjour*, without which no one could remain in the capital. He submitted to routine questions of age, destination, and so on, thoroughly satisfying the authorities that he "had no intention of preaching democratic doctrines." But as one could not remain in St. Petersburgh without permission, neither could one leave without it. He had, according to law, to advertise in the Government Gazette on three successive days his intention of departing. Suspicion was directed toward him because he planned to cross Poland. Who, in God's name, said the exasperated police official, wanted to travel in Poland "for pleasure"?

He left in company with a tall Pole, born in Belgium of French descent, possessing, as he remembered, to a "striking degree the compound *amor patriae* incident to the relationship in which he stood to these countries." Travel was performed in a *kibitka*, a round-bottomed box cradle on four wheels, proudly contemptuous of springs. They bounced over the road that Napoleon had followed in his advance on Moscow, through the immense distances of Poland, over the execrable road past the Dwina River, into Minsk, and beyond it to Warsaw. Like the cities of Greece, Warsaw lay partially in ruins, the result of the latest revolution which had flared up in the eternal "Polish problem." On the night of November 30, 1830, the Poles had begun a badly managed revolution. The leaders were incompetent and irresolute. The fighting was, as in most revolutions, without quarter. In England public opinion was loud in support of the Poles, as it was in France. Louis Philippe, while not disposed to risk his throne in a quixotic

---

[3] ". . . much interesting information from home, and more than all, a budget of New-York newspapers. It was a long time since I had seen a New-York paper, and I hailed all the well-known names, informed myself of every house to let, every vessel to sail, all the cotton in market and a new kind of shaving soap for sale at Hart's Bazar; read with particular interest the sales of real estate by James Bleecker and Sons; wondered at the rapid increase of the city in creating a demand for building lots on one hundred and twenty-seventh street, and reflected that some of my old friends had probably grown so rich that they would not recognize me on my return."

crusade against the vast autocratic power of Russia, did propose to England a joint *démarche;* but nothing came of it. Poland was crushed, Russified, exterminated. And Lord Palmerston grieved, "The poor Poles, so there . . . is an end of the poor Poles."

Stephens, too, had his problems. He had not fully recovered from the illness that had sent him to Europe, and in Warsaw, overcome by malaise, he took to bed. He wrote home from Warsaw, August 15, 1835:

"I have reached this place to be put on my back by a Polish doctor. How long he will keep me here I do not know. He promises to set me going again in a week; and, as he has plenty of patients without keeping me down, I have great confidence in him. Besides having weathered a Greek, an Armenian, and a Russian, I think I shall be too much for a Pole."

So he escaped the doctor, went as far in Poland as the Vistula River, crossed it, and continued over the border into Austria. Passing through Vienna, he went up the Danube into Germany, and then in the cloudy November days took the road that led to Paris.

The preludes of winter had come to France as Stephens, traveling by *coche d'eau,* rolled past the files of poplars that lined the road. In Paris again, he walked with the satisfaction of a cosmopolitan entering his real milieu, the city. He had intended to return at once to America; in fact, he had written his father to expect him on the Le Havre packet in November, 1835, but there was no passage. Emigrants crowding the ships to their gunnels were pouring into America; every ship leaving Le Havre was packed with them. All Europe in 1835 had an unsettled air—the people of Paris were rising against the Bourbons, Belgium and Holland were breaking apart, and Germany was in a state of flux. Everyone who could, fled. In Paris the emigrants sold their wagons and their horses at auction, and then bivouacked on the banks of the Seine, waiting their turn to move on to Le Havre.

Frustrated in this attempt to sail for home, Stephens spent his time among the bookstalls along the Seine, where booksellers offered beautifully illustrated folios at fancy prices. Ever since Stephen had trod the Homeric lands, he had become passionately interested in the antique, and he had carried with him Count Volney's rhapsodic elegies to *Ruins*. All Americans, as Van Wyck Brooks explains, "loved Volney's *Ruins* and as their cities multiplied, hopeful and busy and shining with fresh, bright paint, the more their imagination delighted in these desolate scenes of temples and tombs, lost in the deserts." In one of these expensive folios on the ruins of empire, Stephens discovered some superbly beautiful lithographs "of a most glorious ruin," a city, buried in Stony Arabia, whose palaces had been cut out of the living rock. Its name was Petra. Stephens did not know it then, but that book, *Voyage de l'Arabie Petrée,* which sent him to Egypt, was to change the course of his life. It was also to change the course of American archaeological history.

Chapter IV   At the age of twenty-four Alexander the Great had founded the city bearing his illustrious name. He had been welcomed to Egypt as a young general in 332 B.C. and a conquering demiurge (for he was considered a god-man), and finding a wind-free harbor where Greek ships could enter and carry away the produce of the Nile, he himself designed the city and called it Alexandria. A century after its founding it was peopled with a million inhabitants, the most populous city in the ancient world, and the most industrious: "some," said the ancient geographer, "blow glass, others make papyrus sheets, others weave linen—every man practices a craft." It was still a magnificent city of libraries, baths, and immense buildings when, centuries later, it was captured by the Saracens. "We found it," reported a general to the Caliph Omar, "with four thousand palaces, four thousand baths, four hundred theaters, twelve thousand shops—and forty thousand tributary Jews."

Time and man, both iconoclasts, had changed Alexandria. After centuries of deterioration Egypt saw, for a brief historical moment, General Napoleon Bonaparte; and he, too, passed away leaving behind him a train of wreckage. The latest catastrophe was the cholera epidemic in 1834 that despoiled the city of fifty thousand of its inhabitants. When Stephens—his face covered by a handkerchief—went through the narrow streets of Alexandria in December, 1835, he was overwhelmed by beggars squatting in the shadows of overhanging *mushrabiyas*, exhibiting their sores and begging for alms. He had expected to see, as he walked along the sun-splotched lanes, bazaars offering the fabulous wealth of the Orient. What he saw left him unimpressed: ". . . why, I do not believe that the contents of all the bazaars in one of the largest towns in Egypt were worth as much as the stock of an ordinary dealer in dry goods on Broadway." He made his way to the Ameri-

43

can Consulate, and there met the man who was to give his Egyptian travels direction and content.

George Gliddon[1] (O! *rara avis*) was an intellectual American consul. British-born, like his father, he had succeeded him as the first American consular agent in Egypt. Although his vocation was the care and feeding of American tourists (along with consular invoices), his consuming passion was Egyptian archaeology; his pamphlet, *Appeal to the Antiquarians in the Destruction of Monuments* in 1841 marked the genesis of American archaeological interest in Egypt.

The great American invasion of Egypt began in 1832 when the Nile was discovered as a winter resort for convalescents and a haven for the wealthy. Just three years before Stephens' arrival Colonel Mendes Cohen of Baltimore made the first American collection of Egyptian antiquities; he sailed his own vessel up the Nile to the Wadi Haifa and purchased specimens from the ghouls who raided the tombs of the Pharaohs. Egypt in 1835 was scarcely a tourist's paradise; it offered, in truth, no more security for the traveler than the western wilderness of America. For that reason Gliddon suggested to Stephens—after he had seen the marvels of Alexandria—that they repair to Cairo, have audience with Mehemet Ali, and secure for his person, if possible, a *firman* from the Pasha of Egypt. "I was not ambitious," Stephens confessed, "for a *tête à tête* with his highness, and merely wanted to see him as one of the lions of the country." Still he went, mounted on a superb horse, richly caparisoned and preceded by a *janizary*, in the manner of a Turkish gentleman of quality.

[1] Gliddon, many years in Egypt, helped archaeological travelers. He wrote several books, among them *The American in Egypt* (1840) and *The Races of Mankind* (1851); he gathered skulls for Dr. Samuel Morton, an activity which resulted in his book *Crania Aegyptica*. He was the first to lecture on Egyptology in America, visiting in 1837–38 and 1842–50. He gave the Lowell lectures in Boston in 1843, created a transparent panorama of Egypt which he exhibited in the New York Chinese Museum on Broadway. He was famous, among the wits of Broadway, for the *faux pas* attending the unwrapping of an Egyptian mummy which he declared to be female, but which when unwrapped proved to be a male, exhibiting in its fossil state the erected unequivocal mark of its sex. Later he was associated with E. G. Squier in the Trans-Oceanic Honduras Railway, contracted malaria, and died in Panama. Squier visited his grave in 1857, which he reports in his book.

Mehemet Ali, a grand vizier come to life from the Arabian nights, was surrounded by a eunuch-guarded harem, a company of wives, and a regiment of children, which he continued to beget in spite of his seventy-six years. In a marble hall of a palace built by Saladin, cooled by tinkling fountains and surrounded by scarlet ottomans, Mehemet Ali sat with his full white beard, silken robes, and bejeweled turban, looking precisely what he was not— a kindly patriarch. Of kindred horoscope with Napoleon, Mehemet Ali was born in 1769 in Albania. His schooling was in a Turkish regiment, where, between massacres, he learned the rudiments of speech and good custom. After trying his hand in the Latakia tobacco trade, he was sent as a lieutenant by the Turkish Sultan to command three hundred Albanian soldiers, to aid General Bonaparte's invasion of Egypt. Mehemet Ali played a superb game of oriental trickery; he helped Napoleon against the British; then the British against Napoleon; then when Lord Nelson annihilated the French fleet, he remained in Egypt and consolidated his position. In the chaos that resulted from the Napoleonic wars he aided the Mamelukes against the Turk; then he played off one faction against the other, finally inviting the heads of the factions to his palace in Cairo, where he slaughtered them all. Thus Mehemet Ali; "whose every act," wrote the French Consul to his government, "reveals a Machiavellian mind"; to prove his thesis he gave a copy of *El Principe* to Mehemet Ali, which was translated to him ten pages a day. On the fourth day of reading Machiavelli Mehemet Ali spoke: ". . . in the first ten pages I discovered nothing great or new. . . . I waited. But the next ten were no better. The last ten were merely commonplace. I can learn nothing from Machiavelli. And as regards cunning, I know far more than he about it. Now stop and translate no more."

European powers, contending among themselves for the mastery of the Mediterranean and the gateway to India, found their perfidy matched by Mehemet Ali; even M. Talleyrand, that master of obliquity, paid him a compliment. As for the British, they were usually furious with him. At one time Lord Palmerston threatened that he would "chuck him into the Nile," yet Mehemet Ali survived all threats and all attempted assassinations. He died, as seldom does the tyrant, in his bed at eighty years of age, surrounded by the army of descendants that was his family.

The Pasha received John Lloyd Stephens with marked attention; a water pipe was given to him, and coffee, jet black and sugared in the Turkish fashion, was brought. After chatting discursively on this and that, Stephens suggested that the Pasha might continue his good works by introducing a steamboat from Alexandria to Cairo. "He took," said Stephens, "the pipe from his mouth again, and in the tone of 'Let there be light' said that he had ordered a couple. . . . Considering that a steamboat was an appropriate weapon in the hands of an American . . . I told him that I had seen . . . in a European paper a project to run steamboats from New-York to Liverpool in twelve or fourteen days. . . . He then asked the rate of speed of the steamboats on our rivers . . . and remembering an old crazy five or six mile an hour boat that I had seen in Alexandria, I was afraid to tell the truth."[2]

Mehemet Ali was not quite so naïve as he appeared. As the creator of modern Egypt, his first gesture as dictator was to give back to Cairo its former grandeur, for Cairo was one of the great centers of Islamic culture. The university was housed in the ancient Al Azhur Mosque where, until the Pasha had appeared, only the subtleties of medieval logic were taught. Now it buzzed with progress. Europeans had been brought to Cairo. The curriculum was gradually advanced, with students and officers trained by Europeans. Costi, an Italian, taught drawing and mathematics; an Englishman, Frederick Catherwood, who had drawn to scale many of the country's monuments and repaired some of the mosques, taught architecture; and a Frenchman, Colonel Sève, who had fought with distinction at Waterloo, established a modern army. A printing press had been set up at Bulaq in Cairo's suburbs, where seventy-three oriental works had already been printed.

[2] "I did not venture to go higher than fifteen miles an hour; and even then he looked as Ilderim may be supposed to have looked when the Knight of the Leopard told him of having crossed the Dead Sea without wetting his horse's hoofs. I have no doubt if he ever thought of me afterward, that it was as that lying American."

The fortress of 'Aqaba. *Deathly ill, Stephens arrived here in March, 1836,
on his way to Petra.*

From a lithograph by Leon de LaBorde (1829)

The Roman amphitheater at Petra, *built by the Romans during the reign
of Trajan.*

From a lithograph by Leon de LaBorde (1829)

John Lloyd Stephens dressed as a "Merchant of Cairo." *From an engraving by Stephen H. Gimber (1836).*

El Kasneh, ruins of Petra, Transjordania. *Stephens, the first American to visit Petra, spent several days here in 1836.*

From a lithograph by Leon de LaBorde (1829)

Americans had been known—and respected—in the Mediterranean ever since Captain William Eaton in 1804, at the head of eight Marines, thirty-eight Greeks, and a motley assortment of Arabs, captured Derna. The short war with Tripoli had further enhanced the reputation of the Americans, and many were urged to settle in Egypt. R. B. Jones, later United States consul in Egypt, took service in the Pasha's navy; another American, George Bethune English, took part in an expedition up the Nile to Dongola, the published account of which became the first original American contribution to Egyptian literature. Later, American naval architects were employed at Alexandria building the fleet of Mehemet Ali, used to suppress the Greeks, the same people that other Americans were trying to succor. So John Lloyd Stephens was to Mehemet Ali no *rara avis;* he welcomed him to Egypt, expressed his wish, in Allah's name, that he would enjoy himself, and forthwith gave Stephens his firman as a talisman for his expedition up the Nile.

On January 1, 1836, "with a fair wind and the star-spangled banner made for [him] by an Arab tailor," Stephens started up the Nile. He had hired a *falookha*, and a captain and a crew to sail it, sealing the bargain with a contract in Arabic which neither he nor the captain understood. For the rest he had only a copy of the *Modern Traveller*, Volney's *Ruins*, an Italian dictionary—and Paolo Nuozzo, although Stephens called him Paul. He had first met him in Constantinople in the previous year. When in Malta in 1835, in November, while staying at the vacation-residence of Commodore David Porter, he looked up Paolo and, finding him disengaged, employed him for his hegira to Egypt. Multilingual and arrogant, making a regiment of enemies wherever he went, Paolo was a man experienced in Arabian travel, and Stephens owed to him, in many instances, the safety of his life. "Paolo Nuozzo . . . was a man about thirty-five years old; stout, square built, intelligent; a passionate admirer of ruins of the Nile; honest and faithful as the sun, and one of the greatest cowards that luminary ever shone upon. He called himself my dragoman, and I remember, wrote himself such in the convent of Mt. Sinai and the temple of Petra. . . . He spoke French, Italian, Maltese, Greek, Turkish, and Arabic."

Up the Nile they inched past Memphis and the pyramids of Gizeh. The wind was contrary and the weather cold, so cold that Stephens was delighted to join the swarthy natives at El Minya in a steaming Turkish bath.[3] All through the month of January he continued to ascend the dark thread of the eternal Nile, stopping here and there to examine ruins, enter a pyramid, and otherwise fill his journal with his observations. At the ruins of Denderah, beloved of Hathor, he halted his ship and made an extensive tour of the plains, walking through the green fields of lucerne to the Temple of Denderah. He was enraptured at sight of the carvings of Osiris in high coiffure and Isis etched in rock-intaglio, crowned with the helmet of a bird; and the jackal-headed Anubis, the falcon-beaked Horus, ibis-headed Thoth, and all the other bird-gods, repeated a thousand times.

Archaeologically Egypt was still listed among the unknown. There had been by 1835 little if any systematic investigation of the archaeology of Egypt, and the tombs were frequented only by Arabian ghouls and one Giovanni Belzoni, a Monka coffee merchant turned antiquarian, who entered the tombs with a battering ram. Stephens was permitted to make his own judgments, and he found the Egyptian remains "beautiful, far more beautiful than I had expected."

The ruins of Thebes, a thousand miles up the Nile, he reached at night; he "could not bear that the sun should set before [he] stood among the ruins." In the moonlight with the stars reflected in the water, Stephens walked among the rows of battered statuary of the Colossi that led to the great ruined palace of King Amen-

---

[3] "My white skin made me a marked object among the swarthy figures lying around me; and half a dozen of the operatives, lank, bony fellows, and perfectly naked, came up and claimed me. . . . A dried-up old man, more than sixty, a perfect living skeleton . . . took me through the first process. . . . My arms were laid gently on my breast, where the knee of a powerful man pressed upon them; my joints were cracked and pulled; back, arms, the palms of the hands, soles of the feet, all visited in succession. I had been shampooed at Smyrna, Constantinople, and Cairo, but who thought I would have been carried to seventh heaven at the little town of Minyeh?"

em-heṭ. A new feeling possessed him now as he walked in the disconcerting chaos of carved granite. When he might have been expected to lapse into some sort of Volneyesque meditation on "ruins" in the turgid language of the period, he remained silent and contemplative. The spell was working. After Thebes, he walked to adjacent Luxor and passed among the Great Temples of Amun, which had been erected in 2100 B.C. to honor Queen Hat-shep-sut. Here, a year before, on the summit of the Temple of Luxor, John Lowell of Boston had drawn a long codicil to his will providing for what finally became the Lowell lectures, "to be delivered in Boston upon philosophy, natural history, the arts and sciences," and here Stephens felt a surging interest in unraveling time-lost civilizations.

Above Karnak, where the Nile turns pastel blue, Stephens came to Aswân and the first cataracts into the Nubian country; dark Nubians, sable-skinned, walked under the warm sun entirely naked except for a fringe of leather six inches in width that encircled their loins. A negroid race, early Christianized, who had formed a powerful tribe in Upper Egypt, the Nubians had been conquered by the Arabs, and were converted to Mohammedanism; now under the alchemy of change they were living in a neo-arcadia, their economy regulated to date-gathering on the banks of the Nile. How Pierre Loti would have loved the Aswân of Stephens' day! There was no dam to regulate the flow of the Nile, no flood of water to bury the Temples of Isis at Philae, no flesh-tortured reformers to clothe the ebony nakedness of the voluptuous Nubians. He would have written tantalizingly of the smooth skin, the two large jet-black eyes in unceasing movement, the high, pouting breasts, exquisitely molded; the Nubians would have joined Loti's other exotic heroines—Azyade, Rarahu, Fatou-Gaye, and all the rest—whom he has allowed the world to taste in intoxication, to delirium, even to stupor. But Stephens was not Pierre Loti. He made an effort to keep his observations on a scientific plane: "The Nubian is tall, thin, sinewy and graceful, possessing what would be called in civilized life an uncommon degree of gentility; his face is rather dark, though far removed from African blackness, his features are long and aquiline. . . . I remember to

49

have thought when reading Sir Walter Scott's 'Crusaders,' that the metamorphosis of Kenneth into a Nubian was strained and improbable, as I did not then understand the shades of difference in the features or the complexions of the inhabitants of Africa."

After that anthropological excursion, the inimitable Mr. Stephens came upon a voluptuous Nubian: ". . . she was not more than sixteen, with a sweet mild face, and a figure that the finest lady might be proud to exhibit in its native beauty; every limb charmingly rounded and every muscle finely developed. It would have been a burning shame to put such a figure into frock, petticoat, and the other et ceteras of a lady's dress. . . . I began to bargain for [her] costume. For one of my friends in Italy had been . . . making a collection of ladies' costumes. . . . Now one of the elements of beauty is said to be simplicity. . . . It was impossible to be more simple, without going back to the . . . fig-leaf. I thought nothing of seeing women all but naked, [but] I did feel somewhat delicate in attempting to buy the few inches that constituted the young girl's wardrobe. Paul had no such scruples, and I found too, that in the road to vice, *'ce n'est que le premier pas qui coûte. . . .'* " With that John Lloyd Stephens, attorney at law, knelt down and carefully unhinged the naked Nubian's breech clout.

In Cairo again, after floating for three months on the Nile, Stephens underwent a metamorphosis; he had become, by dress and name, *Abdel Hasis*. He sloughed off his clothes, purchased a red robe, a pair of red morocco shoes for his feet, a tarbouch for his head; and, adding a blue sash to hold a brace of pistols, he became a Turkish merchant, bound for Stony Arabia and the ruins of Petra. For Stephens had not forgotten *that* which brought him to Egypt—the intaglio city of Petra, about which he had read in the pages of León de LaBorde's book. In Cairo he was introduced to Maurice-Adolphe Linant, who had been LaBorde's companion on the journey to Petra in 1827. He told Stephens how they had traveled with a large retinue of camels and horses, with a great display so as to overawe the Bedouins. Their expedition had been the second to Petra since its rediscovery in 1812. For a thousand years that city had lain in Stony Arabia, forgotten in the annals of man and known only to the Bedouins. Yet once, in Roman times, it had been one of the greatest cities of the East.

In 1806 Ulrich Seetzen, a German Orientalist traveling as an Arab, had heard a Bedouin say: "*O! how I weep when I behold the ruins of Petra.*" Excited by its prospects, he had tried to enter the lost city, but his disguise was penetrated and he was murdered. Johann Ludwig Burckhardt, who discovered it, spent two years in preparation, studying Arabic, learning the Koran by rote, and with Teutonic thoroughness even having himself circumcised, for a foreskin was as dangerous as the Bible in Arabia; then under the pretense of being an Arabian beggar named Ibrahim Ibn Abdallah, who had vowed to slaughter a goat in honor of Aaron (whose tomb was at the summit of Mt. Hor, overlooking Petra), he entered the rock-city.

In 1812 Petra was rediscovered for the European world; and this Petra was Stephens' goal. All of Cairo's seasoned residents pointed out to him the dangers of his itinerary. Beyond the Nile, the firman of the mighty Mehemet Ali was so much paper. Yet Stephens persisted. With an experienced camel driver and the faithful Paolo dressed like an Arab, he mounted a vault-ribbed camel and disappeared into the desert. "I am about to cross a dreary waste of land," he wrote in his final letter home, "to pitch my tent wherever the setting sun might find me, and . . . to have for my companions the wild, rude Bedouins of the desert, to follow the wandering footsteps of children of Israel . . . to visit Mount Sinai, and then to the long-lost city of Petra, the capital of Arabia Petraea."

They took the Hejad route to Mt. Sinai. Passing through dirty Suez, they went along the shores of the Red Sea, through a desert land, desolate and anemic. On the sixth day they ran out of water and would have perished had they not discovered a water spring sentineled by a lone palm tree, an episode about which Stephens later wrote with a good sense of the ridiculous and which Herman Melville remembered when he once saw Stephens, "*that wonderful Arabian Traveller*," in church.[4]

[4] "For I very well remembered," Melville wrote in the autobiographical *Redburn*, "staring at a man myself . . . who had been in Stony Arabia and passed

At Mt. Sinai, they took refuge for a few days in the ancient Monastery of St. Catherine, where Stephens scandalized the patriarch by bringing up the subject of Mohammed on the sacred precincts of Mt. Sinai. Then they shaped their desert journey for 'Aqaba.

In the springtime of the world, Strabo, in his geography, divided Arabia into three parts—*Arabia Felix*, *Arabia Deserta*, and that over which Stephens was urging his camel—*Arabia Petraea*. This clinker-bound Arabia, a wedge-shaped peninsula, was pushed by an indifferent geology into the Red Sea, fashioning thus two gulfs: to the west, the Gulf of Suez, to the east, the Gulf of 'Aqaba, an appendix-shaped, sirocco-whipped body of water which terminates in the fortress town of 'Aqaba, squatting at the southern end of the wadi 'Araba, the driest, most desolate place in the world.

Here Abdel Hasis, i.e., Mr. Stephens, met El Alouin, Sheikh of Araba, in whose territory Petra lay. They had met once before in Cairo, when the Sheikh was conducting a pilgrimage to Mecca; then Stephens was unable to bring him to terms. Now no longer interested in the interminable haggling of the Arab, Stephens consented to be conducted by El Alouin and his men, for an undetermined price, to Petra. He dismissed his camel caravan, retaining only Paolo, mounted an Arabian horse and left northward for Petra. During the 150-mile ride the Sheikh tried this and that to make Stephens reveal the amount of money that he carried, and every step of the way he increased his clamor for *bâkshish*. Near

---

through strange adventures there, all of which with my own eyes I had read in the book which he wrote, an arid-looking book in a pale yellow cover.

" 'See what big eyes he has,' whispered my aunt; 'They got so big because when he was almost dead with famishing in the desert, he all at once caught sight of a date tree, with ripe fruit hanging on it.'

"Upon this I stared at him until I thought his eyes were really of an uncommon size, and stuck out from his head like lobster. I am sure my own eyes must have been magnified as I stared. When church was out, I wanted my aunt to take me along and follow the traveller home. But she said that the constables would take us up if we did; and so I never saw this wonderful Arabian traveller again. But he long haunted me; and several times I dreamt of him and thought his great eyes were grown until larger and rounder; and once I had a vision of that date tree."—*Redburn, His First Voyage* (New York, 1924), 4.

the entrance of Petra the leader, by a clever stratagem, told Stephens they would have to choose between fighting their way in or bribing an entrance. He relieved "Abdel Hasis" of five hundred piasters.[5]

The Sîk was the entrance to Petra. An earth convulsion had cleft the rocks of Mount Seir, creating a two-hundred-foot-high chasm; into this narrow-necked gorge Stephens entered, paced by the red-robed Sheikh. It was so narrow that no more than six horsemen abreast could ride through it. After a quarter of a mile, following the bewitching walls of the cleft, the Sîk suddenly ended, and through the narrow slit Stephens could see a temple carved out of the side of the living rock, marble white and moon red, its façade dazzling.

In the shadows Stephens rhapsodized upon this *El Khazneh*, "a temple, delicate and limpid, carved like a cameo from a solid mountain wall." Columns of the Corinthian order held up a richly carved façade which towered a hundred feet high, all cut out of the mountain. Paolo, who had lived among the ruins of Baalbek and Crete, involuntarily cried out when he saw this architectural miracle. The effect on Stephens was equally profound. One glimpse of *El Khazneh* and he was an archaeologist. "The first view of that superb façade must produce an effect which would never pass away. Even [after I] returned to the pursuits and thought-engrossing incidents of a life in the busiest city of the world, often in situations as widely different as light and darkness, I see before me the façade of that temple."

Stephens' wonder grew with each advancing step. He passed through a well-preserved stone door into a large excavated central hall, cut fifty feet into the heart-rock. Pompous portals led into inconsiderable solid halls. Once the tomb of kings, *El Khazneh* now was only the nightstalls of the nomad flocks, blackened with herdsmen's fires. On either side of the central hall, north and south, were additional rock chambers; they, like the other, were solid,

[5] "The precise danger I had to fear," said Stephens, "was that he would get my money piecemeal and when we came among the Bedouins, where it would be necessary to buy my peace, he would go off and leave me to their mercy."

plain, undecorated. On the back wall Stephens found the names of some English travelers—Leigh, Bankes, Irby, and Mangles—who had paid 1500 piasters to gain entrance to Petra in 1818. Below them were the names of León, Marquis de LaBorde, and Stephens' friend Maurice-Adolphe Linant. Stephens was the first American to visit Petra. "I confess that I felt what, I trust, was not an inexcusable pride, in writing upon the innermost wall of that temple, the name of an American citizen."

Beyond the Temple of Isis, the wâdi led to a trapezoidal-shaped canyon, one mile in width, the heart of Petra. At the edge, where the rock walls rose precipitously, a vast crescent-shaped Roman amphitheatre had been carved, as the rest, out of solid rock. Stephens wandered from tomb to tomb. He climbed the Urn Temple, etched with a Greek inscription; he crawled into the *El Khubdha*, the largest monument in Petra, and, like the Temple of Isis, bare within. He saw where the ancients had stripped away a whole sandstone mountain to build another temple, *Ed Der*, severely classical in style. Stephens was lost for words. In his journal he sought for the adjectives that would describe the mere coloring of the rock temples. In the morning they were like great rainbows, flashing out vermillion, saffron, and streaked with white and crimson; at dusk, when the stone was enveloped in its last shadows, it was rose red, shot blue with porphyry, a perfect quilt of swirling ribbons marked like watered silk. "Match me such marvel," sang the poet of Petra; "Match me such marvel save in Eastern clime, A rose-red city, half as old as time."[6]

In the flat, mile-square valley there were the ruins of a temple, an isolated column, some remains of a bridge, an arch of triumph, and part of a pavement thought to be the main road. Potsherds were scattered everywhere. At the end of the valley, the mountain closed once more into another Sîk-like chasm; from this cul-de-sac, the out-road led to Arabia Felix. Through these canyon portals trade poured for a thousand years. Its history was alive and pulsating, especially to an American. Stephens was enveloped by the shades of the past, for here Alexander the Great had tried

6 "Rose Red City, Half as Old as Time," Newdigate prize poem, 1845, by Dean Burgon, fellow of Oriel.

to force an entrance; here the Emperor Hadrian had visited; here Aretas III had minted coins with the name "Petra."[7]

Petra's architecture was so much part of its mountainscape that it seemed more the work of nature than of man, yet it was actually the ancient Nabataeans who had carved the city. In this corner of Arabia Petraea the Nabataeans became merchants, traders, mercenaries, and carriers of trade from Arabia Felix. Their accretions increased their prestige until, by the first century B.C., they were one of the most important powers in the East, and Petra was their capital. The territory of the Nabataeans spread to Damascus in the north, and south to the shores of the Red Sea. They began as fighting nomads, revolted against the Assyrians in the sixth century B.C., and filled the geographical vacuum left by the Jews when they were taken to their Babylon captivity. The Nabataeans seized, occupied, and then fortified the mountain fastnesses of Petra. Since the earliest times they had been carrying on a spiceries trade with Central Arabia. Under the kingship of Aretas III, in 60 B.C., the Nabataeans came into collision with the Romans. Some time in the seventh century the last vestige of Petra's civilization was swept away. By the time of the Mohammedan invasion it was lost to human memory. The recorders of Arabic conquest do not even mention Petra; it had passed into limbo. And there it lay for one thousand years, this jewel of a city, until Seetzen, as has been related, heard the Bedouin's exclamation and set out to find it for himself. Although Stephens spent only two days in the intaglio-city, his descriptions and account of the ancient rock city remained for many years the principal stimulus of popular interest.[8]

After Petra, his path shaped northward to the Holy Land. Jerusalem held him for some months. Then, after a navigation of the Dead Sea (that was to provide helpful suggestions for an offi-

[7] Pliny wrote of "the Nabatei who inhabit a city called Petra, in a hollow somewhat less than two miles in circumference, surrounded by inaccessible mountains, with a stream running through it. It is distant from the town of Gaza 600 miles, and the Persian Gulf 122."—Lib. VI, c. 28.

[8] See the excellent chronological biography given by R. E. Brunnow and A. von Domaszewski in *Die Provincia Arabia* (Strassburg, 1904, 2 vols.), I, 480–510.

cial American expedition[9]) Stephens left for the port of St. Jean d'Acre. Here he fell ill with dysentery and "ague." In a debilitated state he was put under the care of "an old Italian quack . . . with a blue frock coat and great frog buttons . . . who frightened [him] half to death every time he approached [his] bedside." Finally escaping the doctor and dysentery, he was carried on a small vessel sailing for Alexandria. Two years of travel—during which time a new pattern of life had been made for him—had come to an end. Stephens remained in Alexandria long enough to gather his mail and his effects, then he sailed to England, which was at that time the shortest way to New York City.

[9] "To Mr. Stephens of New York, the author of one of the most interesting books of travels which our language can produce I return in this public manner my acknowledgements for a timely letter written when the equipment of the expedition was under consideration."—William F. Lynch, U.S.N., *Narrative of the United States Expedition to the River Jordan* (Washington, 1843), *vi*.

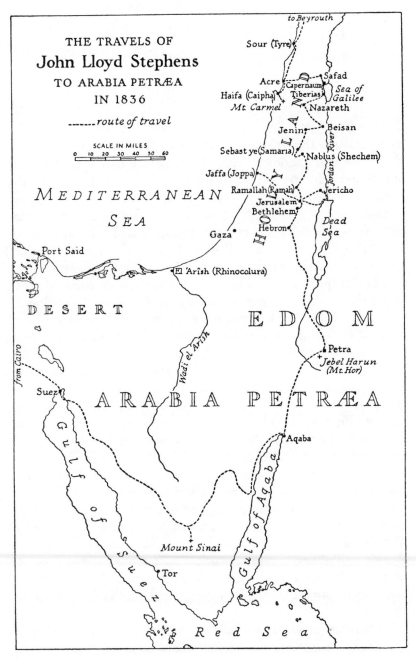

THE TRAVELS OF
John Lloyd Stephens
TO ARABIA PETRÆA
IN 1836

------ *route of travel*

SCALE IN MILES
0 10 20 30 40 50 60

to Beyrouth

Sour (Tyre)

Safad
Acre Capernaum
Haifa (Caipha) Tiberias *Sea of Galilee*
Mt. Carmel Nazareth

Jenin Beisan

Sebast ye (Samaria) Nablus (Shechem)

Jaffa (Joppa)

Ramallah (Ramah) Jericho
Jerusalem
Bethlehem
Hebron *Dead Sea*

Gaza

Jordan River

M E D I T E R R A N E A N
S E A

H O L Y   L A N D

Port Said

El 'Arîsh (Rhinocolura)

D E S E R T

E D O M

Wadi el Arîsh

Petra
Jebel Harun (Mt. Hor)

from Cairo

Suez

A R A B I A   P E T R Æ A

Aqaba

Gulf of Suez

Gulf of Aqaba

Mount Sinai

Tor

R e d   S e a

Chapter v Stephens drank in the sights of London as he had once the fetid water of Idumea. The press of the crowds, the well-dressed women issuing from elegant carriages, the handsome shops, the streets lighted with gas—all poured over him like some sovereign balm. He took his turns through Bond Street, strolled in new clothes (high-collared, tight-fitting grey coat, voluminous neck cloth, trousers strapped under boots) around Piccadilly Circus. He looked in at Tattersall's auctions, rambled through the Mall, gazed in rapture upon the celebrated Elgin Marbles at the British Museum, then strutted on successive nights along the Corinthian path, breathing in the odors of London.

At the American Consulate, he was received with marked attention; he found that his name was already well known. Colonel Thomas Aspinwall of Brookline, consul since 1824, showed him the issues of the *American Monthly Magazine* where his letters had been printed. He found himself the new literary lion. Colonel Aspinwall, a literary consul, represented Washington Irving, Cooper, Fitz-Greene Halleck, and many other writers in London. A capable, friendly, affable man, Aspinwall's appearance was dignified by an empty sleeve, where in the War of 1812 he had lost an arm and gained his military title. He was, like all American consuls of the period, only partially beholden to his government; the rest was private business. He had just received from America, from a new literary historian, a set of books entitled *History of Ferdinand and Isabella*, printed in extra-large type, to offer to British publishers; a great historical narrative possessing, as Mr. Van Wyck Brooks said, "the glow and color of Livy and Froissart." Its author, unknown to those present, was William Hickling Prescott.

There in Aspinwall's office Stephens met an old friend, Rev. Dr. Francis Lister Hawks, like himself a Litchfield graduate. Although Hawks spurned the law, entered the clergy, and was then occupying the pulpit of fashionable St. Thomas in New York, he was a literary clergyman; he wrote books on Egyptian archaeology and phallic symbols, reeled off for Harper and Brothers a series of juveniles under the pseudonym "Uncle Henry," translated Von Tsuchudi's *Peruvian Antiquities* into English, and, in the crowning achievement of his life, edited Commodore Perry's *Narrative* of his opening of Japan. A fashionable vicar, one of the intellectual influences that made John Jacob Astor lay the foundations of the Astor Library, he had, as he himself remarked, a keen literary nose. When he heard Stephens speak of his adventures and listened to him read from his notes on *A Journey Through Idumea*, he was very enthusiastic about the style and content of the material.

"Stephens," he said, "you should write a book."

At that moment, Stephens had no concept of a future other than one wedded to law and politics. He confessed to Hawks that he "did not know how to write, besides he had no intention of becoming an author."

Yet Hawks had planted the virus. As Stephens walked through the streets of London, the thought of writing a book grew and grew in his mind. He did not know, at the moment, whether what he had to tell was worth the telling.

Then Stephens met Frederick Catherwood.

From this meeting of an American and an Englishman was to come one of the most romantic episodes in the history of man's exploration of his past—the rediscovery of the Mayas and the beginnings of American archaeology.

Frederick Catherwood was discovered in Leicester Square, lecturing at a panorama called "A Description of the Ruins of Jerusalem painted by Robert Burford from drawings supplied by F. Catherwood." Here in the late eighteenth century, Robert Barker erected a rotunda in which circular panoramic views of cities, battles, and news events of the time, were painted in continuous canvases, ofttimes two hundred feet in length and ten feet in height. The panorama had passed into the proprietorship of Robert Burford—known in America for his panorama of New

York City—who engaged artists to paint every important city of the world, which he fashioned into panoramas. There Stephens found the new exhibition of a "Panorama of Jerusalem, by F. Catherwood."

Physically and psychically, Frederick Catherwood differed greatly from the American; taller than Stephens, he was solidly built, round faced, sandy haired, and blue eyed—an inheritance of his Scotch ancestry. Using the measured speech of an Englishman, the tones of his voice had a faint trace of the Mediterranean accents, where he had spent the last ten years of his life. Catherwood was excessively formal and restrained. He had a passion for detail and never spoke of anything as a certainty unless he had experienced it, measured it, and weighed it. One took no liberties with Frederick Catherwood. He had, so far as is known, no passionate friendships, and few called him by his first name; some old acquaintances referred to him as "Cath," but Stephens, in his books at least, always referred to him as "Mr. Catherwood." Yet this unsmiling exterior concealed a great burning passion for archaeology, for this enthusiasm had already carried him over every important archaeological site of the Near East. He was a man of many lives: architect, explorer, archaeologist, draughtsman, artist, daguerreotypist, surveyor, and railroad builder; and a precursor in not one but a dozen intellectual fields, and more deserving than thousands listed in the various biographical encyclopedias. Yet he is listed in none.

In the rare moments when Catherwood became autobiographical, Stephens learned that he had been born north of the Thames, out on Hackney Road, in the Parish of Hoxton, in a house at 21 Charles Square on February 27, 1799. Hoxton, with its threadbare gentility, offered little to a boy interested in the arts, yet Frederick Catherwood early in life had exhibited a talent bordering on genius in architectural drawing. So, after a brief schooling—presumably at the Haberdasher's School in Hoxton—he was articled out to one Michael Meredith, architect of Bishopsgate. For five years he followed this journeyman architect throughout the Isles, assisting in this and that and learning, in the unfilled interims, draughtmanship, architecture, surveying, and the study of the human figure

—an essential in that period for an accomplished architectural draughtsman. In 1820, at the age of twenty-one, he left his apprenticeship, took rooms down at Black Friars, and in the year that George III died exhibited his first picture at the Royal Academy. He attended some lectures at the Royal Academy where Sir John Soane gave illustrated lectures on archaeology, and from the influence of that master fell under the spell of the work of Giovanni Battista Piranesi, the Italian master of architectural invention. He followed his friend, Joseph Severn, Hoxton-born as himself, to Rome, after Keats' death.

In 1823 Catherwood left for Greece, in company with other artists, sculptors, and architects, twenty in number, who formed the Society of Englishmen. There Catherwood expanded his knowledge of classical architecture. But revolution was over the land; even as Catherwood was making casts of ancient sculpture, the Turks were laying siege to Athens. Catherwood escaped from Greece, dressed as a Turk. Once free of the civil war that convulsed the whole of the Mediterranean, he made his first tour of the Nile. Two years later, after drawing many of the famous Nilitic remains, the first trained architect to do so, Catherwood returned by way of Rome to not-so-Merry England.

In 1826 the skies of England were darkened by corn, Catholics, and currency. And Catherwood, after five years of wandering, was not happy in the confusion. He remained in London just long enough to realize something on his past five years' work. Then in 1829, accompanied by Joseph Bonomi, Robert Hay, Francis Arundale, and other Britishers, he left again for the East. The next four years he spent about the Mediterranean. The Levant and Egypt became the alembic of Catherwood's genius. Thereafter, dressed as a Turkish officer, he drew, with consummate deftness, many of the ruined sites of the Near East. He sketched the structures of Thebes and Karnak to scale, he excavated Egyptian monuments, he visited Mt. Sinai, drew the ruins of Baalbek in the Levant, which Norman Douglas, a century later, was to make the subject of a novel, *Love Among the Ruins*. Then he became architectural adviser to Mehemet Ali, repaired the mosques of Cairo under the protection of janizaries supplied by

61

the Pasha, and in Jerusalem, and with great risk to life—for pencil and paper were anathema to the Arab—he made a complete plan of the interior of the Mosque of Omar. Catherwood's travels had encompassed almost every civilization in the Near East. There are few archaeologists who have had the acquaintance of classical architectural styles as Catherwood—and no one, then or since, was so thoroughly prepared, by actual contact, to weigh in balance the civilizations of the Old World and the New.

In 1834, with portfolios bulging with drawings, Catherwood returned once again to London. His health momentarily impaired and his purse empty, he turned to the panoramas of Robert Burford, and there in association with the Leicester Square rotunda prepared four huge panoramic canvases.

Stephens was delighted by all that he had heard. He was immediately sensible of all of Catherwood's talents, and their mutual enthusiasms for traveling and archaeological research completely bridged the differences that were inherent in their personalities. Sometime in this genesis of their friendship "America" entered their conversations. Catherwood brought to Stephens' attention a curious book: *Description of the ruins of an ancient City discovered near Palenque in the kingdom of Guatemala.* The book described in wild, extravagant language the ruins of a place called Palenque, its palaces and pyramids buried in the jungle, illustrated with crude engravings. What particularly struck Catherwood were the assertions by the authors that the ruins were either Egyptian, Carthaginian, or Phoenician in origin. Catherwood saw at once from the illustrations, crude as they were, that there was little or no similarity. As for the ruins buried in the jungles of tropical America, they were all new to Stephens; no one in America had ever heard of palaces or pyramids in Mexico. The editors of the book suggested that if, "instead of the researches so repeatedly undertaken in lower and upper Egypt, a small portion of that indefatigable proceedings had been resorted to in . . . America . . . a copious mine of wealth would have been opened." Catherwood and Stephens agreed with the editor that the discovery "opened a new era in the field of historic speculation," and they agreed—although no date was decided upon for such an expedition—to undertake a trip into that incognita of Central America and search out these ruins.[1] Thus, but in not so many words, an archaeological partnership came into being; it was more than just mere arrangement, it was a friendship which had its origin in the mutual admiration of buried civilizations, it sprang from never fully analyzed emotions that stood in awe of past grandeurs struck down in the heights of glory. It drew these two together, cemented their acquaintanceship into friendship, a friendship that was to endure for twenty active creative years. They signed no contract. They appeared before no notary to make public record of a synthesis of their interests—writer and artist merely clasped hands. That was enough. Then Stephens sailed for the New York City he had left over two years before.

[1] "In repeated conversation with me, Stephens said he was called to Guatemala (and Yucatán) by reading the works of Del Río and Waldeck."—Francis Lister Hawks in *Putnam's Monthly Magazine*, January, 1853.

Chapter VI   The New York City of 1836 had visibly changed since Stephens left it to go on his Ulysses wandering. Most of it was a blackened shell. The fire that had gutted it broke out on a winter's night in 1835—somewhere in the vicinity of Maiden Lane—and made an Aetna-like progress. Hampered by severe cold—the water froze in the pipes—the firemen were unable to stem the holocaust as it swept through Wall Street, taking entire blocks of the commercial center. The Merchants Exchange, once the pride of Knickerbocker New York, was left a gutted ruin; Ball Hughes' statue of Alexander Hamilton, that dominated the Grecian foyer, was a mass of molten metal. Stores and houses alike in Beaver Street and Stone Street were gone, as were many of the Dutch houses with their gabled roofs and weathercocks. Delmonico's had disappeared; so had most of South Street, Wall Street, and Lord's Beautiful Row. The losses had been, for so small a city, catastrophic. The *Herald* suggested that they would reach twenty millions. Yet New York, undeterred by fire or politics, was growing out of its traditional bounds; the new census placed the population at over two hundred thousand, and it was stretching beyond the City Hall, once set by the Croakers as the optimum of expansion. Greenwich Village, which had been, in Stephens' boyhood, a parish and a potter's field, had now been turned into a green, and was the fashionable residential section. The Stephens' had long since left Dey Street and now occupied a handsome dwelling, severely classical in style, at 13 Leroy Place, in Greenwich Village.

As for John Lloyd Stephens, he had hardly time to orientate himself and open—for appearance's sake if not for business—a law office at 33 Wall Street, before he was "politicking" again. This was another presidential year, and Martin Van Buren, Jackson's heir, had been nominated and was, according to all predictions, about to carry the election.

Stephens had no difficulty in extending his loyalty to Van Buren. He made speeches, and those he did not speak he wrote; he reappeared at Tammany to inspire a divided hall to the old rallying cry, "Hurrah for Jackson"; and while the more fastidious-minded might object to Stephens' acquiescence to odious politics, it proved an important step in Stephens' American discoveries.

Martin Van Buren, with an impressive mandate from the people, inherited Jackson's office; promptly after taking office he also inherited the crash. Inflation as a concomitant of Jackson's policies had been gaining steadily since 1834; by 1837 paper money had grown far beyond the proportion of specie; there were crop failures and speculation; credit was tightened; gold fled the country; and America was in the grip of the worst depression it had known. Eight hundred banks had, by May, 1837, suspended payment, freezing $120,000,000 in deposits. In a single six months, one-third of the population of New York City was unemployed. Daniel Webster toured the city in a barouche making speeches; Nicholas Biddle, "the insulted and proscribed of Andrew Jackson," held a meeting of merchants at the Merchant's Bank. Gone were the days of "Hurrah for Jackson."

And Stephens? He was for once oblivious to the melee. Somewhat like Pliny, who went on studying Greek while before his eyes Vesuvius was overwhelming five cities, Stephens was talking his quill across piles of paper while his world crashed about him. He was, although with severe misgivings, writing a book.

American literature up to the year 1836 had been, with rare exceptions, the diversion of amateurs; writing of books was generally considered the realm of the dilettante, a gratification of idleness. There were few if any professional authors. A young collegian, it is true, might publish a poem, a scholar a didactic thesis, or a gentleman might write, usually anonymously, some dull octavo volumes, but one did not live by writing.

Those who did write received little money for it. Until 1850 Emerson had nothing from his publications; he lived on his private income and fees from his lectures. Nathaniel Hawthorne, who published *Fanshawe* in 1828 at his own expense, was barely able to sustain himself and had to be given a governmental sinecure. Poe, divided against himself, never solved the problem of writing for money; and Thoreau so managed his life that money, or the lack of it, never troubled him. As for Prescott, who later made a tidy fortune from his writings, he said at the beginning of his career: "Fortunately, I am not obliged to write for bread and I will never write for money." Yet Noah Webster, as early as 1817, was paid $40,000 by Goodrich for his *Spelling Book*, the Reverend Albert Barnes $30,000 for his *Notes of the Gospels;* and Professor Charles Anthon, Stephens' old Columbia mentor, was in the high-income brackets with his translations of the classics.

These constituted (with the singular exception of Washington Irving—and perhaps Fenimore Cooper) the only "paying" litera-ture; belles-lettres was an avocation.[1] It had long been accepted as axiomatic by American publishers that it was injurious to their commercial credit to undertake the publication of an American writer unless the books be "More's *Geographies*, Watt's *Psalms*, or something of that class." For one thing, there was no interna-tional copyright, and books by British writers, who were seldom compensated, could be reprinted in America cheaper than in Eng-land. When Carey and Company in Philadelphia published *The Pickwick Papers*, they sent Charles Dickens in 1837 a draft for £25, "which we beg you will accept not as compensation but as a memento of the fact that unsolicited, a bookseller has sent an author, if not money, at least a fair representative of it." And Dickens, so different from the Dickens of 1842, refused it, asking only one copy of the American edition, "which I shall consider a sufficient acknowledgment of the American sale."

Scott, Thackeray, and Dickens were favorites with the Ameri-cans, as well as Bulwer-Lytton with his spice of elegant deviltry and his glimpses into the deshabille of the aristocracy; yet if the British authors were paid at all by the American publishers, it was only for advance sheets so that they might have the jump on their competitors. "So why," questioned Sydney Smith of *Brother*

[1] Nicolas Trübner, *Bibliographical Guide to American Literature* (London, 1859), discusses the "remuneration of authors."

Jonathan, "should the Americans write books when a six weeks passage brings them in their own language, our sense, our science and genius in bales and hogsheads. . . . In the four quarters of the globe, who reads an American book?"

Stephens was fully aware of this state of American literature, and he had in fact canvassed the possibilities of publication even as he was writing. He visited Harper and Brothers—then the largest publishing house in the United States with its five-floored loft on Franklin Square—and interviewed James Harper on the forms of literature his house favored.[2] Apparently there was an understanding between Stephens and Harper as early as the fall of 1836, for by May, 1837, Harper was already setting up for publication the work "in two duodecimo volumes."

Incidents of Travel in Arabia Petraea, by "An American," was enthusiastically received by the press. ". . . we have," said Fenno Hoffman, editor of the *Knickerbocker Magazine,* "perused

[2] "John L. Stephens, a clever enterprising New-York lawyer, author of Travels in Russia, Greece, etc., and of Central American Antiquities, and afterwards President of Panama Railroad, made his entry into the world of literature in a rather whimsical fashion. He had been, many years ago, in Eastern Europe, upon I know not what business. After his return to New-York he happened one day to be in the publishing house of Harper Brothers, when the senior member of the firm, Mayor Harper, fell into conversation with him about literature—that is, the sort of books he sold most of, which was his special interest in the matter.

" 'Travels sell about the best of anything we get hold of,' said he. 'They don't always go with a rush, like a novel by a celebrated author, but they sell longer, and in the end, pay better. By the way you've been to Europe; why not write us a book of travels?'

" 'Never thought of such a thing,' said the lawyer. 'I travelled in out-of-the-way places and went very fast. I made no notes and should have very little to write about.'

" 'That's no matter,' said the publisher who had taken a fancy that he could get hold of something racy from the fast-talking New-Yorker; 'You went through, and saw the signs. We have got plenty of books about those countries. You just pick out as many as you want, and I will send them home for you; you can dish up something.'

"He did dish up three volumes of very amusing travels and in due time, three more, and the Harpers paid him some twenty-five thousand dollars as his portion of the enterprise—which was by no means the lion's share. Encouraged by this success, Mr. Stephens made an expedition to explore the ruins of Palenque, in Central America, taking an artist with him to do the illustrations. His work on those mysterious antiquities may be more accurate than the Oriental Travels, but it is not half so amusing, and as it was an expensive illustrated work, I doubt if it paid as well."—Thomas Low Nichols, *Forty Years of American Life, 1820-61* (New York, 1937), 211-12.

these volumes with unmixed gratification." He praised the "vivid and faithful descriptions" and the "style free from exaggeration and affectation." For Stephens had not, as Harpers wanted, merely "dished it up." *Arabia Petraea* was a book of some 180,000 words, and despite its disarming title and light touch, a book of considerable erudition. It has remained one of the most delightful travel books in American literature. Stephens in preparation read and used the entire bibliography of the regions through which he traveled so as to buttress his own observations. Volney's *Ruins*, Keith's *Prophecies*, the "Travels of Lamartine," the researches of Pococke, and Keniker's *The Letters from Palestine of Jolliffe*, the *Narratives* of Legh, the published explorations of Burckhardt, La-Borde, Linant, Belzoni, Bankes, and Ulrich Seetzen were read, studied, absorbed, but so thoroughly distilled and so fully digested that their presence is hardly obvious. He did not fill his travels with learned intrusions that would spoil the flow of the narrative; his humor was droll and the sex titillation Boccaccian; his excursus into history masterfully done.

All the reviews—without exception—highly praised the book. General Lewis Cass, himself an explorer in the East, found the author possessed of "admirable qualities for the traveller"; his review with digressions, footnotes, paraphrases, and asides went to seventy-five pages, of which Lewis Cass thought so highly that he published it separately. He found the style excellent ("at times rising into elevation"), and he assured the prospective purchaser of the book that he would not be bored with that "eternal affectation of *knowledge and taste* which distinguished Eustace's *Classical Tour*."

The *Christian Examiner* recommended it most highly to their readers even though the reviewer complained of the "levities with which the book is spiced and which occasionally give a queer air of irreverence . . . about sacred things," as did the *Princeton Review*. The reviewer, Mr. A. Alexander, did not know the "American," but he, too, objected to his "spice of the irreligious," he found him a good Christian and, for that reason, decided to give an extended review in a journal "which is devoted almost entirely to Biblical subjects." But it was Edgar Allan Poe's review of

Arabia Petraea—the only critic who had anything intelligent to say about the mechanics of writing—that made Stephens famous. In his first assignment for *The New-York Review* Poe gave the volumes a twelve-page review, a scholarly article and one that Poe later recalled with pride. He found the book "written with a freshness of manner evincing manliness of feeling," Twelve pages later he concludes: "... we take leave of Mr. Stephens with hearty respect. We hope it is not the last time we shall hear from him. He is a traveller with whom we shall like to take other journies equally free from the exaggerated sentimentality of Chateaubriand, or the sublimated, the *too* French enthusiasm of Lamartine. ... Mr. Stephens writes like a man of good sense and sound feeling."

Poe's literary opinions found a reflection in the reaction of the public; *Arabia Petraea* was so popular that it went through six editions in a single year, and within two years sold 21,000 copies, this at a time when America's population was not yet twenty million. London, too, praised it. The *Athenaeum* found them "two pleasant volumes" with "not a wearisome page in the whole work," echoing Poe's panegyrics on the style: "excellent, unaffected and unpretending, with the flavor of freshness and perhaps something of the carelessness of conversation." It had both vogue and influence, inspiring in 1845 the Newdigate prize poem, "Rose Red City, Half as Old as Time." The British liked *Incidents of Travel in Arabia Petraea* so much that they were still reprinting Stephens' popular book on the Near East in 1866.

Stephens overnight was the new literary sensation and fifteen thousand dollars wealthier from his share—approximately 50 per cent—of the sales. Not one to rest on his laurels (for one of the reviewers asked for more: "... we respectfully suggest—what will occur to many readers of these volumes, that another set of volumnes from the same pen, would not be unacceptable to the public, a lively description of Greece, Italy, Russia, and Poland might be instructive and entertaining and as our author has got the attention of the public, he may calculate upon their continued favor"), Stephens took this advice, plunged in, and wrote two more volumes, entitled *Incidents* as the other, *Incidents of Travel in Greece,*

Turkey, Russia, and Poland.[3] This was published in the following year. He had scarcely a moment for the law. Universally acclaimed as *The American Traveller,* his books circulating widely, his accounts swelled with royalties, with these new accretions he was accepted into New York's literary circles; The Astor House Book Store became his favorite rendezvous.

The Astor House had risen Phoenix-like from the ashes of the fire of 1835 and imposed itself—a huge pile of Grecian pediment —across from the City Hall. Around it gyrated the fashions. With Broadway for its promenade, ladies dressed in coal-scuttle bonnets and short-waisted, tight-fitting spencers walked beside their gentlemen in the full tide of a romantic period which still lived by candlelight. Graceful barouches with spanking horses bowled along the cobblestone streets. Mounted gentlemen pranced the streets, riding their horses on a snaffle, ignoring the horse-drawn omnibuses with high-sounding names that conveyed their passengers within the limited area then New York. One began and ended at the Astor House, for there were the fashionable shops.

At Number Seven, on the ground floor of John Jacob Astor's monument, where the cognoscenti pressed their faces against the window glass, was Bartlett and Welford's, Antiquarian Booksellers. John Russell Bartlett, the senior partner, was a quiet, scholarly Rhode Islander who had quit the banking business in order to open this bookstore. In the last days of the Knickerbockers it became the rendezvous of the literati. Washington Irving was a frequent visitor; Bryant, the poet-editor of the *Evening Post,* spent a good part of his time there; Fenno Hoffman of the *Knickerbocker Magazine,* Park Benjamin, the brothers Duyckinck, and all the other names remembered and forgotten of this period.

Stephens, who often used the well-stocked store for research, soon became an intimate friend of John R. Bartlett.[4] An author as

[3] *Incidents of Travel in Greece, Turkey, Russia and Poland,* by the author of *Incidents of Travel in Egypt &c.,* (New York, Harper and Brothers, 1838, 2 vols.), with woodcuts by Dr. Alexander Anderson. There was a Dublin edition (1838), two British editions (1838–39), a French edition, and a Swedish edition in 1841.

[4] John R. Bartlett, born in Providence, R. I., in 1805 (the same month, day, and year as Stephens), came from an old Massachusetts family, who installed him

well as a bibliographer, Bartlett was one of the influences in Stephens' life, for he was familiar with all antiquarian publications and, being a bookseller, he was acquainted with the world's literature. There had been talk in his bookstore about the early records of New York which lay in Holland, and since Stephens was the literary man of the hour, it was proposed that he go to Albany to get the state to allocate funds to the New York Historical Society to be used to pay his expenses while he dug out in Amsterdam the early records of New York's settlement.

In January, 1839, Stephens was in Albany in audience with Governor William Seward (later Lincoln's secretary of state), using his influence to obtain such funds. So "zealous the attention" of Stephens that when the act was passed, Governor Seward recommended that the New Yorker be appointed its commissioner. The Whigs in Albany thought differently; they remembered Stephens' activities in Van Buren's political campaigns and his defense of Jackson; they refused to confirm him. Fenno Hoffman then wrote to Seward for the position, saying that since his "friend Mr. Stephens lost his chance of the appointment," he would like the position. He failed also. It went to John Romeyn Brodhead, who spent three years in Europe collecting these records. It was just as well, for Stephens was already immersed in preparation for a new adventure—the discovery of the ancient civilizations of America.

What made Stephens at this moment turn to those vague,

after graduation from college in the banking house of Cyrus Butler. A founder member of the Providence Athenaeum, he was more interested in books than in dollars. In 1837, in conjunction with Charles Welford, he established Bartlett and Welford in the new Astor House. His literary activities embraced the universe. He formed the American Ethnological Society and managed the New York Historical Society; he wrote *A Dictionary of Americanisms* (1848), and when he retired from the book business in 1849, he undertook a commission from President Taylor to establish the boundary line between Mexico and the United States. In 1854 he published *Personal Narrative of Explorations . . . during 1850–53*. After having been elected secretary of the state of Rhode Island, he began his work on the publication of the *Records of the Colony of Rhode Island, 1636–1792* (1856–65, 10 vols.). His greatest contribution to bibliography was his *catalogue raisonné* of the library of John Carter Brown: *Bibliotheca Americana, a Catalogue of Books Relating to America, in the Library of John Carter Brown* (1865–70, 4 vols.). Bartlett died in 1886. His résumé of the advance of anthropology, *The Progress of Ethnology*, may still be read with profit.

shadowy monuments which rumor, floating through the learned world, hinted were lying in the jungle? He himself has left us no record. But he had much talk with Mr. Catherwood.

Frederick Catherwood meanwhile had installed himself at No. 4 Wall Street as an architect, and in 1837 he entered into partnership, Catherwood and Diaper, "to carry on together the profession of Architects and Surveyors in the City of New York." After some difficult months he began to prosper. He married, brought his bride over from England, took a house at 488 Houston Street, and sired two sons. He leased a piece of ground from John Jacob Astor on Broadway at Prince Street in front of Niblo's Garden, and there in 1838 he erected his own Panorama. Soon New Yorkers were entering night and day to see "The Splendid Panorama of Jerusalem." It was a profitable enterprise and helped very much by Stephens, who in his eighth edition of *Arabia Petraea* (September, 1838) gave two pages of publicity, in the preface, to Catherwood's Panoramas.

Released then from the mere huddle and vacuity of business, Catherwood had time to dream with Stephens of new adventures. Every available moment they were seen together at Bartlett and Welford's bookstore. John Russell Bartlett was always there urging and encouraging, and he in fact claims, modestly enough, that his was the ultimate influence that turned Stephens to Central America. In his journal, until now unpublished, Bartlett reveals the genesis of the expedition: "I claim to have first suggested it to Mr. Stephens. No book ever awakened a deeper interest in New York than Mr. Stephens' *Incidents of Travel in Egypt, Arabia Petraea, and the Holy Land,* published in 1837. Soon after its publication I one day said to Mr. Stephens, when in my office: 'Why do you not undertake the exploration of Yucatán and Central America? There is a field that is quite unexplored where there are numerous objects of interest in ruined cities, temples and other works of art.'

"Mr. Stephens said he had never heard of these remains and would be glad to know more about them. I invited him to my house where I showed him Waldeck's work on Yucatán, a beautiful work in folio, containing views of some of the ruined edifices in that country which I had imported a short time previous from Paris. Mr. Stephens called at once upon me and examined the book. At the same time, I showed him several other books on the countries in question and pointed out to him in other works references to the ancient remains in Yucatán and Central America. Mr. Stephens was greatly interested in what I showed him and took some of the books home for a more careful examination."[5]

Oblivious to the busy clatter of New York, Stephens propped up the bulky folio tomes borrowed from Bartlett, and in a spirit of wonder and inquiry began to read all that was then known of the ancient Americans. The further he read, the more he was entranced. Stephens was lost in a lost world.

[5] The "Journal of John R. Bartlett," deposited in the archives of the John Carter Brown Library, Providence, R. I.

Chapter VII Stephens was astounded by what he read. Deaf to all other enticements, he had for weeks been absorbed in descriptions of the ruins that were supposed to exist in the jungles of Central America. The adventures of Capitán del Río, who discovered the ruins called Palenque in southern Mexico—*Descriptions of the Ruins of an Ancient City*—he had read in London; now in its rereading he was convinced that as shadowy and inchoate as the descriptions were, some sort of culture existed in tropical America. This was confirmed by yet another book, a huge folio volume written from the accounts of Capitán Guillelmo Dupaix, an officer of the Mexican Army, who had, following del Río, explored the Palenque ruins. In the same volume, *Antiquités Mexicaines*, another ruined city called Uxmal was said to exist in the State of Yucatán. The author of this article was the famous Lorenzo de Zavala, who had been born in Yucatán and had seen these ruins with his own eyes. When minister to Paris, he contributed a *Notice sur les Monuments Antiques d'Ushmal, dans la Province de Yucatán* to the work on Mexican antiquities. And only lately there had appeared in one of the learned American journals[1] the first notices of yet another ruined city called Copán, which, as Stephens said, "instead of electrifying the public, either from want of interest in the subject, or some other cause . . . little notice was taken of it." So three names were engraved in Stephens' mind: Copán! Palenque! Uxmal! Although Stephens could find none of these sites on the existing maps, it was obvious that these ruined cities, hundreds of miles apart, suggested a widely spread culture.

In 1839 all these vague ruins were called by the generic name "Mexican" and their very existence treated with great skepticism

[1] "The Ruins of Copán in Central America," by Colonel Juan Galindo, in *Proceedings* of the American Antiquarian Society, Vol. II (1835), 543–50.

by the scholars of the world. "The first light thrown upon this subject," Stephens reflected, "was by the great Humboldt, who visited that country at a time when, by the jealous policy of the government, it was almost as much closed against strangers as China is now. . . . At that time the monuments of the country were not a leading object of research; but Humboldt collected from various sources information and drawings, particularly of Mitla . . . Xoxichalco . . . and the great pyramid or Temple of Cholula he visited himself. . . . Unfortunately, of the great cities beyond the vale of Mexico, buried in forests, ruined, desolate and without a name, Humboldt never heard, or, at least . . . never visited. It is but lately that accounts of their existence reached Europe and our own country. These accounts, however vague and unsatisfactory, had roused our curiosity."

The acceptance of an "Indian civilization" demanded, to an American living in 1839, an entire reorientation, for to him an Indian was one of those barbaric, half-naked tepee-dwellers against whom wars were constantly waged. A rude, subhuman people who hunted with the stealth of animals, they were artisans of buffalo robes, arrowheads, and spears, and little else. Nor did one ever think of calling the other indigenous inhabitants of the continent "civilized." In the universally accepted opinion, they were like their North American counterparts—savages. No one dreamed that throughout the tablelands of Mexico, in the tangled scrub-jungles of Yucatán, there stood, covered by jungle verdure, ruins of temples, acropolises, and stone causeways of a civilization as great in extent as Egypt's. The names Hernán Cortés, Pizarro, Bernal Díaz del Castillo were but synonyms for rapine; "Aztec," "Maya," "Toltec," and "Inca" were in no dictionary, and in few histories. These civilizations were not only dead, for dead implied having once lived, but, even to the world immersed in searching out the antique, absolutely unknown.

This blanket of oblivion that covered these civilizations had, in part, been woven on the loom of the well-known William Robertson, the eighteenth-century Scottish historian: "Neither the Mexicans nor Peruvians [were] entitled to rank with those nations which merit the name of civilized." As for the palaces ascribed

75

to them by the Spanish *conquistadores*, Robertson dismisses those cities "as more fit to be the habitation of men just emerging from barbarity than the residence of a polished people. . . . Nor does the fabric of their temples and other public edifices appear to have been such as entitled them to high praise . . . these structures convey no high idea of progress in art and ingenuity. . . . If the buildings corresponding to such descriptions had ever existed in the Mexican cities, it is probable that some remains of them would still be visible . . . it seems altogether incredible that in a period so short, every vestige of this boasted elegance and grandeur should have disappeared. . . . The Spanish accounts appear highly embellished."[2]

Yet if the vestiges of ruined stone cities did exist in tropical America—for one could no longer deny the evidence of these publications—and they were not built by the Indians, who built them? The antiquarians from Stephens' books all tried to speak at once: they were built by the Egyptians, the Norsemen, the Chinese, the Mongols who came with elephants, the Romans, the Phoenicians, the Carthaginians, the lost Tribes of Israel—it was an old controversy and one that had raged in the academies, in the priories, and in the council rooms, where blood had, on occasions, been spilled in arguing out a favorite hypothesis. For after America was discovered to be a new continent, and its explorers confronted with a heretofore unknown race of people, the Church found itself in a dilemma. If the flood had destroyed the world's population, as detailed in Genesis, leaving only Noah and his chosen family to repopulate it, whence came the American Indians?

Noting the hawk-visaged faces of the Indians, the Spaniards believed they were looking at Semitic faces and, remembering the well-known skill of the Phoenicians in oceanic travel, the theory was advanced that the Indians were descendants of the lost Tribes of Israel. This fancy was to endure for four hundred years and into our own century, for the doctrines of the Mormon church are based upon it. Gregorio García, writing in 1607 in his *Origin of Indians of the New World*, made the Biblical Orpir, Peru;

[2] William Robertson, *The History of America*, Vol. III (1792), Book VII, 152, 191–93.

76

Joktan (of Genesis) became the Yucatán of the Mayas. Another *fraile*, Padre Durán, sitting among the thousands of Indians that constituted Mexico, wrote that "the supposition is confirmed. These natives are of the Ten Tribes of Israel that Salmanassar, King of the Assyrians, made prisoners and carried to Assyria in the time of Hoshea, King of Israel."

The Dutch soon entered the controversy, and the learned Huig de Groot—the famous Hugo Grotius of international law—muddied the anthropological waters by writing that the Indians of North America were Scandinavian; the Peruvians, Chinese; and the Brazilians, African. He was immediately answered by his countryman, Johannes de Laet, who, stirred to rage over such logic, wrote that anyone except a dunderpate could see that the American Indians were Scythians. By this time the Londoners of Cromwellian England were also involved in the anthropological battle. One Thomas Thorowgood had heard from a rabbi in Holland of an Antonio Montesinos who was entertained by a community of Jews in Peru, Indians who practiced the circumcisional rites; this and other apocrypha he wrote into his pamphlet, *Jewes in America*. But he was soon challenged by another writer whose tract was engagingly titled *Americans no Jewes*.[3]

By the beginning of the eighteenth century it was universally accepted in America that the Indian was the descendant of the lost Tribes of Israel. Roger Williams and John Elliott accepted it as fact and so did William Penn. "I imagined myself," he said when he looked at the Indians, "in the Jewish Quarter of London." Centuries of repetition (with explicit theological approval) and this theory—resisting the assaults of logic—had hardened into anthropological fact. Even as Stephens was studying these works of questionable erudition, there were arriving in America[4] from London copies of *The Antiquities of Mexico*, huge folios that offered "scientific proof"—from archaeology itself—that the Indians were Jews.

[3] Written by Harmon l'Estrange in 1652.

[4] "I am daily expecting from Europe . . . the magnificent works of Lord Kingsborough. *There is not a copy, I believe, in the United States.*"—William H. Prescott (at work on the research for the *Conquest of Mexico*) to Manuel Najera, in Mexico, April 25, 1839.

77

The Antiquities of Mexico, in nine volumes (£30 the folio), had been authored by Edward King, third earl of Kingston, called Lord Kingsborough. An Oxford undergraduate, born in 1795, he was suddenly precipitated into American antiquities by examining in the Bodleian Library an original Aztec hieroglyphic tribute chart. His imagination was fired, his lordly purse opened, and to the publication of these massive tomes he gave his fortune and eventually his life, for he died in a Dublin debtors' prison for his failure to meet the cost of the handmade paper on which the publications were printed. The illustrated material within the huge eight volumes was historically important, for Kingsborough had gathered the whole known collection of Mexican codices in Europe and had them lithographed and then hand colored, following the originals. Kingsborough elucidated this valuable illustrative material with a written text—a potpourri of Greek, Hebrew, Latin, and Sanskrit—interspersed with occasional English words. It took a form which was to milord Kingsborough's mind logic, but to the reader, confusion. To anyone whose patience was able to withstand these millions of words, one could learn, in sum, that America had been peopled by the lost Tribes of Israel.

It was a simple bibliographic fact in 1839 that there was no literature available to the American reader on the ancient American civilizations other than those, recently published, which Stephens had read. The Mayas of Yucatán—which every reader of the Hearst supplement knows now as well as he does the Blackfeet—had been allowed little space in the published works of the Spanish chroniclers, and their histories were in most instances secondhand. The reports on the Maya, voluminous detailed investigations made by priest and soldier, still lay unpublished in the Spanish archives, or if printed, had been issued in editions of such rarity that they were inaccessible to scholars in America. Actually, before one could attempt literary research on these pre-Columbian civilizations, or the history of the Conquest, one would have to create an entire manuscript library. This, in fact, William H. Prescott of Boston was doing at that precise moment. Although Stephens and Prescott were then personally unknown to each other, both were initiating researches into America's protohistory.

While Stephens read and pondered the manner in which to assail the mysterious cities buried in the jungles of Central America, Prescott in Boston had his "heart set on a Spanish subject—perhaps a 'Conquest of Mexico,' an anterior civilization of Mexicans, a beautiful prose epic for which virgin material teems in Madrid." He wrote to Washington Irving, telling him of his plans, but declining to proceed if Irving, as reported, had the same plan. "I have always intended, Mr. Prescott," Irving answered, in a letter dated January 18, 1839, "to write an account of the Conquest of Mexico . . . ever since I have been meddling with the theme—its grandeur and magnificence—these themes are connected with the grand enigma that rest upon the primitive population and civilization of the American continent, and of which the singular monuments and remains scattered through the wilderness serve as tantalizing indications." Prescott was given permission to proceed.[5]

And Stephens, too, had begun. Aztec! Mexico! Ruins! It was in the air. He could feel the throbbing sense of inquiry, as Prescott's letters ramifying into every cranny of the world's learned edifice made men speak and think of Mexican antiquities. Stephens had made his decision. He no longer had to depend on financial assistance from his father, for his two books, continuing edition into edition, were earning magnificent royalties. He was now ready to put into operation the plans that he and Catherwood had formulated so long ago. "Fortunately for [Stephens]," continues the journal of John R. Bartlett, "Mr. Frederick Catherwood . . . with whom he was on intimate terms, was then in New York. Mr. Catherwood had great enthusiasm in anything pertaining to architecture, and was an ardent lover of the picturesque and of archaeological researches. Mr. Stephens made him a favorable offer to accompany him to Central America, which offer he at once accepted."

Then death made John L. Stephens a diplomat. Preparations for their expedition had been about completed, passage on a vessel sailing to Central America had been arranged, when "Mr. [William] Leggett, of New York, our minister in Central Ameri-

[5] "I doubt," said Washington Irving privately, "whether Mr. Prescott was aware that I gave him my bread."

ca, died, and," Bartlett explains, "Mr. Stephens, whose policies were the same as Mr. Van Buren's, applied to the President for the vacant place. He was supported by a large number of prominent men in New York and his name being at the time very prominent before the country by his interesting books of travel in the East, he was appointed to the vacant mission. We had several interviews on the proposed visit to Central America and Mr. Stephens determined that as soon as he had presented his credentials and attended the diplomatic duties with which he was charged, he would undertake the exploration of Yucatán."

William Leggett, whom Stephens had replaced, had been part owner with William Cullen Bryant of the *Evening Post,* a strong supporter of Jacksonian principles—free trade, broader suffrage, and so on—and he had headed, for a brief moment, the radical element in Tammany Hall called the "Locofocos." He had been a violent young man, court-martialed and dismissed from the navy for dueling, and had taken up journalism and the cause of Jackson. He was a clever writer; his biting, caustic comments supplied much of the verbal ammunition of the Democrats. In 1839, Van Buren offered him a post in Guatemala, but before he could even arrange for passage, he died at the end of May, 1839. Four of the previous diplomats had died in office: John Williams, commissioned chargé d'affaires in 1826, spent only a few months in Guatemala; James Shannon, who succeeded him in 1832, died somewhere in Guatemala without even reaching office; Charles G. DeWitt managed to remain for seven years in Central America, but died from malaria in the United States; and then—William Leggett, before the ink was scarcely dry on his appointment. Obviously, this office was no diplomatic plum. Stephens began to question whether he had done the right thing, for, after all, his seeking an official post was only to aid his search for ruins. Perhaps his diplomatic duties might interfere with his primary plans. On August 13, 1839, the Secretary of State, John Forsyth, sent Stephens his instructions:

"Sir: This department having occasion to send a confidential agent to Central America on business connected with our late diplomatic mission to the country, the President has selected you for the performance of the duty and the time had now arrived when you are expected to enter upon the discharge of it." The Instructions were clear even though no one knew whether a Central American government still existed, or if it did, the location of its present capital, or the name of either its president or its minister of foreign affairs. Stephens' duties as outlined seemed uncomplicated: close the legation, ship back its official papers, find the seat of government, present his credentials, and secure the ratification of a trade treaty. So in anticipation Stephens went to a tailor on Broadway and had fashioned for himself a blue diplomatic coat, embroidered with a flow of golden braid and golden buttons. Frederick Catherwood, for his part, purchased a ream of drawing paper, a mound of sepia colors, brushes, a new camera lucida, surveying and meteorological equipment; then, turning over the management of his Panorama to his partner George Jackson, the bookseller, he embraced Mrs. Catherwood and his two sons and impatiently awaited the settlement of Mr. Stephens' "diplomatic matters."

On the third day of October, 1839, accompanied by a few friends, Stephens and Catherwood went to the North River and found their ship, the British brig *Mary Ann* with its anchor apeak and its sails loose, ready to sail. Whaling ships, Pacific bound, were putting out to sea on the ebb-tide. "It was," Stephens remembered, "seven o'clock in the morning; the streets and wharfs were still; the Battery was desolate, and at that moment of leaving it on a voyage of uncertain duration, New York seemed more beautiful than I had ever known it before."

As the *Mary Ann* put out to sea, Stephens opened a letter delivered just before sailing. It was from the wife of the late Mr. Charles G. DeWitt. She referred to all the other diplomats who had died in Central America and then sounded an ominous end: "May you be more fortunate than any of your predecessors have been."

Chapter VIII From the sea, Belize looked enchanting. A thin row of white houses stretched along the shore, framed between masses of coconut-palm fronds, and to Stephens and Catherwood for an unthinking moment it looked, as they rowed ashore in a mahogany dugout, like a Venice or an Alexandria. When they landed, sinking to their boot tops in the muddy streets, and saw the rows of buildings mounted on stilts and had their nostrils assaulted by the heavy odor of human refuse, Belize exhibited its true character. It was an untidy, shabby, tropical port —the postern of Middle America.

Although it had been settled since 1670, Belize gave no indication of mellowing; most of it seemed newly fashioned, like the settlements that Stephens had seen in the Illinois wilderness mushrooming overnight on the banks of the Wabash. The port settlement, intersected by the Belize River, contained most of its principal buildings on the western side. There were two avenues, Front and Back Streets; along these, fierce-looking scavenger hogs were taking mud baths in the undried holes. All the houses were raised on stilts, airily balconied and tastefully planted with tropical flowers; scarlet hibiscus and flaming crotons gave life to the mud and wafted sensual odors to counterbalance the stench of the port. At the extreme end of Front Street was the Government House, the Barracks, Parade Ground, Parsonage, the Free School, and the Burial Ground—in order of their importance. Back of the settlement lay the cohune ridges and savannahs of reddish sandy soil that supported pitch pine, cohune palms, and tall, toughly succulent savannah grass on which the town cattle browsed. Back of this was a solid phalanx of jungle, as effective in defense as the Chinese wall. With no land communications with the interior, Belize hung on the jagged littoral, a brief oasis in the chaos of disorder that was then Central America.

There were no hotels in Belize. Mr. Edwin Coffin of Hulse and Coffin, exporters and consignees of the *Mary Ann,* waved aside this unimportant problem, took the gentlemen to the extreme end of Front Street, and installed them in an empty house. Having passed twice down *the* street in Belize, it did not take Stephens long to see that of the settlement's six thousand population, listed in the *Honduras Almanac,* four thousand were Negro. "They were a fine-looking race," Stephens recalled, "tall, straight, and athletic, with skins black, smooth, and glossy as velvet, and well dressed, the men in white cotton shirts and trousers, with straw hats, and the women in white frocks with short sleeves and broad red borders, and adorned with large red earrings and necklaces." Coming from a land of tightly corseted women who wrapped their bodies cocoon-like in swathes of petticoats, making the ankle the most exciting part of the anatomy, Stephens "could not help remarking that the frock was their only article of dress, and that it was the fashion of these sable ladies to drop this considerably from off the right shoulder, and to carry the skirt in the left hand, and raise it to any height necessary for crossing puddles."

Breakfast found the explorer dining with an assortment of peoples and colors: a white British officer in brilliant red coat, two neatly dressed mulattoes; as for Stephens, he was sandwiched between "two coloured gentlemen." "Some of my countrymen," said Stephens, "would have hesitated about taking it, but I did not; both were well dressed, well educated, and polite."

In Belize there was no rigid demarcation between white and black as in the United States. "Before I had an hour in Balize," remarked Stephens, "I learned that the great work of practical amalgamation, the subject of so much angry controversy at home, had been going on quietly for generations; colour was considered mere matter of taste; and that some of the most respectable inhabitants had black wives and mongrel children, whom they educated with as much care, and made money for with as much zeal, as if their skins were perfectly white. I hardly knew whether to be shocked or amused at this condition of society."

The Negro had been in Belize long before Cromwell in 1655 laid, by his "Western Design," the foundation for British interest in the Caribbean. Negro slaves captured from the seventeenth-century Spanish *asientos* were brought to Belize to "work" mahogany when Belize was still occupied by the Mopán tribes of the Maya, which the more aggressive Negro either absorbed or annihilated. The tropics being the Negroes' milieu, they out-reproduced their white masters, so that soon they became, as they are today, the dominant race-pattern not only of British Honduras but of the whole of the Caribbean. On August 31, 1839, just before Stephens' arrival, the nominal yoke (for their slavery was casual) was removed by the act of general abolition. The event was celebrated, wrote the *Honduras Almanac*, by religious processions and music; Nelson Schaw, "a snow-drop of the first water," the spokesman for the occasion, approached the superintendent of Belize and said: "On the part of my emancipated brothers and sisters, I venture to approach your excellency, to entreat you to thank our most gracious Queen for all that she has done for us. We will pray for her; we will fight for her; and, if it is necessary, we will die for her. . . . Come, my countrymen, hurrah! Dance, ye black rascals; the flag of England flies over your heads, and every rustle of its folds knocks the fetters off the limbs of the poor slave. Hubbabboo Cochalorum Gee!"

For two centuries, Belize, spawned by the gold-thirsting buccaneers, hung precariously on the fringe of the Gulf of Honduras, hidden behind the defenses of razor-sharp coral cays. Belize became in the power politics of its day the pitiful residue of the ill-conceived plans of Oliver Cromwell. The "Western Design"[1] had been conceived for one swift, telling blow—to be struck at all the vulnerable ports of the Spanish Empire in America: Panama, Porto Bello, Cartagena, Jamaica, and Cuba—by which the Lord Protector hoped all America would be wrested from Spain. But it had miscarried. Out of it, however, the British developed a political wedge, the commercial intrusion of Jamaica, hard on Cuba, and Belize in Central America. These footholds were the Achilles' heel of Spain. Jamaica, captured in 1655, became the piratical exchange of the Main, Belize its continental branch. When, in fur-

[1] First conceived by Cromwell's private secretary, John Milton. *Scriptum domini protectoris contra hispanos* (1655).

therance of national interests, piracy was suppressed by William III, the buccaneers broke up into small groups, scattered themselves on the Atlantic coast of Central America. They abandoned freebooting and turned to logging—fustic for dye, mahogany for fine wood—and so Belize became the new piratical capital.

His Catholic Majesty, the King of Spain, soon learned that by suppression of official piracy his ambassadors had done him no service, for now these privateers—the most dangerous of the British fauna—were entrenched along the entire Caribbean, from Belize to Nicaragua, and not only did they carry off his botanical treasures, but when the rains came and they were unable to log, they thought nothing of running down the King's caravels, carrying off his royal fifth, and dumping without ceremony his loyal subjects into the barracuda-infested Caribbean. These irritations led to wars, 150 years of brutal engagements which kept the whole continent on edge. At length, in 1783, Spain was ready for compromise; she acknowledged British rights on the Atlantic coast of Central America and gave them logging rights, official sanction to cut mahogany, dyewoods, and lignum vitae, although it was expressly stipulated that the King of Spain yielded, thereby, no other rights beyond these.

Belize was then organized along the lines of a British crown colony. There remained, however, the "unofficial wars." The collapse of Spain as a continental power brought Belize no surcease, for Spain's former colonies, Mexico and the Federated States of Central America, continued the wars, which in Stephens' time became so aggravated that they almost caused a war between North America and England. These differences were settled, fortunately, by compromise in the Clayton-Bulwer Treaty of 1850; however, it did not settle the claims of Central America—the Republic of Guatemala still regards British Honduras as irredenta.[2] "Why do we bother," asks Aldous Huxley of his fellow Britishers, "to keep this strange little fragment of the Empire? Certainly not from mo-

[2] At the moment of writing, this dispute between Great Britain and Guatemala will be reviewed by the International Court of Justice of the United Nations. Both disputants have agreed to the Court's jurisdiction and its decision. The legal solution of British Honduras will be a long step forward toward the pacification of the irredenta; the dispute has long poisoned Central American diplomacy.

tives of self-interest. Hardly one Englishman in fifty thousand derives any profit from the Britishness of British Honduras. . . . To the overwhelming majority of British voters, taken as individuals, it is probably a matter of indifference whether British Honduras remains within the Empire or not."

Back of British Honduras lay mysterious Central America, a triangle of violent geography, roughly seven hundred miles long, a land of graceful Spanish cities centuries old, skirted by jungles filled with fierce Indians. The land was mountainous, tumbled and indented, with no central mountain range, and covered by a thin earth-crust that burst with threatening inconstancy. Central America was without a central geographic communication, such as existed in the high plateaux of the Andes. And it lacked geographical unity. The high, jungle-topped mountains sent their flooding streams to coalesce into tempestuous rivers—shallow and violent—rivers which did not admit easy navigation. Even the name for this 177,000 square miles of volcano-spiked land was an anachronism; "Central" America was not a geographical description, but a political term, invented in 1823, a republic embodying Guatemala, Salvador, Honduras, Nicaragua, and Costa Rica. The only thing central about it was its position between the two colossi, the North and South Americas.

América Central remained for centuries the focal point of foreign envy, for here, if it was to be constructed at all, was the location for a passage to the Pacific. The British, at the moment of Stephens' visit, had the most effective foothold, and the policy at that moment was directed by the colonies' superintendent, Colonel Archibald M'Donald. Stephens paid Colonel M'Donald a visit of state in a style reminiscent of the time he had called upon Mehemet Ali in Cairo. But this time, instead of a richly saddled horse, he went in a native *pitpan*, a forty-foot-long Indian dugout, fashioned from a single mahogany log powered by eight ebony-colored soldiers, who chanted the wild, half-forgotten barbaric songs of Africa.

Colonel M'Donald met them on the steps of the government house. "One of a race," Stephens observed, "that is fast passing away, and with whom an American seldom meets," M'Donald was a professional soldier, empire-style, handsome, expansive, deluged with military honors. He had fought the twenty years' war with Napoleon, seen action in the Peninsular War at Waterloo. His tunic was rainbowed with campaign ribbons. He also had connections. Sir John M'Donald, his brother, was adjutant general of England, his cousin was a marshal of France, and so his attitude reflected his genealogy. His conversation was full of largess, "like reading a page of history," Stephens thought. M'Donald toasted the Queen, the health of Mr. Van Buren, president of the United States, and the successful journey of the explorers, all this in the hearty manner of the empire builder. Stephens, although "unused to taking the President and the people upon my shoulders," responded to the toast, and the official dinner went on its brilliant way. The American Secretary of State at the moment would have liked to have known more about the plans of Colonel M'Donald,[3] for this excellency was about to put into execution the seizure of the Bay Islands in the Caribbean, and other little imperialistic expansions upsetting the balance of power in Central America.

When they took their leave, M'Donald put his arm through Stephens' in an easy spirit of camaraderie and told him that he was about to enter a distracted country (a euphonious term for the confused slaughter that was going on in the hinterlands), that if danger ever threatened, he was to gather all the Europeans together, run up the British flag and send for him, and he, Colonel M'Donald, with his redcoats, would, in Waterloo style, come and mow the enemy down.

The explorers took their leave of Belize on the old *Vera Paz* which plied among the atolls and cays of the Caribbean. As they moved away, to Stephens' surprise a salute of thirteen guns was given. The soldiers on the docks, blackamoors in flaming red coats,

[3] "Colonel MacDonald is a Soldier, as well as a High Minded, frank and Honorable man. He would have made a fit representative of Greece and Rome in the brightest days of their Glory—But I venture to State, as the result of all I can learn from Enquiry, and of all that I have seen, that neither Colonel MacDonald, nor any other person, connected with the Colonial Government at Belize, can or will venture to set any bounds to [their] claim . . . over the Territories of these states."—W. S. Murphy, special agent to Daniel Webster, secretary of state, January 20, 1842, in *Diplomatic Correspondence of the United States* (Washington, 1933), III, 163.

presented arms, and Captain Hampton of the *Mary Ann* sent off his four-pounders. "You will ask," Stephens wrote, "how I bore all these honours. I had visited many cities, but it was the first time that flags and cannons announced to the world that I was going away. . . . Verily, thought I, if these are the fruits of official appointments, it is not strange that men are found willing to accept them."

After stopping in a Carib village at Punta Gorda, the *Vera Paz*, befouling the porcelain-blue tropic sky with huge wreaths of black smoke, rattled into the crescent-shaped bay where the Río Dulce debouched the interior waters of Lake Isabal into the Caribbean, and turned into the palisaded river. Ghostly herons flew along the shore, iguanas with three feet of whiplash tail clung to the sides of trees, indifferent to the roaring monster that broke the jungle peace. "Could this be the portal," Stephens asked, "to a land of volcanoes and earthquakes, torn and distracted by civil war?" The narrow walls of the river passage recalled to him his entrance into Petra—only the steamboat seemed to shatter the romantic illusion. The age of steam had hardly begun, and already John L. Stephens was apostrophizing its shattering of romance. "Steam boats have destroyed some of the most pleasing illusions of my life. I was hurried up the Hellespont, past Sestos and Abydos, and the Plain of Troy under the clatter of a steam-engine; and it struck at the root of all the romance connected with the adventures of Columbus to follow in his track, accompanied by the clamour of some panting monster."

The Río Dulce continued its narrow passage for nine miles, then opened into a lake. Lying unagitated and reflecting the cloudless sky, Lago Isabal seemed like the polished surface of an emerald. At the end of the lake—harbor and entrepôt of violence and chaos—was the port of Isabal. Among the coconut palms and bananas were scattered the palm-thatched huts of its inhabitants. There was only one frame building, the commercial establishment of Ampudio y Pulleiro, whose principal occupation was to collect the cargo which arrived on the *Vera Paz* and engage muleteers to carry the stuff over Mico Mountain, the principal route into the heart of Central America. The muleteers, ragged and mud splattered, lay sleeping on stinking, sweat-permeated mule blankets, about which swarmed stingless bees slaking their thirst on the exudate. The mules, noisily crunching sugar cane, were doing their best to console themselves for the return trip.

Stephens called upon the commandant with his passport. A soldier, a *minus habeans* of about fourteen years, with a bell-crowned straw hat falling over his eyes like an extinguisher upon a candle, stood at the door as sentinel.

His Excellency, Don Juan Peñol, shirt hanging out of his trousers, commandant of the port, could give Stephens no assurance that the passport he would issue would be respected. The Carrera faction might recognize it, but the troops of General Morazán definitely would not. Stephens was given the impression that there were three contending parties in the scrambled politics of America Central: Morazán, Carrera, and Ferrara. Carrera, an Indian, and Ferrara, a mulatto—"though not fighting for any common purpose, they sympathized in opposition to General Morazán." Altogether the commandant's picture of the country was like something out of Dante's tableaux of horrors. Had not the discovery of ruins been their object, rather than making logic out of the chaos of government, they would have made a *volte-face* then and there.

Their principal object now was to go to Copán and clear Isabal as quickly as possible. For death hung around the place. Catherwood called upon Mr. Thomas Rush, the engineer of the *Vera Paz*, an Englishman of Herculean frame, six feet, four, stout in proportion, who had been struck down by malaria. He wanted, in his nightly bout with the "ague," to have a countryman about. Stephens, remembering that his predecessor in office, Mr. James Shannon, had died in Isabal, set out to locate his grave. On a knoll back of the village, in the cellar-cool forest, under epiphytic arums, was the unmarked grave of the late Chargé d'Affaires. Considering it a "gloomy burial-place for a countryman," and fighting the depression of spirit that the place gave him, he ordered that it be marked, a fence built around it, and a coconut tree placed as a marker.

At daylight they began the ascent of Mico Mountain on mules arranged for the night before by Augustin,[4] their guide. Augustin they had picked up in Belize, a young cutthroat with a machete scar across his face. He had been born in Santo Domingo, sired by a French father. At first they thought him "not very sharp," but as they continued, they found him possessed of a Machiavellian shrewdness. As he spoke French, it became the expedition's lingua franca. Augustin had been over the Mico trail before, and he knew what was required. They mounted their mules and set off into the gloomy, dimly lighted jungle to the raucous calls of the parrots. Stephens and Catherwood were both armed with a brace of pistols. Augustin, also mounted, carried pistols and a sword, while the principal muleteer, who guided the Indians and the pack mules, carried unsheathed a murderous-looking machete. On his naked feet a pair of enormous spurs jingled like the fetters of a convict.

Shafts of morning light filtered through the leaves, as light breaking through the stained-glass windows of a cathedral. The road was a quagmire. Soon they were lost in the thick, leady gloom of the jungle. White morpho butterflies floated ahead of them, and in the distance the bleating of unseen tree frogs gave the darkened jungle aisles a melancholy note. Giant roots of the mata-palos and mahoganies, awash from the black earth, broke across the road, making hurdles for the mules. Stephens, holding on to the pommel, had all he could do to remain in the saddle. "For five long hours," he remembered, "we were dragged through mud-holes, squeezed in gulleys, knocked against trees, and tumbled over roots; every step required care and great physical exertion; . . . I felt that our inglorious epitaph might be, 'tossed over the head of a mule, brained by the trunk of a mahogany-tree, and buried in the mud of Mico Mountain.' " Later Frederick Catherwood, who bore all these discomforts without a word of complaint, was violently thrown from his saddle when his mule failed to clear an exposed root, and struck his back with great violence against a tree. He lay half-buried in the mud, and for a moment there was not a sound from him; then, without moving from the

4 The proper Spanish spelling of this name is "Agustín," but Stephens always made it "Augustin," the French spelling.

mudhole where he lay, he groaned: "If I had known of this cursed Mico Mountain before I agreed to come, you would have come to Central America alone."

Was it possible that this was the great "highroad" to Guatemala City, the road over which all traffic moved to feed the wants of the largest of the Central American states? The muleteers insisted that almost all the merchandise from Europe came over it. Augustin said that the reason for its condition was that it was traversed by so many mules, to which Stephens replied that in most other countries that alone would have been considered a sufficient reason for making it better. During the whole of the first part of the day they encountered no other living person; then, at a turn in the path, they came upon a tall, dark-complected man in a large-brimmed Panama rolled up on both sides. Over his shoulders was a Guatemalan poncho, and in his hand was an unsheathed sword. He had a brace of pistols sticking out of his belt and knife-sharp spurs on his mud-splattered boots, like a fighting cock. To their utter amazement, he doffed his Panama and spoke to them in the cultured tones of an English gentleman. He had lost his guides, his mule had fallen twice, and his nerves were frayed. He asked for a drink of brandy. With his feet buried in the mud of Mico Mountain, he told them that he had come from Guatemala City, where he had been trying for two years to negotiate a bank charter. "Fresh as I was," Stephens said, "from the land of banks, I almost thought he intended a fling at me; but he did not look like one in a humour for jesting; and, for the benefit of those who will regard it as an evidence of incipient improvement, I am able to state that he had the charter secured . . . and was then on his way to England to sell the stock."

The second day found them on the road to Gualán. Geography had metamorphosed the thick turmoil of the lowland jungles into sun-bright, pine-studdied highlands. Purple mountains succeeded each other, elfish, fantastic peaks, some bare, some verdured, reaching into the clouds like scenes from some fabled Walpurgis. Instead of jungle, they now had enormous candelabra cacti, mile upon mile of strange, dully green cacti holding spiny arms stiffly aloft. Cacti were succeeded by pine, and the pine by thickets of mimosa, covered with fluffy pale yellow balls which filled the evening air with an intoxicating odor. The enchanting distance, the hillsides green studded with pine and grazing cattle, reminded Catherwood of the pencilings of George Morland and gave a faint appearance of rural England.

By afternoon they reached the Río Motagua, crossed it, and found themselves in the village of Encuentros, the first habitation they had seen since they had left Belize. Stephens was forcibly struck by the deep simplicity of the people, a natural, fundamental dignity. The courtesy of their women was like that of some well-bred chatelaine. They asked him to dismount and placed their homes—even though only covered with palm thatch—at his disposition. Their every act of kindness seemed to come from an instinctive sense of personal pride. Food was scarce and, when available, monotonous, yet there were always *tortillas* which Stephens was at pains to describe.[5] Corn cakes, black beans fried in grease savored with garlic, with an occasional piece of meat, washed down with jet-black coffee flavored with native raspadura-sugar, was the regime for a day's three meals.

They continued to follow the Río Motagua—on the *camino real*—passing Gualán, through pine and oak regions, after which they entered Zacapa, the largest settlement they had encountered in Guatemala. The streets, cobblestoned and rough, were laid out regularly, and the houses, coming to the edge of the street in the Spanish manner, were neatly whitewashed. The main plaza, planted with scarlet hibiscus and palm trees, was dominated by a large church, built of cyclopean walls and decorated with a Moorish façade. Directed to the finest house, they knocked at a gargantuan gate and were admitted by a French-speaking Santo Domingo Negro. With easy grace the servant said that although his master Don Marino was not at home, the gentlemen must be pleased to consider this their home—at which he placed everything at their

[5] "The whole family was engaged in making tortillas. This is the bread of Central America . . . Indian corn soaked in lime-water to remove the husk; and, placing a handful on an oblong stone curving inward, [the woman] mashed it with a stone roller into a thick paste. The girls . . . patting it with their hands into flat cakes, laid them on the griddle to bake. This is repeated for every meal, and a great part of the business of the women consists in making tortillas."

disposition. So, said Stephens in his droll manner, "we had candles lighted and made ourselves at home. I was sitting at a table writing, when we heard the tramp of mules outside, and a gentleman entered, took off his sword and spurs, and laid his pistols upon the table. Supposing him to be a traveller like ourselves, we asked him to take a seat; and when supper was served, invited him to join us. It was not till bedtime that we found we were doing the honours to one of the masters of the house. He must have thought us cool, but I flatter myself he had no reason to complain of any want of attention."

At Chiquimula, which they reached the following day, crossing deep barrancas in the cicatrized earth, the first object that met Stephens' eyes was a young lady who stood in the doorway of a red-tiled house. She smiled at the party as they rode by. Her face was of uncommon interest—her eyes were like dark pools and the eyebrows finely penciled. Stephens instantly marked her house as their lodging. He suggested it, and she accepted them with graceful courtesy. As yet, Stephens did not know whether she were to be addressed *Señora* or *Señorita*, "but unhappily," he wrote, "we found that a man whom we supposed her father, was her husband," and a ten-year-old boy whom he supposed to be her brother turned out to be her child. "*Es mío*," she said, smiling enchantingly, laying her hand upon his head. "But it was so long since I had seen a woman who was at all attractive," Stephens confessed, "and her face was so interesting, her manners were so good, her voice so sweet, the Spanish words rolled so beautifully from her lips, and her frock was tied so close behind, that in spite of ten-year-old boy and puro [cigar], I clung to my first impressions."

Their direction was now westward along the precipitous branch of the Río Motagua, the ancient river road to Copán. It was a halcyon country, a patchwork of corn and bananas and an occasional plantation of cochineal. Mountains intervened, an interminable and meaningless wilderness of peaks and quiescent volcanoes lay around them, tall and gloomy, their verdure-covered tops buried in the clouds. They met no one. An occasional naked child would peer out from a whitewashed adobe house, only to be snatched in quickly. They passed churches, primitive types of Hispanic-Moorish architecture which appeared in every little village. At the town of Comatán, they came to the seventh church in as many hours. Its whitewashed façade supported eight rococo pillars, displaying its four saints, placed properly in niches. Bells hung silent in the tower; an iron cross, eroded and ancient, crowned the top and fought with the plants growing out of the roof. The grass in the plaza fronting the church was green and unscarred even by a mule path. Back of it, red-tiled houses lay scattered. Fronting the church was the village *cabildo*, an adobe structure forty feet long, roofed with tile. Coolly Stephens tore the chain off the iron door, and they entered a large, vacant room. A table was the only item of furniture. Augustin was sent out to forage for food. He returned with one egg. Later the alcalde of Comatán, carrying his wand of office, a silver-headed cane, called upon them. As was the custom, he asked their business. Stephens displayed his official passport, which the alcalde was unable to read, so he departed with his retinue. The explorers, tired by the long journey, had to be content with the one egg, stale bread, and chocolate for their supper. They arranged their sleeping quarters, lighted some pine slivers, and settled in their hammocks. In the wreaths of smoke from their cigars, they speculated on the fabled ruins of Copán, which they would reach tomorrow.

Suddenly there was a shuffling of feet outside. The door burst open. Into the room suddenly made ablaze with sputtering pine torches, poured a horde of men—alcaldes, *alguacils*, soldiers, Indians, mestizos—all armed and ferocious. A young officer with a glazed hat and sword demanded to see their passports. Augustin gave it to him, explaining in an aside the official character of the endorsements. The toothless Indian alcalde, poking his wrinkled, coffee-colored face over the officer's shoulder, ventured that he had seen a passport before, but that it was printed on a small piece of paper, not larger than his hand, whereas that which he held before him was as large as a quarto sheet. The conversation grew heated. The officer said that the party could not proceed on their journey to Copán. They would remain prisoners in Comatán until more information came from General Cascara at Chiquimula.

Guatemala-Honduras. *The precise route over which Stephens traveled from Comatán to Guatemala.*

From a photograph by the author

Church at Comatán today. *Here Stephens and Catherwood were imprisoned in 1839.*

From a photograph by the author

The Court of the Hieroglyphic Stairway at Copán. *This is a synthesis of various carvings found within the tree-filled courtyard. In the fore-ground, a sacrificial altar; in the background, the terraces of a pyramid.*

From a lithograph by Frederick Catherwood (1844)

In the Court of the Hieroglyphic Stairway at Copán today. *The ruins have now been partially restored.*

Stela and altar at Copán.

From a lithograph by Frederick Catherwood

Stephens was adamant. Rather than lose time, they would abandon the journey to Copán. The officer said that "the Señores would neither go forward or backward." He then demanded the passport. Stephens refused. It had been given to him, he said, by his government for his protection, and he would not surrender it. Frederick Catherwood was now aroused. It was not the custom for Englishmen set upon by uncivilized hyenas to take such effrontery supinely. He made a learned exposition of the law of nations, he touched upon the sacrosanct quality of ambassadors, he passed down the ages, dwelt upon diplomatic immunity; he ended with a threat that this miserable coxcomb would bring down upon him the wrath of vengeance from the *Estados Unidos del Norte*. Through all this the officer never relaxed the supercilious look on his face. Stephens, remembering his difficulties with the Sheikh in Arabia Petra, recalling that it is sometimes good to be in a passion, deliberately put his passport in his breast pocket, folded his arms across his chest, and said: "If you want it, you will have to get it by force."

The soldiers raised their muskets, cocked them, pointed them within three feet of Stephens' head. Had Stephens known how little value was placed on human life in that period, he would have yielded.

Augustin, always bellicose and appearing more so with the pine torches reflecting on his scarred face, shouted in French: "Give me the order to fire, Monsieur; one round will scatter them."

At that moment another officer, older and slightly permeated with reason, entered the room. The soldiers lowered their rifles. At Catherwood's request the newly arrived officer read the passport aloud. It was agreed that a courier, at their expense, should be dispatched to General Cascara. Stephens wrote the letter, Catherwood translated it into Italian, signed the note "Secretary," and having no official seal, Stephens took from his pocket a new American half-dollar and impressed it in the wax. Guards were posted in front of what was now their cell; and they, exhausted by the ordeal, dropped into their hammocks. At midnight the door burst open again. Once more the same routine. There was a repetition of the confusion. This time the explorers, pistols cocked for action, thirsted for battle; there was no need. They were told that they were now free to continue to Copán.

It was an unfavorable introduction to American archaeology, and the incident long rankled with Stephens. He wrote a letter of protest to John Forsyth, secretary of state: "I regret to be obliged to say that on my way . . . I was arrested and imprisoned. I made a complaint to the Government of this State."

Chapter ix   Stephens stood on the edge of the tropical Río Copán, looking, through the interstices of leaf and vine filled with flowering orchids and chattering spider monkeys, upon an ancient wall. It was his first view of time-mythed Copán. But let Stephens speak: "Soon we came to the bank of a river, and saw directly opposite a stone wall, perhaps a hundred feet high, with furze growing out of the top, running north and south along the river, in some places fallen, but in others entire. It had more the character of a structure than any we had ever seen, ascribed to the aborigines of America. . . . I am entering abruptly upon new ground."

For one thousand years Copán had lain there, covered by trees, embraced by roots of the strangler Ficus, engulfed by the detritus of the centuries, centuries which gradually covered up one of the greatest archaic civilizations the world has ever known. Now monkeys were the only tenants of Copán.

Shephens and Catherwood, almost breathless with ecstasy, entered, through a maze of tropical undergrowth, the "Eastern Court" of the acropolis of Copán. It was as silent as a tomb. From invisible stations in the treetops, cicadas quietly raised their rhythmic song. Long-armed black spider monkeys scolded quietly as they watched these strange invaders of their sanctuary. Stones meticulously set formed some kind of amphitheater, and in the distance about cyclopean steps was the ruin of a temple enveloped in the pallid tentacles of a strangler-fig tree. On a broken stairway were stone jaguars rearing up on their hind legs. Above them, a huge stone head, the symbol of the corn god, was fighting for its place with a tree which, scorning the need for earth, had grown out of the interstices of the stone steps. They, who had seen the remains of the classical civilizations, were instantly able to gauge

97

from a decorated stone and a ruined plaza, the value of their discovery.

They climbed over more pyramids and descended into a jungle of trees growing in the principal plaza. There, through the darkened stands of huge-buttressed trees, they discerned the white shadows of great-sized, intricately carved monoliths, still standing erect, disdaining the jungle that usurped their place. Stephens came face to face with a colossal stone figure "about fourteen feet high and three feet on each side, sculptured in very bold relief. . . . The front was a figure of a man curiously and richly dressed, and the face, evidently a portrait, solemn, stern, and well fitted to excite terror. The back was of a different design, unlike anything we had ever seen before, and the sides were covered with hieroglyphics. . . . before it, at a distance of three feet, was a large block of stone, also sculptured with figures and emblematical devices, which he called an altar. The sight of this unexpected monument put at rest at once and forever, in our minds, all uncertainty in regard to the character of American antiquities. . . . With an interest perhaps stronger than we had ever felt in wandering among the ruins of Egypt, we followed our guide . . . to fourteen monuments of the same character and appearance, some with more elegant designs, and some in workmanship equal to the finest monuments of the Egyptians."

Who had built these stone buildings? What race in America had reached so great a height of civilization as to be able to carve such sculptures? To these two archaeological explorers gazing wonderingly on these monuments, the whole history of Copán was a blank. A century of archaeological investigation has answered it, but only partially. The importance of Stephens' rediscovery can only be placed in its proper perspective by an excursion into time.

When the Maya poured into the compact eight-mile-long valley which was Copán, it was empty of people. If man had been there before them, he had disappeared and left nothing of himself. The Maya themselves had been great wanderers. The entire span of their existence, as tribe, as race, had been a ceaseless migration. So remote in time were these first migrations that even their necromancers had been unable to preserve the confused memory of the events; for who among the Maya could remember the cold that once covered his oven-hot world, that epoch of eternal winter with the earth, like the moon, whirling ice-bound through interplanetary space?

It was the end of the Ice Age. A new world was forming. The glacial ice that had held the world in eternal winter was melting and pouring brawling streams of frigid water into the agitated ocean. Plants that had survived it pushed their pallid heads out of the tundra, spores of seeds wafted on the streams of warmer air found root, and under the climatic change rank luxuriance gradually usurped the place of the ice. Over the face of this strange new green earth, after aeons of evolutionary progress, man, real man, Cro-Magnon appeared. He is not out of the pale of world memory. Three hundred centuries ago he was making zoomorphic engravings on the walls of caves, creditable intaglios of bison, mammoths, deer, wolves. In body, Cro-Magnon was a completely formed type not materially different from modern man; he had wit, ornament, a technique of living, he had custom. The massive herds of mammals that roamed the earth soon made the acquaintance of this tool-using primate. He flowed around the Mediterranean and crossed it, and he wandered through the wilderness of the Nile into the sylvan lands of India, Java, China, throughout the whole of Eurasia. Finally he broke into that world-in-itself, Mongolia and northern Siberia.

Slow century followed slow century and the metamorphoses of time were making changes in this primitive man; the descendants of the pithecanthropi were becoming "race." These Siberian dwellers, hair coarse, black, and straight, had beardless faces, flat, with cheekbones in prominence, and indexed by epicanthic eyes. They were already, at this time, in the Neolithic age of human culture, using stone-celts for tools, when some of them mutated from their Siberian world and moved into an utterly new one. Two hundred centuries ago, these men with the mongoloid eyes, following the northern paths of mammals, were making the first invasion of the Americas.

99

Primitive man came to America over its roof. Westward from Alaska are twelve hundred miles of Aleutian Islands; the geologic residue of volcanic action, they stretch out in an endless chain across the Bering Sea within sight of outer Siberia. Once they were a land bridge, a connecting link between continents, and over them for countless epochs had lapped herds of camels, tapirs, and elephants crossing over from America to outer Siberia.

The Ice Age was still the dominant element when ancient man came to America. We know of his presence; he has left his bones commingled in fossiled death with extinct animals. Throughout the centuries following their Siberian migration, these proto-Americans moved down the unglaciated Alaskan corridor into the vast land theaters of America. Within five centuries this man penetrated the most remote corners of the hemisphere, from ice-bound north to ice-bound south, eventually covering America's entire 135 degrees of latitude. Living here on the shores of frozen or of tropical waters at altitudes varying from sea level to several thousands of feet, living there in forests, grassy plains, or deserts; here starved, there in plenty; here with a night of six months' duration, there a night twelve hours long; here among health-giving winds, there cursed with disease—ancient man in America, greatly varying in his cultural milieu, was emerging into a new creature, a Homo Americanus.

In 5000 B.C. this American man did not much differ in his cultural accomplishments from primitive man elsewhere. At the time man in the Nile Valley was cultivating millet and barley and laying down the agricultural base upon which Egyptian civilization was to flower, the American man was selecting the wild plants which would become his maize, potatoes, tomatoes, beans, and squash, on which he, too, would hypothecate his civilization.

In only one respect—and this an important one for American cultural history—did he differ from Eurasian man. In America there was no Metal Age; man here never quit his Neolithic horizon. His tool (despite the Incan invention of soft bronze) remained the tool of the pithecanthropi—the stone-celt.

By the time the Egyptians had reached their cultural apogee and erected the Temple of Amon in 2100 B.C., the Babylonian civilization had come and gone. The legendary Cadmus had left the alphabet, and the glory that was to be Greece was still contained in societies of Hellenic men abysmally primitive.

In America by that time, the period of great wandering had come to an end. Vast spaces of the American earth were menfilled. Out of these cysts of geography, human cultures came into being. In the hyperborean regions, the Eskimo, flat of face and rotund of body, still lived in the environments of the Ice Age; on the North American plains, tall, keen-eyed tepee dwellers regulated their lives to the biology of the roving animal; farther south where the caress of the sun was longer, the Indian, becoming partly sedentary, cultivated his plants and under the shelter of rock eaves erected crudely constructed pueblos. At the other extreme of America, the antipodal south, giant Fuegians, their naked bodies wrapped in guanaco skins, walked the frozen tundra, leaving the imprint of their widely spreading feet—"*patagoes*"—on the fire-bound land.

In the luxuriant jungles of that same South America, naked Indians with filed teeth hunted man and beast. West of these dwelling places of the Amazon and the Orinoco was the evening land of the Andes. There in the high, cold, dun-colored valleys, a huge-lunged people were developing a great civilization. Around a frigid Andean lake called Titicaca, an Aymara-speaking race had, by the year 1000 B.C., laid down the agricultural patterns that would become the monolithic civilization of Tiahuanacu. Below the Aymara and around them, over the rock-hard world, there were other tribes speaking Quechua, a related language. In time these "Incas" would form all the other Andean tribes into an empire. North of the Incas were the Quitus; north of the Quitus the territory of the Chibcha, whose strange customs already included the piercing of the nose septum for the insertion of golden ornaments. They were to create the myth of El Dorado.

Between these two geographic monsters, North and South America, lay Middle America and Mexico, their broken mountains studded with belching volcanoes. This was to be the scene of two of the greatest civilizations of ancient America, the Aztec and the Maya.

Most of Mexico had a homogeneous culture. Whether it was Totonac, Toltec, Zapotec, Otomi, Huasteca, or Maya, tribe was developed from family; animal diet was supplemented by a rude agriculture—plots of ground were burned over, and seeds were inserted in holes made by a fire-hardened stick. Agriculture revolved around corn as the staple. Society was then, as it has remained ever since, machineless. There were no draft animals, the denominator of speed was the foot. Dress was the breechclout. Men walked in sandaled feet. Women wore a short-petticoated cincture of woven cotton cloth; bare breasts matched bare feet.

In all these tribes society was organized on cognate kinship; the unit was the clan, and each clan had a totemic name. Together these clans became a tribe, bound not by the holding of land, but by the ties of blood. Equally homogeneous was their religion. Belief was animistic; everything in their world, animate or inanimate, possessed "soul," everything was alive, sentient, willful. Gods, both good and evil, had to be propitiated, and art, when it evolved, became dedicated to the metaphysics of this theology. Stoneworking was universal among them. The tides of cultural inheritance ebbed back and forth among all tribes of Mexico and Middle America until that which had been the exclusive cultural property of one tribal kin became the cultural currency of all. There was no intrusion of culture from either Europe, Asia, or Cambodia; within itself and by itself America created its own world.

Then out of this mosaic of archaic cultures sometime after 1000 B.C. (we have no means of knowing precisely when), one tribe, the Maya, sprang forward in this struggle of civilizations, and for 2,500 years it never fully relinquished its dominance; the Maya were to be the apotheosis of American Indian culture. They were to create a solar calendar, hieroglyphic writing, temples of carved stone, and a system of agriculture.

A hundred centuries ago—relatively recent for geology—a convulsion of nature tossed up out of the Caribbean a huge bulk of limestone composed of fossil marine animals, and this, converted by the alchemy of geology, became the strangely featured peninsula of Yucatán. The relation of the Maya to their limestone habitat was, in a sense, symbiotic, for limestone when burned became their cement, when crushed into a fine powder caustic it softened the maize kernels for *tortillas*, when split and fashioned, their building material. And even more life-sustaining, the porous limestone worn by erosion opened here and there about the land into large *dzonotes* or *cenotes*, water cisterns.

By 1000 B.C. the Maya were in possession of this tropical glebe; 500 B.C. and they were already possessed of glyphic writing and a 365-day calendar, based on acute astronomical observations, a calendar bound up with a tortuous religious ritual. Societies formed about the wells and planted their milpas. Maize (*"ixim"* in Maya) was the life-giver. Everything in Maya life began and ended with the planting of the milpa, for man no longer fought against the plant world but for it. In his world, the Maya sought to alter nature, not to plunder it, and with this feeling the earth became more than soil, it became the earth-mother. "O, god, be patient with me," the Maya murmured when sowing. "I am about to do that which my fathers and my fathers' fathers have done before me." A profound affinity was set up between spawning and be-getting, between harvest and death. The priests who read the stars and made the permutations of the calendar, filling in the marching adjunct of the stars, became the first chieftains. Under their di-rections, temples were raised to the gods; and under their hypnosis of religious-ecstasy, Maya art had its genesis.

In El Petén, in the humid, wet regions of Guatemala, the Maya built their first known religious center, Uaxactun, a pyramidal structure of rubble coated with a thick layer of plaster, flanked by broad buttresses into which grotesque masks were carved. This was the beginning of the culture of Maya cities. The Maya governmental system was theocratic and its *halach uinic*—its "high-er men"—were hereditary. Maya society was divided into three classes: slave, commoner, and noble. Religion and state were one, inseparable. Everything was god-directed, the prototype of San Agustín's *Civitas Dei*.[1]

---

[1] St. Augustine of Hippo (354–430), who existed at the time that the Maya were erecting their Temple Evii Sub at Uaxactun, would have found here his "City of God" in fact.

At Uaxactun, centuries before Caesar crossed the Rubicon, the Mayas began to erect pyramids, with temples at their summits, stone long houses, faced with stucco, exquisitely ornamented with portraits of their gods. Out of five square miles of jungle-bush immense plazas were fashioned, and stone seats were arranged in the manner of amphitheatres; this became the religious center of Uaxactun. Within the plazas, the priests erected huge monoliths of stone, on which were carved strange hieratic symbols. One stela, older than all the rest, which spoke of time, is dated April 11, 328 A.D. Constantine was being converted to Christianity, the Persians were cutting off Christians heads, while across the Atlantic, unknown to god or man, the Maya had already initiated their culture of cities.

The heart of the religious center was the pyramidal temple. Around it, off from it, in geometric squares, were narrow streets frowned upon by oval-shaped dwellings calcimined into brilliant whiteness; these were the dwellings of the "highly esteemed." The homes of the people, the simple artisan, farmer, and soldier, lay on the periphery until their houses were swallowed up by the shadows of the uncleared jungle. Throughout all this region there was a sudden cultural floresence. Tribal communities multiplied and spread out over Yucatán; cities rose of embellished stone— Xmakabatun, Xultun, and Nakun. But of all these Tikal was the greatest.

Lying twenty miles southwest of the first known Maya city, Tikal was founded one hundred years after Uaxactun (its first stela is dated 416 A.D.), and of all Maya cities it endured the longest —five hundred years. The temples, towering with supreme arrogance on two-hundred-foot truncated pyramids, had high roof combs, intricately carved, protruding above the proudest trees of the Petén jungle. During five centuries the Maya laid out this city-state with an ordered maze of quadrangular plazas and filled it with a wealth of hieroglyphic carvings. Few of the world's archaic peoples lavished so much industry on a religious center. Stone causeways spanned the cicatrized earth for miles upon miles, flanking out on all sides of Tikal. These Maya possessed a city culture, as Spengler has suggested: "All great cultures are town cultures." Maya history was bound up with its primary classes, the priesthood and the nobility, and these were the motivating soul of the city. The simple Maya Indian was without history. He was, in most instances, unable to read the glyphs which the priest set down on his folding charts, nor could he understand the necromancy of the stars. He felt but he did not know the involved ritual of the appeasement of the gods.[2] Yet this simple Indian was the builder of these magnificent stone monuments, the creator of an art which now has taken its place beside all other world cultures.

Around the Petén, religious centers (today only muted necropolises embraced by the jungle) could in a few short centuries be counted in the hundreds. For as the technique of stone-carving was mastered there were ceaseless cultural mutations, colonies extending the sway of "empire," not empire in the political sense (since the tribes of Mayan speech were autonomous) but empire in the cultural sense.

Three hundred miles to the southwest of Tikal and Uaxactun is the Copán valley. It was here that the Maya were to build, over a period of five centuries, one of their greatest cities. Some time in the third century the Maya took possession. The problem of breaking off monolithic slabs from the natural quarries that lay a mile to the north of the site was solved, as was the method of transporting the thirty-ton pieces on wooden rollers. By the time that these huge blocks of stone had been set up for the sculptors, the priest astronomers had already worked out the precise pictographs to be carved thereon. The valley became checkered with maize fields. Ten years after Tikal carved its first dated stela, Copán raised its first inscribed monolith, in 455 A.D.; with appropriate ceremonies (human hearts cut from living bodies and held, still palpitating, to the sun), the people of Copán dedicated their first sculptured stela.

No wars interfered with the Maya. There was no diversion of

2 "The peasant," according to the Spenglerian dictum (and here one can supplant "Indian" for "peasant"), the peasant "is the eternal man, independent of every culture that ensconces itself in the cities. He precedes it, outlives it, a dumb creature propagating himself from generation to generation, soil-bound, a mystical soul, a dry shrewd understanding that sticks to practical aptitudes."

their energy. Having surmounted the most difficult phases of an archaic culture, they were now equipped to express themselves architecturally. The Maya had come to Copán with a perfected calendar, a system of glyphic writing advanced so far that the priestly astronomers could anticipate hundreds of years and the dates on which certain astronomical phenomena would take place. So provided, they began to build their religio-acropolis.

The cultural growth of Copán, like all cities, was a gradual process. It began with temples set on small truncated pyramids filled with rubble, faced with carved stone. Time markers were erected. The earlier monuments exhibit the sculptor's struggle to master the volcanic stuff out of which they were carved. There was nothing primitive about them—for primitive implies lack of refinement—they were merely archaic. So far as the glyphical record is known, Copán began in 436 A.D. The main acropolis was built, a complicated maze of courts, plazas, pyramids, and stairways, during the three and one-half centuries of their occupancy. Through its cultural growth, Copán's pyramids were altered, improved, heightened, and embellished, a great plaza was laid out, eight hundred feet in length, faced with tier upon tier of stone seats, capable of seating most of the population of the city-state of Copán. Within this immensity, huge monoliths of stone were erected, carved, and dedicated, first every twenty years, then every ten, and then in full triumph over their material, every five years. These stelae, carved with incredible profusion of floral, animal, and religious motifs, are as densely alive as the jungle itself. They offer proof that great art is the product of the struggle for the mastery of the materials and that the decline of art comes when that mastery is won.

Then without prelude came disaster. Copán raised its last monument. By 810 A.D., Copán was giving off its death rattle, and then—the great silence. So far as its glyphic history is concerned, Copán comes to an end. "A people is like a man," writes Elie Faure; "when he has disappeared nothing is left of him unless he had taken the precaution to leave his imprint on the stones of the road." The huge pyramids, the embellished figures in the sacred temples, the tall, awesome monoliths that stared upon the empty plaza, were soon reclaimed by the jungle. In the fertile, cultivated earth, sun-loving balsas and cecropias sprang up, their shadings gave impetus to the seeds of other huge-but-tressed trees, wild-fig seeds, imprisoned in bird feces, were dropped within the darkened interstices of the palaces, and these, germinating in the warm tropical air, took root and grew. Within a century the huge, snake-like roots of the strangler Ficus had entangled the palaces of the Maya. Other trees grew up, shaded, and then enveloped the ruins. Within a hundred years Copán was blotted out of human memory.

And there, so far as archaeological history is concerned, Copán lay for a thousand years, waiting for its Champollion. When he arrived, he came in the person of John Lloyd Stephens, New Yorker.

Chapter x   Stephens was fully aware that he stood at the threshold of an unknown world: "I am entering," he wrote, "abruptly upon new ground." If the ruins of Copán existed, then so did Palenque and the other mystery cities of which there had been whispered rumors. It was not merely an archaeological site that he was discovering, but an entire civilization. In emotional delirium he moved around the ruins, passing into the eastern court-yard, examining there the figures of a jaguar, admiring here a colossal head, and climbing over stone seats that recalled the amphitheater of Petra. A feeling of grandeur, of the immensity of human endeavor came over him, possessed him, and never left him. Jean François Champollion, reading the Egyptian hieroglyphics, had made no greater contribution to the history of civilization, nor Heinrich Schliemann, who excavated the plain of Argos to find the topless towers of Ilium. Nor Paul Emile Botta, who excavated the remains of the Assyrian civilization, with their huge, terrible sculptures of winged bulls.

Yet the vestiges of Greece and Egypt were, in some instances, above ground and their greatness within world memory. Even Cretan civilization had been remembered. When Sir Arthur Evans dug out the Palace of Minos, archaeology was illustrating the pages of Homer. But Stephens, lawyer by profession, diplomat through expediency, traveler by inclination, and achaeologist by choice, had discovered a whole civilization, a far-flung civilization with scarcely a published history, a civilization so obscure that it was even without a name. And its rediscoverer, this same Stephens, was also to be the one who would transmit these discoveries by cleverly written, well-illustrated books—books which would arouse a whole generation of incipient archaeologists.

In all this flowering chaos of Copán, how to start? First they must have a place to stay, for the weather was unpropitious, and to clear the ruins of the jungle, they must have workmen. They went back to the village of Copán—a few miles distant from the ruins—and there they were unceremoniously rebuffed. They collided with Don Gregorio, the village tyrant.

It was obvious that Don Gregorio had not been reared on the milk of human kindness. He did not like Mr. Stephens, nor did he like Frederick Catherwood, who spoke Spanish with an Italian accent, nor Augustin's habit of speaking French to his *patrónes*. In the village of Copán, with its six miserable pole-huts thatched with corn husks, he was a man to be reckoned with. Who was this Don Gregorio? He was a man "about fifty, had large black whiskers, and a beard of several days' growth; and, from the behavior of all around, it was easy to see . . . a domestic tyrant." He performed none of the graces of the *posada;* no chair was offered, no invitation to make this their house; his whole manner—and one which infected, at once, the legion of women and children that surrounded him—was that he did not wish them at Copán, for he thought that looking for "idols" was merely a ruse to cover their real political activities.[1] In effect, his manner was to deny them freedom of movement to the ruins.

Stephens, hardly of the temperament to accept such behavior without a violent reaction, was working himself up to a proper rage when Catherwood arrested him: "If we had an open quarrel with him, after all our trouble we would be prevented from seeing the ruins," for Catherwood, who had eight years of experience in dealing with the natives of the Mediterranean, had acquired a diplomatic mask; so "with a great effort," as Stephens expressed himself, "I resolved to smother my indignation until I could pour it out with safety." Don Gregorio relaxed sufficiently to offer them use of the sapling uprights that formed the house to stretch their hammocks. A very small section which Stephens remembered was so insufficient that he had "so little room for mine that my body

[1] "Augustin was very indignant at the treatment we received; on the road he had sometimes swelled his own importance by telling of the flags hoisted and cannon fired when we left Balize; and here he hoisted more flags and fired more guns than usual, beginning with forty guns, and afterwards going on to a canonade; but it would not do. The don did not like us, and probably was willing to hoist flags, and fire cannons too, as at Balize, when we should go away."

described an inverted parabola, with my heels as high as my head. It was vexatious and ridiculous; or, in the words of the English tourist in Fra Diavolo, it was 'shocking! positively shocking!' "

If that inexorable Cerberus did not provide difficulty enough for archaeology, there then appeared a new one: the owner of the ruins of Copán *in propia persona*. A middle-aged man, cleanly dressed in cotton shirt and pantaloons, José María Asebedo by name, told them that he was the owner of the "idols," that no one could enter his land without his permission; he exhibited his title papers. In his best legal manner, Stephens thrust his thumbs into the upper pockets of his long shooting frock, rocked back on his heels and studied José María's title deeds, "as attentively as if I meditated an action in ejectment." Señor Asebedo showed inquiring intelligence; besides, his wife was ill, and he begged something from the Homeric simples of Catherwood's pharmacopoeia for her "ague."

So they quitted Don Gregorio's hovel, crossed the river, and took up a new residence, at José María's. They passed the first night agreeably enough, lying in their hammocks listening to the fall of rain on the corn-husk roof and smoking "cigars of Copán tobacco, the most famed in Central America, of José María's own growing and his wife's own making." Their host was an intelligent man, although his face, his appearance, and the troglodytic dwelling loudly denied it; still, he could "read and write, bleed, and draw teeth." Wreathed in tobacco smoke, naked except for a pair of pants (for his wet clothes were drying over the fire), Stephens lay back in his hammock "brooding over the title-deeds" of Copán. Drawing a blanket over him, he suggested to Catherwood (who lay awake thinking how he might copy the Copán monuments) that he had in mind a gigantic operation. "(Hide your heads, ye speculators in building lots!) To buy Copán! remove the monuments of a by-gone people from the desolate region in which they were buried, set them up" in New York "and found an institution, to be the nucleus of a great national museum of American antiquities! But quere, Could the 'idols' be removed?" Stephens stopped his reverie, asked his host if the river was deep enough to float down the idols. From the darkness came the an-

The fallen "idol" at Copán, *since restored to upright position*.

From a lithograph by Frederick Catherwood

The Great Plaza of the ruins of Copán today.

From a photograph by the author

Stela at Copán.

From a lithograph by Frederick Catherwood

The Maya Lord of Harvest, Yum Kax.

From an original drawing by Frederick Catherwood, owned by the author

The altar at Copán, *with the introducing glyph (between the two central seated figures) 6 Ahua, 13 Kayab* (540 A.D.).

From an engraving of Frederick Catherwood

swer—the Río Copán is filled with rapids. Stephens then returned back to his archaeological reveries. "Other ruins might be discovered even more interesting and accessible. . . . with visions of glory and indistinct fancies of receiving the thanks of the corporation [of New York] flitting before my eyes, I . . . fell asleep."

In the morning, Catherwood left to begin his drawings of ruins, while Stephens remained to fight for the title deeds of Don José María. He explained that he would like to hire a crew of men, build a hut for them in which to live, and bring in spades, crowbars, and ladders in order to excavate the ruins; this he could not do unless he held the title; in short, what would Don José María take for the whole ruin of Copán with all its idols? José María was tempted, for when would he have another chance to sell so unprofitable a piece of real estate, encumbered as it was with acres of stone "idols," too large to be removed or to be broken up? The matter would have been easily settled had it not been for Don Gregorio lurking in the background. Having heard of the negotiations, he wanted to know whether his compadre, Don José, knew that these mysterious men had been arrested in Comatán; was he going to risk his neck by selling land to those who might well be the enemies of the Republic?

Poor befuddled José María was now distressed beyond all bounds; torn between *amor patria* and a chance to convert unproductive property into money, he was a picture of frustrated dejection. Stephens showed him his passport with the flaming red seal of the United States, but shades of suspicion still lingered. Stephens made a final gesture. He opened his trunk, took out his diplomatic coat with its profusion of large golden buttons and slipped into it. "I had on," he remembered, "a Panama hat, soaked with rain and spotted with mud, a check shirt, white pantaloons, yellow up to the knees with mud, and was about as outré as the negro king who received a company of British officers on the coast of Africa in a cocked hat and military coat, without any inexpressibles." José María could not withstand the buttons on the coat, and the household stood in awe as Stephens, with the best diplomatic hauteur, paced the mud floor. They thought themselves in the presence of some illustrious incognito; one more look at the golden buttons, and José Maria succumbed: he agreed to sell the ruins of Copán. You are "perhaps curious to know," says Stephens, "how old ruins sell in Central America. Like other articles of trade, they are regulated by the quantity in market, and the demand. . . . I paid fifty dollars for Copán. There was never any difficulty about price. I offered that sum, for which Don José María thought me only a fool; if I had offered more, he would probably have considered me something worse."

November 17, 1839, is a memorable date in the history of American archaeology, for on that day the first systematic work on the Maya civilization was begun. Under the dark shadows of rain clouds, the new owner of Copán, as befitting his station (he felt, he said, more like the cicerone of the Pitti Palace), left for the ruins paced by two retainers. First the site was measured; Catherwood worked the surveyor's theodolite, while Stephens, cutting the stations, used the tape reel, the same measure that Catherwood had used to map the ruins of Thebes on the Nile. Bruno, whose eyes had the same staring vacancy as the Copán sculptures, felled the trees, while Francisco, whose placidity masked the incipient taste of an antiquarian, put his straw hat on a pole as a guide point for Catherwood's observations; by the second day, the two Copanecos were "thoroughly in the spirit of it."

Out of these operations Catherwood made a most creditable map, accurate when one considers that the whole site was embraced by thick jungle, and even though, in the printing of the map, the cardinal points were reversed 180 degrees, making Catherwood's north, south. These two explorers set the base for all future investigation, and though the thickness of the jungle prevented them from ascertaining the great extent of the ruins, that which they accomplished, told in the delightful style of Stephens and the dramatically accurate drawings of Catherwood, was to stimulate others to reconstruct the ruins of Copán. Not until 1883 —a half-century later—would anyone follow them. Alfred P. Maudslay, a discerning English amateur, went there in 1882–83 "merely as a journey of curiosity . . . with no intention of making a study of American archaeology." Stephens' books led him to Copán. Under the restoring hands of this man, Copán began to reveal some of its secrets. He was followed by an expedition of the Peabody Museum of Harvard, and it in turn yielded to the practiced hands of the archaeologists of the Carnegie Institution. A century after Stephens, Copán took on, although shadowy and amorphous, something of its ancient form.

Copán, a complex of three main courts, is composed of several pyramids, with flattened tops, on which in times past were rectangular-shaped temples. In the Eastern Court—considered the most sacred part of the acropolis—there are tiers of stone seats, not unlike those in a classical coliseum, having on one side an extended platform beside which are two large stone jaguars—with spots sculptured in intaglio—fashioned in a fanciful mood rising on their hind legs. These Stephens found only in fragments, but above the courtyard is a gigantic head of the Maya Lord of the Harvest, Yum Kax, which Catherwood drew with dramatic accuracy. At the end of the courtyard (buried when Stephens was there and uncovered a half-century later by Maudslay) is a temple enlivened by a doorway by all odds the most unique in Maya art. Crouching sculptured human figures form caryatids to the ornamental doorway, holding above their heads a great wealth of sculpture. Stone stairways lead from these courtyards 125 feet down to another section, now called The Court of the Hieroglyphic Stairway (which in Stephens' time was buried under a mountain of debris, although he discovered some of the sculptured figures which ornamented the stairway). It is one of the most magnificent remains of an American people, a stairway rising to almost 100 feet in height, at an angle of sixty degrees, the treads of which are composed of 2,500 separate hieroglyphics so arranged as to be read in lines, rather than as usual in columns. It was built or mayhap completed in 756 A.D. and was one of the last monuments of Copán. It was, doubtlessly, one of the major undertakings of the Maya civilization, and even though much of the text remains untranslated, Dr. S. G. Morley regards it as "an epitome of the principal events which befell one of the greatest cities during the greatest period of Maya civilization."

The encroachments of the jungle in 1839 had erased all architectural form; Catherwood's trained architect's eye was unable to detect the main elements of structure. But it was obvious to him that here, as in Egypt, architecture was dominantly religious and that the relation between sculptor and architect was very close. Architecture seemed to be but a form of sculpture. He did not know then that the Maya had no idea of the true arch, or pulleys or derricks, nor that their architects lacked the knowledge of bonding corners or the formula by which to lay off a right angle. One was quite unable to make a comparative judgment of this civilization with that of Egypt or of Mesopotamia until the technological limitations of the Maya were known.

North of the Stairway Court is the Sacred Ball Court, where during the times of the city's occupancy men played at a game much resembling basketball and called by the Maya *pok a tok;* and beyond this, the acropolis dissolves into the Great Plaza, flanked on all three of its sides with tiers of stone seats. Within this plaza stand the huge slabs of carved limestone—the famous stelae of Copán. Since there were no structures to draw, Catherwood turned to the "idols," those which Stephens, with his two helpers, had uncovered. For the first time in a thousand years light fell upon these strange monolithic slabs (called "stelae" after their Greek prototypes) in the Great Plaza. These sculptures, generally twelve feet in height and three and one-half feet in breadth, standing alone in the jungle, detached from the fallen buildings, made a profound impression on their discoverers. Fashioned in something of the likeness of a human being, they were carved in high relief, the clothing and headdresses incredibly ornate; the sides and backs covered with glyphs. Stephens found eleven of them, with his helpers showing an inborn taste in the arts. Stephens was impressed with "the development of their antiquarian taste. . . . Francisco found the feet and legs of a statue and Bruno a part of the body to match and the effect was electric upon both."

When Stephens returned to where Catherwood was sketching an "idol," he expected to find him excited over his discoveries; instead, "his mood was black." For Maya art, American art, flowering in isolation, developed as Mr. Pál Kelemen has written,[2] "a completely individual ideal of beauty, untouched by histori-

[2] *Medieval American Art,* a master work by a discerning art historian.

cal influences such as co-operated throughout the Eastern hemisphere." Maya art was unique. Its symmetry, its art-patterns were not those of the Eastern Hemisphere; and Catherwood found, as Stephens reported, "difficulty in drawing. He made several attempts, both with the camera lucida and without it, but he failed to satisfy himself. . . . The 'idol' seemed to defy his art; two monkeys on a tree on one side appeared to be laughing at him, and I felt discouraged and despondent."

The tropical luxuriance of the design was confusing; the Maya artist seemed to have a fear of space, a *horri vacui*. He filled it with people, reptiles, flowers, bird plumes, which flowed in and out of the principal design, oozing about like voluptuous ectoplasm. Yet so complete was his mastery over the material that the sculptor treated this thirty-ton stone as carelessly as an oriental craftsman might a piece of ivory.

Catherwood at first tore up many of the drawings, then gradually as the day passed, he began to feel the spirit that pervaded Maya art. He passed from "idol" to "idol," drawing each with extraordinary verity. In the century since he first drew them, few reproductions have surpassed his accuracy; none have ever eclipsed their beauty.

It was the glyphs which drew Stephens' mind into speculative channels. What did they really mean? Stephens could "hardly doubt that its history was graven on its monuments," and he dreamed of another Champollion discovering a Maya Rosetta stone which would provide the key to these curious symbols of American history.[3] The shade of John Lloyd Stephens will never

[3] Twenty years after Stephens questioned these hieroglyphics, a key was thought to have been discovered. It was not a Rosetta Stone but an ancient manuscript found in the archives of the Spanish Royal Academy by the French antiquarian l'Abbé Brasseur de Bourbourg, a manuscript entitled *"Relación de las Cosas de Yucatán,"* written by Fray Diego de Landa. L'Abbé Brasseur de Bourbourg rushed into print, believing that he had found an "alphabet" of Maya glyphs. If Stephens had lived until the time of the Landa discovery and had expected to "read the history on its graven monuments," he would have been sorely disappointed. Landa had found no alphabet for the fundamental reason that the Maya possessed none. Yet the *"Relación"* was of inestimable value in that here were drawings of the twenty days of the Maya month with Spanish translation, and eighteen of the nineteen divisions of the Maya year. Scholars in the nineteenth century tried to work out a system of reading the Maya monu-

be fully satisfied, for when the glyphs spoke, they told only of time. All the vast number of monuments, all the hard armies of stone which archaeological explorers unearthed are merely one vast monument to the Maya's extraordinary preoccupation with time. In the days of their architectural heyday these time-obsessed people raised carved monoliths every *katun* (7,200 days, i.e., 20 years). At Copán these dated monoliths appeared every ten years; then, as the mastery grew, every five years. In the twilight of the Mayan gods, close to the end of their occupancy of the valley, the time fetish spread to the whole of the architecture: not an altar, a step, a doorjamb, a cornice, a lintel that did not have carved in calculiform-shaped writing the date on which the work was either initiated or completed.

No people in history were so fully preoccupied with the flux of time as were the Maya. The Greeks, it is true, mourned the transience of youth, marking the intervals of the Olympiads, yet even Hipparchus' 304-year period was accepted as a unit of time only by those philosophers who speculated on the infinite; beyond that the Greeks would not go. In timeless Egypt, Hecataeus, "thinking to put himself on the very edge of eternity, traced his descendants to a god in the person of his sixteenth ancestor." Yet in America, the Maya priest-astronomers had calculated recurring cycles of millions of days! Did the Maya find time unbearable, so that each day must have a symbol, each month its god? Man everywhere has in some measure studded the calendar round with festivals to break up the constant flow of time, but this obsession of the Maya—.

So preoccupied were the Maya in carving the dates of the monuments that they forgot, or perhaps disdained, to record the precise reason for putting them up at all. Catherwood, who could read Egyptian hieroglyphics, had thought that in these strange characters, the Maya, like the Egyptians, might be historically dis-

---

ments. The librarian of the Berlin Library, Herr Ernest Forstemann, and a newspaperman, T. J. Goodman, on the *Oakland Inquirer*, neither of whom ever actually saw the Maya civilization, nor had tread the Central American jungles, independently worked out chronological tables constructed from the information given by Landa.

cursive. He remembered how King Unis, of the Fifth Dynasty, had covered the walls of his pyramid with hieroglyphic texts that read like Homeric epics, how the deceased Pharoah may fly to heaven as flies a goose or a beetle, and there seat himself upon the throne in the boat of Heliopolis, the sun god. Or elsewhere he had read how the Egyptians conquered this tribe or that, or how an apocalypse rode their lands, killing the people and burying their temples. The Maya, however, said nothing of themselves. Copán, Palenque, Tikal, Uaxactun are not named, nor is there graven, so far as our knowledge permits us to know, the name of a single chieftain in all these monuments, or the name of a city. And yet the dates which the Maya sprinkled through the sun-drenched land have given something of their history. The archaeologist deciphering these dates can follow the gradual growth of Copán; through them he can witness the slow evolution of the acropolis, like the unrolling pages of history. Even in the studied silence of the Maya themselves, one can see the architectural progress of Copán between 460 and 810 A.D.

After 810 A.D. "something happened." They built no more. Everywhere in the Old Empire, within that cultural triangle of Copán, Tikal, and Palenque, activity suddenly ceased. There is no hint of it in the architecture. The technique of the sculptor does not deteriorate, nor does, seemingly, the Maya civilization. For not long before the end at Copán, the Maya erected their greatest monument, the Hieroglyphic Stairway, the most magnificent architectural achievement in all Indian America. Then that "something" happened, after 350 years of occupancy. The Maya left the valley of Copán.

Stephens naturally knew nothing of what we now know. He did not even know the word "Maya." Nor had he, at Copán, any idea of the extent of this civilization. Yet he sensed it. And he showed keen discernment. In the Western Court, where excavation a century later was to uncover amazing huge-headed sculptures in full-round, Stephens stumbled across a rectangular stone altar, which "presents as curious a subject of speculation as any monument in Copán." It was an altar, a single rectangular block of stone 1.42 meters square, 74 centimeters high, resting on four roughly spherical supports, containing sixteen carved human figures, four to each side, sitting cross-legged on glyphs. On top, the altar was divided into thirty-six glyphs which, Stephens (knowing nothing of them) said, "beyond doubt, record some event in history of the mysterious people who once inhabited the city." Nothing for it but Catherwood must stop drawing a stone in the court and come to copy this extraordinary altar. What excited Stephens' interest were the carved figures, for they held in their hands rolls of huun-paper, which were the Maya books: these they held as scepters.

Stephens believed the altar to have recorded a conference, which was confirmed by Dr. Herbert Spinden, who writes that the altar was made to commemorate a congress of priest-astronomers meeting in the city in 765 A.D.; and the sculptor gave great prominence to the Maya date, *6 Caban, 10 Mol,* emphasizing this symbol again on the top of the altar. Changes apparently were to take place in the Maya calendar. It was in that epoch, or close to it, that the decline sent the Maya Old Empire spinning into oblivion. Stephens showed great sagacity in speculating upon the importance of this altar; he allowed it five full engravings. There was something else he discovered about the altar. When he returned to America, he compared its glyphs with the reproduction of a curious polychromic manuscript, called the Dresden Codex, a Maya tonalamatl, written in the eleventh century, which Alexander von Humboldt had published. Placing these two, manuscript and sculpture, together, he deduced—and very correctly—that the people who had written the one had carved the other.[4]

Van Buren's confidential agent to the Republic of Central America remained thirteen days at Copán, from November 17 until November 30. Catherwood had already completed several of his sepia drawings. Stephens could stay no longer, for he had

[4] Prescott, writing to Stephens, August 2, 1841: "I had long come to the conclusion that it [the Dresden Codex] is not Aztec. No one knows from what part of America it came into Germany, and its appearance precisely answers to the description given by Peter Martyr of papyri from Yucatán. From this quarter or some part of Central America, I imagine it came."—Prescott, *Correspondence,* 242.

to perform "a desperate chase after a government." Should he remain too long, he feared that among the ruins of Copán he "might wreck [his] own political fortunes and bring reproach upon [his] political friends." He called a council at the base of one of the "idols" and while the eyes of the stone figure stared down upon them, it was decided that Frederick Catherwood was to remain behind alone, and continue to copy the sculptures, whilst he, John Lloyd Stephens, minister rather extraordinary, was to ride off to Guatemala City in search of the Central American government. After that, they would meet again in Guatemala, and God willing, go off in search of other ruins.

Chapter XI Stephens stumbled into Guatemala City with his clothes mud-splattered and his buttock galled. The streets were deserted; it was as if a plague had swept away the population. The shutters of the one-storied houses were drawn tight, and the clatter of the horses' hoofs sounded like the pounding of drums. The capital city of *La República* was as silent as a tomb. "Perhaps," Stephens reflected, "no diplomatist ever made a more unpretending entry into a capitol."

He found with difficulty the house of Mr. Hall, the British vice-consul, which like the others was sealed as tightly as an Egyptian pyramid. Augustin's knocking brought out a head; Stephens shouted his name and business. Eventually, after much rattling of bolts, the British Consul, terribly agitated, opened the great doors just wide enough for Stephens and Augustin, with their mules, to slide in. Rafael Carrera's unpaid soldiers, he explained, were in revolt; they had only the previous day exacted a "loan" from his French neighbor to meet their salaries. They had called the British standard a "*bandera de guerra*," fired on it, and Mr. Hall struck his colors. (Stephens wondered why he did not run them up again and send for Col. M'Donald in Belize to come with his gallants and lay about him.)

The City of Guatemala he found enchanting. "I have seldom been more favourably impressed with the first appearance of any city." Even at five thousand feet altitude it was tropical with a diaphanous air, the gardens within its one-storied houses canopied with glowing bougainvillea. As was usual among Spanish colonial cities, the center was the principal plaza, where on its four sides, as symbols of power, stood the old vice-regal palace, residence of the capitán-generál under the Crown, the cabildo, which disposed of the city affairs; on the third corner was the palace of the ci-devant, the Marquis of Aycinena, and completing the square in all majesty, the cathedral of three arched naves built in 1790. Where the octagonal fountain, heavy in style and bad in taste, now shot up a stream of cold water piped down from two league's distance, once stood the equestrian statue of Charles IV. It had been torn down in the first ebullitions of independence, and although the rider was gone, the horse remained.

Conquest had come early to Guatemala. No sooner had Mexico been reduced by Cortés than he sent Pedro de Alvarado southward, guided thence by Montezuma's tribute charts, to Guatemala. In 1524 Alvarado found three principal tribes inhabiting the villages about Lake Atitlán. Living in fierce opposition to each other, the tribes sought to use Alvarado to liquidate one the other. They were scarcely aware that the principle of *divide et impera* was an old Spanish custom. Alvarado played tribe against tribe until he had completed his conquest. "Seeing," wrote Don Pedro to his liege, "that by fire and sword I might bring these people to the service of his Majesty, I determined to burn the chiefs." After this he branded all the leaderless captives as slaves and exacted such gold as they had, turning over the royal fifth to the King's treasurer. It was all very legal. Pedro de Alvarado, following the manner prescribed by the rules of conquest, built churches, baptized the conquered, and established towns. In a lovely valley beneath the volcanoes Fuego and Agua, he built his capital, "The City of St. James, of the Gentlemen of Guatemala."

The Guatemalan-earth land was rich then. Impecunious Spanish grandees came to America to take their ease in Guatemala's sun, raise cochineal and cacao, enlarge Catholic Spain's orbit, and fill therewith their own empty coffers. In time the city became a sea of sienna-red roofs, and the City of St. James grew in beauty and power until by the middle of the eighteenth century it contained, if the statistics can be trusted, 100,000 souls. The City of St. James progressed through the periods of perukes, powdered wigs, and ten-syllable couplets until, in 1770, the restless inner earth broke its thin crust and tumbled most of its 6,000 houses, its 20 public foundations, its college of San Tomás, the churches, its nunneries, its convents of Merced, Franciscanos, and Domini-

121

canos, into a shapeless mass. Then the Spaniards, like the Maya, moved en masse twenty-five miles to the south, and there in the very year that a shot in Concord "was heard around the world," the Capitán-Generál laid the foundation of modern Guatemala City.

John Lloyd Stephens entered into his diplomatic duties (somewhat delayed by discovering other civilizations) by taking possession of the American Legation. He was very much pleased with its single-storied house. One entered it by going through a large double door which led into a paved courtyard emblazoned with bougainvillea. He found the salon of the legation tastefully furnished and lined with large bookcases filled with books in yellow bindings, which gave him "twinging [sic] recollections of a law-office" in New York. There, too, he found the archives of the legation, and following his instructions (it must be owned for the first time), he prepared to ship them back to the United States.

Now it became incumbent upon him "to look around for the government to which [he] was accredited." The prescribed protocol suggested that he slip into his blue diplomatic jacket with the golden buttons, the one that had so overawed Don José at Copán, and present himself formally to the Minister of Foreign Affairs. But where was this person? And where, for that matter, was the President of the *Confederación de Centro América?* In answer, the French minister, Baron Malelin, shrugged his shoulders. Frederick Chatfield, the British chargé d'affaires, stated flatly that such a government was non-existent. And then, all speaking at once, they tried to initiate him into the mysteries of this political limbo.

They did not begin from exactly the beginning, for they missed the deluge, but they followed the American conquest, entered the stormy times of Philip II, the revolt of the Maya Indians at El Petén in the late seventeenth century, and then, by riding over the reign of Carlos III, they came full gallop into the times of Napoleon. Well—Napoleon had deposed Carlos IV, and then in 1808 he had, with the instruments proper in that case, unthroned King Ferdinand too. At this the American colonies rose in royal rebellion; that is, they declared themselves the loyal vassals of Fernando VII and would obey no Code Napoleon. A governmental junta was formed in Central America, headed by Lieutenant General José Bustamante y Guerra (famed more in history as second-in-command of the ill-fated oceanic expeditions of Alessandro Malaspina than for his statecraft), who was actuated in the royal name to collect the King's revenues and to suppress revolts. The revolutionary standard was raised for a brief moment in 1811 in San Salvador, when Manuel José Acre captured a few thousand new muskets and $200,000 from the royal treasury with the intention of seeking independence, but Bustamante was an old hand at suppressing mutiny. The revolt was strangled.

The Captaincy-Generál of Central America did not have to fight, as South Americans had, for its independence, for when Fernando VII was re-enthroned in 1821 a delegation actually journeyed to Spain where the Central American Junta gave the unhappy King the conditions under which they would remain within the Empire. He refused, recanted, hesitated; then it was too late. Mexico was in revolt. South America was independent. By the time the delegates had returned to Guatemala, all of Central America was part of the new Mexican Empire under "Emperor" Iturbide. Fifteen months later, with the rise of the liberal Republican *Cacos*, the five Central American provinces adopted a constitution, formed a federation, abolished slavery, and elected Marinas Gálvez president. With revolutionary social aims they prepared to launch the ship of state. The coat-of-arms of the federation consisted of five volcanoes, each representing one of the five republic states. The liberty cap of the *sans culotte* occupied its center, and, like a messenger of hope, a rainbow formed a lunette over the symbols of federation.

The state of Guatemala, filled with Indians, aristocrats, and clerical *fueros*, the largest member of the federal system and saddled with the expense of maintaining a central government, lost within a year its enthusiasm for it. The years that followed, 1825 until 1835, were filled with revolutions and counterrevolutions. Out of these conflicts came two vividly contrasting personalities: Francisco Morazán, the liberal, a son of a French Creole, born at Tegucigalpa in 1799; and his antithesis, Rafael Carrera, the half-

Indian bastard of a Guatemala *ci-devant,* the personification of frustrated resentment.

Francisco Morazán had twice been president, rising spectacularly from the post of secretary general of Honduras, which he held at twenty-five years of age, through higher offices to senator. He became the leading liberal and was elected president in 1831 and again in 1837. But his liberal reforms were launched too quickly. The people had hardly time to consider their newly won liberties when Morazán established the Livingston code,[1] trial by jury, and broke the power of the clergy by exiling the archbishop with a regiment of friars to Havana! Reform followed reform with such rapidity that the people absorbed none of them. Neither King Ferdinand nor the Pope recognized the Central American Federation. And even though America, Great Britain, and France gave diplomatic recognition, the federation was so torn by unceasing civil war that the republic doomed itself to failure.

In 1837, with Francisco Morazán fighting revolution everywhere, cholera broke out in Guatemala. Morazán was charged by the opposition, mostly the clergy, with having poisoned the wells so as to liquidate the Indians. This date marked the rise of Rafael Carrera. The army of the federation marched with Morazán. He entered Guatemala just a few months before Stephens had made his unspectacular arrival in the city. In a series of sharp battles he dispersed the half-Indian army of Carrera. Solemnly he announced the revolution's end. Yet no sooner had Morazán retired to Salvador than Carrera came out of hiding, assembled the army again, and terrorized the whole of Guatemala.

Stephens was now brought up to date; for he had entered the city just when the unpaid soldiers of Carrera were exacting "loans" from the citizenry. His diplomatic colleagues had painted a very simple picture. The differences were more fundamental than ap-

[1] Adopted from the *Code* of Edward Livingston (1774–1836). His *Project of a New Penal Code,* published in America in 1823, was immediately reprinted in France, England, and Germany. The *Confederación de Centro América* translated one of his codes, *Codigo de Reforma y Disciplina de las Prisiones,* in 1834, and in his honor Francisco Morazán named a village "Livingston" at the mouth of the Río Dulce in the Bahía de Amatique.

peared on the surface; and Stephens, used to politics at home, tried to draw for his own government a clearer, less prejudiced picture.

The Federal party in Central America, he explained, "like our own Federal party, was for consolidating . . . the powers of the general government. . . . The Central Party consisted of a few leading families, which, by reason of certain privileges of monopoly for importations under the old Spanish government, assumed the tones of nobles. . . . The Centralists wished to preserve the usages of the colonial system, and resisted every innovation and every attack, direct or indirect, upon the privileges of the Church. . . . [They] contended that, with their ignorant and heterogeneous population, scattered over a vast territory, without facilities of communication, it was a hallucination to take our country as a model." And the Liberals, "ardent, and cherishing brilliant schemes of reform, aimed at an instantaneous change in popular feelings and customs, and considered every moment lost that did not establish some new theory. . . . [They] forgot that civilization requires a harmony of intelligence, of customs, and of laws."

Mr. Stephens carried on his farcical diplomatic mission by attending a sitting of the Guatemalan Assembly. There in lofty tones they spoke of restoring the tithes of the church; "what was raised by God should be given to God alone." The presence of many black-frocked priests, constituting half of the elected assembly, very much affected Stephens: "the scene carried me back to the dark ages, and seemed a meeting of inquisitors." As an equipoise to politics he dined often at the home of "an interesting young widow."

Guatemala was very tense, for Rafael Carrera was expected. Through the whole city ran a feeling of expectancy, as if the city waited for a hurricane, roaring out of nowhere, to sweep the town or for the rumbling volcano de Fuego to burst its serrated peak. The churches, offering solace, had an unprecedented attendance. Stephens met an American woman, born in Pennsylvania, who carried him to La Concepción to witness the taking of a veil of one of her dearest friends. And he saw the "beautiful spectacle . . . [of] rows of kneeling women" on the padded *prie-dieu*, "with

125

faces pure and lofty in expression, lighted up by the enthusiasm of religion." After the long ceremony he was told that his friend's friend would in a few days appear at the grating of the convent to embrace her friends. Stephens mischievously asked to be included. The lady from Pennsylvania "promised to take me and procure me a share in the distribution."

Carrera or no Carrera, Stephens returned at the specified time "for the purpose of embracing a nun." The convent was crowded. The delicate girl, dressed simply in black, stood in the midst of her friends who sobbed quietly into their handkerchiefs. Soldiers burst in during the ceremony, put down their rifles, took her embrace, and left; then came the turn of Stephens. First the woman from Pennsylvania embraced her friend, whispering something in her ear, flipped away a tear that coursed down her powdered face, then introduced Stephens as her countryman. "I never," Stephens recalled, "had much practice in embracing nuns; in fact, it was the first time I ever attempted such a thing; but it came as natural as if I had been brought up to it. My right arm encircled her neck, her right arm mine; I rested my head upon her shoulder, and she hers upon mine; but a friend's grandmother never received a more respectful embrace." The next morning he paid a visit to "El Carnicero."

Rafael Carrera was sitting at a table counting stacks of silver pesos when Stephens, dressed in his blue, gold-laced diplomatic coat,[2] was ushered into the presence of the absolute master of Guatemala. His guards were fitted out with red bombazet jackets, tartan-plaid caps, which with their dark skins reminded Stephens of the organ grinders' monkeys which he had seen as a boy about Bowling Green. Colonel Monterosa, Carrera's aide-de-camp, in a dashing uniform, sat by his side piling up the silver as it was shoved to him by his master.

Rafael Carrera was surprisingly young (Stephens guessed twenty-five), with the straight black hair of the Indian and the copper-colored skin of a mestizo ("His friends, in compliment,"

---

[2] "And which by-the-way," Stephens added, "owing to the abominable state of the country, I never had an opportunity of wearing afterward, and the cost of which was a dead loss."

Back of stela at Copán.

From an engraving of Frederick Catherwood

Front of stela at Copán.

Stela at Copán today.

From a photograph by the author

Side of stela at Copán.

From an engraving of Frederick Catherwood

Stephens wrote, "called him a mulatto; I, for the same reason, call him an Indian, considering that the better blood of the two."). He was beardless, short, bandy-legged, and barrel-chested. His attire was military, which, when he rose to welcome Stephens was seen to be a black bombazet roundabout jacket with matching trousers. He told Stephens that two years ago he had "begun" with thirteen men, with muskets so old they had to be fired with lighted cigars, as one fired ancient harquebuses. Within a year he had a praetorian guard of Indians who carried banners crying, "*Viva la religión y muerte á los extranjeros*"—"Long live religion and death to foreigners"—which, as it was no idle threat, soon sent the foreign population flying from the country. But when Carrera finally met and talked to some of the foreigners his war cry was modified. Now he numbered quite a number of Englishmen among his acquaintances, which exhibits, said Stephens, "a happy illustration of the effect of personal intercourse in breaking down prejudices against individuals or classes."

Carrera was the prototype of *caudillismo*, a form of personal government—*personalismo*, the Latin Americans call it—which has plagued Hispanic America since its independence; Carrera, Rosas, Francia, López, and in modern times Francisco Villa, Vicente Gómez, and Trujillo all spring from this moloch-theology of *persolanismo*. Carrera began as a highway robber (after having been drummer boy and pig herder), terrorizing the country. Trade was disrupted. Few traveled beyond the environs of the cities. The Centralists, in their hatred of Morazán, clasped Carrera to their aristocratic bosoms, thinking that if each would war on the other, both would be eliminated; it is not the first time in history that one faction has embraced the apocalypse for the purpose of ridding itself of a temporary problem. Carrera, at the time of Stephens' audience, was riding the crest of a wave of triumph. Feeling was still bitter. When he found a broadside pasted on an adobe wall calling him a bandit and an *antropófago*, he demanded that the last word be defined; when, after several attempts, its meaning—"man-eater"—seeped through his brain, his wrath was Jovian. It was only calmed by a flow of blood.

After two years of unprecedented power he could read, scrawl his name, "Carrera," ending it in a flourish in the antique style. His dress improved, and he established himself as guardian of Guatemala. "Considering Carrera a promising young man," relates the Presidential Agent, "I told him that he had a long career before him, and might do much good to his country; and he laid his hand upon his heart, and with a burst of feeling that I did not expect, said he was determined to sacrifice his life for his country."

One can only applaud the political sagacity of Stephens, for although he liked neither the man nor his tactics he gauged, very accurately, the future of Rafael Carrera. "I considered," he wrote, "that he was destined to exercise an important, if not a controlling influence on the affairs of Central America." Carrera in fact remained in power for twenty-five years, from 1840 when he was a mere *caudillo* until 1865, when he died in office as president. In 1854 he was declared *Presidente vitalicio*. His title: His most Excellent Señor, Don Rafael Carrera, President for Life of the Republic, Capitán-Generál of the Forces, General Superintendent of the Treasury, Commander of the Royal Order of Leopold of Belgium, Honorary President of the Institute of Africa. Unfortunately he had established the political formula for the *coup d'état*. It was given a quaint touch by a presidential aspirant in 1898, who walked into a cabinet meeting, laid his pistol on the table, and said: "Gentlemen, I am Estrada and the new president of Guatemala."

Befitting his person and calling, Mr. Stephens took a diplomatic tour of the country. He went to the ruins of Antigua, climbed the volcano de Fuego to obtain a panorama of the country, and later in a very gay company he rode to the city of Mixco, where *simpático* "Meester Estebens" won the hearts of the ladies and, we judge by the compliments given him, the respect of the men. Everywhere he allowed his curiosity full license: he went to the Indian markets, he talked to the padres, and between his calls of courtesy wandered in the mountains.

However, Van Buren's confidential agent had still to find the central government; Carrera, although he exercised life and death powers, possessed no office. The members of the Guatemala Assembly wanted Stephens to change the meaning of his instructions so as to be represented to Guatemala alone. This had little effect on Stephens. Morazán represented the federal government and still had a force in the field, and he was, rumor said, in San Salvador. So in conformance to his instructions, Stephens, on Sunday, the fifth of January (1840), as he wrote in his journal, "rose to set out in search of a government."

A French ship, the *Melanie*, was sailing for Salvador, and he accepted with alacrity the captain's offer of passage. From the miserable port of Istapa, where Pedro de Alvarado built his ships for the expedition to Ecuador, Stephens sailed.

For the first time, fever was upon him. His head ached, there was a severe pain in the lower extremity of his back as if he had wrenched it, a feeling of numbness in his legs—in his blood stream were swarming millions of protozoa, multiplying asexually at an appalling rate and exploding his red blood cells; the germs were the Plasmodia of malaria. Central America had given Stephens something other than archaeological immortality; it had given him malaria, a tropical kiss of death.

The *Melanie* was a trim little schooner with four cabins, one of which the French captain arranged for Stephens. The neatness of the ship and its ordered life offered great contrast to the turbulent war-torn shore. As it moved southward toward the neighboring state of San Salvador, the gentle heaving of the ship put Stephens to sleep. Yet the fever hung on. In the morning the captain put his guest under ship's discipline; the steward stood before him: "*Monsieur, un vomitif*"; in the afternoon, "*Monsieur, une purge*," so that by evening he was for all practical purposes out of the battle.

San Salvador, the smallest of the *Federación*, about the area of Maryland, had been an Aztec colony and trading center, and like Guatemala was conquered by Pedro de Alvarado. San Salvador faced the Pacific, and although volcano-studded, the land was fertile, the Indians more easily absorbed than those of Guatemala, a fact which contributed much to its liberal point of view. It was an easy, somnolent country, and Stephens, riding under the huge shadows of the ceiba trees that lined the road to Sonsonate, felt quite at ease with the world. He used the smoking Izalco volcano as a guidepost, and this led him, after a fiercely hot day, to the edge of the town. Outside it he passed a horseman superbly mounted on a saddle tooled in silver over which was thrown a scarlet Peruvian pellon. He was much struck with the appearance of the man, and they exchanged bows; he did not know it then, but that gentleman was "the government." The next day they met again at the house of a Costa Rican exile. He was introduced as Don Diego Vigil, the vice-president of the Federation. Vigil was in fact a vice-president without a government. They talked at length (since Stephens' Spanish had improved), and Vigil made him aware that his diplomatic quest was hopeless; there was little semblance of a central government. That night Stephens addressed a letter to John Forsyth, secretary of state, from Sonsonate:

Sir: January 17, 1840

    I have the honor to inform you that I arrived at this place on the 12th instant, on my way to Cojutepeque or the seat of Government. Unexpectedly I found Mr. Vigil, the Vice-President of the Federal Government *in ease*. He came not as Vice-President, but as the friend of Morazán to make terms with one Ranon, who has kept the borders of St. Salvador in such a state of alarm as to break up all travelling by land from Guatemala. Ranon demanded $4,000 in money, a commission as Col. &c &c &c to all which Vigil assented, only substituting a state paper for money. The terms were considered settled when Ranon without giving any notice of his intention, mounted his horse and rode out of town. The Commandant has barricaded the Plaza and principal streets in apprehension of an attack.

    I have seen Vigil several times. He has treated me with more delicacy than was shown me in Guatemala, when the state officers endeavored to avoid giving me a passport for St. Salvador and finally made it out without describing my official character. Vigil contends that the Federal government still exists but instead of urging me to present my credentials, advises me to wait till my return from Nicaragua and be governed by the proceedings of the convention at Gracias a Dios.

    My own opinion is that the convention will not do anything. At present however it is useless to go to Cojutepeque, for during the absence of Vigil, there is no one to answer to the name of the Federation. I am suffering from an attack of fever and have the opportunity of making a short voyage down the coast of the Pacific. I shall return by land and expect to reach the seat of Government in about six weeks.

To inspect the "canal route" at his own expense, he sailed to the Gulf of Nicoya. With his unshakable companion, malaria, he debarked at Costa Rica, visited the points of interest, and then, with a curious ogre named Nicolás as a guide, rode north by horse through Costa Rica into Nicaragua. There he examined the canal route that had agitated the press and Congress alike for fifty years. In Granada he met John Baily, a British ensign, residing on half-pay in Nicaragua, who had made the first scientific survey of the Nicaraguan Route, and from him obtained the list of depths, altitudes, and other data from which he fashioned a complete and exhaustive report on the canal project for the United States. It was an excellent summary, one worthy more of an engineer than a lawyer, and although he had the assistance of Horatio Allen (famed as the engineer of the Croton Aqueduct) to assist him in the technical portions, his grasp of the complicated details exhibited the practical side of his nature.[3]

Stephens estimated the cost of the canal at $25,000,000, rather optimistic alongside of the present estimate of $750,000,000. Yet Stephens put the "dream" into something resembling logic; he challenged the bankers who once laughed at "Clinton's Ditch" to undertake this gigantic project. He wrote that such a canal would lend balance to blood-drenched Central America, that it would bring commerce to its cities and contact with peoples of other lands. He envisioned great cities growing up in the heart of the country, and the "valleys now weeping in desolation and waste" coming into fruitfulness, he saw steamboats sailing through the canal into the Pacific and feeding the whole vast range of the Pacific coast; "I would not speak of it with sectional or even national feeling; but if Europe is indifferent, it would be glory surpassing the conquest of kingdoms to make this greatest enterprise ever attempted by human force entirely our own work . . . to furnish a new field for action of that tremendous power which, first brought to being under our own eyes, is now changing the face of the whole moral, social, and political world."

[3] *Incidents of Travel in Central America*, I, 396–424, where Stephens gives descriptions, elevations, diagrams, and historical details. This was the first accurate report issued to North America.

Then the dream of progress ended. Stephens, once more in Salvador, saw the Confederation of Central America, blood drenched, dissolving before his eyes.

With Nicolás guarding the door with a machete, Stephens was trying to sleep. The little town of Ahuachapán which had felt the rumbling of earthquakes before was about to feel another. For Francisco Morazán had been terribly defeated in Guatemala, and like the gentle trembling of the inner earth before the shocks increase in violence, rumor passing from house to house gave substance to tension in the air; "Francisco Morazán had been defeated by the forces of Carrera." Morazán's army had been cut to pieces, and what was left of it was returning in full flight to Salvador, with Carrera in pursuit.

At one o'clock in the morning, Stephens was violently awakened by a pounding on his door. In burst Colonel Molina, jacket torn, hat gone, eyes dilating with horror.

"They are coming," he shouted, "the men of Carrera are coming."

Outside, Ahuachapán was in turmoil. The *Federalistas* were running for their lives. Mules with supine indifference, weighted down with movable chattels, were followed by weeping women in black mantillas, flitting along like black bats in the deep shadows of the houses. Nicolás dropped his machete with his bravado—he blubbered with fright. The gods were athirst.

Stephens ordered the horses to be saddled while he took counsel with his companion, Don Saturnino Tinocha, a tall, thin, Quixotic figure of a man, a Costa Rican merchant Guatemala-bound, who, like Stephens, was caught in the maelstrom of revolution. He suggested that they disassociate themselves from the refugees, lest they be considered one of them. Let them ride out of town and appear as they in actuality were, travelers. Now the church bell was tolling. Its mournful clanging rang for those halt and blind, very young and very old, who were unable to flee. The *cura* gathered them in the sanctity of his church. There they waited for the blood-drunk men of Carrera.

At dawn a little boy ran hysterically through the street shouting, "*La gente viene.*" Stephens climbed the church tower and from that height saw a single file of men nearing the town. One of their scouts cautiously approached, and Stephens, unarmed, climbed down to meet him. He told him the village was deserted, and forthwith he surrendered Ahuachapán formally.

The main body of troops entered, headed by General Figueroa and followed by a hundred or more mounted lancers. They were fierce-looking soldiers, mestizos and Indians. As they passed Stephens, they shouted "*Viva* Carrera!" in his face until Stephens became suddenly aware that his life depended on its echo; he feebly responded, "*Viva* Carrera."

Hardly had they settled themselves when Francisco Morazán counterattacked. The troops who had entered Ahuachapán only a few hours ago with so much arrogance now quickly developed the fugitive complex. A broadside of musketry rolled down the streets and bullets ricocheted off the heavy stone church. At full gallop General Figueroa led his lancers out of Ahuachapán. The foot soldiers lost all soldierly shape; they were reduced to dirty bundles of shivering humanity. A soldier, here or there, as if jerked out of the line by the Fates, would, at the crack of a rifle, spin about, clutch the air, and fall into the cobblestone road. Stephens and his friend in misery fell behind three-foot-thick stone walls, while the shots burst all about them. Only when they heard "*Viva la Federación*" and knew that Morazán had returned did they fling themselves into the open.

Morazán's troops, thoroughly disciplined, bivouacked in the plaza and took up defenses where they could not be surprised by any counterattacking force. They were worn by fighting. Morazán, with 1,400 troops (showing on what a pitiful scale were these battles[4]), had entered Guatemala a few weeks before and laid

[4] To form a concrete idea of these losses: The wars fought between 1821–48 were in Guatemala alone recorded as 52. In all of these, only 2,291 men were killed and 471 wounded. On March 19, 1840, when Carrera triumphed over Morazán in Guatemala City in a battle considered the most sanguine of all struggles during the period, the losses for both sides were only 414 killed and 172 wounded. The aggregate losses involving all of Central America's 143 battles, over a period of thirty years, was 7,085 killed and 7,785 wounded. More people died, in fact were assassinated, than were killed in battle. (Figures obtained from Morelet, *Voyage dans l'Amérique Centrale*.)

seige to the plaza which he took by storm. Reinforced, he waited for the expected counterattack which, when it came, was led by Rafael Carrera; the carnage was unprecedented even for the wars of Central America. A war without rules and without quarter, the dead filled the streets and the houses, even the embassies of the foreign legations. Morazán lost half his troops and almost all his officers. When the battle-maddened troops of Carrera advanced, Morazán placed men to cover his retreat into San Salvador. It was more than Francisco Morazán that was defeated in the final battle of Guatemala on March 17, 1840; it was the whole fabric of federation that tumbled with him.

In the plaza of Ahuachapán, Stephens performed the last duty of his office of American minister: he met and talked with the man who had been the president of the government to which he was accredited. He came up to where General Morazán, surrounded by his remaining officers, was drinking chocolate. Morazán was a handsome man of middle age with something of the look of Bolívar about him. He was of middling height, animated by dark, expressive eyes in a cameo face that was mild and intelligent. He wore a dusty, faded military frock coat laced with grapeshot; one epaulet, dangling gold lace like an unwound spring, was torn from his shoulder. Like his prototype, Simón Bolívar, he was very impetuous and impatient, and, like him, endowed with great perseverance.

Stephens greatly admired Morazán, but his presentation to him, in the flickering light of candles, surrounded by battle-worn soldiers, was far different from the way he had pictured it. In New York, where he had had made the diplomatic coat, he had then pictured himself being presented formally before the head of a state. Now he was aware, as well as Morazán, that they attended the last rites of the republic. Stephens hardly knew how to address him. At this moment Morazán revealed his greatness. He apologized to Stephens for the condition of his country. He spoke of the treaties with North America, the projected Nicaraguan Canal, and all the details of ordered progress that he had planned for his people; not one word did he utter about his own misfortune nor the rotting bodies of his troops that he had left upon the road in his flight from

Carrera. Stephens saw him once again the next morning before he left for Guatemala. Morazán exhibited not the least despondency. He was bound for Sonsonate, the capital of the federation, yet he did not know then that he would be coldly received, insulted publicly, by a people who knew of his defeat. "I bade him farewell," said Stephens, "with an interest greater than I had felt for any man in the country. . . . His worst enemies admit that he was exemplary in his private relations, and, what they consider no small praise, that he was not sanguinary. . . . The great outcry against General Morazán was hostility to the church and forced loans. For his hostility to the church there is the justification that it is at this day a pall upon the spirit of free institutions, degrading and debasing instead of elevating the Christian character. . . . I verily believe, and I know I shall bring down upon me the indignation of the whole Central Party by the assertion, . . . that they have driven from their shores the best man in Central America." These words were written when Morazán had not more than a handful of friends in Central America. It does great credit to the perspicacity of John Stephens. After a century, this is precisely the view of Central Americans themselves.

Forced into exile, Morazán went to Chile, but soon returned to northern Panama, waiting there for a change in the political barometer. When he saw the gold that was taken from the graves of Coclé, he formed a company to excavate these archaeological treasures, which, if he had found what Dr. Samuel Lothrop found a century later, would have provided him with a full treasury. However, his destiny was differently cast. Returning to Costa Rica with a small band of armed followers in April, 1842, he issued his stirring manifesto. He was elected acting chief of state, but only for a brief moment, for Central America rose against him. Besieged with his followers, he, in order to save further bloodshed, surrendered. One of his wounded officers was tied to a chair; and Morazán, with his hands tied behind him, gave the firing orders for his own execution. On September 15, 1842, on the anniversary of the founding of the *Federación*, shouting "posterity will do us justice," Morazán died, perforated by a dozen bullets.

The meeting with Francisco Morazán at Ahuachapán ended

Stephens' diplomatic mission. Arriving in Guatemala, he summed up for the Secretary of State the whole distracted picture of Central America, ending his letter with:

"The Federal Government was thus entirely broken up. There was not the least prospect of its ever being restored, nor for a long time to come of an other being organized in its stead. Under these circumstances, I did not consider myself justified in remaining any longer in the country. I had no public business. . . . According I secured the Books and Archives of the Legation and forwarded them to New York—having done this, I leave for Guatemala and will travel at my own expense into the Mexican provinces of Chiapis and Yucatan, for purposes of my own and at my own expense."

Chapter XII   By April, 1840, Stephens' and Catherwood's plans were complete. Their itinerary, in fact, had been
published, whether by design or accident, in the *Official Gazette*
of Guatemala. There, among the complicated rituals of government, one could read that Señor Juan L. Stephens, *Ministro de
los Estados Unidos*, with his dauntless companion, the Englishman, Frederick Catherwood, were resuming their archaeological
journeys, this time to the mysterious (the editor said *"fabulosa-
mente rico"*) ruined city of Palenque located in the Department
of Tzendales, state of Chiapas, in Mexico.

As a precautionary measure to insure his safety to Palenque,
Stephens called upon Rafael Carrera who, after the massacres of
Quetzaltenango, had taken up residence in Guatemala City. He
had obtained letters from the Archbishop of Guatemala to all the
padres along the route, but just in case that God was on the side
of those with the best artillery, Stephens obtained a passport signed
in the unalphabetic scrawl of Carrera:[1] "It had taken him longer
than it would have done to cut off a head, and he seemed more
proud of it. Indeed, it was the only occasion in which I saw in
him the slightest elevation of feeling."

On April 7, 1840, they set off to Palenque. On muleback they
followed the ribbon trails that wound through the high, pine-stud-
ded mountains of Guatemala, the whole breadth of the state.
Within a week they reached the environs of Lake Atitlán.

[1] During Stephens' absence, Frederick Catherwood had discovered the ruins
of Quiriguá, thirty miles north of Copán, near to the Río Motagua. Unquestion-
ably a colony of Copán, Quiriguá is noted for its superb stelae carved out of
red sandstone. Although Stephens, himself, did not visit the ruins, he was able
to write correctly: "The general character of these ruins is the same as at Copán."
Catherwood limned those monuments now known as Stelae "E" and "F." Later,
when Stephens found that they were near a river, he began negotiations with
Señor Payes, their owner, for the purchase of the entire ruins. The negotiations
were still in progress when they left Guatemala City, bound for Palenque.

Atitlán lay shimmering between towering volcanoes, sparkling like a colored mirror of lapis lazuli. It was one of the great population centers of the pre-Conquest Guatemala. The Indians flowed around the environs of the lake, living the uncomplicated lives of a primitive people. The centuries had not changed Atitlán, except, perhaps, the Indians' masters. Their houses of sun-dried bricks still spotted the lake, they dressed as they did in the time of the Maya gods, and they still trudged up the panting sides of mountains to plant their milpas.

A right-angle turn on the main road brought them, guided by a huipil-clad Indian, to the ruin of Utatlán, two miles southwest from the village of Santa Cruz de Quiché. The ruin of Utatlán was the center of the Quiché tribes which Pedro de Alvarado had assaulted in 1524. The explorers reached it by climbing the precipitous hill on which it was perched. Catherwood found little to sketch among the ruin which the Guatemalan historian, Juarros, in a rush of undisciplined imagination, had pictured as greater than anything in Peru or Mexico. "The point to which we directed our attention," wrote Stephens, "was to discover some resemblance to the ruins of Copán and Quiriguá; but we did not find statues, or carved figures, or hieroglyphics, nor could we learn that any had ever been found there. If there had been such evidences we should have considered these remains the works of the same race of people, but in the absence of such evidences we believed that Copán and Quiriguá were cities of another race and of a much older date." Still Catherwood made drawings, for here was another record.[2]

At the end of their second day they saw a rotund figure panting up the steep sides of the ruins of Utatlán under the cover of a huge red silk umbrella. An old black coat which fell to his heels, rubbed bare by constant use, a broad-brimmed, glazed black hat, and a pair of plaid trousers covered the body of this extraordinary person who laughed outrageously as he came toward them. The natives quickly uncovered, and the explorers were aware that they were in the presence of the *cura*—despite his extraordinarily un-

[2] In 1834 the ruins had been thoroughly explored by the government of Guatemala, at the insistence of Francisco Morazán. Señor Don Miguel Rivera y Mistre, a man of some scientific attainments, gave Stephens a full copy of his report, which Stephens used in his book.

clerical dress—of Santa Cruz de Quiché. In high spirits he introduced himself and passed around cigars. He asked the news from
Spain and then in the cultured tones of an Andalusian (using the
seseo and *yeísmo* of Castilian Spanish) he told them his personal
history. He was a Dominicano. In his youth he had seen the battle
of Trafalgar, and he laughed every time he thought of it; the
French were blown sky high and so were the Spanish. He had had
enough of war and revolutions, and he had asked the Father Superior to send him to America. On the high seas they were chased
by a French corsair; in the waters of America they were shot at
by an English ship; and then landing at Omoa, in Honduras, they
were assailed by the revolutions which he thought he had escaped.
He laughed at the irony of his position, and with tears of merriment, making the world the butt of his joke, he passed around
more of those dark, rich-leafed cigars. His laughter was irresistible, and he directed his biting humor at everything. Stephens and
Catherwood finished their measuring and followed the laughing
padre with his red silk umbrella to the convent.

In the padre's room, a chaos of books, clothes, and religious
effigies, they continued their conversation on politics, on history,
and especially on the mysteries of the Indian. It was rather unexpected to find a priest in this out-of-the-way place so well versed,
so learned in archaeology, and so eager to impart that which he
had learned in half a lifetime spent in Los Altos. There were, he
said, some ruins peopled by a mysterious race of Indians beyond
Santa Cruz de Quiché. Somewhere between the cordilleras of
Guatemala and the flat jungle-bound lands of El Petén was a living city, occupied by Indians who still lived in their stone palaces
just as they had before the coming of the Spaniard. The padre
had heard of it at the village of Chajul in Vera Paz, and when he
was young he had climbed the highest peak of the Cordillera, some
12,000 feet, and there as the clouds parted he could see the flat
plains of Yucatán and the undulating blue of the Caribbean. Below him the padre avowed he had seen the white towers[3] of a great
city rising from the vivid green jungle, glittering white in the sun.
These Indians, he said, allowed no white man to come into their

[3] He probably saw the ruined buildings of Tikal in the Petén.

country. Money was unknown to them. They kept their roosters underground so that their crowing could not be heard and guide the hated white man to their jungle city.

The telling had a great effect on Stephens. Four days from there—a great city—Indians living precisely in the same state as before the discovery of America! This was no ordinary man who told them this tale, but a well-educated padre, skeptical and balanced. They who had seen the marvels of Copán, Quiriguá, and the cloud-perched ruins of Utatlán, now were told of a living city of Indians.

When the padre took down a map and pointed out the location of the site, Stephens could no longer contain himself—"One look at that city was worth ten years of an every-day life. . . . there are living men who can solve the mystery that hangs over the ruined cities of America; perhaps who can go to Copán and read the inscriptions on its monuments. . . . Can it be true? Being now in my sober senses, I do verily believe there is much ground to suppose that what the padre told us is authentic." Stephens was not a man to be stampeded by another's imaginings. Yet he thought that "two young men of good constitution" who learned the language of the Indians, who were willing to give five years of their lives, might find the mysterious white city. He thought himself of climbing the cordilleras to get a glimpse of this mysterious white city, yet they would not be diverted: "Palenque was our great point."

Enter Phineas T. Barnum: Some years after the above narrative was published in Stephens' book, Barnum picked up this fragment. Soon on exhibition were two "Aztec children." They had been found by "two young men of good constitution" in that mysterious city mentioned by Stephens. Barnum cleverly published a pamphlet supposed to have been from the pen of "Pedro Velásquez of San Salvador."

Unwittingly Stephens had authored a hoax, for Barnum provided the fictional "two young men of good constitution," whom he names as Mr. Huertis of Baltimore, "possessing an ample fortune . . . who had travelled in Egypt, Persia, Syria . . . and . . . Mr. Hammond, a civil engineer from Canada." These two were supposed to have sailed from New Orleans in 1848 to join Pedro

Velásquez in Guatemala. After adventures dreamed up only in the mind of P. T. Barnum, these three entered the jungle of Petén and discovered the *living* city of Iximaya, "with walls sixty feet high . . . covered with the sculptured annals of the city . . . of four thousand years." There were statues sixty feet high "of the ancient kings of Assyria . . . and of their descendants in the Aztec empire." There were hanging gardens, vestal virgins, drawbridges, parapets, all the rhetorical trimmings of a Gothic romance. The two Americans were killed trying to carry away the glittering booty of Iximaya, but Pedro Velásquez kidnapped two royal "Aztec" children, whereupon the Indians gave chase. Velásquez reached Salvador with the children, where "they became objects of the highest interest to the most intellectual classes of that city." Eventually they were brought to New York, exhibited at Barnum's American Museum, then sent to England "as the greatest ethnological curiosities in living form that ever appeared among civilized men." Albert, prince consort of Queen Victoria, dignified the hoax with a personal inspection, and Barnum even wheedled a letter out of Baron von Humboldt. London journals complained about the "Yankee experiment upon the credulity of our British public," and blamed the whole exhibition on Stephens, a charge which Frederick Catherwood was quick to refute: "The story of their capture . . . is scarcely worth while to refute. . . . It has not even the semblance of truth."

Stephens and Catherwood left the laughing padre and his heavenly discourse to take the highroad across Los Altos. It was quite a procession; Bobon, an Indian, part buffoon, part guide, carried on a long stick, like a standard, a stuffed quetzal bird given to Stephens as a parting gift by the padre of Quiché. Juan, half-Indian, was the factotum of the expedition who kept the peace with the muleteers. He had a gargantuan appetite, and nothing edible was safe in his presence, until one time he wolfed a hamper of fresh bread that brought on a terrible attack of indigestion, and Stephens found him rolling on the ground wailing, "*Voy morir, voy morir*,"—"Mother of God, I am going to die." After that he settled down to a routine appetite which was terrible enough. As for Stephens and that faithful "Mr. Catherwood," they were gradually losing all appearances of foreigners. They had added to their native attire a piece called *aguas de arma*, undressed goatskins, embroidered with red leather, which covered their persons when it rained, and they wore the large hats of the country.

After riding over wild abyss-filled country where the odors of spiked agave plants in bloom and begonias intermingled, they came, during Holy Week, to heaven-high Quetzaltenango. "The-Place-of-the-Quetzal" (once "Yelahu"), so named by Montezuma's grandfather, had been in ancient times subject to the Aztecs. A picturesque city, the largest between Guatemala City and Mexico, it was a sea of red-tiled houses facing smooth, well-paved streets, and delightfully located; huge mountains rose at the end of the streets acting as a dramatic backdrop. It had an imposing cathedral, a tastefully arranged *cabildo* facing a wide plaza, and a large fountain where man and beast slaked their thirst. Catherwood was so impressed by its picturesque qualities that he made a fine panoramic water color of it.

Quetzaltenango was still shuddering under the shock of Carrera's massacre. The *cura*, a mild-looking friar with beet-red nose, told Stephens in a hoarse whisper the horrifying details. When a courier had arrived in Quetzaltenango with the intelligence that Francisco Morazán had retaken Guatemala City, the townspeople, sickened by the tyranny of Carrera's soldiers, enveloped his garrison, forcing them in a bloodless *coup d'état* to lay down their arms. They did not know that Morazán had been defeated by that time, and knew no more until Rafael Carrera himself, bent on revenge, appeared at the town's edge with an army of blood-drenched soldiers. Without a semblance of trial, hundreds were massacred in the plaza, Carrera himself striking down with his saber defenseless men. Directed to the place of execution, Stephens saw stone and wall still dyed with their blood. He was horrified by it and worked himself into a proper rage.[4]

They would not have stayed for the barbaric Good Friday procession except that decorum demanded it; besides, their Indian carriers were taking part in it. The procession began with two Indians walking abreast carrying huge lighted candles. Be-

Great Square of the Antigua Guatemala.

From an engraving of Frederick Catherwood

The city of Quetzaltenango.

From an engraving of Frederick Catherwood

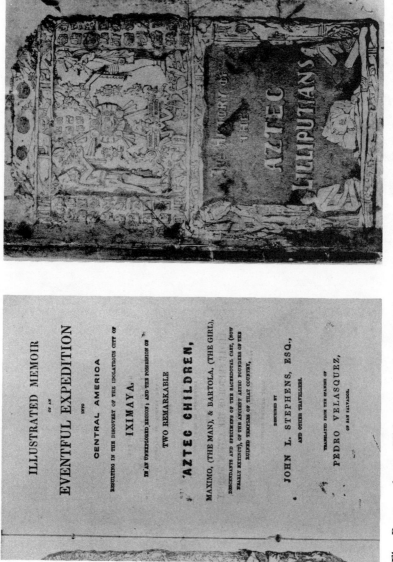

The Barnum hoax. *Title page and frontispiece from the boax perpetrated by P. T. Barnum, in which he used Stephens' name and Catherwood's illustrations.*

hind them, in almost literary symbology, were the effigies: Judith, with bloody sword; the archangel Gabriel, dressed in red silk; Indians dressed in black paper to simulate the Moors; Indians in silver paper to appear grotesquely as knights; four little bronze-faced Indian girls, scrubbed down to their second epidermis, dressed in white gauze to resemble angels; then the figure of the Christ drenched in simulated blood, bearing his cross. It was not a procession specifically calculated to erase an American's feelings about "the poisonous infection of Popery." When the effigy of the Christ passed Catherwood, who stood inconspicuously at the corner, a native slid up to him and with an order like a whip-lash striking at his face shouted: "Take off your spectacles and follow the cross."

They were happy to quit Quetzaltenango.

There was a grandeur, a magnificence about the raw earth. Mountains burst out of the high plains, abysses cut away the soil, leaving yawning chasms around which mule paths followed on the very edge. And the pungent smells of pine and cypress, begonia and trumpet flower, filled the raw, thin air. At Huehue-tenango, not far from the Mexican border, where the expedition stopped to rest the galled mules, they were taken by a gentleman of the city to a river bank where not many months past he had excavated the bones of a mastadon elephant; then he accompanied them to ruins called "Las Cuevas"—The Caves. The practiced eye of Catherwood made out at once amorphous mounds, once pyramidal in shape; they were quick to note that the ancient structures were not, as at Copán, made of cut stone, but of stone fill cemented with stucco. The owner of the ruins was delighted to give them permission to excavate, if he be allowed all the treasure which he felt they would discover.

---

4 Wrote Stephens: "I have avoided speaking harshly of Carrera when I could. I consider myself under personal obligations to him, and without his protection I never could have travelled through the country; but it is difficult to suppress the feelings of indignation excited against the government, which, conscious of the enormity of his conduct and of his utter contempt for them, never dared call him to account, and now cajoles and courts him, sustaining itself in power by his favour alone."—*Incidents of Travel in Central America*, II, 209.

The treasure they found was not incised pottery and funeral urns of Chorotegan pattern, but strangely enough an American, a living, vital North American. He burst in on them and greeted them in English, calling them by name. It took a moment for Stephens to recognize him. He was dressed in Guatemalan costume, a sort of jodphur with well-spurred jackboots, a woollen poncho, large, gray, brimmed hat. A young man under thirty, his face was covered with a full black beard. It was his blue eyes that jogged Stephen's memory; he remembered now—this was the American who was major-domo of a cochineal plantation near Amatitlán; he introduced Henry Pawling to Catherwood. Pawling had seen Stephen's journey announced in the *Official Gazette*, and suddenly he was overwhelmed with nostalgic memories of home and his own people.

He had been born in Rhinebeck Landing on the Hudson, clerked in his father's store, then in New York, and finally drifted to Mexico City. There he met the owner of Handy's Traveling Circus, who, impressed with Pawling's excellent Spanish and knowledge of the country, made him a proposal. Anxious to see something of the world, Pawling traveled before the circus distributing handbills to the startled Mexican audiences and arranged places of exhibition. He had deserted his circus profession in Guatemala and had taken over the cochineal plantation near the environs of Amatitlán. Pawling spoke of America and home with great feeling. Disgusted by the chaos of the country, he had put all that he owned in his saddlebags, bought another mule, and ridden night and day to catch up with Stephens. Pawling's excellent command of Spanish, his technique in handling Indians, not to mention his pair of pistols and short-muzzled, double-barrelled blunderbuss, were very welcome. "Fortunately," wrote Stephens, "my passport was broad enough to cover him, and I immediately constituted him the general manager of the expedition."

The last of April, after climbing Sisyphus-like over the mountain trails of Guatemala, they crossed the Río Lagertero that marked the frontier, passed, without stopping, the first Mexican village of Zapolouta, then rode in, dust covered and famished, to the town of Comitán.

144

A frontier town of Chiapas, Mexico, Comitán was a city of some substance, with a huge church, a well-filled convent of Dominicanos, and a population of 10,000. The largest store was owned by an American. He was introduced to them as Don Santiago Maquena; and when Stephens spoke to him in English, he answered in Spanish, until at last the wheels of memory threw him back to heavily accented English speech. He was Doctor James M'Kinney of Westmoreland County, Virginia. He had gone many years before to Tabasco for a vacation and somehow wandered into Guatemala, which was then waging a war with the cholera. The government employed him for two years to help quell the epidemic, and wanted to make him the chief surgeon of the government, but when the revolutions came, he fled to Mexico, settled in Comitán, married a beautiful woman ("the only tie that bound him was a dark-eyed Spanish beauty," said Stephens in parenthesis, ". . . for whom a man might forget kindred and home"), and presumably decided to settle there for his eternity. M'Kinney accompanied them to the commandant to arrange for Mexican passports. The official character of Stephen's mission worked its magic, passports were issued with the complimentary remarks that Mexico would regard him and his party in the same light as if he had been accredited to it, and he was free to travel where he pleased. It is quite understandable why Stephens told those who might follow him: "I recommend all who wish to travel to get an appointment from Washington."

But when they touched upon their proposed visit to the ruins of Palenque, the gifts of diplomatic immunity were exhausted. M'Kinney had told them that they would find it thus. Only recently three Belgian antiquarians had been turned back from Comitán while attempting to get to Palenque. The commandant had an order from dictator Santa Ana that no one—whatever his credentials—was permitted to visit the mysterious city of Palenque; and so he, as much as he desired it, in view of this decree could do nothing. He suggested that Stephens visit Mexico City. The expedition held a council of war. To ride a thousand miles to Mexico City and then, if granted permission—which was doubtful —to double back again was not an inviting prospect. The ruins of Palenque, buried in the jungle, would certainly not be garrisoned. To Palenque, then—in defiance of Santa Ana!

Santiago Maquena (i.e., Dr. M'Kinney) had been very right in his figure of speech: the road to Palenque was made only for birds. The landscape was scarred with barrancas, cut by rivers, and, as they dropped to fifteen hundred feet altitude, enveloped by jungle. There were no bridges, suspended or otherwise, every abyss had to be crossed by descending and ascending. Nor was the thin ribbon of trail, used mostly by natives running contraband from Campeche, helped at all by the rain. Storms, sweeping in from the Caribbean—for it was the beginning of the rainy season—deluged them night and day, upsetting Henry Pawling so much that he wanted to desert the expedition, only returning to it when Stephens made him an attractive offer. They were already among the archaeological preludes of Palenque, for at Ocosingo, three days from Comitán, they discovered the vestiges of what had once been a stucco-embellished city, still bearing traces of the ornaments that had enlivened it. Had they stopped longer (although Catherwood made several drawings of the ruins), they would have found near by a constellation of archaeological sites,[5] but they were drawn to Palenque. With Indians as carriers, following the mountain ridges, they moved over the same trail taken by Capitán Dupaix on his expedition in 1807 to Palenque. The poor Capitán, doubly bedeviled by rain and fatigue, said that "the roads, if they can be called thus, are only narrow and difficult paths, which wind across mountains and precipices, and which it is necessary to follow sometimes on mules, sometimes on foot, sometimes on the shoulders of Indians, and sometimes in Hammocks. In some places it is necessary to pass on bridges, or rather, trunks of trees badly secured and over lands covered with jungle . . . and entirely dispeopled. . . . After having experienced in this long and painful journey every kind of fatigue and discomfort, we arrived, thank God, at the village of Palenque."

Thirty years of rain and revolution had made the trails to

[5] About Ocosingo within a ten-mile radius there are ruins, probably colonies from Palenque, at Ubala, Chacal Chib, Campomtic, Pamtela, Tonina, Laltic, Cololte, Quechil, etc.

Palenque even worse than then pictured by Capitán Dupaix. Indian carriers had to be changed at every village—for none wished to go beyond the limits of their tribe—food was almost nonexistent. The labors of Sisyphus; they went up, they went down. On the eighth day, they reached the heights of Tumbalá. Below them a ravine dropped thousands of feet. In the distance, some hundred miles away, they could see the Laguna de Terminos and the Caribbean Sea. Below them, buried somewhere in that immensity of jungle, were the ruins of Palenque.

On the tenth day, they echoed Capitán Dupaix: "Thank God, we arrived at the village of Palenque."

Chapter XIII After the horrible journey the village seemed a paradise. It was a small Eden perched on a grass savannah, rows of little wattle and daub houses magnificently shadowed by huge ceiba trees, as peaceful as fabled Arcadia. As they entered the village, crossing the Río Michol, they discovered the townswomen bathing in the limpid stream, braiding their long black hair under vine-festooned trees; garbed only in a blue skirt that clung to their wetted loins, they seemed like sea-born Venuses surrounded by naiads. In Palenque, there was, as expected, a church, thatched with palm, a belfry and wooden cross before it; the whole aspect was curiously halcyon, "the most dead-and-alive place I ever saw," said Stephens.

Directed to a house no different from the rest, Stephens aroused the alcalde and presented his passport. The irritations of the alcalde were known far and wide—he was an inexorable Cerberus, and in addition he had been awakened from a siesta. He asked what he had to do with Stephens' passport. Since the question was rhetorical, he himself answered it: "Nothing." They asked for food, he said there was none; specifically they detailed corn, coffee, chocolate, to which he answered the same *"No hay"* —"None." Conscious of what must be passing in their minds, he told them complaints had been made against him before, but it simply was of no use; they could not remove him from office, and if they did, he did not care. He recommended them to the prefect of the village. The *prefeto* was the other side of the moon; he was courteous, helpful, and solicitous. He offered Stephens a chair and a cigar. He was not in the least surprised to see the American, in fact he said he had expected him for some time. This was very puzzling to Stephens; how, in this corner of American earth, as isolated as Saturn, could this official have known that he was coming to Palenque? Very simply he was told. The *prefeto* was informed thus by Don Patricio. Gradually it dawned on Stephens that by Don Patricio was meant Patrick Walker of the Belize colony. Then the information that he and Captain Caddy had been killed by Indians was not true. It was not, the *prefeto* assured him. They had spent two weeks at the ruins where Captain Caddy had made some drawings, then they had left for Belize.[1]

Santo Domingo del Palenque, from which the ruins near by got their name, had been founded on the savannahs of Tumbalá in 1564 by Pedro Laurencio, a Dominicano missionary. Nothing, even in that early time, was known of the great stone city that lay eight miles distant. The memory of it had disappeared long before the arrival of the white man. Even the original name of the site was unknown; no one knew what the Maya called it. "Palenque" ("palisaded" in Spanish) was given it by early explorers only because it approximated the village of Santo Domingo del Palenque. The memory of Palenque had been blotted out so completely that when Hernán Cortés made his famous march from Mexico, through Yucatán to Honduras, it was unknown even to his Indian guides; even though they passed within thirty miles of it, for "if it had been a living city," thought Stephens, "its fame would have reached his ears, and he would have turned aside and from his road to subdue it and plunder it."

Sometime in the eighteenth century, the Indians who lived in scattered communities in the geographical violence of the Tumbalá hills, where they planted corn twice yearly, discovered the ruined stone buildings. For years thereafter, the favorite tale of

[1] John Herbert Caddy made a report on his explorations, *The City of Palenque*, 36 pp., with portfolio 15 x 21 inches containing a plan of the palace, twenty-four sepia paintings of buildings and sculptures, a folding map of the peninsula of Yucatán, and a sketch map of the ruins. The paper was read before the Society of Antiquarians in London on January 13, 1842, but the prompt appearance of the Stephens-Catherwood work forestalled publication. In 1932, Dr. Marshall Saville, the late American archaeologist, had the good fortune of meeting Miss Alice Caddy, the explorer's granddaughter, in New York, who placed the portfolio in Saville's hands for publication. The Caddy drawings contain, said Dr. Saville, some sketches not found in Stephens' work, and a number more accurate than Catherwood's. Saville died before he could arrange their publication, and they are now, supposedly, buried with the rest of his effects. See "Bibliographic Notes on Palenque, Chiapas," *Indian Notes and Monographs*, Vol. VI, No. 5 (1928), 137-38.

those who traveled through Chiapas, "either for Commerce or God," was of the fabulous ruins of Palenque.

But it was not the fashion of the time to expend energy on things of the past, people were too much employed in cutting out a place for themselves in unsettled America. Count Constantin de Volney had yet to write his romantic rhapsody on *Ruins* that was to send antiquarian-minded men scurrying to forgotten lands to discover moldering ruins on which to meditate the transience of empires. Besides, all sensible men of the eighteenth century disliked "wild nature." There is good reason why the discovery of the ruins, wafted from tongue to tongue, did not move the Capitán-Generál of Guatemala. In the past, too many, far too many, expeditions had been sent out in search of golden El Dorado. Still the rumors persisted.

The Canon of the Cathedral of Ciudad Real de Chiapas could no longer resist them; he gathered together a retinue of poncho-clad Indians, had them fashion a rude palanquin, and on it he was carried from Ciudad Real to Palenque. Arrived, he tucked up his habit and accompanied by machete-wielding Indians, cutting his way through to the stone palaces of Palenque. So impressed was Fray Ramón de Ordóñez y Aguiar in 1773 by what he saw that he wrote a *"Memoria"*[2] which he addressed to Don José de Estachería, president of the Royal Audience of Guatemala. This report reached his periwigged Excellency about the time that his own city was being overwhelmed by earthquake; he had little time for ancient ruins when his own was whelmed with destruction. However, when he had established in 1776 his new capital, he wrote an official directive to José Antonio Calderón, mayor of Santo Domingo del Palenque, directing him to survey the ruins.

In the meanwhile the padre discoverer of Palenque sat in his stone cell in the Chiapas convent and moved his pen across reams of paper, which after many years became "A History of the Creation of Heaven and Earth," unimportant to us save that the padre,

---

[2] A quaint document of twenty-three pages deposited in the Real Academia de Madrid, entitled *"Memoria relative a las ruinas de las ciudad descubierta en las immediaciones del pueblo de Palenque de la provincia de los Tzendales del obispado de Chiapa, dirigida al Ilmo. y Rmo. Snr. Obispo désta dioceses"* (1784).

in order to explain Palenque, had a race of people appear out of the Atlantic, guided by a distinguished leader whom he called, heaven knows why, "Votán." It was he, according to this chronology, who penetrated Central America and—without opposition from the original natives—halted his expedition at the base of the Tumbalá Mountains and there built a stone city. The metropolis of his incipient empire he called "Nachán"—"the city of serpents," now called Palenque.

José Antonio Calderón knew nothing of this "Votán," when, following the directive from Guatemala, he visited Palenque in December, 1784. He was accompanied by Antonio Bernasconi, the Italian-born architect, a resident of Guatemala. Their report, an intelligent one, was, like all the rest, never published but forwarded to Spain, where the royal historiographer, the most able Juan Bautista Muñoz (whose bibliographical labors were to assist Prescott), used the manuscripts to fashion a report on American antiquities. Next a royal decree sent Captain Don Antonio del Río to the ruins in 1786. He came in a three-cornered hat and a powdered periwig, wafting through the jungles of Palenque an aroma of the latest fashionable scent. Captain del Río made up for his lack of antiquarian training by his zeal; he assembled two hundred Tzotzil Indians, armed them with adzes, hookbills, and mattocks; with these he assaulted tree-engulfed Palenque. With an energy matched only by the flamboyance of his language, Del Río tumbled the trees, cut the vines that bound the ruins, and for the first time since they had been abandoned in the seventh century A.D., the pallid, embellished stuccos of Palenque were exposed to the sun. "And so in pursuance of my desires to explore the place," quoth Del Río, "I effected all that was necessary to be done, so that ultimately there remained neither a window nor a doorway, nor a room, corridor, court tower, nor subterranean passage in which excavations were not effected from two to three yards in depth; for such was the object of my mission."

This report of Del Río, illustrated by pencil drawings, was sent to Madrid, where it promptly disappeared into the mountains of unpublished reports; but in Guatemala, where it was copied before being sent to Spain, the manuscript report of "Palenque" was set upon by Dr. Felix Cabrera, a gentleman of fatuous erudition. He carefully edited it, expunging Captain del Río's barracks language, filled it with learned asides, and wrote a preface which he called "*Teatro Crítico Americano*" wherein, following the prevailing cosmogony of the time, he ascribed the ruins of Palenque to people of Egyptian culture. This was to remain in manuscript until Dr. Thomas McQuy, a British resident of Guatemala City, obtained the Del Río manuscript and sent it to London, where in 1822 it was published with crude line engravings by Waldeck. This was the first published book on the ruins in Central America, although Humboldt had noticed Palenque in 1810. It was destined to inspire the expeditions of John Lloyd Stephens.

Yet between the long interval of Del Río's expedition and the publication of it in London, the rumors of the "great stone city" now attentuated into full-blown fable had become, in reality, a new El Dorado. The Spanish government, finally alive to the importance of the civilizations that their *conquistadores* had leveled, sent Guillelmo Dupaix, a retired *capitán* of the Mexican Dragoons, to Palenque, but he fell under the suspicion of Viceroy Iturrigaray, who thought his expedition was mere cover for a revolution. He was afterward jailed. Luciano Castañeda accompanied him as engineer-draughtsman; and in 1807 they reached Palenque, where they felled the trees that had, once more, enveloped the ruins. Castañeda then made drawings of the ruins in the technique of Piranesi. These illustrations went the way of much of Spanish science, for Castañeda, before he was run through with a lance, put them in the Cabinet of Natural History in Mexico, and there they lay, being consumed by fungi and cockroaches until, thirty years later, they were rescued by Monsieur l'Abbé Baradre from an unearned oblivion and published in France.

Palenque had, curiously enough, limited attraction; even though reports appeared in various European journals, none very much excited the imaginations of an antiquarian-minded generation, until Jean-Frédéric Maxmilien, Count de Waldeck, was drawn to the mysterious ruins. Born in Paris, in April, 1766, of German *émigré* parents, Waldeck was a descendant of the dukes of Waldeck-Pyrmount, the tiny German principality embedded in Prussian territory between Westphalia and Hanover. For centuries the Waldecks had been born and inbred in the shadow of the Hegekopf, until one branch of them, which gave issue to Jean-Frédéric, came to Paris by way of Prague. At the age of fourteen, excited by the prospects of adventure, he fled Paris and gained a position in the African exploring expedition of François Le Vaillant. After five adventurous years, Waldeck returned to Paris in 1875 and, excited by what he had seen in Africa, began a study of art under Jacques Louis David. In the studio of this master he filled his paint brushes as well as his head with republican ideas. With a tricolor cockade in his three-cornered hat, Waldeck continued his art studies with Pierre-Paul Prud'hon, the French Correggio, while the bloodstained besom of the revolution swept up the debris of the *ancien régime.*

After their majesties had deposited their severed heads in Monsieur Guillotine's basket and the crescendo of revolution produced, as an act of reprisal, General Bonaparte, Waldeck became a soldier artist and went off to fight the Campaign in Italy. A year later, as scientific observer, he went with the Napoleonic Expedition to Egypt, where, in company with other French savants, he made a survey of ancient Egyptian art. Waldeck's passions were so aroused by the wonders of the antique that when Napoleon's venture came to an end with the destruction of his fleet at Aboukir, Waldeck, with four companions, deserted, and fled up the Nile beyond the rapids of Aswan. In 1801 they attempted to cross the Sahara to Portugese North Africa. All perished except Waldeck.

After an additional fifteen years of travel, exploration, and shipwreck (which included a sojourn on Madagascar), Waldeck at his half-century mark fell in with South American revolutionists; he joined the fleet of Lord Cochrane, the British lend-lease admiral to the Chileans. For two years he fought the Spanish in the Pacific. Some time later, about 1821, he went to Guatemala, where he made his first acquaintance with the architectural remains of the Maya, and a year later he was in London engraving the illustrations for Del Río's book on Palenque. There he met the young Lord Kingsborough, who was assembling materials for the huge nine-volume work on Mexican antiquities that was to bear his name. Since both Kingsborough and Waldeck believed that the North American Indian was of Mediterranean origin (Kingsborough said "Semitic"; Waldeck, "Egyptian"), it was a relatively simple matter for milord of fabulous wealth to extend sufficient pounds sterling for Waldeck to make an expedition into Mexico.

It was the Mexico born out of its latest revolution. Spanish rule had ceased, Agustín de Iturbide had been proclaimed Mexican emperor, and within two years he, too, was only a memory. The day of the *caudillo* was at hand; the government rested in a junta of Anastasio Bustamante and Antonio López de Santa Ana. In this flaming cauldron of politics Waldeck, now sixty years of age, still as ruggedly built as a Brittany fishing sloop, settled in Mexico. He was no longer *Citoyen* Waldeck but *Comte de Waldeck*, who in a velvet coat and a neckcloth of Brussels lace assumed the management of the silver mine at Tlalpujahna, near Mexico City. Between the intervals of mine operations, he painted backdrops for the Mexican theater, and at other moments gave himself over to his monogamic devotion of searching out antiquities.

In 1831, he was given permission by Bustamante to visit the ruins of Palenque, to which official rubric was added a stipend from the Mexican treasury. Within the year Waldeck took up residence at Palenque, building himself, on May 12, 1832, at the foot of the pyramid of the Temple of the Cross, a small, palm-thatched lean-to. There, between exploring the ruins of Palenque and the bed of a dark-skinned, firm-breasted *mestiza*, Comte de Waldeck, at an age when most men would seek comfort, weathered the climate of Palenque for two years.

Drawing the ruins while keeping elaborate notebooks,[3] he tried to ravel out the complicated Mayan glyphs. He made sketches of the flattened heads of the Indians, the naked bodies of the Indian women, animals, and birds; in short, everything that his cos-

[3] These are still extant in the Edward E. Ayer Collection, in the Newberry Library, Chicago, along with a sizable number of Waldeck's original drawings. I intend to publish, before long, the tombs, travels, and troubles of Jean-Frédéric de Waldeck.

mopolitan enthusiasm embraced. His drawings of the Maya sculpture, typically period pieces, were beautifully done in the facile manner of a Jacques Louis David, but as archaeological drawings they were very inaccurate and most inventive, a crime in archaeological science. A broken Maya stone head became, under the alchemy of Waldeck's brush, a vibrantly alive modern sculpture, a tumbled ruin metamorphosed into a building of classical finish. As archaeological drawings, they were relatively useless, but as works of art, superb; "I had a *soupçon*," said William Prescott, "that Waldeck was a good deal of a charlatan," and that "his coloring" does not "bear the true weather-tints of antiquity."

Not alone Prescott, but General Santa Ana. He was too suspicious of him, for in Waldeck's two-year absence from Mexico City, Bustamante, his patron, had been replaced by Antonio López de Santa Ana, "replaced" being a euphemism for assassination. All of Bustamante's "works" came under suspicion, including Waldeck. Santa Ana set his police upon him, sequestered most of his drawings (although Waldeck managed somehow to keep his original sketches). Fleeing to Yucatán, where he continued his archaeological wandering, Waldeck vociferously complained of Mexico's treatment of him, calling them "barbarians who want to be considered an enlightened people." And so with bitter hatred he sailed to Paris, where in 1838 he published, at the age of seventy-two, his first book, *Voyage Pittoresque*. Little appeared on Palenque in Waldeck's first book; this was reserved for his dotage, for Jean-Frédéric de Waldeck lived to be a veritable Methuselah, publishing his second book on Maya archaeology on the anniversary of his own centennial. He died in 1875 from a stroke while looking at a girl in a swishing petticoat on the Champs Élysées; he was 109 years old.

Such were the romantic overtones to the ruins of Palenque, of which for all practical purposes John Lloyd Stephens was to be the rediscoverer.

Chapter XIV At dawn, in the proper military fashion, while the jungles were still opaque with vapors, they advanced on Palenque. First came Stephens with the Indian guides, his pants rolled up above his boots and trailing a blue line of smoke from his "morning cigar." Then Catherwood, trying to keep his spectacles dry despite the deluge from the water-laden branches. Next Henry Pawling, who in his capacity of manager kept his eyes on the many poncho-clad Tzotzil Indians, carrying on their backs the impedimenta of the expedition. All were nervously expectant—all, that is, except Juan, for upon him of the gargantuan appetite was to fall the entire preparation of the food. They had cornered in the village the entire market of fowls, beans, rice and corn, chocolate and sugar, and the alcalde had unbent sufficiently to allow them the use of a water jug; but what they really wanted they could not get—a woman. No woman "would trust herself alone with us," Stephens complained. "This was a great privation; a woman was desirable, not, as one may suppose, for embellishment, but to make tortillas."

In the luxuriant forest, rills were cascading down between rock and root. Birdcalls echoed in the stillness. The delicate trill of the modestly plumed hilguero broke out, rang the length of its avian scale, and broke midway in its song as a flock of scolding toucans, huge beaked and black of wing, fluttered noisily down to see who broke the jungle peace. Howling monkeys barked in deafening paroxysms.

Stephens seemed hardly aware of the tumbling Río Michol which brawled noisily on his left or of the throbbing moans of the howling monkey, for his mind was "set on Palenque." Within three hours they had reached the part of steep ascent; they dismounted, left their mules behind, and turned left at the smaller Río Otolum, which was filling the jungle with its tinkling music.

Sculptured stones began to appear in the shaded aisle of the forest, a certain index of Maya occupancy. This stirred Stephens' imagination on the wrecks of empires and the world's mutations, for here once was a gleaming white road over which feather-bedecked people had come in the pageantry of empire.

He was suddenly brought out of his reverie by the Indians shouting: *"El palacio, señor, el palacio!"*

Above the stream which poured from a vaulted culvert, sixty feet upward at a dizzy angle was the vague, shadowy outline of a huge white building. Stephens, in his eagerness to lead the rest, clambered over a stone terrace, reached the top first, and gained the edge of the "Palace."

Palenque was barely visible in the sea of the jungle. It seemed to hang on the edge of the mountains, set at the very edge of an outlying finger of a jungle range projecting from the Tumbalá escarpment. It looked down over a gentle undulating plain, where once, a thousand years ago, checkered milpas supplied the builders and later the occupants of the acropolis of Palenque. Eighty miles distant lay the Laguna de Terminos. The Maya craftsmen had shown great architectural daring to set their buildings at the very edge of a steep gorge six hundred feet above the coastal plain. Palenque hung there like an unshed tear. Above it, back of it, the forest-clad mountains rose abruptly, huge and dominant, projecting verdure-covered heads three thousand feet into the sky.

The Palace, which Stephens seized upon as a residence, consisted of thick-walled, many-chambered rooms grouped about four main courtyards forming the Palace cluster. From the center rose a three-storied, square tower—unique in Maya architecture—engulfed by the roots of strangler-fig trees. On the main stairway were gigantic figures in bas-relief. On the frieze and roof combs, crumbled by time, were fragments of stucco—serpents still tinted in violent polychromy battled headless gods. From within the darkened ruins there poured out a moldy dampness, like the smell of a potato cellar. Three huge fruit bats, disturbed by the noise, detached themselves and circled the ruins, and with that the Indian guides gave a startled shout and ran down the side of the pyramid. They were quickly swallowed up by the jungle.

On the walls of the *"Palacio"* Stephens found the names of those who had visited the ruins before them: Count Waldeck's led the list with a faded drawing of a woman, under which he had scribbled the date, "1832"; there were the names of Captain John Herbert Caddy and Patrick Walker, who had arrived a few months before, and Noah O. Platt, a New York merchant looking for logwood, who had come miles out of his way to the living enchantment of the ruins. In another corridor Stephens found a piece of doggerel which "breathed a deep sense of the moral sublimity pervading these unknown ruins," written by a young Irish merchant of Tabasco, William Beanham, later found murdered in his hammock.

Darkness came suddenly. The night was indigo black with storm, the earth rocked with claps of thunder. The winds roaring in from the Caribbean blew out the candles. As they lay in their hammocks besieged by the darkness, wondering what next would descend upon them, large luminous fire-flies, *cucuyos*, began to flick on their lamps.

In the cold light of the *cucuyos*, the ruins appeared to be enchanted; the stucco bas-reliefs seemed invested with life. Headless warriors stepped out of their walls, stalked through the somber, tree-glutted galleries. They lay awake in the darkness, their ears strained to pick up the strange night sounds. Outside there was the tinkling, it seemed, of silver bells, which was the bleat of tiny tree frogs, and something like a plaintive voice called in the distance. Then, as if from the ruins, came a sob almost human, then a birdcall, limpid and dulcet. Silence. Now the distant roar of thunder. On fierce gusts of wind, the rains came, pouring in through all the interstices, wetting them, drenching them in the chill of a falling barometer. They could not hope for too much sleep that night, so Stephens composed himself with a cigar. "Blessed be the man," said the irrepressible Mr. Stephens, "who invented smoking, the soother and composer of a troubled spirit, allayer of angry passions, a comfort under the loss of breakfast, and to the roamer in desolate places, the solitary wayfarer through life, serving for 'wife, children, and friends.'"

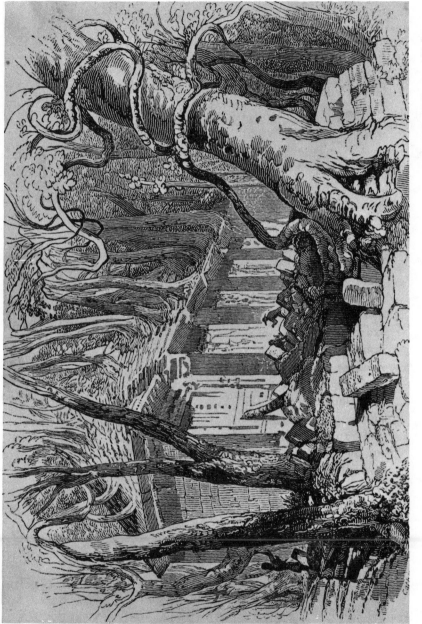

Casa No. 1 at Palenque.

From an engraving of Frederick Catherwood

Schematic drawing of Palenque.

B. Temple of the Inscriptions   *C. Temple of the Bas-Relief*
D. Temple of the Cross   *E. Temple of the Sun*
The Palace is in the right foreground.

The ruins of Palenque in the Tumbalá Hills, Chiapas, Mexico. *Directly in front is the famous palace with portions of its ruined tower. Temples are atop each of the truncated hills. The heights are exaggerated.*

From a lithograph by Frederick Catherwood

Temple of the Sun, Palenque.

From an engraving of Frederick Catherwood

The reconstructed altar of the Temple of the Sun.

From a drawing by Frederick Catherwood

The architectural complex called the Palace, with its thick-walled rooms grouped about four main courtyards (the outside measurement of which Stephens correctly estimated as 228 feet by 180 feet in width), was, as their archaeological residence, the first to be investigated. Stephens, with the aid of Henry Pawling, used the measuring rods to lay the mathematical basis for Catherwood's floor plan which is amazingly accurate even when compared with those taken by better-equipped twentieth-century explorers. They erected the scaffolding to hold Catherwood's camera lucida, and he then began to draw the stucco portraits of the priests that ornamented the walls. At Palenque, Catherwood found the Maya artist unusually restrained, the luxuriant complexity of detail that so befuddled him at Copán did not exist here. Architecturally this site seemed of later date if not more advanced than the others he had seen. The huge stone bas-reliefs in the main court, colossal figures with sloping foreheads and protruding lips, Catherwood had no difficulty in drawing. Although assailed by small black flies that hovered before his eyes, or larger ones that bit his ears, or the mosquitoes that plunged their stings into his pallid skin, these annoyances were not enough to quench his interest; Catherwood stuck to the Palace.

In the first ten days the crumbling mass that the chaos of a thousand years had tumbled was being measured, drawn, and explored by these three. They carried on despite wind and rain, insects and bats. But sleep or the lack of it was having a telling effect on everyone. Catherwood would suddenly slump at his easel, and only the persistent whirling buzz of insects could awaken him. They soon found that they could no more exist without sleep than that nitwit of Aesop's fable, who, at the moment he learned to live without eating, died.

And there was another enemy—niguas. The explorers were well armed against what they believed to be their real dangers, prowling jaguars, or Indians for whom they had laid traps should they try to ambush them in the blackness of a thunder night. Yet who would believe that they could be felled by niguas? Early in their conquest the Spaniards had made acquaintance with the nigua, horrible insects which "ate their way into the Flesh under the Nails of the Toes then laid their NITS therewithin, and multiplied in such manner that there was no ridding them but by Cauteries," and they even inspired some badly cadenced verse:

> *Minutest fleas that inwardly drilling*
> *Bury themselves 'twixt skin and flesh*
> *feeding . . .*
> *Until they are as large as peas*
> *Then*
>   *go spreading through the soles*
> *And multiplying their generations.*

Stephens thought he had the gout, his toes pulsated like those of an eighteenth-century debauchee, but Pawling, soon correcting this ridiculous first impression, announced that he had niguas, and set about with a knife to remove them. Stephens' foot was inflamed and swollen to twice its size; he was soon hammock-ridden. It was decided that he, with the aid of Juan, was to return to the village.

All Santo Domingo had been expecting the arrival of the padres to pay their annual visit. People crowded the street of the village, and when Stephens appeared, three men rode out to meet him, mistaking him for not one but three padres. "If the mistake had continued," said Stephens, remembering his empty stomach, "I should have had dinner enough for six at least." But he was given a hammock and a poultice of hot salt water, and in two days the swelling of his foot was reduced sufficiently to allow him to appear among the three hundred inhabitants who welcomed the padres to Santo Domingo.

A retinue of a hundred Tzotzil Indians, clad in uniform pinstripe knee-length ponchos, accompanied the three padres who had come over the mountains with the express purpose of visiting the ruins of Palenque. The black-bearded padre from Tumbalá was a young man of twenty-eight. Weighing one-eighth of a ton, he had been carried in a palanquin over the mountains to Palenque, requiring the services of fifty Indians. The Dominicano from the Indian village of Ayalon was somewhat older, with a majestic manner which befitted him, for he was not only a priest but a member of the Mexican Congress. He had taken part in the revolutions that had unhinged New Spain from the mother country and had been twice wounded on the field of battle, where he varied his conduct in the struggle between killing and then confessing the dying. The third was a black-cowled padre from Ciudad Real.

"It is a glorious thing in this country to be a padre," said Stephens, "and next to being a padre oneself is the position of being a padre's friend." For now Stephens, as resident-explorer of the ruins of Palenque, was invited to take chocolate with them inside one of the white calcimined houses. The *cura* of the village soon appeared, a tall dark-visaged man, an Indian of uncertain mixture with dark eyes. He presented a very unclerical appearance with his checked shirt and yellow buckskin shoes, his black waistcoat and pants held two inches apart by a protruding stomach. He was as charmingly affable as he was singular in appearance, and tossing his old straw hat into a corner he pulled out a pack of much-used cards and suggested a game of monte. The whole scene was like a tableau out of the life of Jérôme Coignard, the lovable abbé of *La Rôtisserie de la Reine Pédauque*, who played *ombre en philosophe*, reflecting "that at play men are much more sensitive than in serious business and that they employ the whole of their probity at the backgammon board." At first the padres' game of monte began easily, with witty, earthly discourse; then it "settled down seriously," said Stephens, who watched on the side lines, and "I left them playing as earnestly as if the souls of the unconverted Indians were at stake."

The next day, the padres put away their cards, donned their surplices for a Mass in the tumbled village church. Afterwards they appeared for dinner with the "padre's friend" (i.e., Mr. Stephens) at the home of Santiago Froncoso, the Croesus of Palenque. Although the inventory of Don Santiago's entire stock—macaroni, flour, and nails—could not have totaled thirty dollars, he was well dressed in red slippers, white coarse-cloth trousers, and a white shirt, the bosom embroidered red with little animal figures in the Maya fashion. He was a man of immense courtesy, with an erudition entirely out of place in this tiny termite-eaten village. His most intimate "foreign relations" were with New

York City. The padres, in anticipation of Don Santiago's dinner, arrived rather noisily, the 240-pound *Cura* of Tumbalá carrying a violin which he at once offered politely to Stephens asking him to play some musical airs of his country. Since Stephens could not perform, the padre put the warped fiddle under one of his six chins and played while the other padres continued their game of monte. Considering himself on a social footing, Stephens said: "Señores, in my country, were you seen playing cards on Sunday you would be read out of the church."

"An Englishman," replied the priest politician, hardly looking up from his cards, "once told me the same thing. He also went into some detail of the manner of observing the Sunday in England. You will pardon me Señor Esteebans but we think it very stupid." And they fell to playing again with grains of maize as counters until the other guests arrived. Stephens, reflecting on this scene, said: ". . . the whole Spanish American priesthood has at times been denounced as a set of unprincipled gamblers, but I had too warm a recollection of their many kindnesses to hold them up in this light. They were all intelligent and good men, who would rather do benefits than an injury; in matters connected with religion[1] they were most reverential. . . . I would fain save them from denunciations of utter unworthiness which might be cast upon them. Nevertheless, it is true that dinner was delayed, and all the company kept waiting until they had finished their game of cards."

In the morning Stephens led the padres and their Indians over the escarpments of the Tumbalá mountains, from whence, after much vexatious bickering, they labored to the pyramids and to the Palace.

Catherwood, drawn by all the clatter, came out on the projecting steps. In his emaciated state he was hardly recognizable. He was as gaunt as a skeleton. The insects had played havoc with his face, it was swollen about the eyes, spotted with red blotches where furious Diptera had sucked his blood. His left arm hung

[1] One is reminded here of l'Abbé Coignard's creed: "Always bear in mind that a sound intelligence rejects everything that is contrary to reason, except in matters of faith, where it is necessary to believe blindly."

paralyzed from rheumatism. In no mood for pleasantries, he gave the priests a cold welcome. He did not like the way they pored over his drawings—for despite the horrible conditions he had kept on working—but the food they brought was welcome, and he and Pawling fell upon it like famished wolves. Fortunately the divine visitors did not long remain, and they departed lavishing praises on the ruins in typical Spanish hyperbole.

While Stephens had been nursing his niguas, Catherwood had "finished" the *Palacio;* now they were ready for the other structures of the site, none of which were wholly visible. Everything was obscured by the eternal forest, entangled, engulfed, blotted out by a profusion of trees, strangling yet protecting the architectural work of the builders of Palenque. It was only when Stephens climbed the triple-storied crumbling tower that he discovered, to the southwest through its disorder of fallen rubble, another building. Well over one hundred feet high, it lay obscured by a chaos of vegetation on top of a pyramid. This structure was the next to be uncovered. To the accompaniment of the soft patter of rain, they cut their way through the encumbering brush, slowly mounting the stones of the pyramid until they burst upon the Temple. Plants grew out of the roof, trees with naked roots tried to dislodge the stones. Even though it had suffered greatly from the sapping of roots and creepers, this, The Temple of Inscriptions (Stephens called it "No. 1 Casa de Piedra"), was the best preserved of the isolated temples of Palenque.

The front of the Temple, facing north, was entered by five doorways which were decorated by four stuccoed reliefs. All had lost their faces. The elaborate garments of the figures could be made out even though exposed to a thousand years of alternate fierce rain and fierce sun, enough of form and figure for Frederick Catherwood to draw. The stucco mosaic was once violently colored; it still exhibited something of its yellows, obtained from the ocherous earths, and its scarlets taken from the cochineal insect, and its purples extracted from the immemorial Purpura, the thick-shelled snail of the Yucatecan coast. But imagination alone could recreate what barbaric beauty this temple must have had with its stuccoed sculptures tinted with violent colors alive and sentient, with a towering mountain as a backdrop. Catherwood carefully copied the figures, making little attempt at restoration. He drew what time had spared in outline and shaded in the parts irretrievably lost. Then they entered the darkened interior vault.

They paused, for a brief moment, before the great door and peered into the inky blackness of the interior. It was as black as pitch. A lizard came out of the fetid vault, blinked its eyes, and ran into the open. The only sound was the baleful screech of the fruit bats hanging from the ceiling. Juan went forward slowly, the pine torch in his hand, and the shadows of their figures danced on the ancient, eroded walls. They examined the seventy-foot-long vault; it was empty and clammy as a tomb. Juan gave a startled cry. They followed his pointing finger to the side wall, where under green-gray moss were two huge, flat limestone slabs. They were covered with glyphs. The expeditious Juan, silenced by the solemnity of the moment, brought up a pair of brushes. He dipped them into a pool of water and began to rub off the verdure of centuries. There was no sound within the vault except the swish of the brushes. Catherwood leaned against the eroding stucco walls, waiting expectantly. Stephens, holding the pine torch, had forgotten for the last minutes to puff upon his cheroot. "The impression," he remembered later, "made upon our minds by these speaking but unintelligible tablets I shall not attempt to describe."

Slowly the carvings revealed their form. They were written, or better, sculptured in characteristic pebble-shaped glyphs, each completely filling its appointed square, wildly grotesque face symbols coupled with bars and dots as if trying to ape Roman numerals. There was no mistaking these; Stephens knew them to be the same as they had found at Copán and Quiriguá. It was perfectly maddening to Stephens that they could not read them. He was certain that "the hieroglyphics . . . tell Palenque's history."

But there was no Maya Rosetta stone. And Stephens, standing before these newly found Maya glyphs, was beside himself, for they had no key to the unraveling of these strange face-glyphs, which Stephens fervently believed would tell something of the people who had built this stone city. In hope that they would find an answer, he had Catherwood copy them accurately. Stephens would have been disappointed today, for these glyphs, partially deciphered, give nothing but dates; the builders of Palenque say nothing of themselves. Only one stela, one dated sculptured monolith, has been found at Palenque and the earliest date yet found is 642 A.D., but the latest date to be found there is only 783 A.D., which suggests that the Maya were in possession of Palenque for only 150 years! If this is true, it had the shortest occupation of any of the Maya cities, for the Maya lived continuously at Uaxactun for 492 years; at Tikal for 381 years; and at Copán for 345 years. Stucco was developed late in Maya technics, and this suggests Palenque as one of the last cities to be built in the Maya "Old Empire."

When Frederick Catherwood had finished copying the tablets ("of the law," the padres called them) within The Temple of Inscriptions, they stumbled down the pyramid into a *quebrada*, where the river stream had been artificially sewered by the Maya. A few hundred yards away and upward they discovered the base of another pyramid.

They had suspected, in reading the works of Dupaix and Del Río, that there were more buildings to be found in Palenque, yet there was nothing to follow in the jungle save instinct. Juan stumbled across a profusion of cut stones, his shouts drew Stephens, who was inspecting a ten-foot monolith, and he passed the call along; the four drew together, moved toward the purple shadows of an artificial rise of ground. Dodging between trees and ducking the lianas that crossed their path like bell ropes, they found, after climbing the sides of another pyramid, a crumbling building, an edifice of three doorways—the Temple of the Cross. A magnificent building with a roof crest forty-two feet high, a roof comb boldly conceived, it became "Casa No. 2" in Stephens identification. The Temple was once decorated with a stucco design of bewildering complexity, but carved wooden lintels of sapote wood had decayed, causing the whole of the façade to tumble down in a mass of rubble. Catherwood thought that he had been forestalled by time, until, looking within the vaulted interior, he found a stone triptych on the wall. This was the carved tablet with a cross that was to cause so much weary logomachy, more learned controversy than any other piece of art in America.

The principal decoration of this triptych was a cross, resting on a symbol of a death's head (suggested by two fleshless jaw-bones). On top of the cross was a grotesquely sculptured quetzal, the famous golden-green trogon, sacred bird. Two life-sized Indians, carved in exquisite low-relief, flanked the cross; figures fashioned without distortion of features which are among the prime and faultless masterpieces of Mayan art. The grotesqueries were reserved for the "cross" which caused a learned controversy, since the presence of a "cross" at Palenque proved to those who held such a view that Christians before Columbus had lived in America. Yet the Maya "cross" is not a cross at all, but a conventionalization of a tree combined with the sun and death symbols which point their four corners in the direction of the four principal earth directions. Catherwood drew the ten-foot-long tablet.[2]

In Stephens' mind there was no longer any doubt of what he saw. As art, it ranked with all other cultures. "What we had before our eyes was grand, curious, and remarkable enough. Here were the remains of a cultivated, polished and peculiar people, who had passed through all the stages incident to the rise and fall of nations; reached their golden age, and perished. . . . We lived in the ruined palaces . . . we went up to their desolate temples and fallen altars; and wherever we moved we saw the evidences of their taste, their skill in arts. . . . In the midst of desolation and ruin we looked back to the past, cleared away the gloomy forest, and fancied every building perfect, with its terraces and pyramids, its sculptured and painted ornaments, grand, lofty, and imposing, and overlooking an immense inhabited plain; we called back into life the strange people who gazed at us in sadness from the walls; pictured them, in fanciful costumes and adorned with plumes of feathers, ascending the terraces of the palace and the steps leading to the temples. . . . In the romance of the world's history nothing ever impressed me more forcibly than the spectacle of this once

[2] Another tablet, somewhat similar, was discovered at Palenque fifty years later, which its discoverer, Dr. Alfred P. Maudslay, called "The Temple of the Foliated Cross."

great and lovely city, overturned, desolate, and lost . . . overgrown with trees for miles around, and without even a name to distinguish it."

Thus mused Mr. Stephens while sitting on the steps of the crumbling ruin of The Temple of the Cross. In the distance, veiled by a thin, persistent rain, the howling monkeys gave out a pulsating moan; cicadas beat upon their membraned drums, and the air resounded with the calls of unseen birds. Two huge white hawks circled the ruins on extended wings. All the while Stephens, lost in a trance, sat dreaming his archaeological dream. The rain had snuffed out his cheroot, it lay smoldering like a burnt match.

Stephens was unaware that close to Palenque lay another ruin, Dchulzum, and that thirty miles distant on the Río Usumacinta there were other ruins of the period of Palenque. On that river which drained most of Los Altos of Guatemala (and which Louis Halle, Jr., called the "River of Ruins") there were other Maya cities buried by the jungle—Yaxchilán, Piedra Negras, El Desempeño—which, because of the stimulation of Stephens' book, others in a later century would discover. Within the Maya area marked by the extremes of Copán and Palenque, there lay a vast sixty thousand square miles which hid the remains of thousands of these ancient structures.

Although Palenque was distant three hundred air miles from Copán, separated by a bewildering clefted space of mountains, jungles, rivers, and savannahs; although Palenque's medium was stucco while that of Copán was stone, they who built them wrote the same language. Stephens had explored the two extremes—north and south—of the Maya cultural empire. He had, in Dr. Spinden's words, "proved the homogenity of Maya art despite differences of space and geography."

Above the well of mellow sound there were the muted calls of human voices. Henry Pawling and Juan, who had disappeared in the jungle, had found another ruin. They could not be seen. They could only be traced by their voices. Stephens turned to Catherwood, who was just finishing the last glyphs of the "cross," waited until he had done, then, gathering up the easels, they made their way down the pyramid. So thick was the forest that they had been unable to see, from the heights of one, the pyramid of another. Following the sound of Juan's voice, again they climbed a truncated pyramid to another temple. Stephens quickly took its measurements, noted the slanting stucco roof, the high lattice-work roof comb, the two vacant niches where two huge carvings, which he had first seen in the village (and which were to be the cause of a humorous sequel), were once placed. At either end were two huge glyphs—somewhat battered by centurial erosion—proclaiming to those who could read them that the building was erected in 692 A.D.

Within a darkened room giving out the fetid staleness of centuries, they found the apothesis of Maya art: in a vault constructed to hold it was a huge altar, a sort of altar within an altar. A stone mural dominated by two life-sized figures flanked the Sun Face symbol, its tongue protruding Gorgon-like, backed by two spears and a double row of glyphs. The carved Indian figures offered in the Sun's homage cross-legged mannequins. Glyphs coursed the sides. There were other typical Maya intrusions and distractions, yet on the whole it was magnificent. Catherwood, who had seen much of ancient art, said it was as fine as anything he had seen in Egypt. One can find little else in Maya art so perfect in its essential simplicity, so fluent, so completely achieved. It had a delicacy, an almost epicene quality. The Maya artist knew here the value of empty space. Stephens was deeply impressed. If they did not go through their usual exchange of enthusiasms, it was only because after twenty-eight mostly sleepless nights and often foodless days, their bodies would no longer respond to these old enthusiasms. The copying of the relief at The Temple of the Sun was almost the last thing that Catherwood accomplished at Palenque. It was to be his Maya masterpiece. So impressed was he by the design of the Sun that he had it stamped on Stephens' book.

The rains were now the Furies unbound. The wind whipped gusts of water into the ruins, and there was not a single dry place of refuge. Catherwood worked as in a trance. He allowed himself to be dragged a few hundred feet more through the jungle to yet another ruin—an architectural fragment now called The Temple of the Beau Relief. There he was able only to make a feeble sketch of an allegorical piece of a stucco—which unknown to them Count Waldeck had done five years before (ending his work by chopping off the face of the piece). After that, Catherwood, like a massive oak deprived of its roots, fell slowly to the ground. The hurricane lashed across the exposed hills, toppling trees, pulling down whole sections of forest. Above the din of the storm the howling monkeys sounded like roaring banshees. And Juan, to top the disasters, tipped over the pot of grease—that was the end.

On June 1, 1840, they quit the ruins.

Chapter xv There was no satisfying Stephens' lordly ambitions. Since he had possessed himself of the ruins of Copán
for fifty dollars and was in negotiation for the purchase of Quiriguá, he thought he might as well add Palenque to his archaeological real estate. Thus far he had been frustrated in his attempt
to remove some of the monuments to take back and set up in
America an archaeological museum. While Catherwood recovered from an illness brought on by exposure at the ruins, Stephens
negotiated for the Maya-land. He informed the prefect of his plan
and ascertained from him its value: "The tract," Stephens re-
counted, "containing the ruins consisted of about six thousand
acres of good land, which, according to the usual appraisement,
would cost about fifteen hundred dollars, and the prefect said it
would not be valued a cent higher on account of the ruins. I resolved immediately to buy it." Yet this was not so simple as in
Honduras. Here, in Mexico, the land laws required that a foreigner
must be married to a woman of Mexico before he could purchase
property. Although Stephens was a young man of thirty-four,
attractive to women and very much attracted to them, he retained
a firm grip on his bachelorhood. "On principle I always resisted
such tendencies, but I never before found it to my interest to give
way." Yet his dark eyes flashed mischievously, "The ruined city of
Palenque was a most desirable piece of property."

Archaeology must have had a deep hold on Stephens if he was
willing to allow his principles to be usurped by the purchase of
Palenque. Apparently in a serious mood he began to look over
the ladies. But Santo Domingo was a small village with few prospects and the prettiest girl on which his eye had long rested and
who had contributed most to his happiness ("she made our cigars")
was only fourteen, hardly a deterrent, except that she was already
married. The only remaining possibilities were the two neatly

dressed ladies occupying a pink calcimined wattle and daub house which contained on its stucco front and embedded in the walls the two carvings from the Temple of the Sun. Stephens liked the house. He liked the ladies. He especially liked those Maya tablets. He might have either lady: a widowed sister of the congressional delegate Señor Bártolo Bravo, or the other, a *soltera*, both displaying a mere whisper of lip down. To whom would he make the first proposal? Apparently Stephens plumbed the possibilities, in more ways than one, for reporting to Catherwood on the progress of this nebulous archaeological romance with the sisters Bravo, he said: "Both were equally interesting and equally interested." Yet nothing finally came of it, and Stephens, as a last resort, instructed the prefect that he would try to arrange the purchase when he departed, through the American consul at Laguna. He allowed his firm offer of fifteen hundred dollars to stand.

North of the little village of Santo Domingo del Palenque, the elfish pinnacled Tumbalá Mountains melt into the ground and become palmetto-studded savannahs. Here and beyond is a tangled skein of rivers pouring down from the Guatemala highlands onto the Tabasco-Campeche plain. In a confusing pattern of water, these lands are transformed by the caprice of weather into either desert-hot savannah or hyacinth-covered lakes. A historic land, this section; here tribes of Mayance speech in historyless times moved down from Vera Cruz to lay tribal claim to all of Yucatán. Here in 1519 on the shores of Tabasco, at Cintla, Hernán Cortés made his first landfall that was to eventuate in his conquest of the Aztec, and here, too, not many years afterward, he struggled through the quagmires of Tabasco on his way to Honduras to punish Cristóbal de Olíd, who had revolted against his rule. And here, in June, 1840, following an immemorial route of Indian, conquistador, and colonist, John Lloyd Stephens led his three fatigued expeditionists across the savannahs.

After traveling most of the day through quagmires of stump grass and palmettos, they came at night, with the rain, to the village of Las Playas. Not so much a village as a single street on which frowned huts of leaf-thatch, the rain-soaked town was filled with ill-fed dogs and scavenger pigs. Unable to find a *posada*, they took, with the blessings of the padre, refuge in a church which stood, or rather tumbled, at the end of the street. On its crumbling stone cornice, rows of buzzards plumed in funeral black stretched their ugly necks to look down on them as they entered the darkened church.

In the morning, night yielding up its mysteries to the dawn, they quitted Las Playas. In a thirty-foot-long canoe loaned to them by the alcalde; poled by three men, they began the descent to the sea.

Beyond Las Playas is the Catazaja Lagoon, a broad sheet of hyacinth-covered water surrounded by forest. In the distance the mountains of Palenque were visible, forming a perfect trapezium against the horizon. Catazaja was an Elysium for birds. There were web-footed and long-legged wading birds, swimming, plunging, flying about the diurnal invaders of their peace. There, in small flocks, was the tantale with its hard, crooked beak, infinite varieties of ducks, cranes walked slowly and stately by, stopping to stare, quite unafraid of the canoe gliding through the maze of lily pads. Over them ran the graceful jacana, with its yellow-tipped wings and iridescent green neck, tripping dexterously over the floating leaves, fluttering down like a butterfly to the next lily pad. The shy spoonbills kept to the shore. Near the flamingo with its flaming wings, ghostly herons rose in effortless flight. Even in their discomfort, Stephens and company could feel the beauty of the moment. There was little of the naturalist in John Lloyd Stephens; his preoccupation was man—the measurer of all things. He could pass through the entire length of a jungle without once conveying that life, in bewildering forms, swarmed about him. But now, with hundreds of varieties of birds about him, nameless and unknown, he felt the lack of knowledge. At the Catazaja Lagoon he decided, should he ever come to Central America again, to bring a naturalist with him.

Following the channel, they glided past alligators floating on the surface like partially submerged mahogany logs. Then they entered the Río Chico. It was a sluggish, stagnant channel, so narrow at first that the trees arched overhead and the lianas interlaced; the muddy stream flowing through the thick jungle walls was more like a tunnel. Monkeys peered down at them through the interstices of the leaves, and a huge green iguana, with three feet of whiplash tail, looked at them briefly—and continued to climb the sides of a smooth-trunked tree. There was no other sound above the dip of the paddles except the pallid whisperings of the river.

Toward evening the Río Chico grew wider and became, no one knew why, the Río Chiquito; with a roar it joined the turbulent Río Usumacinta, one of the noblest rivers in Central America. The Usumacinta, drains three-quarters of the Guatemalan highlands, gathering most of the tropical waters, streams, and rills to it, and flows through the provinces of Yucatán, Campeche, and Tabasco to empty into the Gulf of Mexico. It was a wild country, uninhabited and desolate. The howling monkeys screeched the whole night, a gigantic screaming wail that quivered and rose, fell and rose again, trailing its banshee echoes across the brawling river.

Moving through the heart of the logwood country, they came to the village of Palizada, which lay on an open plain. Willows hung over the banks, a herd of cattle all but hidden grazed on the tall, luxuriant grass. The tall straight *bojón* trees stood on the banks with their spreading umbrella-shaped tops reminding Catherwood of Italian pines, and the ghostly-stemmed Cecropias looked like gigantic candelabra. So much an idyll they did not even mind the atrocious cuisine of moldy biscuits, tasajo, black beans, rum, and cigars.

In Stephens' time Palizada was a small hamlet of straggling palm-leafed huts; in a few years it became a boom town, for a forest of logwood—the *Haematoxylum campechianum* of botanists—was discovered there. Logwood had been a source of Spain's wealth and misery for centuries. The red dyes obtained from the *palo de tinta* were much in demand by the rest of Europe. Pirates —British, French, and Dutch—when not sacking Spanish galleons, would come into the dyewood country to log; their continued presence throughout the peninsula caused endless diplomatic disputes between England and Spain and resulted eventually in the Crown Colony of Belize. Campeche had been for centuries the port of fine woods; so great a supply was on hand that when

Grandmont captured the city in 1684, he burned a thousand logs in honor of Saint Louis.

They went down to the sea, with a cargo of these dyewoods. Stephens hired Don Peluco—an engaging fellow devoid of all front teeth except his canines which gave him the look of a jaguar when he opened his mouth, which was frequent—to take them to Carmen. With Don Peluco went his bungo, a flat-bottomed, two-masted schooner, a horribly patched and unseaworthy craft, cluttered with logwood, bananas, mangoes, and papayas, and with the bungo went the crew—whom Stephens called "breechless marineros," miserable, half-clothed *lazzaroni* who scarcely knew a jib from a halyard. Don Peluco, grinning like a tiger, prefaced each command with: "Gentlemen, do me the favor . . ."

Down to the Laguna they went with this Yucatecan Charon, through an inferno of mosquitoes and alligators, along the furiously rushing river where bamboos and aquatic *jahuacte* palms rose above the grasses and the willows. The wind whistled through the rigging, rain, biting like hail, came with the wind, increasing in violence as they reached the Boca Chica of the Lagoon. At this point they disdained the breakfast of ship's biscuit, shark's flesh seasoned with a dash of vinegar, and a little glass of rum, although Stephens accepted a cigar "to assist the digestion." The blasts of the Carib wind god Huracán were agitating the whole lagoon when the bungo plunged into it. Don Peluco reefed the tattered sails of the bungo, shouting his commands above the wail of the wind: *"Señores, hagame el favor."* Waves broke over the vessel, and Stephens thought they certainly would not reach Carmen alive. He put the balsa-wood life preserver on Catherwood, they took off their boots and coats and waited. Don Peluco, helm in hand, seemed to enjoy it thoroughly; with his ragged shirt beating in the breeze, he laughed and showed his two teeth as they moved to Carmen.

Into Laguna de Terminos, fifty miles long, hundreds of jungle-spawned rivers debouch their sediment-filled water. It had been discovered in 1518 and named by Bernal Díaz del Castillo, the famous soldier historian of *Historia Verdad*. He had at first fancied it an arm of the ocean encircling Yucatán, which they then believed to be an island. Terminos was partially enclosed by the island of Carmen, a low, flat, sandy island seven miles long, lying like a shriveled appendix facing the Caribbean. The city port of Carmen lay at the eastern end, an outsize village of two thousand persons, nurtured by the commerce of logwood, for the *palo de tinto* was floated down into the Laguna, stripped of bark, floated into Carmen, and lodged in warehouses.

After tacking under a close-reefed sail, the bungo was brought into the open roadstead of Carmen. They were happy to be quit of her. In their water-soaked clothes they walked the entire length of the town, past hotels, cafés, even barber shops. The houses, mostly frame, were huddled close together, banana trees spread their luxurious shade, and red and white flowers like periwinkles were tastefully planted in and about the piazzas. The streets ended in the jungle. At the very end of the town in a neat, freshly painted house was the United States consulate. In attendance to its problems was Don Carlos.

Charles Russell, Esq., called familiarly "Don Carlos," was a Philadelphia-born American, long resident of the tropics. He had been an importer of logwood, a partner of the well-known house of Gutiérrez and Compañía; "he married," went on the letter of Mr. Noah Platt of New York to the State Department, "a Lady belonging to one of the first families in the country." On Mr. Platt's recommendation, Charles Russell assumed charge of the consulate at Laguna, Island of Carmen, Campeche, on March 1, 1839.[1] A merry, blue-eyed man, with gray-streaked hair and grizzled eyebrows, he was intrigued by Stephens' description of Palenque. He had always wanted to go there but now the cold of many winters had diminished the enthusiasms of his younger years and Palenque remained unvisited. He agreed to the scheme to buy the site of Palenque for fifteen hundred dollars in Stephens' name, for, being married to an *hija del país*, he could conform to Mexican law.

The matter of plaster casts entered the conversation at this point. Henry Pawling finally agreed (for he desperately wanted

---

[1] Charles Russell, according to the records of the State Department archives, died at his post on February 8, 1843. His official dispatches number sixteen, of which several are missing.

money to return to the United States) to undertake the commission to return to Palenque and there make casts of the principal sculptures. Catherwood, who had made plaster casts of Greek monuments while shut up in Athens during the Greco-Turkish War, instructed Pawling in the technique of making plaster-cast impressions of the sculptures. Apparently Henry Pawling was well instructed. He left for Palenque in July, 1840. Months later, he had made thirty casts, when he ran into trouble. He had completed his part of the mission when the self-appointed "patriots' committee of Palenque" had seized all the plaster casts. They had written to the governor of Chiapas telling him that Pawling's molds "are so much like the originals that at first sight it may be observed that they may be taken surely for second originals, and no doubt serve to mold after them as many copies as might be wished and in this manner supply the world with these precious things without a sixpence expense. . . . we suggest to your excellency, that Sr. Enrique Pawling pay four or five thousand dollars which would be applied to benevolent works and to the embellishment of this town. Allow him, in no manner to take away any of the moulds of Plaster of Paris he has made and continues making. Indeed if this treasure is ours, and by rights belongs to this town, why should it not be benefited by it?"

In November, 1840, Pawling was forced to leave Palenque without the casts of Palenque sculpture. The demand for tribute reached Stephens too late, for having raised twenty thousand dollars among his New York friends to finance a proposed museum, he would have been willing to make an offer of money—"for the embellishment of the town of Palenque." Stephens was furious at that two-faced *herm*, Santiago Froncoso—one of the "three patriots"—for he had written Stephens on his departure: "Farewell, my friend, and Dearest Sir, Command whatever you wish and from whatever distance." And it was he who demanded the destruction of Pawling's casts of Palenque. Seven years later the fragments of these molds were seen by the French naturalist Chevalier Arthur Morelet, traveling in Chiapas in 1847. "They were," he wrote, "totally destroyed . . . depriving science of facsimiles of great interest."

There is a sequel. Captain William Brown of New York, master of a logwood vessel which operated between Tabasco and New York—and married to a Mexican lady, Doña Trinidad Garrido (thereby placing himself within the orbit of Mexican law)—journeyed to Palenque and offered the "three patriots" ten thousand dollars if he be allowed to "extract four or six principal stones from Palenque." This American Lord Elgin was not successful either, but he did bring away one of the three slabs which made up the famous stone triptych in The Temple of the Cross. This reached New York in the bottom of one of Howland and Aspinwall's vessels. It was offered to Stephens, but he refused it, for his idea of laying the foundation of the Museum of American Antiquities had not been consummated.[2] Palenque he could not purchase. From Copán, which he owned, he could extract nothing. Quiriguá's purchase had become impossible since its owners had placed a fabulously high price upon its monuments. These sounded the death knell to his hopes, so the Palenquean tablet found its way into the newly formed Smithsonian Institution. There it remained until 1908, when Mr. Elihu Root, then secretary of state, as a gesture of friendship returned it to Mexico. It has since been joined by the other two sections of the triptych of The Temple of the Cross, and all are now on permanent exhibit at the National Museum of Mexico.

[2] Stephens, *Incidents of Travel in Central America*, II, 469: "The author considers it proper to say that, immediately on his return home, a few friends, whose names he would have great pleasure in making known if he were at liberty to do so, undertook to provide the sum of $20,000 for the purpose of carrying that object into effect. Under their direction, the author wrote to his agent at Guatimala, to purchase the ruins of Quiriguá, or such monuments as it might be considered advisable to remove, at a price beyond what would have been accepted for them when he left Guatimala; but, unfortunately, in the mean time, a notice taken from Mr. Catherwood's memoranda, and inserted by the proprietors in a Guatimala paper, had reached this country, been translated and copied into some of our own journals, and one eulogistic paragraph, probably forgotten as soon as written, was sent back to Guatimala, which gave the proprietor such an exaggerated notion of their value that he refused the offer. From vague conversations with foreigners who had never seen and knew nothing of them, he conceived the idea that all the governments of Europe would vie with each other for their possession; and still entertaining the foolish belief that the author was acting on behalf of his government, said that, if the President of the United States wanted them, he must pay $20,000 for them; in the mean time, he resolved to wait for offers from England and France. By the last advices he was still under the same hallucination."

It was Stephens' intention to continue his explorations—the search for ruined cities—into Yucatán, for he had heard whispers of a great walled city called Uxmal. It depended wholly on Frederick Catherwood, who was racked with malaria. Rather than break up the expedition, Catherwood insisted that he was well enough to take the journey. Fortunately there was a vessel rocking in the open harbor at Carmen, a sailing vessel under consignment to Charles Russell. The Consul agreed to load Captain Obadiah Femsley's brig *Gabrielacho* in two days if the master would take Stephens and Catherwood 120 miles northwest and land them at Sisal, entrepôt to Mérida, the capital of Yucatán.

They reached Mérida on the eve of the fete of Corpus Christi, having bounced in from the coast in a springless buckboard affair, a *valon-coché*. At dusk, the twilight scarcely intervening, they passed under the ruins of three lofty stone gateways, miniature arches of triumph for the explorers who had, thus far, braved two thousand miles of Central American geography. The whole flat, drab countryside was pleasantly animated by the approaching *fiesta*. The white-clad Indians whom they passed in the streets doffed their straw hats, uttering *"Dios botik"*; the women, neatly dressed in white huipils, waved to them. On the horizon, above the stern-spiked pads of the maguey, they could see the church spires of the city. The houses lined the streets, neatly calcimined in pastel shades of pink, cream, green, and yellow, "very pleasing to the eye," Stephens admitted. The streets, nicely paved, were, with the advent of Corpus Christi, decorated with pine branches. On the roofs of the corners of the buildings stood models of animals—elephants, deer, flamingoes—which served in the absence of the natives' being able to read Spanish as street guides: "Meet me at the street of the flamingo." Simple monolithic houses turned their posterns to the street—in the Spanish-Moorish fashion—the iron-studded doors and grilled windows gave them a forbidding mysterious appearance, yet once within the gates lovely patios were aflame with riotous tropical flowers. "The streets," Stephens remembered, "were clean, and many people in them well dressed, animated, and cheerful in appearance; calêches fancifully painted and curtained, having ladies in them handsomely dressed, without hats, and their hair ornamented with flowers, gave it an air of gaiety and beauty.... we felt as if by some accident we had fallen upon a European city."

The capital of Yucatán, titled by the King as "The Very Loyal and Very Noble city of Mérida," had been one of the first cities built after Yucatán's conquest by the Montejos. They had, it is true, begun the conquest on the ground floor; Francisco de Montejo, the elder, had landed with Hernán Cortés at Cintla in 1519, fought in its first battle, and had been chosen a year later to take back to Charles V the first loot to impress the council with the wealth to be found in the Mexican land ruled by Montezuma. An amiable gentleman, this Montejo, with his blue eyes and a scar across his face which gleamed scarlet when he was angry, and a *conquistador* with connections at court.[3] Montejo, after successfully accomplishing his mission, remained in Spain, where he married a widow troubled equally by the weight of a fortune and a violently demanding womb. Then in 1524, just before Cortés was to make his heroically quixotic march across one thousand miles of Mexican geography to find and punish those who had revolted against him in Honduras, he sent for Montejo. He could refuse nothing to his old companion in arms and agreed to make yet another representation for him before the Court. While he was on his way back to Spain, in skirting the jagged littoral of Yucatán, the sirens of conquest called again to Montejo, and this time he was unwilling, as Ulysses was, to stuff his ears. He returned to Salamanca, where he enticed his Croesus-rich wife to sell her estates and pawn her jewels. The madness of conquest possessed him.

In those halcyon days—before the age of reason—the King of Spain, by virtue of the papal bull of Pope Alexander VI, was the greatest real-estate holder in the world outside of God. He owned all the lands in the "new founde worlde" (except those of Brazil) west of the arbitrary line drawn by the papal geographers. The new conquests operated something like realty subdivisions. Montejo, whose qualifications were well established, paid a sum of

[3] ". . . somewhat middle-sized, and his face merry, and he was fond of rejoicings and a businessman, and a good horseman; when he came over to Mexico he might have been about thirty-five: and he was liberal and he spent more than his income warranted."—Bernal Díaz del Castillo, II, 467.

money to the Crown, agreeing to conquer and then colonize the whole of Yucatán at his own expense. He was named *capitán-generál*—only one of his sonorous titles—and given a grant of arms with a bequest of one thousand square miles of land, *para siempre jamás*, that was his "for ever more." The Crown, as was the usual practice, was to have its "royal fifth," which was to be used to build schools, convents, roads, and a host of other complicated governmental projects which would weld the newly conquered province to the state. And so it came to be, or, factually, not to be.

The conquest of Yucatán took fifteen years, fifteen years of close battle, for the Maya had learned to take the measure of the Spaniard; they had among them a talented practitioner of perfidy, Gonzalo Guerrero, a Spanish captive of the Maya who had lived through the rituals and tortures to emerge a war chieftain. The Maya turned to him when pressed by the Spaniard, and he devised defenses that blunted the offensive power of horse and gun. By posing as a captive slave, unwillingly held, he smuggled to the Spaniards scrawled messages always ending: "I remember God, and you, Sir, and the Spaniards. I am your good friend. . . ."

Still there was no staying the conquest. Tutul Xiu, one of the most powerful chieftains of the Maya, was induced into alliance with the Spaniards that their aid might be brought against his traditional Maya enemy. That marked the end of Maya independence. In January, 1542, Montejo chose the site for his capital, the Maya religious center of T'ho; its huge plaza of stone buildings reminded him of Mérida in the Spanish province of Badajoz (the ancient *Augusta Emerita* of *Lusitania*) with its Roman ruins. He called it Mérida. In the rigidly prescribed "manner of founding a town," the town council was appointed, streets laid out, a gallows erected, and the Indians employed to tear down their temples so that the stone might be used in building the cathedral.

On the south side of the plaza, the Montejos, uncle and nephew, selected the site for their palace. Over the doorway was an elaborate façade of carving; the Montejo coat of arms in the center, and on the sides two mailed knights standing on the heads of conquered Indians. It was not truly symbolic. The conquest of Yucatán was long drawn out and bitterly waged by the Maya, who never really submitted. They resisted the conquest of their souls as they resisted the conquest of their land. On Sundays they went through the ritual demanded by the white man's God, and on weekdays in the shadows of the jungle they still worshiped as they had always worshiped. In the deep recesses of the forest they carried the images of the Maya gods that had escaped the rapacity of their new masters, and here in the blue haze and the aromatic perfume of burning copal incense they sought solace.

There was little progress in their spiritual conquest until Fray Diego de Landa appeared on the peninsula. A rigidly efficient monk lacking both humor and humility, Landa with one hand lighted the torch that destroyed Maya culture, and with the other preserved it. He assiduously studied the Maya language, and armed with it, and it alone, walked the riverless land of Yucatán attempting through these pagan shibboleths to bring the Maya around to his ways. When this method did not succeed, in terrible fury he tore down with his own hands any vestige that remained to remind the Maya of their gods. In this way the beautifully built stone pyramid at Izamal was destroyed under his direction and used to build the Franciscan monastery. Landa spared no one, not even the Spanish authorities, when he found them violating the principle of the Laws of the Indies; Indians, least of all. For failure to appear at Mass, they were lashed. For continuation of their pagan ways, they were given soul-breaking tasks to perform.

When Diego de Landa learned that the people at the village of Maní, the font of the Tutul Xiu dynasty, were still offering obeisance to their ancient deities, he descended upon the village, and found to his horror idols of clay and wood and books, folded books, on which were written in glyphs (such as Stephens found carved in stone), histories, calendars, tables astronomical and astrological, illustrated so as to assist their mnemonic processes. These were the cornerstone of Maya learning, books which had so far escaped the zeal of the missionaries' hands. Landa gathered them together under his own auto-da-fé. "We found," he said, "among them a great number of books . . . and because they contained nothing but superstitions and falsehoods about the devil we burned them all."

"We burned them."[4] The accretion of two thousand years of knowledge built up from a cultural zero perished in those flames at Maní. Landa had dealt a blow that all the king's horses and all the king's men had failed to accomplish: the end of Maya culture. For while socially important secrets are seldom in the hands of a single man, as Aldous Huxley aptly pointed out, "in many communities elements of higher culture are in the hands of a few." The latest world war has given more than one example of how delicate is the balance of civilization, how easily it can be uprooted. The very existence of an industrialized and urbanized society depends on the knowledge and skill of, at most, 1 per cent of its members. ". . . a selective massacre of three to four hundred thousand technicians," Huxley wrote, "would bring the whole economic and social life of England to a standstill."

Yet, paradoxically, the same person who helped so generously to stamp out Maya culture also did the most to preserve its history. Diego de Landa carefully compiled—with a host of Maya amanuenses—all the details of their lives as well as—and this the most important—an analysis of their written language. When the Spanish authorities learned of his self-administered burning of Maya antiquities, he was recalled to Spain and made to answer before higher ecclesiastical authorities. Confined at the convent of San Francisco in Guadalajara he wrote a manuscript, in reality his apologia, which he called *History of Things of Yucatán*,[5] this proved to be (but only in part) the Rosetta stone for the deciphering of the Maya glyphs. Stephens, who begged for a Champollion to unravel the linguistic mysteries, little knew as he looked upon a tomb in the cathedral at Mérida that his "Champollion" was a monk; and his name was Diego de Landa.

But it was the rumor of another ruin that lay close to Mérida that had brought them to the capital of Yucatán. It was the last of the three ancient deserted stone cities[6] that had entered the

[4] In like manner Fray Juan de Zumárraga had burned the Aztec books at Tlotelolco.

[5] See the excellent edition of Landa's *Relación de las Cosas de Yucatán*, translated with elaborate notes by Dr. Alfred M. Tozzer, Papers, Peabody Museum publications (Cambridge, 1941).

[6] Copán, Palenque, Uxmal.

literature, mentioned by the famous Lorenzo de Zavala, who had actually seen it. The ruin was called Uxmal and it lay fifty miles from Mérida. They were taken to Don Simón Peón, the gentleman on whose vast estates Uxmal lay, and Stephens presented his letters of introduction. Furnished with a guide to lead them through the scrub jungles, they arrived two days later at the hacienda near Uxmal. Catherwood was too ill in the morning to go to the ruins, but for Stephens the cornucopia of surprises had not ended. When he saw through the interstices of the scrub forest the outlines of pyramids, standing stark and bare in the fierce sun, the nerve-tingling sensations he had experienced at Copán and at Palenque again possessed him. ". . . to my astonishment [I] came at once upon a large open field strewed with mounds of ruins, and vast buildings on terraces, and pyramidal structures, grand and in good preservation, richly ornamented, without a bush to obstruct the view, and in picturesque effect almost equal to the ruins of Thebes."

Stephens could hardly contain himself. He rode back to the hacienda and burst in upon Catherwood, who lay with a wet cloth over his head. Stephens, using all the adjectives his enthusiasm could summon, drew for Catherwood his glimpse of Uxmal. Catherwood sat up unsteadily in the hammock, looked at him from bloodshot eyes: "Stephens, you are romancing."

Even malaria which alternately chilled and fevered the body of Catherwood was not enough to keep him in his hammock; weakened but unyielding, he went out the next day to Uxmal, inspected the vast ruins lying under an oven-hot sun. He agreed that the "reality exceeded Stephens's description."

As in a trance, so accustomed had he become to working under depressing conditions, Catherwood put up his easel and began with practiced hand to draw a panorama of the pyramid of the House of the Dwarf. His fever mounted and his head felt as if it were being incessantly clubbed with tiny hammers. At three in the afternoon Stephens found him collapsed beside his unfinished drawing; the first expedition to Central America came to an end.

On June 24, Catherwood was put aboard the Spanish brig *Alexandre* bound for Havana, with Stephens, in "great apprehensions for his health," taking over his care as well as the guardianship of his drawings and notebooks. As if the gods willed their perishing, the *Alexandre* ran into the equatorial doldrums. It sat for days like a Muscovy duck on a sea of glass. By the thirteenth of July, the drinking water ran out. Sharks, as if summoned by some strange telepathic instinct, began to course the ship. In the afternoon a wind came up in gusts, yet was not strong enough to move the vessel, but about the time Stephens had given up, thinking that their discovery of the Central American ruins would be lost on the *Alexandre*, the wind strengthened and another vessel hove into sight. Stephens hailed it in English, and it turned out to be the *Helen Maria* of North Yarmouth, New York bound. It came about, the sailors pulled Catherwood and Stephens aboard, then it sped north, reaching New York harbor on the last day of July, 1840.

Chapter XVI If one were looking for atmosphere, New York City possessed it. It was not, unfortunately, the atmosphere to best serve the writing of Stephens' archaeological discoveries. It was a presidential election year and the "city," like the rest of America, was in constant political turmoil. Every hour of the day and the night had its parades. Young men, in wide-awake hats, pulled log-cabin floats through the streets, joined by old men in beaver hats and frock coats in good-natured song: "Tippecanoe and Tyler too." At night there were bonfires . . . "Great Moral Meetings" . . . "for all the virtuous, moral and honest friends of General Harrison." The Hard Cider campaign was under way, with the contagious motif of log cabin and hard cider. Martin Van Buren, there was not the slightest doubt, was going to fall. He sat through the Whig onslaughts calmly enough, "eating expensive soup from a silver tureen with a gold spoon," said his detractors, driving rather haughtily through the streets of Washington in his maroon coach with outriders. Martin Van Buren was being treated to the same buncombe that he had once used against John Quincy Adams. He was now utterly bewildered. He had no antidote against the mass libido for "Tippecanoe and Tyler too!" The nation seemed to be determined to vote for anybody, anybody but Martin Van Buren. And "anybody" became William Henry Harrison.

A Virginia-born aristocrat, now in the bucolic period of his life, a gentleman from Ohio, General Harrison had once in the Indian wars won a battle. Well meaning but bumbling, Harrison was precisely the figure to coalesce conservatives, Whigs, and antislavers into a political party to win the election. They formulated everything save a platform. They needed none. People sang their way through the campaign:

And have you heard the news from Maine
And what old Maine can do?
She went hell-bent for Governor Kent,
And Tippecanoe and Tyler too.

Issues were swept aside. Arguments dissolved in front of bonfires. The hard-pressed Democrats, trying to inject a show of humor to the campaign, repeated the remark of a Whig printed in a Baltimore newspaper: "If General Harrison were given a pension of $2,000 a year and a barrel of hard cider he would be perfectly content to spend the rest of his days in a log-cabin studying moral philosophy." The people were instantly aroused at the sneer at log cabins and hard cider which symbolized the common man. Overnight, it seemed, the Whigs were parading themselves silly pulling log cabins. There were log-cabin watch chains and log-cabin earrings; there were log-cabin songs, hard-cider quick steps. It was in vain that the Democrats pointed out that General Harrison was an aristocratic planter, did not live in a log cabin, and that the remark originally emanated from the Whigs, showing contempt for their clodpoll candidate. It was useless.

In the midst of this political lunacy, the Maya discoveries dropped like a bomb shell. John L. Stephens, the well-known traveler, had discovered in the jungles of Central America ruins of ancient cities as imposing as those of Egypt! "Marvel of the Century!" And these American ruins had not been found by an ordinary traveler, but by The American Traveler, the celebrated author of *Arabia Petraea*. And if Mr. Stephens' epoch-making discoveries needed any verification, there were the beautiful sepia drawings of Mr. Frederick Catherwood, the gentleman who had accompanied him on his journey. The editor of the *Evening Post*, Mr. William Cullen Bryant, had seen them with his own eyes and found them of remarkable and unimaginable beauty.

The whole of America's intellectual world was stirred by these discoveries. The venerable Albert Gallatin, who had been Jefferson's secretary of the treasury, visited Stephens, and went away entranced by what he had seen and heard. Gallatin had just completed, at Baron von Humboldt's request, the first comparative treatment of Indian languages of North America, and he had a great interest in primitive American civilizations. Henry Rowe Schoolcraft was also a visitor. An upstate New Yorker with a leonine head sitting on a foreshortened body, he had early interested himself in the American Indian. He had been sent by the government with General Lewis Cass to the upper waters of the Mississippi, and published in 1821, as a result, his *Narrative Journal*. Later he married the daughter of an Ojibwa chief who assisted him in interpreting the American Indian. Dr. Samuel Morton of Philadelphia came also, begging for skulls of the civilizations that Stephens had discovered. Morton, intellectually nurtured in Philadelphia, had just published *Crania Americana*, one of the first books on anthropology. It was an excellent book, even though marred by the "phrenological illusion," and in many ways an astonishingly unique American production; its lithographic illustrations were masterpieces of anatomic art, and have never been excelled. Humboldt thought it equally wonderful for its beauty as well "*par l'absence des rêveries poétiques.*" Dr. Morton was all questions. He remained with Stephens to the small hours of the morning until a severe headache, from which he intermittently suffered, drove him back to his hotel, but not before Stephens promised to collect skulls on his next expedition to Yucatán.

A cryptic letter from Philadelphia followed Dr. Morton's visit, a letter written in the dithyrambs of a dying man; it was signed "Rafinesque." He asserted his priority over discovering the symbols of the glyphs, for he had written to Champollion, the discoverer of the Rosetta stone, as early as 1832: "On the Graphic Systems of America and the Glyphs of Palenque in Central America. . . . You have become celebrated by deciphering the glyphs and characters of the ancient Egyptians," he wrote to the famous Frenchman, "you first announced your discovery in a letter. . . . I am going to follow your footsteps on another continent." And so this "botanist-naturalist-geologist-geographer-historian-poet-philosopher-economist-philanthropist" (so he labeled himself) entered the area of the Maya as he had every scientific field in America.

Constantine Samuel Rafinesque-Schmalz, who had been born in Constantinople of a French father and a German mother (nee

Schmalz), had as a youth been an exporter of olive oil; on the side he collected fishes and birds. He married a Sicilian woman, came to America, only to be wrecked off Long Island, lose his collections, and find when he had wrung himself dry that his Josephine had run off with Giovanni Pizzarrone, a strolling player. A slightly mad natural philosopher (Audubon called him "eccentric"), he described twice as many plants, shells, and fishes as anyone else in the far-flung regions he had traveled. He claimed to have found a botanical formula for the cure "of my chronic complaint, the fatal *phthisis*," a questionable specific which, while living in abject poverty in a garret in Philadelphia, he peddled from door to door. By the time Stephens could reply to his letter "on Rafinesque's Maya priority," Rafinesque had died of stomach cancer. Even as the mailman was seeking to deliver Stephens' letter, Rafinesque's friends were lowering the cadaver out the garret window to save it from sale to the local medical school where his landlord threatened to send it to pay for his arrears of rent.

Public interest in the Maya discoveries was as intense as the curiosity which prevailed during the twentieth-century raid on the grave of Tutankhamen. Stephens had promised the public a book on his adventures, and the public sat back impatiently waiting for it. The Messieurs Harper—all four—called upon Stephens following his return. They insisted that he lose not a moment before beginning on his book, for the publicity attending his return had been such that soon it would send others flying off to Central America to find ruins; he might be forestalled. As Harper and Brothers' best-seller, Stephens was in a position to insist on certain conditions: the work must be in two volumes, larger in size, "suitably octavo" he said; it must be well printed, and yet priced within the range of the common man, for Stephens' other significant contribution to the subject of archaeology was to tumble it from its fabulous price heights. Lord Kingsborough's massive nine-volume work at $150 the volume, Waldeck's folio at 3,200 francs were beyond the means of the man Stephens wished to reach. Catherwood was to have charge of the illustrations; he must personally choose the engravers, inspect the final work, reject, select, and design the binding.

Poor Catherwood was at that moment still confined to his house at 89 Prince Street. His wife (he referred to her only as "Mrs. C."), who bore him two sons, had patiently waited for him and took charge of his wasted body. Whether it was the tumultuous political parades that drove him from his bed or his rugged constitution or his wife's loving care we do not know; he recovered, anyway, in time to meet with Stephens and arrange the illustrations for the book.

Catherwood's Panorama also had prospered during his absence, for New York was now a cosmopolis of 300,000 and was growing daily with the influx of capital and immigrants. The papers daily carried his advertisements for

> *The Panorama of Jerusalem.* A splendid painting of the largest class, covering a surface of ten thousand square feet, painting from drawings taken by Mr. Catherwood in 1834.

> Parents may bring their children; Sunday and other school teachers their scholars, and that all may have an opportunity of viewing this transcript of the Holy City.

Catherwood's Panorama gave competition to P. T. Barnum, who offered, up the street, an "Extraordinary combination of Novelty and Attraction, Mr. Nichols the original ventriloquist and *La Petite Celeste* the celebrated *danseuse*," and to Peall's Museum across from the City Hall, which promised "The Great Anaconda," and to Catlin's Indian Gallery exhibiting a collection of Indian portraits and Egyptian exhibits by George Gliddon. But the Panorama prospered, allowing Frederick Catherwood the leisure to direct the illustrating of Stephens' book. He selected five well-known engravers to make the illustrations from his sepia and wash drawings, and employed Dr. Alexander Anderson to do the woodcuts.[1] And so with eighty or more plates to prepare for the work, Catherwood left Broadway for some months and disappeared into the engraver's world filled with its scrapers, burins,

[1] Dr. Alexander Anderson to his daughter Julia, October, 1840: "We are acquainted with Stephens who is a fine young fellow. I have been engraving for his last work, Travels in Central America and description of the ruins of a great city in Yucatán."

roulettes, and copper plates. In the meanwhile Stephens, with his sister Elizabeth in quiet attendance sharpening his quill pens, kept to his manuscript.

America's literary air was suddenly becoming vibrant with Hispanic-American themes. James Fenimore Cooper had left his Leatherstocking world to write a lurid, heavy tale called *Mercedes of Castille*. Herman Melville had sailed that year on the *Acushnet* around South America into the Pacific. And in a different milieu, fashioned by the same forces, Walt Whitman was grinding out such literary potpourri as *The Inca's Daughter* and *The Spanish Lady*. But it was in Boston, in a brick house on Beacon Street, that the literary theme of Spanish America was the most insistent. There, in a darkened room of a fashionable house, William Hickling Prescott was dictating the first pages of *The Conquest of Mexico*. William Prescott had decided, after completing *Ferdinand and Isabella*, to write on Cortés and the Conquest of Mexico. He began, since his connections were boundless and his purse ample, by writing to a London bookseller and placing fifteen hundred dollars at his disposal for the purchase of books on the subject of Mexico. He soon learned (as did Stephens) that little was purchasable in book form, but he had the aid of Don Pascual de Gayangos, a learned Spanish scholar living in London who, with persistency and devotion, ransacked the libraries in England, Spain, and France on the subject of Hernán Cortés.

A Harvard classmate, Arthur Middleton, fortunately in Spain as secretary of the American legation, put Prescott in touch with a German historian, Friedrich Wilhelm Lembke, who knew the Spanish archives thoroughly as a result of his researches on his own *Geschichte von Spanien*. Responding to Prescott's request, he put to work a corps of copyists. In time, they amassed a huge box of unpublished material for transshipment to America. "This learned Theban," wrote Prescott, "who happens to be in Madrid, has taken charge of my own affairs and, like a true German, inspecting everything and selecting just what has reference to my subject." In France there was Henri Ternaux-Compans, the French historian, to assist from his vast library, as well as his compatriot Count Adolphe de Circourt. In Mexico, Najera lent his advice, as did

Doorway to the Temple of the Magician (Dwarf), Uxmal.

From a lithograph by Frederick Catherwood

Schematic drawing of Uxmal, *showing the Temple of the Magician (Dwarf), Monjas, and the Palace of the Governor.*

From a panoramic drawing

Ruins of the Maya city of Uxmal as they appear today. *The long façade of the Governor's Palace appears in the center of the picture.*

The House of Nuns and the Temple of the Dwarf, Uxmal.

From an engraving of Frederick Catherwood

Lucas Alemán, Carlos de Bustamante, and the whole crop of Mexican historians who were summoned to the aid of the muses. The whole retinue of the learned world was soon pouring material into the study of Prescott, out of which was to come, in his words, "a beautiful prose epic on the Conquest of Mexico."

"I am most generously supplied," he wrote to Angel Calderón de la Barca, the husband of the famous "Fanny," "from Spain with ammunition for the Spanish invasion: 5,000 pages of fair manuscript . . . all contemporary on which the public breath has never blown; the united collections of Muñoz, Vargas, Ponce and Navarrette." By 1839 Prescott had ended his collecting of material for the *Conquest*, a search which had engaged most of the world's scholars; and at the very moment that John Lloyd Stephens was composing his personal narrative of exploration in the legendary field of Mexican archaeology, Prescott was feeling his way through the antiquities of Mexico, "a fathomless gulf," as he called them.

A suave-mannered gentleman who wore on his morning walk a gay blue waistcoat which well fitted his tall, graceful figure, Prescott's handsome face did not reveal the sightlessness of one eye—hurt by a sky-larking student at the Commons in Harvard—nor the irritations of a scholar whose infirmity permitted him to read only ten minutes a day. Yet if he could not travel to see the geographical milieu of his subject, he had the eyes of friends who supplied him with the sensuous detail of the conquest topography. Prescott was a spectator, not a man of action, and so the news of the discoveries of John Lloyd Stephens, in the very earth in which he struggled, came as a most providential coincidence. The first letter Stephens wrote announcing his discoveries went to Prescott:

Feb. 2, 1841.

. . . I have delayed publishing for I am engaged in a scheme for bringing to this country some very interesting monuments, which might be defeated by newspaper paragraphs reaching Guatemala and giving the owners exaggerated ideas of their value, but if I have any knowledge worth your perusing I shall be most happy to communicate it.

My route was from Belize in the bay of Honduras to Guatemala diverging to visit the ruins of Copán in Honduras, from Guatemala to Istapa and down the Pacific to Costa Rica the Southmost state of Central America. I returned by land to Guatemala, followed the road to Mexico as far as Comitán in Chiapis, turned off to Palenque and the Laguna in the Lake of Terminos and thence to Sisal and Mérida the Capital of Yucatán.

I have drawings taken by Mr. Catherwood of the ruins of Copán, Quiriguá, Tecpán, Santa Cruz del Quiché or Utatlán and Gueguete- nango in Guatemala, of Ocosingo and Palenque in Chiapis and of Uxmal in Yucatán, all entirely new except those of Palenque and Uxmal and the former much more complete than Del Río's or Capt. Dupaix.

I wish you could see these drawings and still more that I could have a few hours conversation with you. Robertson [the eighteenth- century Scottish historian] is entirely wrong. Some of the sculptured columns at Copán and Quiriguá are equal to the finest of the Egyptians and the buildings at Palenque and Uxmal are very large and really one can hardly help speaking of them extravagantly, but I am afraid they are not as old as I wish them to be. . . .

Please do not mention my schemes for . . . the monuments.

In March 1841 Prescott answered him:

You have made a tour over a most interesting ground, the very forum of American ruins, none of which has been given to the public, even in descriptions I believe, except Palenque, Uxmal, Mitla, and Copán—and there are no drawings of these latter. . . . It would help us much if all of the Conquistadores had condescended to give some particulars of the state of the buildings in Yucatán at the time of their arrival. But I have found nothing beyond a general allusion to remark- able buildings of stone and lime and curious architecture scattered over the country. Their eyes were occupied with looking after gold dust. *Your opinion as to the comparatively modern date of these re- mains agrees entirely with the conclusions I had come to from much more inadequate sources of information, of course, than you possess.* There is evidence in the old growth of trees about them, and in their dilapidated condition of centuries no doubt. But I have met with no facts to warrant the antiquity assigned by Waldeck and other travelers of thousands of years, like the Egyptian. What you say of the wood in them is a strong argument, certainly against this, though I suppose hard woods, like the cedar, will last in a dry spot a very long while. One can never read of such antiquarian speculations, however, without thinking of Membrino's basin helmet [the barber's basin asserted by Don Quixote to be King Membrino's helmet].

I was not aware that the buildings were so well executed as to equal in this respect the Egyptian. Robertson[2] underestimated everything in the New World. It was little understood then, and distrust which had a knowing air at least was safer side for the historian. The French and Spanish travelers however, write with such swell of glorification and Waldeck's designs in particular are so little like the pictures of *Ruins*, that I had supposed there was some exaggeration in this respect. No one can be a better judge than yourself, however, who are familiar with the best models in the Old World, to compare them with."

Encouraged by all of America's scholars, Stephens kept to his book, but try as he would he could not keep the secrecy, as he wished, for the publicity attending his discoveries had already inspired others to emulate his expedition. To Boston in 1840 had come an elegant young Viennese with scented sidewhiskers, the Baron Emanuel von Friederichsthal, where he was presented to Prescott. "An Austrian gentleman is here just now," Prescott informed Calderón de la Barca, "and proposes to visit Palenque which he has been studying in my Lord Kingsborough. He may possibly visit Mexico in which case I shall take the liberty to give him a note to you. He is an accomplished man in whose society you and your wife will take pleasure."

Friederichsthal, known for his botanical travels in Greece and Serbia, had, upon hearing of Stephens' triumphs, decided himself to make the tour. After visiting Prescott, he left for New York, where he purchased a daguerreotype apparatus and in midyear, "animated by Mr. Stephens' account," as he acknowledged, Friederichsthal left for Yucatán. His archaeological tour, in the manner of a man of fashion, was scarcely profound, although he was the first European to visit Chichen Itzá. Before he died, of a disease contracted in Yucatán, he issued a small brochure on the Maya.[3]

[2] William Robertson (1721–93), Scottish historian: "Neither the Mexicans nor the Peruvians were entitled to rank with those nations which merit the name of civilized." Their houses were "more fit to be the habitation of men just emerging from barbarity . . . low straggling huts . . . scattered about irregularly."—*History of America* (1792), III, 152.

[3] "*Les Monuments de l'Yucatán*," by M. le Chevalier Emmanuel de Friederichsthal, Eyries, *Nouvelles Annales de Voyages*, Vol. 92 (Paris, 1841), 291–314.

He also exposed for the first time in history daguerreotypes of the Maya structures in Yucatán, twenty-five of which he exhibited at the British Museum on his return. The tour, however, left a bad taste in Stephens' mouth: "I gave Friederichsthal," he said to Prescott, "a *carte du pays* for Yucatán and letters and the result is a publication in the newspapers impeaching the correctness of Mr. Catherwood's drawings. I did not see him when he passed through this city and cannot believe that he authorized the unfounded publication."

Still this did not prevent Stephens from assisting yet another casual explorer, who, "excited by the expedition of Catherwood and Stephens," was Yucatán bound. Stephens received Benjamin Norman in his study at 13 Leroy Place in Greenwich Village in a room littered with manuscript (which his sister, Elizabeth, tried to keep in order). Norman had come well recommended to Stephens. He had been born in Hudson, New York, where his father had been a bookseller. He had lost his wife in the yellow-fever epidemic that had swept New Orleans, and unable to bear the city without her, in the depth of his grief, he found himself excited by Stephens' discoveries. He contacted Stephens and had the pleasure of an immediate reply, giving him an introduction to Yucatán.[4]

In May, 1841, Stephens' manuscript, equivalent to five good-sized novels, was finished. It had been written with Trollope-like speed but was destined to be one of the notable books in American literature, not alone for the influence it would exert on American archaeology; it was to give Americans their first real glimpse of Central America.

The opening gambit in Stephens' archaeological epic was simple and without literary artifice: "On Wednesday," he wrote, "the third of October, 1839, I embarked on board the British brig Mary Ann, Hampton, master, for the Bay of Honduras." Once in the stream of narrative he wrote quickly, easily, spontaneously, for Stephens' writing was like his conversation: alive, full of anecdote, much the antithesis of Oliver Goldsmith "who wrote like an angel and talked like poor Poll." It was rich with detail. Persons

[4] B. M. Norman left for Yucatán in November, 1841. Later, in 1843, a volume appeared with quaint, inaccurate lithographs, entitled *Rambles in Yucatán*.

and places flowed through the book; Francisco Morazán and Rafael Carrera and other personages of Central America, who heretofore had been only bodyless names in that Central American chaos, took on life. There were descriptions of roads and commerce, details of cochineal growing, political struggles between liberals and conservatives, prospects of canals and railroads, along with his personal survey of the much talked-about Nicaraguan Canal—all this, with the discovery of the Maya ruins.

The theme of the book was the personality of Stephens. Through all his difficulties, his imprisonment, his disagreements, he showed a natural playfulness, a native exuberance. The detached amusement was always at his own expense. His perception of incongruities was deft and penetrating. In the depths of seriousness he was always able to achieve a solvent laugh. One was won over immediately to his enthusiasms, and his curiosity was infectious. Before everything Stephens was a New Yorker, analogies were always made—be it banks, women, canals, or ruins—with New York; Gotham became his measurer of all things. And sprinkled throughout the manuscript was the piquant condiment of sex, for Stephens had the eye of a Giacomo Casanova. The picture of a young man of serious interests in that sentimental and malodorous period, sandwiching between his adventurous travels and the discovery of ruined cities his salacious encounters with women, added doubtlessly to the popularity of his writings. He had achieved an impossible synthesis: sex and archaeology.

Yet it was the archaeological sections—by far the greater part of the manuscript—that time, the only test for masterpieces, has made classic. In ten months he had discovered, and then uncovered, several lost Maya cities. Discovery of this ancient civilization remains one of the greatest achievements in American history. His fame rests not alone on sterile discovery; he cut through the web of fabled history to prove the homogeneity of Maya culture. He showed that the people who built Copán in Honduras also built the stucco-embellished city of Palenque in Mexico, even though they were separated by hundreds of miles of jungle and mountain. He was the first to speak of the Maya remains as "works of art." He took issue with the world's authorities—the Lord Kingsboroughs, the Robertsons, the Grotius', the Waldecks—when he insisted upon the American origin of the ruins. They were neither Egyptian, Roman, Grecian, or Cambodian—"for unless I am wrong," he wrote at the end of 300,000 words, "we have a conclusion far more interesting and wonderful than that of connecting the builders of these cities with the Egyptians or any other people. It is the spectacle of a people skilled in architecture, sculpture, and drawing, and, beyond doubt, other more perishable arts, and possessing the cultivation and refinement attendant upon these, not derived from the Old World but, originating and growing up here without models or masters, having a distinct, separate, and independent existence; like the plants and fruits of the soil, indigenous."

With that Shephens laid the groundwork—the archaeological Monroe Doctrine, so to speak—of American protohistory. What he saw, he described well and accurately; what he did not know, he hypothesized with great perspicacity, as Dr. S. G. Morley, the greatest living Maya authority, has said: ". . . although he was unable to decipher the hieroglyphic inscriptions, that discovery being reserved for another generation, Stephens accurately gauged the importance of what he saw and left behind him a vivid glowing description of its wonders, which will stimulate research in this field for all time."

"*June 25, 1841,*" Philip Hone confided to his Pepysian journal; "Mr. Stephens' great work appears today entitled *Incidents of Travel in Central America, Chiapas, and Yucatán.* This is the gentleman who wrote a book of travels in Egypt, Syria, and the Holy Land which was exceedingly popular and an earnest of success in this more important undertaking. He was accompanied on the present occasion by Mr. Catherwood who has furnished the drawings from which a large number of lithographic prints have been added to the work."

The *Knickerbocker Magazine* was the first to get hold of a copy. "Wonderful, wonderful!" the reviewer wrote ecstatically. "What discoveries of the present century can compare with those laid bare by Stephens?" The *New York Review* found it possessed "both literary and scientific merit united . . . of a higher order."

They found him "an uncommonly pleasant writer . . . possessing in an extraordinary degree the power of imparting to his reader the charm of his own disposition."

Nor did the reviewers forget to comment on the appearance of the book: "The style does honor to the publishers" (the two volumes were illustrated with many excellent engravings, and the cloth bindings decorated with the glyphs from Copán, and the sides stamped with the sun god from Palenque). "Mr. Catherwood's drawings are so distinct, so perfect that they spoke of the practiced eye and obedient pencil of Mr. Catherwood reflecting in the proportion of their parts such exact likenesses of the original objects they represent that even Mr. Stephens thinks it useless to add to them any explanations. . . . This book, on account of its doubly national character, will find its way into libraries of all persons who read anything else than a novel."

And so it was with all other reviews. The *North American Review* found interesting "his wonted curiosity . . . personal adventures . . . never flagging vivacity." Everyone seemed to like the easy conversational style of the book, and its lack of pretensions; one of the critics was delighted that Stephens did not "cram his pages with solemn philosophical disquisitions. . . . For what," asked the reviewer, "what under the sun has Dickens and Stephens to do with philosophy or deductive reflection or any other parcel of learned lumber?" The *Knickerbocker Magazine* wrote without reserve: "Stephens's volumes will take their stand at once among the foremost achievements of American literature not only in the estimation of his own country men but in that of the whole enlightened world."

These encomiums from the press were reflected in the sale of the *Incidents;* the two-volumed work went through twelve editions in three months, quite extraordinary when one considers that the population of America then was only 17,000,000 and that of New York City just stretching above the 300,000 mark. The American reading public, at best, was only 10 per cent of the population, and for a five-dollar book (the best room in the Astor House could be had for one dollar) to have sold 20,000 copies within three months attests the public interest in archaeology. *"Bartlett &*

Welford, booksellers, told me," said Philip Hone, "that he [Stephens] had already cleared $15,000.00 by his latest work."

Edgar Allan Poe was in a pique when he reviewed *Incidents of Travel in Central America* for *Graham's Magazine*. The spectacle of one such as Stephens, who had no discouragements, no disappointments, no failures, whose every literary effort stirred ever widening circles of recognition and, along with the acclaim, checks the size of sibylline leaves, was quite too much for one who was lately awarded a paltry one-hundred-dollar prize for "The Goldbug." "Mr. Stephens' book *Arabia Petraea*," he wrote, "was everywhere well received and gained him high reputation—[a] reputation not altogether well deserved. No one can deny his personal merits as a traveler, his enthusiasms, boldness, acuteness, courage in danger—perseverance under difficulty. His narration is also exceedingly pleasant, frank, unembarrassed and direct without pretensions or attempt at effect. But neither were his reflection characterized by profundity. . . . We are not prepared to say that misunderstandings of this character will be found in the present *Incidents of Travel in Central America*. Mr. Stephens may know, no doubt does know as much as the most learned antiquarian. Here all is darkness. We have not yet received from the Messieurs Harpers a copy of the book. We can only speak of its merits from the cursory perusal which has been afforded by a friend. The work is certainly a magnificent one—perhaps the most interesting book of travel ever published."

Prescott—who was in the midst of dragging his hero, Hernán Cortés, over the blood-strewn Mexican earth—was wildly enthusiastic about Stephens' book. He almost ruined the sight of his one good eye by reading it himself. On August 2, 1841, he wrote Stephens from Boston:

I cannot well express to you the great satisfaction and delight I have received from your volumes. I suppose few persons will enjoy them more, as very few have been led to pay attention to the subject. You have indeed much exceeded the expectations I had formed, which were not small, and besides throwing much additional light on places and remains before known, you have brought others into notice and much widened the ground for general survey and comparison. It is no little result of your labors too that you have shown how accessible many of these places are, and have furnished a sort of *carte du pays* for the future traveller. I have no doubt that your volumes will be the means of stimulating researches in this interesting country, which has been looked on as a kind of enchanted ground guarded by dragons and giants. It is encompassed by difficulties enough however to intimidate anybody but a resolute lover of science—and one not much given to rheumatism, for which a night in the ruins, under a drenching thunder-storm, would be an indifferent recipe, even though he should have the luxury of a corridor to swing his hammock in. . . .

I will not trouble you with remarks on the spirited and most interesting sketches of the numerous scenes you have passed through, as any criticism of mine would be impertinent after the general suffrages of all your countrymen. But I may say that I think you have been most judicious in confining yourself in the body of the work to a literal description of the monuments, leaving disquisition to the close. Your true business, the most difficult and diplomatic thing in the matter, was to furnish the public with the actual materials for speculation. There will be castle-builders enough to improve on it. Too much praise cannot be given to Mr. Catherwood's drawings in this connection. They carry with them a perfect assurance of his fidelity, in this how different from his predecessors.

The *Incidents of Travel* continued to go through edition after edition, with William Prescott showing as much enthusiasm for it as if it were his own book. He sent copies to the blind Italian historian, Marquis Gino Capponi: "A work has recently been issued here, Stephens' Travels in Central America. . . . they [the ruins] have attracted great attention, you know, among European scholars and formed the subject of magnificent publications both in Paris and London. . . . I think Mr. Stephens' work will add very important materials to the knowledge of these antiquities." And then to that lively lady with the tart tongue and poison pen, Fanny Calderón de la Barca, who had just quit Mexico with her husband and taken up residence in Cuba, he also sent copies: "I suppose you have hardly seen *Stephens'* work yet. It contains drawings of the remains of Palenque, Copán and other places in Central America. . . . the narrative is spirited and sketchy. . . . Stephens is no antiquarian, fortunately, and doesn't affect to be one—most fortunately for his readers. . . . The work is calculated to give higher ideas of the state of civilization in primitive America than preceding works. It exhibits many drawings in addition to those in the great French work, *Antiquités Mexicaines*, and Lord Kingsborough's, and is put at so low a price that it will be accessible to the public. I have no doubt it will attract much attention on the other side of the water as well as ours."

Fanny Calderón thanked Prescott for the books: "I received *Stephens'* . . . and found them a great resource in our voyage. . . . The Travels are very amusing, and dashed off in a most free and easy style. I hear they are criticized as being very incorrect by those who know the country. One thing is evident—that he could not speak Spanish, which must have caused him many difficulties, but he might have got someone to *spell* it for him. I observe that there is not a word of Spanish spelt right, even by chance." Fanny, a most exacting woman, was correct about the execrable Spanish orthography, but entirely wrong about the veracity of the book, for the Mexicans, despite the unpopularity of things North Americans after our rape of their land, published the *Incidents* in Mexico, and have reprinted it thrice in a century, even celebrating the centennial of its publication, in 1941, by a special commemorative publication to which many famed Americanists contributed.

In England, the *Incidents* had a great vogue. Stephens had sent copies to Colonel Thomas Aspinwall, the American consul, who took them to John Murray (the publisher of Byron, Darwin, and most of the British literary luminaries of the day). There were no copyright protections, then, for Americans. A British publisher merely put a book through his presses—without so much as a "by your leave" to the author—and put it on the literary mart under the fiat of *caveat emptor*. But John Murray paid Stephens for his work, a rare event, as Colonel Aspinwall pointed out to Prescott: "Stephens' *Central America* was saved from such piracy only by the number of and the peculiarity of its plates and the circumstance that they were engraved by an Englishman."[5]

[5] Wrote John Murray, the London publisher, to Edward Everett, American minister to England: "Mr. Stephens sent over the American edition of his work on chance and I have already sold 2,500 copies."

The British were delighted with this new contribution to American literature. The London *Athenaeum*, whose criticisms were dicta in the literary world, was elated to find another book from Stephens' quill: "The readers of the Athenaeum," wrote the reviewer, "have not to be told in what high esteem we hold Mr. Stephens." They spoke of him as "cheerful ... manly ... observant ... graphic" and one who "never indulges in the rhapsody of fine writing. A new book from his pen is something like a godsend." As was the custom of the day, the review was mostly composed of excerpt and summary; huge sections of the book were given verbatim by the reviewer, he being "unwilling to abridge the picturesque descriptions." The next issue of the *Athenaeum* found the review still running. The reviewer, almost tearfully, tore himself from it: "It is positively grievous to quit a store so brimful overflowing. . . . the sooner a second edition appears and gives an excuse for returning to these *Incidents* the better."

The *Quarterly Review* spoke almost paternally of Stephens: "In his former publications, Mr. Stephens described himself as a young American and there were throughout the book many indications that he *was* new to the world and there was also that want of taste and steadiness of purpose which accompanies youth. Now four added years have done great things for the author." There were many encomiums for the "lively spirit" and the "healthyminded tone." The readers were well aware of these history-making discoveries and closed the "book with regret" but not without some highly complimentary remarks. "We well know the extreme cuticular tenacity which characterizes our Transatlantic brethren. . . . the occasional freedom of our remarks upon their literature, among other subjects, has placed us somewhat low in their good graces. . . . But it will be better sustained by their giving to the public a few more volumes such as these. Let our good friends of the New York send out half-a-dozen such travelers as Mr. Stephens and we predict that the records of their wanderings, discoveries and adventures will do more to elevate the literary character of America than the angry philippics of all the reviews and newspapers throughout the union."

Still it was not all smooth sailing before the critics. By gainsaying the fatuous antiquarians who filled America with Egyptians, wandering Jews, and Carthaginians, and by making the ruins wholly "American," Stephens had trod on some sensitive toes. "Mr. Stephens as it seems to us," said the *Spectator*, "was not amply provided in funds or appliances proportioned to the object but trusted American-like to the chance of good-natured help"; and the *New Quarterly Review* thought that if "Stephens and Humboldt say that the *ruins* lie out of prehistory then they reject the biblical origin of mankind." They thought that the reading of the hieroglyphics was the key to the understanding of the enigma; "However dreamy and extravagant may be the speculations which these ruins excite, it is certainly a scandal to American letters that something has not been done toward deciphering these hieroglyphics." In a querulous review, George Jones, who was then writing a book to prove the "Identity of the aborigines with the people of Tyrus and Israel, and the introduction of Christianity, into pre-colonial America, by the Apostle St. Thomas," insisted in the pages of the *Edinburgh Review* that Stephens' book "stimulates rather than gratifies curiosity . . . and even though in justice to him Central America was in violent disorder . . . it seems questionable whether he, even under the most favorable circumstances, would have shown himself possessed of the necessary precious acquirements."

This same George Jones, who had never set foot in America, had more to say. When his book appeared, dedicated to his grace, the Archbishop of Canterbury, a book which he entitled most modestly *An Original History of Ancient America*, he solemnly declared the "soul of history is wanting in Mr. Stephens. . . . He has given indeed by his pen and the artist by his pencil, a reflection of the Ruins, but it is from a mirror of polished ebony, simply a *fac-simile* resemblance,—light and shade . . . only . . . a specimen of Daguerreotype! No one can mistake the rapid manner in which the true copy is impressed upon the mind, and that by the most easy and agreeable means—viz., the fascination of style; but the colouring of life is not there . . . the soul of history is wanting! The Promethean spark by which the flame of historic truth should illuminate his work, and be viewed as a gleaming beacon from afar, to direct wanderers through the dark night of wonders."[6] And so on and on, this Mr. Jones who had wafted Tyrians and Israelites to America's shores with St. Thomas. "We may thank heaven for Stephens' fault," said one American, "when we consider the said Promethean spark in the work of the immortal Jones."

There is no accounting for the result of publicity. Even though Stephens was a militant Jacksonian Democrat, his acclaim, so at least it seemed to the Whigs in power, softened, dissipated, attenuated his political blind spot. Stephens' latest book showed him possessed of an unusual grasp of Central American political problems and Daniel Webster, secretary of state, who was above local prejudices provided they did not incommode him, invited Stephens to Washington to discuss with him a political appointment. This was a curious reversal of opinion about Stephens' diplomatic virtues, for the former Secretary of State, John Forsyth, who attempted to guide Stephens' footsteps in Central America, was frankly, and rather openly, contemptuous of the results of Stephens' work as the confidential agent of President Van Buren in Central America.

Stephens had made little attempt to hide the fact that his diplomatic appointment was only a façade under which he could move while discovering ruins. Yet considering the turbulent conditions of Central America, Stephens acquitted himself well. When he had reported to John Forsyth after his return, all Washington was gloomy over the prospects of Van Buren's re-election. "John Forsyth of Georgia, a good Southern politician, talented, facile, and endowed with strong political loyalties, which served him in place of principles,"[7] had hoped that Stephens might bring back the signed "General Convention of Peace, Amity, Commerce and Navigation between the United States and Central America," an item of importance that Van Buren might bring before the public to divert them from "Tippecanoe and Tyler too," but Stephens, apart from the return of the consular archives, had brought noth-

[6] George Jones, *An Original History of Ancient America founded upon the ruins of Antiquity; the Identity of the Aborigines with the people of Tyrus and Israel, etc.* (London, 1843).

[7] Arthur M. Schlesinger, Jr., *The Age of Jackson*, 104.

ing from Central America to Van Buren but reports, no matter how fascinating, of ruins. Since the President himself was now almost a ruin, Forsyth regarded this *lapsus diplomatica* as most unpolitic.

Eighteen hundred forty-one was the "turn of the Whigs." General Harrison having died after only a month of the presidency, his Vice-President, John Tyler of Virginia, took office. "His Accidency," the austere, unbending John Tyler took over the Harrison cabinet, carried through the project of purgation of the civil service, and made revisions upward of the tariff. But of Biddle's Bank of the United States of detestable memory, he would have nothing. He vetoed Henry Clay's Bank Bill in September, 1841, and that, as he knew it must, brought open war between Clay and himself. The cabinet resigned (all save Daniel Webster, who remained as secretary of state) and Tyler was read out of the Whig party. Washington had something of the chaos of Central American politics when John Lloyd Stephens arrived in Washington to see the Secretary of State.

Daniel Webster was an unforgettable figure with his "deep smouldering eyes and mastiff-mouth." His political position was equivocal at the moment, but it did not affect his meeting with Stephens. Webster had a grasp of the significance of Stephens' Maya discoveries, and, as an author himself, he was pleased to see talent and profit, at least in one American, had coalesced so pleasantly. He made Stephens an offer of an appointment. It was flattering, but in the gathering war clouds that would follow the declaration of "Manifest Destiny," Stephens was not too sure. By September he was again in New York, and he wrote to Prescott:

"When I wrote you last I was perplexed by an offer which had been made me of the office of Secretary of Legation in Mexico, but fortunately I declined in time to save my credit, as affairs took another turn in Washington, and my Minister that was to be will not be wanted."

This out of the way, Stephens could now turn his full attention to the formation of a new expedition to Yucatán. There had been a lack of decision for a while, but now it was clear. He would take another expedition to search out more Maya ruins.

Chapter xvii   At this moment, Dr. Cabot appeared.
Stephens, in consequence of desiring a naturalist to accompany
his expedition, had placed in the Boston Courier, in the month of
September, an advertisement for a naturalist to "accompany a
gentleman to Yucatán." Now he had an answer. It was signed "Dr.
Samuel Cabot, Jr." Dr. Cabot's qualifications were excellent. He
was a Harvard graduate (class of 1836), where he had taken a
medical degree. He then went to Paris to study tracheotomy, but
his greatest interest, he wrote, being hardly able to hide his enthusiasm in the polite forms of the day, was in ornithology; he had
for many years corresponded with the great naturalists of Europe.
His age, he wrote, most apologetically, was only twenty-six. Stephens refused him peremptorily because of his youth, then, discovering that the Cabots were friends of William Prescott, he recanted.

Something of the excitement in the Cabot family over the expedition can be seen in the letters Samuel Cabot's mother wrote
to her other son, Eliott,[1] then in Germany studying medicine:
"Sam . . . sailed with Stephens for Central America the middle of
this month [October, 1841], it was quite unexpected to me for
altho he had thought of it . . . it was understood that Stephens had
given up the idea of returning [to Yucatán], untill one day Sam
came out late to dinner and said that he had a letter from Stephens
telling him if he could bundle up his traps and come so as to sail
Saturday (this was Thursday noon) he should be glad to have
him. . . . Sam thinks he shall have a chance to operate on some
unlucky subjects, tho' Stephens told [him] that it could be only
fancy work. Your father went to N York with Sam & saw Stephens & Catherwood; he was much pleased with their reception

[1] Letter to Dr. Elliott Cabot, dated October 28, 1841, in the Cabot Papers,
Massachusetts Historical Society.

of Sam, they were in the midst of packing all sorts of things amongst others, two daguerreotypes . . . just what they want for copying the ancient monuments found in Central America."

Stephens instantly warmed to the modest young doctor, and Cabot returned the compliment; "they remained," said Cabot's son, "very warm friends and he greatly admired Stephens' resourcefulness, dauntless courage and determination." Cabot was a well-built, athletic young man taller than Stephens (he had been a champion bare-knuckle boxer at Harvard for two years). In a fine head, high and broad, the blue eyes were kindly and the mouth wide with well-shaped lips. It was a studious sort of face and one which reflected his shyness. Dr. Cabot was destined to be one of America's most distinguished surgeons. As the United States drifted into the inevitable Civil War he was to become also one of the more militant abolitionists helping slaves to escape to Canada. He was also secretary of the Emigrants Aid Society, the function of which was to assist men, who could be counted on to vote Kansas in as a "Free State," to emigrate there. A well-balanced man, surgeon, liberal, and naturalist, he married and sired eight children. He was destined to outlive by more than a quarter of a century (he died in April, 1885) the other members of the expedition to Yucatán.

By October 9, 1841, Stephens had secured passage for himself and the others on the bark *Tennessee* bound for the port of Sisal in Yucatán. They went off quietly, almost secretly. He had warned Prescott: "You would oblige us . . . by not mentioning our purpose. We wish to get off without any newspaper flourishes, and without directing attention to our movements. . . . We wish to complete what we have begun before others can interfere with us." The *Tennessee* sailed with hardly anyone knowing it, that is, any except the all-knowing, all-seeing Philip Hone.[2]

[2] "October 13, 1841. . . . Our townsman John L. Stephens, the traveler, with his friend Mr. Catherwood have sailed again to Central America to pursue farther their researches among the interesting Antiquities of that country and have taken with them a complete set of Daguerrotype apparatus."—Philip Hone, Diary, XVIII, 316.

The Governor's Palace at Uxmal.

From a lithograph by Frederick Catherwood

The walled city of Tulum, *on the east coast of Yucatán, today.*

The Maya explorers at Tulum. *Catherwood, to the right, holds the measuring tape; Stephens, in white pants and blue cutaway jacket, is carrying the tape; and far to the left, almost lost in the background, Dr. Samuel Cabot is setting out after an oscellated turkey.*

From a lithograph by Frederick Catherwood

John Lloyd Stephens at the ruins of Kabah, *directing the carrying out of a stone doorjamb now in the collections of the American Museum of Natural History.*

From a lithograph by Frederick Catherwood

Gateway at Labna.

From an engraving of Frederick Catherwood

The Wells of Bolonchen. *In the dry interior of Yucatán, wells such as these once supplied water for the Indians. The ladder is now in ruins, and the wells no longer frequented.*

From a lithograph by Frederick Catherwood

In Mérida, Doña Micaela was delighted to have back in her pension Señor "Esteebens" and his two friends. She met them at the door on the cobblestoned "Flamingo corner" in a red-embroidered, freshly-pressed huipil, and exhibiting the latest style of high-heeled shoes from Paris. In high spirits Stephens gave Doña Micaela an *abrazo*. Music, celebrating the last hours of the fete of San Cristóbal, floated down from the plaza as the three expeditionists raised their hammocks in the cool, sparsely furnished room which was to be, for a short period, their home. Having arranged their mosquito netting they went out into the streets of Mérida. White-clad, broad-headed Mayas with eagle-hooked noses and dark epicanthic shaped eyes filled the streets. The women, short and sturdy, inspiringly neat in their gay huipils, hurried by, walking with graceful, lissome carriage. Young Dr. Cabot, his face more boyish than ever under his large Panama (the ends of which undulated in the persistent breeze like the fluttering of a white-winged gull), followed these strange people with wondering eyes; from the very first he was delighted that he had come with the expedition, for the sight of the egrets, pelicans, and ducks (not to count the first wild occellated turkey) on the Yucatán coast at Sisal,[3] where they had arrived on the twenty-fifth of October, "was alone," as he told Stephens, "worth the voyage."

The air of the fete was about them. The narrow, cobblestoned streets were garlanded with pine sprays, the pastel-shaded houses exhibited portraits of their particular saints, lanterns hung from the balconied houses. Pretty, dark-skinned girls peeked out from the grillwork. On the Alameda, the place of promenade, where the broad stone avenue was shaded by *ramón* trees, the expeditionists sat down and watched the ladies, with their flower-bedecked hair, ride by in red-wheeled carriages. In the rush of progress Stephens had almost forgotten the charm of this "primitive Knickerbocker state," but he had hardly forgotten how much, on his previous short visit, he had been charmed by the women. With the eye of a connoisseur, he wrote: "near . . . us was a bevy of young

[3] "We have a short letter from Sam in which he refers to a letter just after arrival at Sisal giving all particulars of his voyage."—Mrs. Cabot to Elliott Cabot, December 1, 1842, in the Cabot Papers.

girls beautifully dressed, with dark eyes and their hair adorned with flowers, sustaining, though I was now a year older and colder, my previous impressions of the beauty of the ladies of Mérida." Let Stephens catch sight of a woman or a ruin and his pulse began to beat wildly; "all these mestizas exhibited . . . a mildness, softness, and amiability of expression that created a feeling of promiscuous tenderness." And there was so much charm about that mestiza dress—no stays, flounces, furbelows, petticoats, or garters —. . . it was so clean, simple and loose, leaving "every beauty free to sink or swell as Nature pleases"; quoth Mr. Stephens, "I was particularly alive to these influences."

While Stephens carried on with these aesthetic dalliances, a momentary prelude to discovering the Maya, Dr. Cabot followed with his trained ornithologist eyes the gyrations of a white-winged king vulture, and Catherwood was experimenting with the daguerreotype. At the edge of the plaza he was trying to expose a picture of the palace of the Montejos.

The daguerreotype had caused a sensation in Mérida. Many had heard of the new invention, for Mérida had good communications with New York, Cuba, and the outside world, yet with the exception of the Baron von Friederichsthal, who had arrived with one in the previous year, the invention was entirely new in Yucatán. At first the expeditionists had experimented on themselves until they grew tired of seeing "their own faces. . . . It was a new line for us," explained Stephens, "but no worse for an editor of a newspaper to turn captain of a steamboat; and besides not like banking—we could not injure anyone by a failure." Catherwood, persevering, pertinacious in his interest in any new scientific gadget, raised no objection to Stephens' suggestion that they photograph, in their rooms—merely for experience, of course—the ladies of Mérida. They took down their hammocks, pushed back their baggage, and opened the shutters. Into the room poured the warm "creative sun" of Yucatán, further "lighted up," said the irrepressible Stephens, ". . . by the entry of three young ladies with their respective mamás and papás."

The women were dressed in the Creole, Yucatec-style, the huipil cut square at the neck and low, low enough to show the shadow of the division of their olive-tinged breasts. Their hair was pushed back and tied in a "bun," exposing the ears bejeweled with elaborate earrings. The two of traditional Spanish coloring did not arouse Stephens, although he admitted "all were pretty"; it was the third, "the delicate and dangerous blonde," with whom he fell in love; "simple, natural, and unaffected. . . . her name was poetry itself." He remembered her especially, for she gave him, on their departure for the ruins of Uxmal, a huge cake, three feet in circumference, which he gallantly stuffed into his saddle bags, ruining thereby his few clean shirts. She of the beautiful name (although he forgot to say what it was), became the first daguerreotype experiment. Catherwood disappeared like a Mephistopheles behind the huge black box, ducked his head under a black cloth to focus the subject, and from under it, in a muted voice directed Stephens in the seating of the model. Nothing for it but all the *papás* and *mamás* must crawl under the cloth and look at the reflected image on the ground glass. The plate exposed for one minute and thirty seconds, Catherwood, the maestro, disappeared into another room to immerse it in a mercury bath from which it was passed through a bromide solution to "fix" the image.

There could be, in the Stephens logic, no better method to experiment with the daguerreotype for its proposed use—the photography of the Maya ruins—than the taking of portraits of ladies. The first was an unqualified success, so Catherwood put the whole unwieldy black apparatus into a high wheeled *volan* and drove to the home of the next experiment. For Stephens proposed for science that they picture the whole family, from mother—with a faint soupçon of a moustache—down to the Indian servants. The result, however, was so disappointing that Catherwood, a perfectionist, declared against further experiments on people. It was at precisely this moment that the people of Mérida discovered that the amiable young man, Dr. Cabot—who spoke French but no Spanish and who seemed more interested in bird-skins than ladies—was a surgeon. He had, they soon learned, studied in Paris, under Docteur Guerin, and knew how to cure the "squint-eye."

Mérida, as most of Yucatán, had an unusually high quota of persons who were cross-eyed, an atavism doubtlessly of their Indian ancestry, for in the ancient world of the Maya it was deemed attractive to be cross-eyed. Maya mothers attached small balls of red-feathered wax between the eyebrows of their newly-born to cause the eyes to cross. So beloved was the "squint" among the Maya that Itzamna, the god of writing (among his other protean aspects), was always represented as fiercely cross-eyed. A fourteen year-old boy, the son of a Mérida family that had befriended Stephens, was the first strabismus patient. A handsome, liquid-eyed boy, his features were singularly spoiled by the squint. After honing off the rust that had gathered on his finely tempered Parisian instruments, Dr. Cabot explained to the parents, through Stephens, the *modus operandi* of the strabismus technique: the eye was secured in its orbit by six muscles, which regulated its movements up, down, inward, and out. Any overcontraction or underdevelopment of one of these eye muscles produced an obliquity in the eye called in their language *bisco*. He, Dr. Cabot, was now to cut without, unfortunately, any anasthesia, one of those eye muscles, after which, God willing, the eye would "fall" back into its normal position. As these muscles lie under the surface of the eye, it would be necessary to pass through its membrane. It was obvious that for so delicate an operation one could not use either a broadaxe or a machete. "In fact," Stephens concluded, "it requires a knowledge of the anatomy of the eye, manual dexterity, fine instruments, and Mr. Catherwood and myself for assistants." A cut of Cabot's knife, a piteous scream, and the boy, his eyes bleeding, got off the improvised table without the squint. *Milagro!* The success of Cabot's miracles swept Mérida.

The next morning betimes, their room was surrounded by a regiment of people and many squint-eyed boys. With two local medicos, Drs. Bado and Muñoz, in attendance, patients selected at random yielded their inheritance of Itzamna to Dr. Cabot's knife. One, a huge gargantuan fellow, with widely spaced teeth, almost lost his eye when he jerked away from the incision; another, a small boy clad in the traditional white Yucatán shirt and drawers and only ten, could be heard among all the others saying in his small voice: "*Yo quiero, yo quiero*"—"I wish it, I wish it," climbed on the table and lay heroically immobile while he was cured of the strabismus. Then came an old general, the oldest in the Mexican Army, a flood of gray hair foaming over the collar of his frayed regimentals. He had fought as a volunteer with General Jackson at New Orleans, and that, in Stephens' eyes, was enough to allow him precedence; he submitted to two operations. The old general, leaving his blood behind him, was followed by a pretty young girl. She came with her *dueña*. Terribly overwrought, the young lady jumped up from the operating table, then calmed by the *simpático* Señor Stephens she submitted. "It is easy enough to spread a boy upon the table," said Stephens, "but not so with a young lady . . . vastly different with combs and curls. As the principal assistant of Dr. Cabot this complicated business devolved on me. . . . I laid her head upon the pillow as carefully as if it had been my own property. . . . When the doctor drew out the instrument I certainly could have taken her in my arms."

After that Dr. Cabot declared he had had enough. And so did Stephens whose head "was actually swimming with visions of bleeding and mutilated eyes." Yet it was not as easy to stop as it had been to begin. Their doors were crowded throughout the day with numbers sufficient to blot out the warm Yucatecan sunlight, with clamoring white-clothed Maya people, all with squint eyes, demanding to be treated. "They became . . . as clamorous as a mob in a western city about to administer Lynch Law." Everywhere they went in Mérida after the strabismus operations, they were followed by small boys who shouted: "There go the men who cure the biscos."

The reception of Messrs. Stephens, Catherwood, and Cabot by the people of Mérida was in the warm, extravagant Spanish manner of unrestrained enthusiasm. The local papers, *El Boletín Comercio* and the *El Siglo Diez y Nueve*,[4] had reprinted most of

[4] *El Siglo Diez y Nueve, Periodico official del Gobierno de Yucatán, Mérida, martes 9 de Noviembre de 1841: "Mr. Stephens celebre viagero, autor de la interessante obra sopre las antiguedades de centro América, Chiapas y Yucatán, de la que el* The Herald *da una idea, en su artículo que empezamos hoy a reproducir en nuestras columnas, se halla hace algunos dias en esta capital: parece que ha venido con el exclusivo objeto de visitar las admirables ruinas de los suntuosos*

the news stories emanating from New York of Stephens' discoveries in Central America, and contrary to Madame Calderón de la Barca's observations that "his *Travels* are criticized as being incorrect by those who know the country," the people of Mérida were pleased with the accuracy of his descriptions, "*llena de la verdad*"—"full of truth," as one editor expressed himself ("his gallery of our costumes is of total exactitude"). The publicity attending them, the daguerreotype, the strabismus operations, not to forget the personal charm of Señor Stephens—all became of inestimable importance to their archaeological discoveries. They were assisted by almost everyone.

Just before they left for the ruins of Uxmal, Don Simón Peón, who was to provide them generously with indispensable aid, suggested that he present Stephens, officially, to the governor of Yucatán. Don Simón himself possessed great power, for he was an *hacendado* of great holdings, enough in Yucatán to be classed as fabulous wealth. And he actually owned the site on which the ruins of Uxmal stood, or better, lay. Don Simón had an aristocratic bearing, for his father, in colonial times, had been a gentleman of the Order of Calatrava. When independence arrived, he had been one of the members of the junta which proclaimed the Yucatán peninsula free from Spain. Even though Yucatán was nominally a republic, attached or detached, as political caprice suggested, to Mexico, Don Simón still retained all the prerogatives of the aristocracy. His dress was simple and elegant, his suede roundabout jacket had buttons of chased gold. Although he had not the slightest interest in Mayan antiquities, evidences of which were scattered everywhere on his great estates, he none the less recognized their importance in the history of the land and the people. He helped most ably to expedite the Americans' plans.

His Excellency the Governor, Don Santiago Méndez, had read of Stephens' travels in the papers and was honored, as he expressed himself in mellifluous Spanish, to welcome him again

palacios de Uxmal y Chichen, y otras menos notables esparcidas casi en toda la extensión de la Peninsula: tal vez este sabio anticuario descifrará algunos geroglíficos de los muchos que adornan las fachadas de aquellos edificios para que pueda penetrar la densa obscuridad en que se halla hasta el presente envuelta su historia."

to Yucatán. Although he did not now come in any diplomatic capacity, the Governor informed him that his search for the horizons of Yucatán's ancient history assured him of every consideration within his country. Learned, facile, and gracious, Don Santiago was about forty years old, although his tall and slender body, somewhat cadaverous in appearance, seemed to suggest a more advanced age. He had recently been elected governor by a party calling themselves, after his name, the *Mendistas,* for he of all other candidates was, like Caesar's wife, above reproach. His pale Iberian face suggested the scholar, although he had been in fact first a *comerciante* in the port city of Campeche, where he was born in 1798. Later in life, influenced by the renaissance of Maya interest created by Stephens' writings, he was to author a book on the customs of the Maya Indians.[5]

Now his thin head rested uneasily on his political shoulders, for he had proclaimed Yucatán a separate republic in 1840, and Yucatán was now seeking political union with Texas. Méndez expected for his audacity an attack on Yucatán by Mexican troops under the command of *el cojo,* Dictator Antonio López de Santa Ana. Yet Méndez was to survive Santa Ana's attacks as well as the War of the Castes that was to break out in 1846 (when the Indians stung soul-deep by centuries of ill treatment rose in successful revolt) and die in the place of his birth in 1872.

Santiago Méndez had always had a flair for politics. He was in Mérida in 1820, when Juan Rivar Vertíz returned from Spain with Yucatán's new constitution; he was with, but did not take part in, the mob that stormed the Franciscan monastery (for the conservative Church was always linked with the established regime) and witnessed the revolutionists' removal of the monks, three hundred in number. Méndez, like many other liberals, applauded, in print and voice, Yucatán's admission to the Mexican confederacy. Yet when chaos grew with Mexico's internal fights between Santa Ana and Bustamante, and small-scale wars were fought between the Texans and the Mexicans and then a short, ridiculous skirmish with France, "The Pastry War," Yucatán grew

[5] *Noticias sobre las costumbes, trajabos, Idioma, Industria, Fisonomía, & de los Indios de Yucatán* (1861).

213

restive, and the movement for complete independence shaped rapidly on the peninsula. The secession of Texas, by its successful revolt in 1836 (resulting in the capture of the terrible-tempered *el cojo*), gave the necessary impetus to Yucatán independence; in 1840 Yucatán severed relations with Mexico and elected Santiago Méndez as governor. At the moment that Stephens was in Yucatán, the Texas schooner-of-war *San Antonio* had arrived, in response to Yucatán's plea for a military alliance. Texas suggested an $8,000 contribution to the Texas Navy to protect Yucatán from Santa Ana's inevitable counteroffensive. The whole peninsula was now more or less in a state of alarm. The government was arming the natives, preparing for defense. The land of the Maya was an incipient volcano and hardly the place for foreigners to ride about, unattended, in search of ruins.

Yet Stephens seemed not the least bit deterred by the situation. They were going into an unknown land, a region almost entirely devoid of white population; into an ancient land, where the natives, after three centuries of ill treatment, were making their first mutterings of revolt. They loaded their brace of brass pistols, tied their baggage to pack animals loaned by Don Simón, received from Doña Micaela an *abrazo* and a large manuscript map of Yucatán, and prepared to set off in a blazing sun into the scrub jungle of the interior. To complete the idyll, their landlady refused to accept rent from them. "The pleasure of your society," she said, "was compensation enough." Between friends house rent was not to be thought of. Whereupon, Mr. Stephens: "we ne'er shall see her like again."

The view of Uxmal, from the top of the House of the Magician, inspired a moment of great exhilaration. They had climbed the two hundred stone steps in panting expectation, and now at a height of one hundred feet there opened before them a vast panorama of flattened jungle. As far as the limits of the senses allowed, until the horizon was opaqued by a purple haze, they could see the limestone land of Yucatán stretching out, *tortilla* flat, mile upon flat mile. Not a river, not a stream, not even a rivulet broke the anaemic flatness of the land. Only below, and im-

214

mediately about them, was the eye relieved. Scattered in a two-mile-square area were stone buildings mounted on terraces once completely faced with precisely cut stone; and mounds, now amorphous and indistinct, that were once in the springtime of a world the meeting-places of the Maya people; stone buildings still revealing something of their once proudly elaborate façades. These were the buildings of Uxmal, the work of a historyless people who once dominated the land. About them, under the sinking sun, the world seemed preternaturally quiet, as if nature wished to impress upon its visitors the dread monotony of space and time. Each man in his own way was awed by Uxmal; Stephens, his dark eyes high-lighted with interest, hypnotically puffing at his twisted cheroot, Catherwood unobtrusively taking the angle of a ruined building with a pencil, young Dr. Cabot, his face flushed brick red, leaning forward with half-open mouth drinking in the strangely new old-world that spread out below them.

The House of the Magician on which they sat was a truncated pyramid on which a rectangular building squatted, dominated by a magnificent doorway. Stone stairways proudly mounted its sides, leading into rooms, thick walled and windowless, the sacrosanct chambers where priests in ancient times celebrated the Eleusian-like mysteries of the Maya gods. The ornamental doorway, an allegorical mask, had for its mouth an open door, while about its sides, in an elaborate contrapuntal pattern, were other masks, long-nosed fantasies, symbols of the long-nosed god, Itzamna. It was wonderfully conceived. The broken surface of the decoration, still bearing the violent polychromy of barbaric colors, stood out dramatically from the unornamented limestone wall. In the Maya heyday, without question, it was the most beautiful in the whole cultural realm.

From these heights one looked down upon a quadrangle about which lay the House of the Nuns, the Nunnery in short, a name given to it by the padres because of the cell-like chambers of the architectural complex. The building, resting on an unsymmetrical artificial terrace, turned its ornately carved façades inward to the enclosed court. Entrance into the court was through a grand archway. Each side differed in decoration. One, as decorative motif, had small models of Maya houses; on another side an entwined feathered serpent wound in and out of a frieze of ordered design; and in yet another, the masks of the rain god, the nose fantastically elongated, dominated the corners of its severely plain sides. No one knew the purpose of the building. South of the Nunnery was the battered remains of a ball court, and beyond it, all but swallowed up in the scrub brush and raised on an earth podium, was a rectangular building called the House of the Turtle from a decoration of turtles that was carved, unusually realistically, in the upper cornice. And far beyond this, enveloped in the blue haze of evening, were the hulks of two pyramids, truncated in the typical Maya style, topped by pinnacled buildings ruined beyond all form. Destroyed, too, was the building at their western base, the serrated nine-gable roof comb, called the House of the Doves, named in analogy by the perforations in the roof comb that recalled a dovecote.

It was the Palace of the Governor, the greatest building of Uxmal and perhaps the most impressive in the entire Maya area, that commanded the most attention. It was a huge trapezoidal building, 320 feet long by 40 feet in width, covered in its entire length by a façade of exquisitely cut stone, so intricate in design that it was in fact a mosaic of some 20,000 sculptured stones. The recessions and projections of the white stones were set, much like the "flecking" of the impressionists' canvases, so that the façade would be enlivened by the subtle play of light and shadow along its entire length. Seven hundred and twenty feet of gigantic counterpoint in sculptured stone! It is one of the greatest monuments the Indian has left in his walk across the American earth. The Palace of the Governor was doubtless meant for occupancy, since its length was pierced by nine doorways which led into rooms and two gateways that permitted egress into the alternate courtyards.

In its original state, the lintels of the doorway had been fashioned out of a single piece of *chicozapote* wood, hard and richly brown. These "talking lintels," carved with glyphs, when exposed to air had become almost as hard as limestone until termites, fungus, and dry rot, conspiring with time, destroyed them. They were consumed, rotted, and destroyed, and with their collapse the stonework over the doorways fell, too, leaving ragged arches above the doorways to mar an otherwise resplendent unbroken façade of carved stone.

None of these architectural features escaped the trained eyes of Catherwood. There were certain features of the buildings, technics of a civilization which he recognized as stemming from the same source as that which had reared other stone cities such as Palenque in the Tumbalá Mountains. There was here none of the massiveness of Copán. None of the sculpture was carved in full round, nor did Uxmal possess the lovely sculptured stuccoes they had found at Palenque. Nor were there any monolithic stelae bearing the telltale glyphs. Still there were unmistakable features in the structures that whispered in rock-hard tones that the civilization that had reared the others had also erected Uxmal.

They were to spend six weeks here, from November 15 until January 1, six weeks of painstaking surveying, mapping, and drawing. Stephens was to expand in Uxmal. With the huge folio of Cogolludo's *Historia de Yucatán* (loaned to him by Prescott) under one arm and in the other hand a machete, Stephens was raveling out the enigma of yet another mysterious ruin.

Uxmal, unlike the ruins of Copán and Palenque, was endowed with history, a laconic history to be sure, one founded on tenuous traditions, a history full of tantalizing hiatuses—yet still a history. Fray Antonio de Ciudad Real, a priest of facile intelligence, had visited Uxmal at the conquest's end, in 1588, following the vague rumors of a great city buried in the jungle, and had found Uxmal, which in the distance "looked like a painting of Flanders." He had written *Of the Very renowned edifices of Uxmal,* in which in terms of unassuming modernity he had described the Temple of the Magician and its "one hundred and fifty stone steps, which are very steep," and all the other "muls" (he called them), "carved with wonderful delicacy." He saw and marked well the high lintens "made of the wood of the chicozapote which is very strong and slow to decay." Padre Ciudad Real discovered, too, the glyphs: "certain characters and letters which the Maya Indians used in old times, carved with so great a dexterity as surely to excite admiration." But all of this was not available to Stephens, for it was not rooted out of the Spanish archives where it had lain for three hundred years until 1875, after Stephens had set the character of the Maya renaissance. It was unfortunate; for knowledge of Ciudad Real—"Royal City" would be the translation of his name—would have helped Stephens immeasurably.

The padre discoverer of Uxmal had been born in 1551 in the city of his name in the province of Mancha. He had been one of the youthful God-inspired *frailes* that had been sent to Yucatán at the discretion of the notorious Bishop Diego de Landa. After the Bishop's death in 1582, Ciudad Real was elevated to commissioner general and secretary of the Franciscan order, in which exalted capacity he traveled much over the land of the Maya. As soon as he familiarized himself with the Maya language, he began a compilation which he called *Calepino*, six volumes of linguistics, history, and ethnology with variations on a theme of Jehovah.

Before his death, in 1617, he had written a *Brief Relation*, in which, among theologic excursions, Uxmal was examined in some detail. He found in the ancient rooms of fetid smell, murals of naked Indians dressed in ancient Yucatecan huipils, "by which," the padre wrote, "it is shown that these buildings were built by the Indians." But who, if they were Indians, were the builders of Uxmal, no one knew! "The Indians," said Ciudad Real, "do not know . . . who built these buildings, nor when they were built. . . . The truth is that to-day the place is called Uxmal. . . . An old Indian declared that according to what the ancients had said, it was known that it was more than nine hundred years since the buildings were built." The Indian was hazarding no guess; he was consulting the Popul histories of the Chilam Balam Maya. So he knew! For Uxmal had been first built sometime in the seventh century, which (considering that Ciudad Real was writing in the sixteenth century) made the Indian's time estimate of Uxmal's first building a most remarkable coincidence, for Uxmal, which means "thrice built," had begun to lay its foundation at the very century that disaster was overtaking the Maya Old Empire.

It is not precisely clear what happened. Scholars have taken, in turn, each theory: disease, earthquake, war, climatic change, soil exhaustion, and decadence; and from a consideration of all these phenomena, social and physical, they have attempted to reconstruct the mystery. Why should a people who had raised with incredible labor such exquisitely conceived religious centers suddenly, and seemingly without outward cause, abandon them? Not one, but all of the magnificent cities of the Old Empire? Copán of all the fabulous monolithic stelae, Tikal, Quiriguá, Palenque, and all the other cities within the 25,000 square miles which was the realm of the Old Empire. There had been no slowing down, no obvious decadence, no clue to the decline and fall.

The last period of greatness, between the eighth and ninth centuries, had been one of incredible achievements: astronomy had advanced, and with it sculpture and book production (for they made paper books by beating out tapa-like the soft white fibers of the mulberry into pliable paper on which the scribes wrote their calendaric histories[6]). Cultural advance seems to have been general throughout Mayadom. Cities of the cultural empire were mutating, throwing out colonies such as Copán had a Quiriguá, then, without prelude—disaster. One by one the Old Empire cities were abandoned. Slowly but relentlessly they were abandoned. In great migrational waves the people were returning once again to their original homes—the flat, riverless, limestone-bound peninsula of Yucatán. Gradually, too, the jungles, which the Indian had fought for centuries, took over the cities, and slowly the jungle drop curtain was lowered on centuries of culture.

A century later almost all Maya activity was centered in the northern tip of Yucatán. Chichen Itzá, which had first been built in the fifth century, was reoccupied in approximately 987 A.D., mostly because of the discovery of two huge-mouthed, sixty-foot-deep *cenotes*, inexhaustible in water supply. Southward other cities were rising in splendor: Kabah, Labna, Sayil, Izamal, Uxmal —wherever, in fact, a *cenote* was found, a religious center arose in the scrub jungle. For two centuries, the lords of Chichen Itzá ruled this new cultural empire. Trade, an essential part of the cultural growth, was under their dominance; large canoes, carrying the manufactures of their realm, set southward beyond Honduras

[6] See *The Aztec and Maya Papermakers*, by Victor Wolfgang von Hagen (New York, 1943).

on trading expeditions, Indian slaves, smothered under mounds of produce, carted it into interior Mexico. Chichen Itzá levied tribute. Chichen Itzá set the calendaric festive days. The religious center of Chichen Itzá rose to Old Empire splendor.

Then on the horizon of the Maya—competition.

The highland people of Mexico did not stand still culturally or materially while the Maya moved forward. Most of Mexico, broken up into tribes or confederations of loosely strung temporary alliances, was building, expanding, and learning to dominate nature. Most of interior and coastal Mexico was spotted with religious centers, built with the same precision although not with the artistic mastery of the Maya. Gradually, through trade and contact, all facets of Middle American culture were becoming common currency. Contact, too, had been made with the people of South America; metal, in the form of weapons of bronze and artifacts of gold, was dribbling in along the long narrow neck of the Isthmus.

In the twelfth century, when the Mongols in the other world were moving over the scarred face of Eurasia, while Barbarossa sought to impress his will on Europe, and while the Second Crusade was bleeding itself out on the spiked partisans of Saladin, in America, too, great movements of conquest were to begin. The Aztecs had yet to appear effectually on the scene; instead on the horizon of the Maya appeared the Toltecs. A shadowy people who had once been consigned to the limbo of fable, the Toltecs were a widely conquering people. They lived in the valley of Mexico. Teotihuacan was their capital. A people of great artistic attainments, the Toltec became the first tribe in Middle America to see the advantages of predatory warfare. They had for years been biting at the outward edges of the Maya realm, then suddenly, under the leadership of Quetzalcoatl, they appeared in force and, either by treaty or by victory, took over Chichen Itzá.

Never has the Spenglerian theme of "raw man" conquering effete "overcivilized man" been so well illustrated as in the Toltec conquest of the Maya. Under that mysterious figure Quetzalcoatl (immortalized by Lew Wallace in the *Fair God*), the architectural designs of the Maya buildings were altered by the use of the "plumed serpent" motif. For the first time in Maya history, there were martial decorations, "Temples of Warriors," on whose pillars, etched in low relief, are spear-carrying soldiers. Under the Toltecs life was quickened. The Maya became suddenly belligerent. Wars fought with the bow and arrow, introduced by the Toltecs, began to take their fearful toll until they were checked by the foundation of a league between the leading city-states: the League of Mayapán, an alliance of Uxmal and Chichen Itzá. This treaty, lasting for two centuries, ushered in a renaissance of trade and architecture. Maya culture continued its splendid march between the twelfth and fourteenth centuries until the Xiu family, who established Uxmal in 1007 A.D., found occasion to break with the League, which resulted in 1451 (ninety years before the coming of the Spaniard), in the complete destruction of Mayapán. Then the victorious people of Uxmal deserted their city, moved on to the village of Maní, which remained the capital of the Tutul Xiu dynasty until the coming of the Spaniard. And it was at this same Maní that Diego de Landa, in that year of infamy 1561, burned the glyphic histories. Maní—"it is finished."

Stephens' excursus into prehistory had the object of finding "who were the people who built these ruins." Uxmal for the first time provided him with proof, real proof, that the buildings were erected by those Indians inhabiting Yucatán at the time of the conquest. Although he knew nothing of Padre Ciudad Real, he nosed about in the archives of the villages and discovered a Spanish transcript of the Books of Chilam Balam, verbal Maya histories recited to a Maya-Spanish amanuensis in the sixteenth century. There he learned that "On the Tenth ahau Ah Zuitok Tutul Xiu founded Uxmal." He found at Maní "a large volume which had an ancient and venerable appearance being bound in parchment, tattered and worm-eaten, having a flap to close like that of a pocket-book," written in Maya, dated 1556. He had it translated to him by a Maya-speaking padre, and again had confirmation that Uxmal was part of modern Indian tradition. Later Stephens discovered an Indian map of Maní drawn in 1557; Uxmal appears therein, not as a drawing of a church, but in the unmistakable design as one of the Maya ruined buildings. Then he dug into the title deeds of Don Simón Peón—"a formidable pile, compared with which the papers in a protracted chancery or ejectment would seem a *billet-doux*." He found that in 1673 the Indians still repaired to Uxmal, "worshipping the devil in those ancient buildings . . . where they burn copal . . . performing other detestable sacrifices." In Padre Cogolludo's *Historia de Yucatán*, that thick folio of foxed pages, he discovered the padre's writing of Uxmal, which he had visited while it was still smirched with "offers of cacao, and marks of copal, which is their incense, burned but a short time before, an evidence of some superstition or idolatry recently committed although we could not find out anything about it among all of us who were there. God help those poor Indians, for the devil deceives them very easily."

Stephens asked rhetorically: "What was Uxmal?" To him it "was clear beyond all question" an ancient city built by the Indians who were in Yucatán at the time of the arrival of the Spaniards, who frequented it, long after the conquest, to pay homage to their ancient gods. Neither Roman, Greek, Jew, Carthaginian, or Egyptian built these cities; they were built by the American Indian. Stephens did not yet fully grasp the connection between Uxmal in Yucatán, Copán in Honduras, and Palenque in Mexico, except that the structures were built of stone. But there was then one connecting link—the glyphs. The mysterious ideographs that cumbered the stones at Copán, that he had seen in the awesome grandeur of Palenque, he also found at Uxmal. Even though he could not read them, there was no doubt that they were the same pebble-shaped glyphs ("the general character is the same"). Stephens discovered in the extreme northeast chamber of the Governor's Palace a wooden lintel, carved with glyphs, which "so far as we could understand them were similar to those of Copán and Palenque." In the whole ruins of Uxmal here was the "one point of resemblance." They found the lintel in the darkened corner of the room where Count Waldeck had hidden it in 1836. Stephens resolved to preserve this beam and took it back to New York, only to see it destroyed in the fire which overwhelmed Catherwood's Panorama. Even then, before Catherwood determined by architectural analogy the homogeneity of the cultures

Modern photograph of Chichen Itzá, *the most famous Maya site in Yucatán.*

Temple of Kulkulkan, Chichen Itzá.

From a lithograph by Frederick Catherwood

Restoration of the Temple of Kulkulkan. *The restored stairs can be seen on the right, the unrestored steps on the left. Two of the four stairways have been restored.*

Las Monjas, Chichen Itzá.

From an engraving of Frederick Catherwood

The Circular Observatory, Chichen Itzá.

From an engraving of Frederick Catherwood

they had discovered, Uxmal, to Stephens, was somehow allied to the other ruins they had found.

They were miserable, hungry men, these three—Stephens, Cabot, and Catherwood—sitting in their sumptuous palace, until the arrival of Chaipa Chi. Over and beyond their nightly struggles with bats and mosquitoes, there were other annoyances: the young boy assigned to them could speak no Spanish and they no Maya; and he could not prepare food. They seemed unable to begin the conquest of the Maya with any *esprit* until Chaipa Chi arrived. They saw her coming through the brush, with "a small boy as her *dueño*." Dark-skinned, ample-rumped and -bosomed, she had the profile of a thousand stone Maya portraits, hook-nosed, slanting forehead, dark epicanthic eyes. She came up the steps, carrying her clothes on her head, nodded a greeting to them—for she spoke no Spanish—and retired to the makeshift kitchen. After that they were in the hands of Chaipa Chi.

As they lived in it and as it was close at hand, the Governor's Palace was the first to feel the measuring rod of scientific accuracy. They had spent some days making a map of the ruins (a work impaired by the thick scrub jungles and the distractions caused by Dr. Cabot, who, at the precise moment of reading, would drop the surveyor's tape to take off after a bird). Now the survey was finished, and they could turn to the Palace. Catherwood seemed the most content of the explorers, for he was at last in his element. At night, by the flickering lights of the candles, he worked upon the Uxmal map, while during the day, as Stephens and Cabot cleared the other buildings, he worked upon the Palace. He began by making a panorama of the front of the building, a drawing made to scale. When it appeared in Stephens' book, it was engraved so as to extend beyond the book format. In this, his past experience with panoramas had come to his aid. He made detailed drawings of the whole building, supplemented by daguerreotype views, and soon he had in his possession "the materials for erecting a building exactly like it." He sketched the stone tracery of the façades, made a floor plan, and measured the walls, performing incredible feats of architectural labor. He was impressed by the bigness of the buildings on the outside, the smallness of the rooms, and the lack of windows.

He recognized as an architect that the massiveness of the construction was necessitated by the lack of knowledge of thrusts, strains, and stresses. He marveled that while their priests could calculate the advent of equinoxes, solstices, and eclipses, and invent a complicated hieroglyphic language, they had been unable to conceive the wheel or the principle of the arch. For this architectural blind spot—not utilizing a rounded arch with a locking keystone that would co-equally divide the stress—made the Maya fall back on massive walls. These were tapered into an inverted *V* of stone, making it almost impossible to construct rooms of any great size. Eventually the time-full pressure of the walls and the overhead roof combs, weighted down by the great mass of rubble, pushed in the roofs. Yet this action left intact the wonderfully conceived friezes of cut stone, "a sculptured mosaic," Stephens called it, "ornaments, I have no doubt, with a symbolical meaning —each stone a part of history, allegory, and fable."

After the Palace they went to work on the House of the Turtles, a rectangular boxlike building lying to the right of the Palace on an earth-stone podium; after the Turtle House, the Nunnery. By the time it was reached, Stephens, with the aid of Cabot and a fifteen year-old squint-eyed Maya boy called Bernaldo had cleaned much of the ruins for Catherwood's inspired brush.

Stephens, his work far ahead of Catherwood's, rode off to the fair at Jalacho and discovered more ruins, including the site of Maxcanu. On the way with Dr. Cabot, he had raided, like a ghoul, a native cemetery, to obtain craniums for Dr. Morton's anthropological collection. Don Simón Peón, the liege of Uxmal, then paid them a visit, attired in tight-fitting buckskin breeches ornamented with silver lace. He had a practical view of the ruins of Uxmal and dilated on them at some length, adding that if these ruins were situated on the banks of the Mississippi, picture the immense fortune one might have from them by selling the sculptured stone blocks for paving the streets of New Orleans! But Don Simón did not long remain at Uxmal. The Maya ruins had an unhealthy reputation, especially in the rainy season when all the dry *aguadas* became filled with noisome water and the air hummed with insatiable blood-seeking mosquitoes. Dr. Cabot, to preserve their health, had suggested the burning of fires within the stone rooms of the *Palacio*, hoping to kill the malaria within the ancient stone walls, for the fever was thought then to be just that, *mal aria*—bad air—fetid humours that seeped up from the earth to overcome by noxious fumes. They took the precaution of sleeping under fine-netted *pabellones* to save themselves sleepless nights. These were precautions—but they fell short.

During their third week at Uxmal, Stephens was visited by an old enemy. It did not come at him in the open, with lowered lance, to do battle on honorable grounds, but moved with stealth, carried in the long probosces of night-loving mosquities; it insinuated into his blood stream swarming millions of malarial parasites. There was no warning of its presence until his teeth shook and he grew pale and cadaverous looking. That night Stephens' body was on fire. His blood boiled like lava. In the morning the heat subsided, and he quaffed quantities of water. Then came the great cold—the second phase of malaria. Stephens felt as if he were encased in ice. His teeth chattered, his lips grew blue, and he shivered violently even though the placid Chaipa Chi took off her shawl and added it to the heap of clothes piled upon him. All the liquid excitement had gone out of his eyes. At that moment, like the presage of death, a tall thin priest in the habit of a *Franciscano* walked slowly into the Governor's Palace.

The *cura* of Ticul, a village midway between Uxmal and Mayapán, was paying the visit that he had promised. The padre was mortified to find his host, the temporary liege of Uxmal, suffering with the *calentura*, and he administered immediately a simple concoction of sour orange juice flavored with cinnamon and lemon juice to allay Stephens' great thirst.

Fray Estanislao Carrillo was worthy of his cloth, for he was a man of rare integrity of soul, beloved equally by Indian and master. He still wore the frayed blue habit of the *Franciscano* with its huge cross; he had refused to abandon it even though in the time of social revolution it was no longer physically safe to wear it. For many years he had interested himself in the Maya, and was

225

eventually to write several important historical papers on the ruins of Nohpat. As curate of the village of Ticul, he had transformed it into a small oasis of prosperity in a desert of indifference. But now at forty-three years of age, this ascetic life had taken its toll; his brilliant eyes lay sunken in his head and his habit hung loosely on his thin frame.

Padre Carrillo was the very epitome of kindness. He insisted that Stephens must leave the *Palacio* and return with him to his convent at Ticul where he could nurse him back to health, and when Stephens weakly objected, he raised a long, bony hand and worked his index finger back and forth like the ticking of the pendulum of fate. Stephens was hypnotized by that moving finger and made no further remonstrance. The padre issued an order in Maya to his Indian retainers, and they quickly ran down the tumbled steps of the *Palacio*, eager to comply with his wishes.

As they waited for a shoulder palanquin to be built to convey Stephens to Ticul, the padre told his story. He had been born in 1798 in the village of Teabo in Yucatán. There he received elemental instruction. At ten years of age he had decided, when he saw an Indian whipped until the cords of his back muscles lay bare as twisted henequen fibers, that he would join the priesthood and attempt to alleviate their suffering. In 1823 he entered the Franciscan order. After the destruction of the convent of Mérida and the scattering of the order, friends tried in vain to have him secularize himself. He refused. Now he resided in Ticul on the forty dollars a month allowed him by the order to live and extend hospitality to strangers. Unusually active in mind and body, without affectation or parade, he had, fortunately for science—and for Mr. Stephens' reputation—interested himself in the antiquities of the country. Stephens owed him much, which he fully acknowledged in his book and, in addition, by having him elected an honorary member of the New York Historical Society.

Three days in the cool gardens of Ticul with the padre's warm infusions of cinnamon-orange-lemon concoction had worked wonders. Then quinine was not used in Central America, nor was it known there as a malaria specific; when fevered, one merely rested, waiting for the fever to abate, as it did in time, when the malarial germs took temporary refuge in the spleen, ready, at the moment of bodily exhaustion, to swarm out again into the main blood stream. Stephens, on the third day, was taking his first stroll in the garden when an Indian ran into the monastery and, between violent pantings, told them that another *"Ingles"* had taken the fever. They found Dr. Cabot on the convent floor. Was this the young doctor with the flushed, eager face, tanned by the Yucatán sun, whom Stephens had left at Uxmal three days ago? Cabot's eyes, staring out of their sockets, were wild with fever, his face was flushed brick red, and even his sturdy body seemed to have dehydrated. He did not recognize Stephens. Too weak to stand, he was crawling about like a wounded animal; when Stephens weakly leaned over to pick him up, they fell together in a twisted pile of fevering legs and arms. On the third day, out of the hearing of Cabot, the padre told Stephens, in a hoarse whisper, that the expression of the young doctor's face was *fatal*. In Spanish, this meant "unfortunate," but to Stephens the word conjured up a terrible picture. The next day Albino, their newly acquired retainer, appeared—also with the *paludismo*. He had become so pallid that his swarthy-bronze skin seemed depigmentized.

Catherwood was now the only survivor of the expedition. He held the ruins alone, with only the ceaseless *tortilla*-slapping of the silent Chaipa Chi to break the silence. A very heroic figure in the annals of American archaeology this Catherwood. He endured, for two years, revolution, sickness, and the bites of a thousand nameless insects; malarial fevers, bad food, sleepless nights— during all the time, without ceasing, he copied, with amazing fidelity and with charming composition, the ruins of the Maya people. Now, once again he was alone, the last of the expedition. He kept at his drawing, spending days tracing out the intricate stone sculptured frieze of the House of the Nunnery.

But as the sun entered Capricorn, the malignant influences of Uxmal were working on Catherwood. On New Year's Day, 1842, after six weeks of demoniac activity, Catherwood was carried, in delirium, from the ruins.

Chapter XVIII It was at Kabah that Albino first exhibited his worth. Ever since he had entered the archaeological service of the *Norte Americanos* at the suggestion of Doña Joaquina Peón, Albino had done little expediting, since he, like the more vulnerable white men, was constantly under siege of "that devil malaria." An amiable cutthroat this Albino, blacksmith by trade, soldier by avocation, he had been at the siege of Campeche, of late memory, where he had received a saber-cut on his brown skinned rump, "which rather intimated," said the observant Stephens, "that he was moving in an opposite direction when the sabre overtook him." Albino's army career ended abruptly. Having received neither salary nor pension for his services, he renounced the army and entered the employ of Señor Stephens. A thick-set, dark-skinned man with lustrous amorous eyes, he was an important adjunct to the expedition. His broad-bladed machete had cut down the scrub jungle around the ruins of Nohpat, where they found a frieze of skulls and cross-bones; he had chopped down the trees that hid the ruins of Xcoch, revealing a huge pyramid, and so he went from new ruin to new ruin until he was finally affected by the enthusiasm of the *Americanos* which grew with each new discovery. He soon found it an exciting game.

Kabah, where they discovered the remains of the once beautiful Maya city that lay outside of the Indian village of Nohcacab, revealed the inner talents of Albino, for he knew how to handle the natives, being removed, as Stephens noted, from the Indians only by a tiny rivulet of "white" chromosomes (externally shown in his fierce mustachios). Stephens had desperate need of Albino's diplomacy, for their arrival at Nohcacab, where the pure Indian populace had never before seen *"Ingles's,"* was as sensational as would have been the return of Kulkulkan. The Indians poured out like ants from their wattle and daub houses, followed the mule train to the convent, where, crowded into the patio, they chattered in excited Maya sibilants, pointing to the tripods, sextants, camera lucidas, and the mysterious black-boxed daguerreotype. Rumor, skimming over Yucatán, had already told the people of Nohcacab that there were loose in the land men who "cured the squint-eye," who captured the visible souls of people in a black box, and, who, in final madness, searched for stone cities in the jungle.

They were also disturbed by their interest in *campos santos*, for Stephens' ghoulish activities in carrying away specimens of Maya skulls for Dr. Morton had aroused them to open resentment. They attributed Padre Carrillo's illness—the malarial fever—to his acquiescence in this. The shades, angry over the rape of the skulls, had possessed the body of the fevered padre. It was rumored that while Carrillo lay in delirium he cried out in a sepulchral voice every five minutes, *"devuelve esos huesos"*—"restore those bones." Albino applied himself at once to dissipating these diabolical illusions, for not only were their very lives in danger so long as these ideas persisted, but as the Indians were the only source of labor, the excavation of Kabah was in the balance. Unfortunately, too, for their work, Nohcacab (which translated "Great-place-of-good-land") had lived up to its name; the milpas had yielded a fine corn crop, and, swollen by food and giving themselves over to the pleasant madness of rutting, the Indians were not at all tempted to work. But Albino applied himself. He managed to acquire Indians with mattock and crowbar to file out to the ruins every morning to do the bidding of these white-skinned madmen who cured the squint-eye.

Kabah was now the new word. Gone from their vocabulary were Palenque, Copán, and Uxmal, for at Kabah they discovered a site whose very existence, even in Yucatán, had been unknown. Stephens took as much delight in his new ruin as if it were the first that they had discovered. An important religious center in the tenth century (to judge by the number of its monuments) Kabah was part of the tri-citied League of Mayapán. It had been connected, at the height of the League's power, by a road to Uxmal over which runners once carried glyphical messages—talking paper rolls—and over which commerce and people alike flowed. Kabah extended over a vast area. Where cattle cropped the sparse herbage, great buildings once stood; remains were still to be seen of immense terraces, triumphal arches, stately palaces, and pyramids, badly ruined and mutilated by man and time alike, yet still preserving enough of their grandeur to quicken the pulse of the discoverers. Combined operations of axe and machete soon cleared most of the ten structures of vegetation. This allowed full sight of the buildings.

The first, which Stephens described as *"Palacio 1,"* was a 150-foot-long structure unusual, even in Yucatán, for the ornamentation of its façade—entirely constructed of "horridly smirking stone masks"—an ornamentation so elaborate that the architecture of the structure entirely disappeared under it. There were six tiers of open-mouthed stone masks revealing a rounded object which was a conventionalized tongue. It was a bold and daring conception. Equally ingenious was the stone molding, scalloped and zigzagged, conceived so that the chiaroscuro of the Maya day could enliven the whole fantastic stone mosaic. Stephens was deeply impressed by this pattern. ". . . the cornice running over the doorways . . . tried by the severest rules of art recognized among us, would embellish the architecture of any known era, and, amongst a mass of barbarism, of rude and uncouth conceptions, it stands as an offering by American builders worthy of the acceptance of a polished people." Catherwood copied it faithfully, and the motif was stamped on the binding of their book on Yucatán. A century later Mr. Pál Kelemen, the author of the monumental *Medieval American Art*, used the same design to ornament the dust jacket of his own work, "in homage to these pioneer explorers."

Kabah yielded other archaeological surprises. There was the solitary monument, a sort of *Arc de Triomphe*, which they discovered and Catherwood pictured; Stephens thought it something "like the proud memorial of a Roman triumph." Latter-day archaeologists politely smirked at this monument because they could not find it. It is now known to be very real, for Mr. Lawrence Dame, in 1941, found it again and photographed it, just as Catherwood had drawn it. And there were carved lintels in sapote wood such as they had found at Uxmal, and superbly worked wood panels, a great rarity in Yucatán because of the voracious termites.

At Kabah they had further proof of the Maya architecture; whether found in Honduras, Guatemala, Mexico, or Yucatán, there was a "striking resemblance in details" between the figures and ornaments of Palenque and those at Kabah. And, too, they found again the mysterious enigmatical glyphs carved on wooden lintels. There they found, in three sections, a beautifully conceived figure carved on sapote wood, ornamented by a headdress of quetzal plumes. The figure was standing on a writhing serpent. So unusual was the subject that Catherwood—fortunately for archaeology—drew the carving. It was one of the specimens burned in that calamitous fire in Catherwood's Panorama, for it was sent back—with the other wooden lintels found at Kabah—(along with the "talking" hieroglyphical lintels from Uxmal)—to New York.

Another singular architectural feature at Kabah was the carved stone doorjambs which Stephens found in the structures on the grand terrace at the south end of the site. The slabs, six feet high by two in width, were delicately carved in low relief of pinkish-gray limestone, representing a curious allegory of a kneeling figure holding a mask in front of his eyes, dominated by a warrior priest enveloped in a headgear out of which quetzal feathers flowed in golden rhythm. Stephens decided that these slabs should form the base of his projected Museum of American Antiquities; accordingly the 500-pound monolithic slabs were lowered from their niche in the palace, wrapped in grass and straw, and under the supervision of Albino removed to the convent at Nohcacab. By running a long tree trunk along the stone and tying it to the limb by means of strong lianas, Indians in relays of eight laboriously carried it to the coast. Catherwood remembered the incident when years later he published his famous lithographic *Views;* Stephens in full beard and short blue jacket is seen directing the removal.

These Maya sculptures had a singular odyssey. Arriving in New York on one of Howland and Aspinwall's Caribbean packets with the idea of being exhibited at Catherwood's Panorama, they came too late. The rotunda had burned and with it all other specimens of Maya art collected so laboriously in Yucatán. So Stephens gave the stones to his friend John Church Cruger, who carried them by steamboat to his estate—Cruger's Island in the Hudson near Barrytown. There he had built, under the influence of the "romantic agony," a moldering cuspidated wall, constructed to simulate a ruin, surrounding it with a glade of trees, so as to weave a texture of mystery and romance. Here in the wall he buried the "Stephens' stones." There they were seen by the Swedish traveler, Fredericka Bremer, in 1844: "on a point projecting into the river a ruin has been built in which are placed various figures and fragments of walls and columns discovered in Central America. . . . This ruin and its ornaments in the midst of a wild romantic rocky and wooded promontory was a design in the best taste." Perhaps, but hardly the place envisioned by Stephens for his Museum of American Antiquities.

In 1918 Stephens had his wish, posthumously: Dr. S. G. Morley, the great Maya scholar, pondering the disappearance of the "Stephens' stones," read the travels of Fredericka Bremer, visited Cruger's Island and found, still embedded in the "romantic wall," the slabs of Kabah along with other Maya sculptures. One of the octogenarian daughters of John Cruger, "who remembered Stephens patting her head when she was a little girl," agreed to their removal. For ten thousand dollars the American Museum of Natural History purchased the "Stephens' stones," and they formed—as they were originally intended to form—the nucleus of a Maya exhibit and may now be seen in the Middle American Hall at that museum.

After Kabah, the explorers traveled lightly. Catherwood was mounted on a horse of placid disposition (he could sketch without dismounting), and Dr. Cabot rode an ugly-headed sorrel of so lethargic a spirit that he could discharge his shotgun without its doing anything else than move its ears. Stephens drew a trotter. Even Albino traveled like a caballero, as the word suggests, mounted, his cicatrized rump in a wooden saddle. Only little Bernaldo walked, for after all someone had to retrieve Cabot's birds. Their only pack animal carried the daguerreotype and the mosquito nets. This strange procession traveling southeast, "moving toward Campeche," was going to perform an archaeological reconaissance which has never been matched in either daring or extent.

The creative sun, as they rode across the land, was a great molten ball burning through the first days of February. It was the transitional period of wet and dry. The sky, sometimes blackened by rain-bearing clouds, heralded the preludes of the other season. The flatness of the Yucatán plain was now broken by limestone reefs and depressions on the undulating ground; they were passing through the section called a *dzekel,* "a place abounding with loose rock," a well-drained calcareous land with pockets of deep, heavy, waxy clay. They rode through the groves of *ramón,* a true fruited mulberry with small yellow berries shaped like miniature oranges. *Ramón* was fed to mules in absence of other forage. These trees alternated with the spiked pads of the agave, for in Yucatán the century plant was king, the immortal maguey of the Aztecs which yielded its tough gray fibers for a hundred uses. In the straggling villages they met with the ceiba, the "god tree," thick trunked and hugely buttressed, whose cool shadows offered the traveler succor on an oven-hot day.

In appearance and purpose, the houses, oval shaped, constructed of reddish clay over a wattle of branches, and roofed with palm leaves, were as unchangeable as the landscape, for in the time of Diego de Landa, of immortal memory, he wrote that "they built their houses . . . covered with palm leaves and they have steep slopes so that the rain may not penetrate. And then they build a wall in the middle dividing the house lengthwise . . . half which they call the back of the house, where they have their beds." It was a form of structure so unchanging that the sculpture-architects of Uxmal used a model of the "thatched house" as a decorative motif in the frieze ornamentation at the Nunnery at Uxmal. Around each house were planted bananas. They were also papayas, with acanthus-shaped leaves shading the melon-sized green fruit; guayabos and sour-orange and spined fruits of the chayote. These were their gardens. Basic food came from the milpas fashioned out of the scrub jungle which they burned in April and planted in May when the rains came, insinuating the corn grains into the reddish soil as their ancestors had done for centuries, with a fire-hardened, pointed stick. Bean vines used the growing corn as support, and between the rows of corn, later in the season, sweet potatoes, jicamas, and cassava, bitter and sweet, were cultured to add to a diet wholly vegetable. The Yucatecan earth was not a hard taskmaster. A farmer could satisfy the whole of his family's needs by three hundred hours' work in the entire year.

In every village there was the incessant patting of the *tortilla* maker. It was a sound above all else heard over the land, as the Indian women molded the lime-swollen corn grains, making the grayish paste into a rounded corn cake the size and symmetry of a stove lid, which was then put to bake on the hot *cumal*. Stephens liked the sound. It brought visions of food, and they were almost always hungry. And it evoked visions of the women bent over the stone metate, furiously kneading the corn mass, while within their loose-fitting huipils their breasts kept time in fearful agitation.

So they passed from village to village, from ruin to ruin. They came to Sayil (Stephens wrote it "Zayi"), another site once bound to the League of Mayapán, and found a palace of three beautifully proportioned and ornamented stories, graced by a broad thirty-two-foot grand staircase, leading up from terrace to terrace. Then not far distant they found another ruin at Sabactche,[1] smothered by flowering plants which grew out of the tumbled stone walls. And even later, when they passed beyond the checkered corn-milpas of a village, they discovered another ruined city which, too, had once been in the orbit of Mayapán. This was Labna,[2] famous for its arched gateway, a city contemporary with Kabah and Sayil and like them a necropolis even before the white man appeared to spread his doom. Labna had a spreading, complex building, "the palace of the ruined house." Neatly tied columns set off the doorways, along with serpent motifs, incised rosettes, and frets in relief with human heads emerging from opened alli-

---

[1] ". . . we have just received a letter from Sam [Cabot] dated February 7th. he says they find the country infinitely more interesting in ruins than they had any idea of but begs us not to repeat anything in his letters because Stephens does not want to be anticipated. . . . Sam is in good health enjoying himself highly."—Mrs. Cabot to Elliott Cabot, Boston, April 26, 1842, Cabot Papers.

[2] *"Labna"* means in Maya "ruined house."

gators' mouths. The building, set off by the russet-colored hills behind it, rested on a stone podium and rose to several stories. It spread to a length of four hundred feet across the scored land. A flying façade still held fragments of its stucco figures and still exhibited some of the barbaric colors with which it had been painted. "If a solitary traveller from the Old World," wrote Stephens, "could by some strange accident have visited this aboriginal city when it was yet perfect his account would have seemed more fanciful than any in Eastern story, and been considered a subject from the Arabian Night's Entertainments."

As they rode southward toward the Campeche border, they discovered, in a single month, a dozen more ruined cities: Kevic which reflected the influence of Mayapán, and Chunhuhub with its single-storied building, and Xampon where, in the overcast of an approaching storm riven by flashing lightning, Catherwood drew with the dramatic overtone of a Piranesi a ruined temple, even while, before his eyes, a deer with blood-frothed tongue was set upon by ravenous dogs. When they reached the village of Iturbide they found "the grandest structure that now rears its ruined head in the forests of Yucatán," the elaborate three-storied edifice of Santa Rosa Xtampak which Stephens called simply "Lab-pahk." In the many rooms of the ruined building, where roots had broken through the interstices, the walls still held the polychromy of its murals, which reminded Stephens of those he had seen in Egyptian tombs. About the ruins, the natives had leveled the forest to grow tobacco, and in the rooms of Xtampak, reduced to ignobility by the iconoclasms of time, they dried their tobacco. Xtampak would have entailed less work to draw than all the previous sites, since it was open and free of the entangling web of the jungle, but it was not to be done easily.

Catherwood fell ill again. He had collapsed the week before, and Stephens had found him lying in the road, Albino by his side, "with the ague upon him," cold and pallid, wrapped in all the clothing he could find, including the stinking saddlecloths of their horses. Carried to a convent, Catherwood took the simples offered him by Dr. Cabot, yet resolutely refused to allow his fever to abate before he was up again. Now he no longer could bear the sun, and while he worked, the patient Bernaldo held a sunshade over him. Catherwood's personality, too, had undergone a change. Always of a retiring nature, never given to impassioned colloquy except when enraptured by a superb piece of architecture, Catherwood had grown moody and querulous.

Then there came the serious quarrel with Dr. Cabot, himself unwell. It had developed over a knife, for news had come that an Indian had crushed his entire hand in the toothed jaws of a cane-crusher, and Cabot, always giving his skill generously to whosoever asked it, thought that an amputation was necessary. He then discovered that he had left his own amputating instruments behind. The only knife present was Catherwood's, a spring knife, Paris made, of admirable temper, which Cabot proposed to hone down to lance thinness. Catherwood, who had acquired the knife twenty years before when he was an art student in Rome, which he always associated with those dazzling days of Keats and Shelley and Count D'Orsay, and all those titled ladies who had made so much over him, would not hear of its being converted into a surgical instrument. The argument developed fiercely and for a while was serious enough almost to break up the expedition. Even when the moment passed, with Catherwood refusing to sacrifice his knife to save the Indian's hand, the tenseness between them did not relax. Then at the ruins of Santa Rosa Xtampak, Catherwood became ill again. Stephens suggested that they break up the expedition, but Catherwood, in a surprisingly firm tone, would have nothing of it. They must go on. While Cabot and Catherwood were beset by malaria and sought to regain their strength, Stephens "determined at once to change the scene." He set off for the festival at Ticul "with only a sheet, hammock, and Albino."

Music was already filling the small plaza, which, tastefully planted with hibiscus and palms, was ablaze with spluttering pine light. The dance of the mestizas "had already begun in the plaza." The good-natured Padre Carrillo was there, fully recovered from his attack of malaria, and the English-speaking member of the Peón family, Don Felipe. They came up to Stephens, took his hand, and led him to a chair where he could face the dancers.

"After a month," Stephens wrote, "in Indian ranchos, toiling among ruins, driven to distraction by garrapatas, clambering over a frightful sierra . . . I settled down at a fancy ball amid music, lights, and pretty women in the full enjoyment of an armchair and a cigar. For the moment a shade of regret came over me as I thought of my invalid friends, but I soon forgot them."

Before his eager eyes, the mestizas were going through a *contradanza*. Over loose white huipils with red, worked border around the neck and shoulder, they added men's black straw hats, gold necklaces, and bracelets. These tinkled with their movements. The young men, in tight-fitting drawers of pink-striped muslin and low-crowned hats trimmed with a golden cord, beat the boards with buckskin shoes, while their fingers snapped in rhythm to the hypnotic drum beats. Stephens suddenly "became alive to these influences."

At daylight there was a ringing of church bells, firing of rockets, High Mass, then a bull fight. At midday was another dance called *el baile del día*. It began with a pantomime by the older men of the village, dressed in mimicry of those who, in pre-Columbian times, attended the Maya caciques. They wore dirty, ankle-long huipils and sandals; under huge-brimmed hats dangled black horse hair which simulated the coiffure of their ancestors. With their long whips of eight lashes they were the masters of ceremonies; upon their commands the dance evolved. They called out persons, here and there, and made them perform some buffoonery which sent the crowd into hilarious laughter. After they had made a circle of the room, their eyes fell upon Stephens. He had been sitting placidly, smoking his cheroot, eying a delicious morsel who raised her head occasionally to meet his brilliantly highlighted eyes. Before he knew it, the master of ceremonies stood before him. The room suddenly hushed as all eyes turned upon them. The time of *el Ingles* had come.

All day Stephens had tried to avoid it, but now it was here. In anticipation of the fun he would have with Stephens, the mestizo stood before him, legs apart, cracking his whip. He opened with a Maya harangue. Whatever he said sent the people into laughter. Caught off guard, Stephens flushed with surprise, embarrassment,

237

then anger. He did not like being singled out. But he quickly recovered. In the same voice of harangue he answered the mestizo with an English oration. The effect on the mestizo was startling, as he had never heard English spoken. He seemed to be straining his ears to understand it. As soon as Stephens stopped, he started up again in Maya. Then Stephens interrupted him by stammering out a stanza of Greek poetry. The crowd roared, the mestizo's mouth dropped open. He called him "*amigo*" and asked that they speak outlandish tongues no longer, but only musical Spanish. Then turning to the orchestra—a viol, a flageolet, a rebec, ancient harp, and drum—he summoned the dancers.

Stephens, seated between a padre and Señor Peón, allowed his eye to wander again. He appraised each mestiza as she glided by, ran his eye expertly up and down her person, cocking his head expressively when some outstanding attribute awakened special interest, then he saw something that commanded his entire attention. "She was not more than fifteen, delicate and fragile, with eyes so soft and dovelike that it was impossible to look upon them without a feeling of tenderness. She was sent into the world to be cherished and cared for and closeted like the finest china. . . . I had learned that she was the *crianza*, the natural daughter, of a padre (who strictly speaking ought never to have had any daughters)."

But there was another who also eyed her. From across the room an elderly satyr came forward and cried out loudly in dionysian ecstasy: "I am going to dance with you, my pigeon."

She danced but with lowered eyes; her eyes never once meeting his. And he, with a wild wolfish gleam, moved about her, beating the floor with his heels—in a pathetic imitation of a *flamenco*. His face became rapt, fixed, intense. The girl alone existed for him. She, with floor-cast eyes, moved gracefully while he wildly tore off his clothes and flung them at her feet. He was totally unmindful of the ludicrous spectacle of an old man, unable to abate his phallic energy, giving a Faustian display of it in public. In desperate ecstasy he tore off the sash that held up his cotton drawers, threw it at her feet. The music stopped. The room vibrated with the roar of the crowd. And the young girl, still

238

Iglesia, Chichen Itzá.

From an engraving of Frederick Catherwood

The Ball Court at Chichen Itzá.

From an engraving of Frederick Catherwood

Dr. Samuel Cabot hunting a wounded jaguar *under the full-lipped god once on the side of a pyramid at Izamal. Now destroyed, this is its only illustration.*

From a lithograph by Frederick Catherwood

without looking at him, bowed and with eyes still demurely cast downward walked over to where Stephens sat and quietly took her place beside him. The old man, still holding up his pants, stood in the center of the floor, swaying slightly, utterly inebriated by sexual intoxication. Lips parted, he stared droolingly at the young girl.

"*Amigo,*" he shouted to Stephens, "Have you any such as her in your country? Would you like to take her home with you? No, No! I can't spare this one. But you can take your choice among the others—" and he let go of his pants with one hand and swept the room. He insisted loudly for Stephens to make a selection of one of the pretty women: "Choose one, *amigo,* choose the one you want and I promise to deliver one to you at the convent."[3]

All that next morning, as he rode to the Wells of Bolonchen, Stephens thought of the festival of the mestizas at Ticul, for an extraordinary thing had happened. He had met, between the other nonarchaeological episodes of the *fiesta,* a very unusual man. His name was Juan Pío Pérez. He had journeyed all the way from Peto to see him. Before Stephens left, Pío Pérez pressed into his hands a manuscript copy, expressly prepared for him, of *Cronologia Antigua Yucateca—The Ancient Chronology of Yucatan—* which Pío Pérez, while he was a local administrative official at Peto, had copied from the ancient Maya chronicles called the *Book of Chilam Balam.* The numeration system of the Maya, which he worked out, (extraordinarily carefully when one considers that he was on unknown ground) was the system of Maya chronology.

The Maya had a lunar, solar calendar based on twenty months of eighteen days each, with an extra five-day month called *Uayeb* (the "five empty days of the Aztecs"), which made the 365-day year. The leap year was calculated but not interpolated. The Maya starting point of creation was placed at 3300 B.C. (just as the mythical date of the Biblical creation was once set at 4004 B.C.); from that date of thirty-three centuries before our "B.C." the Maya calculated their time sequences in an elaborate pattern of

[3] As it appears, transposed only to the present tense, in *Incidents of Travel in Yucatán,* II, 105.

the face-glyphs which Stephens had found on stelae at Copán, on sculptured stucco reliefs at Palenque, and on the carved wooden lintels of Kabah. The outstanding feature of Maya science was the perfection of their calendar, combining day names, month names, and numbers figured from their mythical genesis, by which they were able to designate a particular day which could not be mistaken for any other day throughout thousands of years. This elaborate time-counting system, which went beyond the sterile accomplishment of day counting to tables of solar and lunar eclipses, was lost—more accurately, destroyed, by the Spanish conquerors. The Maya "Rosetta stone," which was to assist in the deciphering of the Maya glyphs, still lay in the archives in Madrid, for the manuscript of Fray Diego de Landa was not to come to light until 1865. John Lloyd Stephens took the studies of Pío Pérez out of unmerited obscurity, had them translated, and put them in his second publication on the Mayas. He did not know it then, but Stephens was supplying a piece of the Maya Rosetta stone himself.

Juan Pío Pérez, born in Mérida in 1798, the son of Gregorio Pérez and Doña Juana Bermón, had attended the Colegio de San Ildefonso, where he studied under Pablo Moreno. Of a Maya-speaking family, although pure Spanish in origin, Pío Pérez was made interpreter to the government. After the revolution he was sent to Peto, in Central Yucatán, as administrator with the resounding title of *Jefe Político*. There, and at the ancient Maya town of Maní (the last capital of the Maya after they fled Uxmal and where Diego de Landa burned many of the Maya documents and books), Juan Pío Pérez found an ancient painting on cloth in the town archives, along with other records written in Maya-Spanish script. These, dating from 1557, showed the titles which the Spaniards gave to the Maya chiefs to supplant their lost prerogatives. It proved unequivocally that it was the Mayas who had built the ruined buildings. When Pío Pérez fell into disfavor with the government at Mérida and was deprived of his sinecure at Peto, he remained at Maní, making the copies of these manuscripts, which eventually were placed in the hands of Stephens. They were to become the historical woof of the great tapestry of archaeological discovery. This small gentleman, Don Juan Pío Pérez, who spoke of his scholarship with a deprecating air, turned over all of his material to Stephens (it still exists in manuscript in the archives of the New York Historical Society), and Stephens honored him by having him elected to three important American scientific societies.

Although racked by a dry cough which seemed to tear him apart, Don Pío outlived both Stephens and Catherwood. Self-effacing to the last, he allowed most of his work—his Maya grammar, his *Cronología Antigua Yucateca*[4]—to be used by others. He finally coughed up his lungs in Mérida in 1858.

Stephens' brain was still whirling with ancient astronomical systems when he rode into Bolonchen. He found to his great delight that both Dr. Cabot and Catherwood were now "free of the ague" and eager to continue their explorations. They had heard of the mysterious underground wells of Bolonchen, and these were marked as next on their exploratory itinerary.

The mouths of the Wells of Bolonchen opened up in the small plaza of the village, a village of oval-shaped houses with grass-thatched roofs. There were nine wells—hence the name of the village: *Bolon* (nine), *chen* (wells). Every afternoon Maya women of lithesome carriage, draped with black *rebozos*, would come to the wells to draw water. Here the newly gathered gossip was exchanged, and so water-drawing had, to these quiet, simple people, an important social as well as a life-giving function. All over Yucatán water was taken, as in Bolonchen, from cisterns.

"God," said Diego de Landa, "provided Yucatán with many very nice sources of water.... Nature worked so differently in this country in the matter of rivers and springs which in all the rest of the world run on top of the land, that here in this country all run and flow through secret passages under it." And so it is. The 50,000 square miles which is the Yucatecan peninsula is one gi-

[4] Juan Pío Pérez's (1798-1859) attempt at Maya chronology was thirty years in advance of all other attempts (for Diego de Landa was not published until 1865). His work however, does not touch upon the glyphs, and he is in error as regards the Katun time unit, for he makes the Katun $24 \times 365 = 8,760$ days, when, in point of fact, the Katun is $20 \times 360 = 7,200$ days. (See H. J. Spinden, "Origins of Civilization in Central America and Mexico," in *The American Aborigines*, 219-46.)

gantic limestone shelf. This limestone, as porous as a sieve, is unable to retain water on its surface, and rain percolates through it to some fifty feet below the surface of the land. During the dry season, while the land above is as anaemic as a desert, below, underground rivers rush to the sea in subterranean channels. What made human culture possible in Yucatán were the huge-mouthed, natural wells which here and there opened in yawning chasms, as Landa says: "On land God provided openings in the rock which the Indians call *cenotes* which reach down to the water, through the cut in the living rock." Around these natural *cenotes* or wells, Maya society first took root. Cities and religious centers were in fact hypothecated on or about a *cenote* well. And, as to be expected with water as the alpha and omega of Maya economy, it took on, naturally or supernaturally, a mystical flavor. Sacrifices were made periodically as *emolientes* to the water gods, and victims of this fetish, jeweled and bedecked as befitting one's visitation to the gods, were hurled into the cenotes. They were expected to commune with the water god and return to the surface with a prophecy; for a community's rise or fall depended on the water supply.

Bolonchen was one of these ancient villages founded about a *cenote*. Once in the past it had had its great city, now ruined and dispersed and covered with corn-milpas. The wells in the center of the village were active only eight months out of the year, the reasons for which were a complete mystery to the Indians. To supply themselves with water the other four months of the year, the Indians fell back on the most ancient of the wells which lay a half-league from the village. It was these huge wells that Stephens and his friends—guided by fantastic rumors—had come to explore.

They came—with a large retinue of Indians—to the mouth of Bolonchen in the flush of a quiet dawn. On the edge of a rise of ground was a huge, gaping, jagged hole large enough to have swallowed the Astor House of Stephens day. The three, surrounded by a horde of torch-bearing natives, slipped off most of their clothing and followed the Indians down the steep ladder. Bats startled by the light fluttered by. It was close and hot. The sounds of their footsteps echoed deep down in the unseen bowels of the cavern. Paced by the Indians, they came to a second ladder, so steep they had to descend backwards; it was a hundred feet down. The lights below looked utterly unreal, like the flickering lights of lanternbugs. The ladder, wide enough for twenty men to climb abreast, was without nails; every wooden traverse was bound with withes. Up these, Indians were climbing with water jugs strapped to their heads. At the bottom, the cavern was flooded with a light-shaft, which came from a hole directly overhead at a distance revealed by the inquiring tape-measure of Catherwood as 210 feet. The rock exuded tepid water from all its ramifications, and this formed rills at the bottom from which the villagers gathered their water during the dry season. It was a dramatic setting, "the wildest that can be conceived," said Stephens, "men struggling up the huge ladder with earthen jars of water strapped to back and head, their sweating bodies glistening under the light of the pine-torches." Catherwood could not resist drawing it. Using the back of Bernaldo as a drawing board he began the sketch, which became one of the finest illustrations of his portfolio.

While Catherwood sketched the posterior of the wells of Bolonchen, Stephens, attended by Dr. Cabot, followed another ramification. They were stripped to the skin. Albino, who carried the torch, could only be dimly seen by the white scar on his buttock. They followed a tortuous Sisyphus path, sliding down slippery ladders, going ever downward. Cabot took the measurements of descent. They had reached a depth of 450 feet and had come, according to Stephens' calculations, 1,400 feet from the mouth of the cavern. They passed the catch basin called Chacka—"red water"—where they bathed, then another called Pu uelha, meaning that it ebbs and flows like the sea, for the Indians said in whispers "it goes with the south wind, comes with the north." Mystically-minded Indians moved silently here when seeking water, for if they made a noise, they whispered, the water disappeared—a legend Stephens promptly punctured by stripping and jumping into it. At each level was another catch basin, each with a specific name. These were the wells and the watery supplement of Hell which supplied a community of seven thousand in the dry season.

243

It is strange that the Maya never completely solved the problem of water. The level of their engineering technics was far enough advanced to build huge stone reservoirs, but they never attempted it—or if they did, time has obliterated the effort. They did, however, construct small subterranean water reservoirs, which Stephens first discovered in the province of Maní. Here at Maní, where the topography of the land changes and where there are ranges of low hills, relatively heavily forested, were what the Mayas called the Puuc lands. Water gathers in the hollows during the rainy season and they are formed into *aguadas*, filled with blue water hyacinths and animated by the ghostly presence of white herons. Under these the Maya built narrow-throated water reservoirs, lined with mortared stone, twenty-five feet in depth, forming a sort of huge subterranean demijohn. Water was retained here when it evaporated elsewhere. Catherwood, who had extensive knowledge of the whole of Mediterranean archaeology, was astounded by this example of engineering knowledge. They searched for other subterranean reservoirs in the immediate vicinity, finding over forty, which Catherwood stylized into five types and which he made into diagrammatic drawings.

Then Stephens discovered the mysterious stone roads of Yucatán. He had, at first, discounted the rumor of stone roads built by the Maya that connected their ancient cities, for one grows skeptical in the face of Spanish hyberpole, but after the discovery of the underground water-cisterns he was ready to follow, no matter how fantastic, the suggestions of the wonder-loving padres. At the ruins of "Sacbey" he discovered his first road, "one of the most interesting monuments of ancient antiquity in Yucatán," he wrote; "It is a broken platform or roadway of stone eight feet wide . . . called by the Indians Sacbey [correctly "Sacbeob"]. The Indians say it traversed the country from Kabah to Uxmal." Then at Chemax in central Yucatán, the padre resident again observed the remains of road "running to the southeast to a limit that has not been discovered, but some aver that it goes in the direction of Chichen Itzá."

It was not until a hundred years later that archaeologists following Stephens turned their attention to these roads. A Mexican archaeologist[5] undertook a traverse of a stone causeway, the Yaxuna-Cobá road, and confirmed that which was known to the early priest chroniclers, that the cities of the Maya in Yucatán were bound together by well-kept roads mysteriously winding their way through jungles and swamps. Diego de Landa had seen them: "there are signs today of there having been a very beautiful road from one [set of buildings in Izamal] to the other"; and Fray José Delgado had traveled over them in 1605: "I followed roads through the swamps which had been built in ancient times and which were still well preserved"; but it was Stephens who brought their existence to the attention of the modern world. He believed that most of the cities had been linked by roads. Investigation showed that the causeways, wide enough for several people to walk abreast, were built of stone filled with rubble and cemented with white earth-cement, called *"sahcab,"* from which the name *"sac-beoob"* ("white roads") was derived. As the Maya had no beasts of burden, the roads were built for foot-travelers. Priests borne in palanquins passed from one province to another. Rest houses were erected at regular intervals along the road, and small reservoirs of water were built in the shadowed side of the highways. Stone markers guided the travelers. There were no roads in all Europe to compare, in the same period, with them. With the aid of the *sacbeobs* the Maya wove all their independent realms into a cultural synthesis. One of these great roads, in actuality a *via sacra*, wormed its way across the jungle to the environs of the great city of Chichen Itzá. And following it, in part, where its stones still cumbered the jungle, went Messrs. Stephens, Cabot, and Catherwood on the Ides of March, 1842, for the end of their archaeological tour.

[5] Alfonso Villa, "The Yaxuna-Coba Causeway," *American Archaeology Magazine*, October, 1934, 189–208.

Chapter xix　Chichen Itzá was now the new word, for, as Stephens wrote, "Ever since we left home we had our eyes upon this place." And well they might. For Chichen Itzá was the largest ruined city within the entire Maya realm and easy of access. It lay on a flat plain sixty miles from the sea, close to, in fact connected with, Vallodolid (the second largest town in Yucatán) by a good stone road.

As the greatest city of the Maya New Empire and a religious center to which all the Maya, at least once in their lifetime, made pilgrimage, Chichen Itzá rivaled all other cities in the barbaric splendor of its monuments. So great was its fame that its traditions remained in chronological order even though the confused memory of events erased all else from Maya minds.

Chichen Itzá had been settled long before the "medieval period" of the Maya New Empire. Three large *cenotes* (one, more than 150 feet in diameter) marked it, in that waterless land, as an ideal site for settlement. Chichen Itzá was discovered (it is written in laconic glyphs) 6 *Ahua*, 13 *Yaxkin* (455 A.D.), in the same period that Copán, Tikal, and many of the other city states were rising to prominence in the wet zone. The Maya spread along the storm-lashed northeast coast of Yucatán and took possession of the islands of Cozumel, and established, during the colonization period, the walled city of Tulum.

Stephens had heard, too, about Tulum, the ruined city that could be seen from the sea, the walls of which, overgrown with trees, clung to a limestone cliff facing the lashing waves. Juan Pío Pérez, his friend of Maní who had given him the ancient Maya documents, told him that a friend, a *"muy anciano,"* Juan José Gálvez, had found it some years previous to Stephens' visit, but as he was neither antiquarian nor writer, the site remained for all practical purposes unknown. Located on the same latitude as the

246

ruins of Uxmal, seventy-five miles from Chichen Itzá and thirty from Cobá, Tulum was as old as Chichen Itzá; a stela, first discovered by Stephens, 8 *Ahua*, 13 *Pax*, was deciphered as January 29, 564 A.D.

They went to Tulum by sea in a small coastal craft in which they paddled and bailed with the care of dynamic death. They skirted the coral-studded shore, windswept and rain driven, passed the Isle of the Women (Mugeres) where Bernal Díaz del Castillo, the doughty companion of Cortés, landing in 1519, "went on shore and found in the town hard by, four temples, the idols of which represented human figures of large size, for which reason we named the place 'The Point of Women.'" They found one of these temples of Díaz del Castillo, and Catherwood drew it before they sailed southward to the next island, Cozumel. There, among screaming petrels and diving blue-footed boobies, they saw remains of time-battered Maya ruins which the *conquistadores* had seen in 1518.[1] And on this island where Cortés had bivouacked in 1519 on his way to the conquest of Mexico, Catherwood made a single sketch.

Tulum, in the Quintana Roo Province of Yucatán, they found hanging on the very edge of a limestone cliff facing the Caribbean Sea. Huge mounds of water broke against it in agitated froth. In its rear the jungle lapped about the ruins, hiding all but a section of the wall. It was in June, 1842, as it was in the springtime of the New World when Juan Díaz and his retinue of bearded *condottiere* bound for conquest and glory saw "three towns separated from each other by 2 miles . . . many houses of stone, very tall towers and buildings thatched with straw."

In the few days allotted Stephens *y Compañia*, they made a plan of Tulum, discovering a great wall enclosing the central part of the ruined city and running to the edge of the cliff. Despite the privations—"the sun beat upon us, moschetoes, flies and other insects pestered us"—Catherwood was able, with the assistance of

[1] ". . . at sunset we saw a large white tower which appeared very high. . . . we entered the village where all the houses were built of stone. Among others, we saw five very well made, and commanded by small towers. The base of these edifices is very small at the top. They appeared to have been built a long time."—Bernal Díaz del Castillo.

Cabot and Stephens, to figure at least seven of the principal buildings. The Temple of the Diving God was dominated by a strange deity made of stucco, which hung over the entrance; it had the tail of a bird and feather wings on his arms, and was flying earthward. The interior of the temple was covered with geometric figures painted on a barbaric blue and scarlet background. And the *Castillo*, also frescoed, was approached by a great stairway, which was now swathed in the tight embrace of snakelike roots of the strangler-fig tree; "watch-towers," near the end of the wall which command the view of the sea. It was only when they were leaving, being unable to endure further the onslaught of the mosquitoes, that they discovered another. Dr. Cabot, in search of an ocellated turkey—made famous by Audubon—had gone off with his shotgun into the jungle. He discovered the Temple of the Frescoes. Catherwood had only time to make the exterior drawings, the frescoes of geometric Mexican design, in a barbaric color display —actually a rhapsody in blue, the dominant color. But the real survey was left for a later century.[2]

And so, although they discovered further ruins on the mainland such as Ake, Silan, and Izamal (where Catherwood drew a colossal full-lipped head now destroyed), and thus extended the Maya cultural area hundreds of miles further, it was at Chichen, at the wells of Itzá, where the concluding moment of their great discoveries came to a dramatic end.

Chichen Itzá's buildings lay under the heat of *El Criador Sol*, as bright as snow in the glare of the sun; the truncated pyramid of Chichen Itzá rising one hundred feet above the flat, jungle-covered plain, the Nunnery, the most massive structure of them all, a huge solid block of masonry two hundred feet high, covered with ornate sculptures, and the Great Ball Court, as large as a football field, where once, in the classical past, man was pitted against man in the Mayan Olympiad. For three square miles, they saw the most extensive city-state in Mayadom, the Temples of the Warriors, guarded by the strange, reclining figures of the

[2] Eighty years after Stephens, Samuel K. Lothrop subjected Tulum to a very thorough archaeological examination. He published, in 1924, a superb monograph, *Tulum, an Archaeological Study of the East Coast of Yucatán*, published by the Carnegie Institution of Washington.

Chacmool, and the circular Carcol, a Maya observatory by deduction if not by tradition. Although Stephens had seen forty ruined Maya sites, none stirred him as did Chichen Itzá, for here, as at no other there was a feeling almost European about the city. It had a lightness, a restraint in decoration with which he almost felt a kinship. They were to remain eighteen days at Chichen Itzá, and were to lay down a scientific approach that would endure as long as man was stirred by the archaeos.

The runes of their fame had spread across the land. At the hacienda of Don Juan Sosa,[3] whose great fief included the site of Chichen Itzá, they were welcomed with touching hospitality; Indians squatting by the hacienda gate exhibiting their infirmities had waited for days for Dr. Cabot to appear; young ladies dressed in their Maya best, with hibiscus-trimmed coiffure, ogled Catherwood that they might be pictured by his daguerreotype. Catherwood's fever had abated as had Dr. Cabot's, and everything—the people, the surroundings—was as halcyon as the turquoise blue sky. It was, after all the others, an archaeological idyll; within a few days they had made an elaborate, scaled map of Chichen Itzá.

There were here no lingering doubts concerning the identity of the people who erected Chichen. At the first structure they investigated, the low, flat, rather undistinguished building, the Temple of Akabtzib, they found in one of the eighteen rooms, where the sculpture was polychromed in violent reds, blues, and yellows, an inscribed stone lintel; its motif was a seated Indian with quetzal-feathered headdress and outstretched left hand in the act of explaining something. Around him flowed those same glyphs they had found at Copán, Palenque, Uxmal, and Kabah. It became immediately obvious that Chichen Itzá was inextricably bound in cultural relationship with Copán, hundreds of miles to the south; and with Palenque, hundreds of miles to the north.

Architecturally, too, there were specific resemblances. The cornices of the annexes of the massive ruin of the Nunnery had the motif of Itzamna, the long-nosed god. It was at this building,

[3] Within five years, the hacienda of Sr. Juan Sosa was only a memory; in the War of the Castes the revolting Indians leveled the hacienda and killed the inhabitants.

called ludicrously the "Church," with its lavishly decorated façade, that Frederick Catherwood's architectural art reached its
height;[4] his drawing of the *Iglesia* has never been equaled, in detail or dramatic intensity, by any photograph.

The pyramid, which one reached by following the remains of
a stone road from the sacred *cenote*, bore a general resemblance
to other structures they had seen, except that this *castillo* was
taller and more massive, and the building atop its truncated pinnacle exceedingly well preserved. Four great stairways with a continuous balustrade of the plumed-serpent motif led to the top,
approaching its four entrances, which were oriented to the earth's
four directions. The interior, which Catherwood sketched by Albino's spluttering pine torch, was decorated with sculptured doorjambs, its sapote-wood beams were carved with a delicate tracery
of figures. Stephens and Catherwood spent an entire day within
the Temple of Kulkulkan, wandering out at various times during
the day to survey the vast panorama of the necropolis of Chichen
Itzá. A few hundred feet to the east of the pyramided temple of
Kulkulkan, they discovered, in Stephens words, "the most remarkable unintelligible remains we had yet met with."

Fighting their way through the incessant web of low scrub,
they found groups of small square columns "in rows of three, four,
and five abreast, many rows continuing in the same direction,
when they changed and pursued another." When Stephens had
counted to 380 of the six-foot-high sculptured columns, he was
completely bewildered; neither he nor Catherwood (who made
a single diagrammatic sketch of it) could comprehend its significance. But they had discovered the Court of the Thousand Columns and the Temple of the Warriors. Stephen did not know, he
merely surmised that the columns at one time "upheld a raised
walk of cement, but there were no remains visible." A century

---

[4] "We have a long letter from Sam dated April 2nd from Valladolid. . . .
[they] visited a great number of ruined cities. He speaks particularly of a ruined
palace three stories high with two staircases much like those of modern buildings.
They found paintings [there] which Mr. Catherwood says are by a master hand
also beautiful carvings both in wood & stone. . . . we hear they have sent specimens home. . . . you must not speak of them for Sam is very particular to enjoin
us to silence in regard to Mr. Stephens monuments. They mean to embark June
1st [for home]."—Mrs. Cabot to Elliott Cabot, May 15, 1841, Cabot Papers.

later the Carnegie Institution of Washington reconstructed the whole of Stephens' discovery and found it once had been "encompassed by a covered colonnade, roofed, like the inner sanctuary of the Castillo . . . supported by the [square pillars] . . . carved and brightly painted with life-size figures of armed warriors." It is one of the most magnificent monuments of the Maya, now restored and the subject of a very complete monograph: *The Temple of the Warriors.*[5]

After Catherwood drew the Caracol, a round structure, rare in Maya architecture, he, pacing Stephens, followed a cow path which led between verdure-covered mounds to a huge structure with 28-foot parallel walls enclosing a field 450 feet long by 120 feet wide. At one end of the east wall, forming a narrow esplanade in front of it, was a ruined structure to be known in archaeological parlance as the Temple of the Jaguars. While Catherwood put up his camera lucida to obtain a panoramic view of the whole structure, Stephens wandered along the great walls. Overhead the black clouds obscured the sun. The mass of vegetation—palms and agave —growing on top of the structure bowed in obeisance to the winds. Even as Stephens stood there in the awesome grandeur of Chichen Itzá, the sky was rent, riven by a bolt of lightning.

All the while Stephens was walking the length of the walls he pondered their use in the Maya economy. At a height of twenty feet above the ground, he discovered attached to the wall two massive stone rings, four feet in diameter, pierced by a large hole. Around its border two snakes, fiercely entwined like those of the caduceus of medicine, were carved in low relief. (Catherwood was deeply impressed by the circular carving. When he designed their second book, he placed the circular stone on the cover of the *Incidents of Travel in Yucatán*). It was when Stephens found that these two rings faced each other across the 120-foot-wide court that he remembered that he had seen at Uxmal similar rings; Stephens had discovered the Great Ball Court of Chichen. "I shall call it, as occasion requires, the Gymnasium or Tennis Court." He

---

[5] E. H. Morris, Jean Charlot, and A. A. Morris, *The Temple of the Warriors at Chichen Itzá*, Carnegie Institute of Washington Publication No. 6 (Washington, 1931).

later found by reading in the closely printed pages of Herrera y Tordesillas (the incident-loving Spanish chronicler) that the Aztecs played a ball game called *tlachtli* with hardened rubber balls; "On the side wall they fix'd certain Stones like those of a *Mill* with a Hole quite through the Middle." Herrera had remarked, too, that "Every Tennis Court had a temple." Stephens believed that this was a ball court. He said "tennis" (for basketball, to which the Indian game bears a resemblance, had not yet been invented). This exhibits an excellent analogical sense: to be surrounded by a structure of which man knew nothing, and yet to judge it so clearly. Time has confirmed his discoveries; Stephens accurately described the ball game of the Mayas called *pok-ta-tok*.

Catherwood could not resist copying down the superb carvings, in low relief, that circled the walls of the Ball Court; warriors, carrying bundles of obsidian-tipped arrows, accoutred in flowing quetzal-feather headdresses. The Maya sculptor showed great virtuosity in composing these space-filling figures; and Catherwood, who had seen most of the archaic sculptures of the Mediterranean area, felt no hesitation in saying: "these are as finely conceived as those of the Egyptians." The Maya artist seemed capable of much stylistic deviation depending upon the geographical milieu in which he worked. Yet no matter how much the variation, Maya art remained, even at Chichen Itzá (where it was influenced by the Toltec), basically Maya. The reliefs were as barbarically beautiful to Catherwood as Mexican art had been to Albrecht Dürer. He, in 1520, upon seeing some of the gold pieces brought back by Cortés, wrote in his diary: "I have never seen in all my days what so rejoiced my heart as these things."

So it is aesthetic moonshine for Elie Faure to write of this American art as "sometimes beautiful, almost always monstrous, contorted, blown up, crushed-in, warped. . . ." Faure, presuming that the art forms of the Maya were of Eurasian derivation, believed that the American Indian had lost his "world-memory" and that the Indian sculptors never saw anything "but mutilated trunks, dislocated members, scalped heads, skinned faces, empty eye-sockets and grinning teeth. . . . In Central America," he rhapsodizes, "where the earth is soaked with the water of hot rains, where the vegetation is heavier, the miasmas deadlier, and the poisonous thorn bushes impossible to traverse, the dream is still more horrible. . . . In the sculptured rocks one distinguishes *nothing* but heaps of crushed and palpitating flesh, quivering masses of entrails . . . a confused pile of viscera."[6]

After ten months' travel in Yucatán,[7] Havana was an oasis of delight. In the four days given them before the *Ann Louisa* sailed for New York they were able—despite the yellow fever that placed Havana in a sort of state of siege—to make the "rounds." Cuba, one of the last Spanish strongholds in America, was overflowing with an entourage of *Condes* and *Marqueses*. There were masked balls, Italian opera with Fanny Elssler as its *danseuse*, and drives along the Malecon, particularly in the evening, in open voltantes, where Stephens could ogle the various pretty girls, "black-eyed and with beautiful figures." Difficulties developed over declaration at customs of Stephens' collected material (transferred from the *Alexandre* which had brought them from Yucatán to Havana), and posed at first insurmountable problems. There were Dr. Cabot's bird skins, hundreds of them, the first ornithological collection ever made in Central America by an expert; and Catherwood's huge portfolios of drawings that he had made of forty ruined cities, his archaeological notebooks crammed with drawings, observations, maps, and diagrams; and Stephens' collections from Kabah, Uxmal, and Chichen Itzá, and his own notebooks.

But the Spanish customs officials, warming to Señor Stephens' *simpático* nature, bridged the difficulties and allowed all their collections to be taken from the *Alexandre* and transferred without going through customs to the *Ann Louisa,* New York bound with its famous passengers.

The night of June 4, before they sailed, they paid their respects to another discoverer; "after dark by the light of a single candle, with heads uncovered, we stood before the marble slab enclosing the bones of Columbus."

[6] *Medieval Art* (New York, 1937), 188–205.
[7] Stephens remained with Catherwood and Dr. Cabot eighteen days at Chichen Itzá, from March 11 until March 29; during that time Catherwood completed a map, various plans, and over fifty drawings.

Chapter xx Life in New York had quickened. Stephens felt it the moment he returned from the quiet lost worlds of Yucatán. New York's streets were longer, noisier, and dirtier. Business was brisk. Talk of expansion filled the air, and Stephens' friend, John O'Sullivan, editor of the *Democratic Review*, had given it literary substance by coining "Manifest Destiny"—"We are a nation of human progress—and who will, what can set limits to our onward march?" In a single ten years, the period that Mead Minnigerode so aptly called "The Fabulous Forties," Americans received in bewildering succession the telegraph, the daguerreotype, and steam (as mechanical power); then the trek of the Mormons across the plains, the absorption of Texas into the Union, the Mexican War, California, and Oregon; and, at the end of the expansion rainbow, as an unbelievable climax, the discovery of gold. There was, too, the cultural gold: Emerson, who had published his first book, *Nature*, in 1836, was beginning to feel his strength; Hawthorne, after publishing two books, gave up his sinecure at the Customs House in Boston to go to Brook Farm to devote himself to writing; Walt Whitman was on the *Brooklyn Eagle;* Melville was living with the cannibals in the Taipi Valley in Tahiti. With the decline of the Knickerbockers, the Irvings, the Coopers, the Pauldings, America had a more representative *Zeitgeist*—Thoreau, Melville, Whitman, Emerson, and Poe; and the historical Titans—Bancroft, Ticknor, Prescott, and Sumner—were beating the sonorous brasses of America's renaissance. John Lloyd Stephens pointed out still another direction, "the visible past of a Pan-America," as Van Wyck Brook has written, "scarcely aware of its own existence."

Stephens' final book, *Incidents of Travel in Yucatán*, was more demanding than the other, for it required wider reading. He dug into Spanish chroniclers—Cogolludo, Herrara y Tordesillas, and Bernal Díaz del Castillo. He called out the old Spanish historiographers from their limbo to make them witnesses to his theme: That the civilizations of Yucatán are American, built by Americans, the same people who built them and occupied them during the Spanish conquest, that these civilizations took nothing from Egypt, nothing from China, nor Greece, nor Carthage, that their art was like the plants of America, indigenous. *Yucatán* was going to be filled with many archaeological "firsts": the first accurate map of Yucatán, the first illustrations of Maya sites, the first visits to forty-four ruined cities, the first confirmation of ancient Maya *sacbeob* roads, and the first publication of Juan Pío Pérez's *A True Exposition of the Method Used by the Indians for computing Time.*

At Catherwood's Panorama, in the meanwhile, there was placed on exhibition for an excited public to see, the carved wooden beams from Uxmal, Kabah, and Labna, along with other pieces of Maya sculpture that they had collected in Yucatán. These were placed beside his Panorama of Thebes, so that New Yorkers might themselves see the cultural similarities or differences between the two civilizations. While the proprietors of the other amusements on Broadway looked with undisguised jealousy, people poured into the circular Rotunda to see Catherwood's Panorama and with their own eyes the wonders that had been discovered. Then, on the night of July 31, after closing time, it caught fire.

Up in flames went the collections that were to be the base of Stephens' Museum of American Antiquities, up in smoke went the priceless "dated" sapote beam from the ruins of Uxmal (the only known wooden beam carved with a glyphic inscription) from the Palace of the Governor ("Its loss simply cannot be overestimated," says Dr. S. G. Morley); up in smoke went all the other carvings from Kabah, Labna, and some of the delicate stones which they had managed to salvage from the ruins. Up in smoke, too, went a huge section of the life of Catherwood. The loss to him was calamitous. "This fire," wrote the *New York Herald* the following day, "is likely to prove much more disastrous than we at first anticipated. . . . Catherwood was insured for only $3,000.00. His own private loss will be at least $10,000.00 more."

255

"I had," said Stephens the morning after the fire, poking among the ruins for the wooden Maya beams, "the melancholy satisfaction of seeing their ashes exactly as the fire had left them."

Stephens took time to go to Boston to consult personally with Prescott over the new vistas opened by his discoveries. And he stopped for a few days with the Cabots,[1] for "Dr. Sam," as they called him, was very ill. For some weeks they despaired of his life. Back in New York by October, Stephens again was at the manuscript, writing despite the incessant political crisis. He was already into "volume two" when the Croton Dam celebration burst; on October 12, 1842, upon New York City. It was impossible to write through this public delirium. "Water, Water," wrote Philip Hone in his chronicle, "is the universal note sounded through every part of the city and infuses joy and exultation into the masses. . . . Nothing is talked of or thought of in New York but Croton water; fountains, aqueducts, hydrants and hose attract attention. Political spouting has given place to water spouts." It took Stephens weeks before he could again pick up the thread of his narrative of Yucatán. At last it was done, and, on February, 1843, the first copies were in Stephens' hands, one of which he sent Prescott[2] on March 23, 1843: "I sent you yesterday, by Harnden's Express, a copy of my Yucatán, Before passing judgment upon it I beg to remind that you committed yourself before I set out on my expedition by saying that if I should make *half as good* a book as the last, my voyage would not be in vain." To which Prescott replied:

My Dear Mr. Stephens:
    I am truly obliged to you for your welcome present. It opens rich and promising, and I am sure from the sample will be worthy of

[1] "Sam's friend Mr. Stephens has been staying some days with us and we found him quite agreeable he is just what you are led to expect from his books, frank & good natured and with good sense . . . we wanted him to stay longer but he is in a hurry to get out his book which has been delayed because of [recurrent] fevers . . . he still expects to get it out this fall."—Mrs. Cabot to Elliott Cabot, September 19, 1842, Cabot Papers.

[2] "A good deal of gossip was heard in literary circles regarding the forthcoming publication of Prescott's *Conquest of Mexico* and how it was to be translated into French, Spanish, and German as soon as issued."—Hone's *Diary*, July 14, 1843.

the elder brother *Incidents of Travel in Central America*, 1841. I shall read the work through, however, carefully, as it concerns some of the matters to which I shall have occasion to advert, and I shall take occasion to give you my opinion of it in a manner I hope not displeasing to you in my notes in the Conquest.

A month later Prescott had finished one volume of *Yucatán*.

I have accomplished one volume of your work and a part of second. I read slowly, or rather it is read to me, which is a slow process, and I have but little leisure now. It is all interesting to me as the old ruins have ever more attractions than the lively narrative of adventure. Most readers find the adventures told with even more spirit than in your preceding work. You have made a good advertising sheet for our friend the doctor [Cabot]. I hope he may live to profit by it. He mends very gradually. I know not what to think of the ruins, they leave my mind in a kind of mist, which I shall not attempt to dispel, till I reread the book leisurely when—thanks, no rather no thanks to you—I shall have to tinker on my chapter on American Antiquities, the last of the work.

. . . I believe that there is but one opinion of the work here and all agree. It is better than its brother.[3]

The press echoed Prescott's opinion. "Consider these superb volumes on the ruins of Yucatán," wrote the *Democratic Review*, "within a month who has not devoured them at ease in the quiet possession of his or a borrowed copy?" In such tenor the reviews stimulated purchase and, like its "elder brother," *Central America*, the two-volume work on Yucatán galloped its way through edition upon edition, until Catherwood's engravings becoming worn from use made the last editions in 1865 only ghosts of the originals. The plates were destroyed in Harper's disastrous fire in 1854, but the type was reset and reprinted by the publishers every two years until, during the Civil War, *Yucatán* was buried under a mountain of grapeshot. In England, John Murray printed an edition, and translations appeared in France, Germany, Sweden, and in the very theater of his operations—Mexico. The work has lived for

[3] The letters of Stephens and Prescott: *The Correspondence of William Hickling Prescott* (1833–1847), ed. by Roger Wolcott, 210, 239, 240, 258, 287, 339, 340, 341, 366, 381, 427, 464, 486, 504. And in addition other letters not printed in this edition in the Prescott Collection, Massachusetts Historical Society.

more than a century; one hundred years after its publication translations, *"Viaje á Yucatán,"*[4] still come from Mexico's presses.

Messrs. Harper prepared themselves for their second publishing event. On the second of August, Prescott's work was completed; in December of the same year it was published. Within the month, 130 reviews were received from all over the country. The three-volumed, high-priced book sold 4,000 copies in a single month! By 1855 it was in its twenty-third edition! "One of the wonders of the Golden Day," it was praised throughout all Europe. Prescott was received into the circle of the international scholarship with Guizot, Sismondi, Thierry, Hallam, and Milman. Henry Hallam immediately exhibited marks of recognition, comparing the Conquest with Gibbon's *Decline and Fall.* "I received a copy of your *History of the Conquest of Mexico,*" he wrote Prescott; ". . . Mr. Stephens' work had already turned our minds to speculate on the remarkable phenomena of a civilized nation decaying without, as far as we can judge, without leaving any record of its existence."[5]

[4] The latest edition was completed in 1938 from the original translation of Justo Sierra O'Reilly, who first translated it in 1846.

[5]

William H. Prescott,
Boston, Mass.
My Dear Sir,

67 Wall Street
December 24, 1843

    I have said behind your back what I shall now dare say to your face and take this means to tell you that I have pronounced the *"Conquest"* the best book that was ever issued from the American press. I told the Harpers that it would be so, and am rejoiced that it has turned out "all right." Really you have done justice to your subject, which is as high praise as I can bestow. Cortez is *used up.* No one will ever mount him again and your names will go down together till octavos are swallowed up by cheap literature. I give you my hearty congratulations. I am not mixing much with the world but in my circle, particularly in my own family I hear nothing but praise. And by the way, sometime since Mr. [George] Griffin in speaking of the expected work said to me, rather disparagingly (of the subject I mean) "Why, what can he make of the life of Cortez?" I met him five minutes ago and he said "What better book is there on this side of the water, *or the other?"*

    I think this will *do* for the present. I should like to talk with you on some points but it is too much to write about them. Please give my best respects and warm congratulations to your father & families.

Very Truly
Your Friend
John L. Stephens

258

A most notable publishing year: First Stephens, Prescott, and then Fanny Calderón de la Barca; her witty, informative *Life in Mexico* created out of a series of letters which she had written while resident in Mexico with her ambassador husband. Prescott had insisted they were worthy of a book, and he added a preface for it. Charles Dickens, himself, carried the manuscript of it to Chapman and Hall; that same year, 1843, it was published. Little did Fanny Calderón de la Barca know that her *Life* would prove to be so exact that hundreds of copies were to be printed for the invasion of Mexico three years hence as a "guide to Scott's officers."

It was at this point that Stephens launched an ambitious project which, had it been fully completed, would have taken its place beside Audubon's *Birds of America* as one of the most monumental publications in American history. Catherwood's dramatic sepia drawings of the Maya ruins had commanded so much attention that Stephens believed that they should be published in heroic size, for much of their detail had been lost in the engravings of reduced size for his book; Prescott himself had remarked that "it only remains that the exquisite illustrations of Mr. Catherwood should be published on a larger scale like the great works on the subject in France and England." Stephens conceived a gigantic project. He announced in a letter to Prescott on March 25, 1843:

"I am thinking of sending out a prospectus for publishing by subscription a great work on *American Antiquities* to contain 100 or 120 engravings (folio) to be issued in four numbers, quarterly. Price $100! Nine hundred subscribers will save me from loss, which is all I care for. I have no room for details and can only say that Mr. Catherwood has made several large drawings, which in the grandeur and interest of the subject and in picturesque effect are far superior to any that have ever appeared. It is intended that the execution shall be creditable to the country as a work of art. From the specimens of engravings which we have seen of *Audubon's* new works [he had just issued a smaller edition of his monumental *Birds of America* in seven volumes] we think that ours can be done in this country; if not, Mr. Catherwood will go over to Paris and have them executed there. The text is to be in English and French. Hon. Albert Gallatin will furnish an article and he will endeavor to procure one from Humboldt with whom he formed an intimate acquaintance while minister to France. I have written to Mr. Murray [John Murray, publisher] requesting him to apply to Sir James Wilkinson the best authority on all points of resemblance or supposed resemblance between American signs and symbols and those of Egypt. . . . The fourth and only other person to whom I thought of applying is yourself. I do so purely as a matter of business and in my estimate of expenses have allowed $250 and a copy of the work for an article from you. Please understand that I should not be willing to accept it without paying this sum which is fixed, not as the price of its value, but in reference to probable ability to pay. It need not contain more than 20 or 30 of your octavo pages and will not be wanted in less than a year [1844]."

Even the contemplation of such a work—Humboldt, Prescott, Gallatin, Wilkinson, Stephens, and Catherwood uniting in a single publication illustrated by one hundred engravings—is breath taking! To draw together such titans as these for a work on the ancient civilizations of America was in itself a grandiose project. Prescott readily accepted: "*American Antiquities* is a noble enterprice, and I hope it may find patronage. I believe there are several persons more competent than myself who could aid you in it. But if you think otherwise, I will supply an article of the length you propose, say five and twenty pages octavo, if it will be soon enough any time in May 1844. . . . Should you abandon the project hereafter from want of patronage, which is possible, you will let me know?"

The "great project" seemed assured. (Humboldt wrote that he would oblige "my dear friend Gallatin" as well as in "admiration of Mr. Stephens"). Even subscriptions at $100 to the "great project" were taken. But a new world was being born. And the *accoucheur* was Manifest Destiny.

James Polk—no one knew precisely why—had been nominated on the Democratic ticket for president and soon the Oregon question, summed up by the slogan "54–40 or fight," swept the land.

Texas was annexed by the outgoing President, John Tyler as a last act of office. Charles Goodyear perfected the vulcanizing process for rubber. Cyrus McCormick exhibited his reaper, and S. F. B. Morse put into practical application "that which God hath wrought." These were the voices of Manifest Destiny, the siren call of Expansion. No one could resist it. Antiquities, which had so long a hold on American imaginations, gave way with dramatic suddenness to the dynamic present. In the swelling, discordant voices of Expansion, Stephens' "great project" was drowned out; and the magnificent work-in-progress, the one hundred Catherwood engravings that were to be animated by the prose of Humboldt, Prescott, Gallatin, Wilkinson, and Stephens disappeared into history. Yet not altogether. Catherwood decided to continue the "great project" in a minor key. He left for England, bearing a letter of introduction from Prescott to Edward Everett, the American minister.

The "project" did not find receptivity in London, either, swept as that city was with Reform riots and its own expansion mood. "As regards the large work of Stephens and myself," Catherwood wrote to Prescott, "nothing has been finally agreed on. The booksellers say trade is bad, etc., the old story but I fear a very true one." Failing all else, Catherwood decided to publish the work himself. It was to consist of a series of twenty-five hand-colored lithographs, with map and letterpress by Stephens. Catherwood took the last of his savings, employed the finest of London's artists, and thus published the magnificent collection of lithographs on the Maya civilization.[6] In March, 1844, Catherwood's *Views of Ancient Monuments in Central America, Chiapis, and Yucatán* was published in London. Stephens, deeply immersed in Polk's election, was unable to supply the text, but Catherwood dedicated it to "my good friend, John L. Stephens." When the work was sent to Prescott, Catherwood asked for news of his friend.

"Stephens," Prescott wrote, "I have not heard from lately but Dr. Cabot who has entered the state of matrimony with every

[6] This work, *Views of Ancient Monuments in Central America, Chiapis, and Yucatán*, I have prepared for republication as part of the book *Frederick Catherwood, Archt.*, which I expect to publish soon.

prospect of happiness saw him the other day in New York and said his spirits seemed pretty good. I thought him rather under a cloud when I saw him there in April last. He shows great depth of feeling certainly. I think while his father lives he will not be much disposed to ramble again, at least so he told me. And in the meantime he is taking care of his own and his father's property and courting the law, but it is not easy to win much professional business when it is known that a man does not need it."

Stephens did more than "court the law"; he was courting that strumpet politics; he had succumbed to the enticements of "party." He was throwing (for a reason which will later reveal itself) his immense prestige behind the election of James Knox Polk for president. Few Americans had ever heard of Polk. A stiff, angular functionary with sharp gray eyes sunk in a lean face, his grizzled uncut hair—Tennessee fashion—overlapping his dandruff-covered black coat collar, Polk was not an impressive figure. His prestige, whatever there was of it, came from the fact that he was a strict party man, a friend of Old Hickory, whose legislation he had sponsored, while speaker of the House, with an almost mathematical precision. He was, to Americans at large, as obscure as Lincoln. When he was nominated, a steamboat on the Ohio River came bearing the news. An ardent Democrat called to a friend on the boat:

"Hullo, Smith, who is nominated for president?"

"James K. Polk of Tennessee."

"First rate. What, what did you say his name was?"

"All right," he said, turning to those Democrats about him, "three cheers for James K. Polk of Tennessee, the next president of these United States."

Henry Clay, the Whig candidate, opposed him in the election. If there had been no issues in the previous presidential election, they were abundant in 1844. "There are four great measures of my administration," Polk told George Bancroft, striking his thigh four times in emphasis, "a reduction of the tariff, the independent treasury, the settlement of the Oregon boundary dispute, and lastly the acquisition of California." It was this last issue with which John L. Stephens had political sympathy, for his interest in an interoceanic canal was hypothecated on a United States of America that stretched from sea to sea.

New York was the key state in the election; if Henry Clay should carry it, he would be elected. Stephens threw himself into the campaign with his wonted enthusiasm, for he felt that the acquisition of California depended on Polk's election. He knew, from information received in Washington, that England or France might forestall America. New Zealand had been acquired by the British in 1840, the French had taken the Marquesas, and the barbaric Hawaiian monarchs, hitherto friendly with American whaling men, had placed themselves under the protection of Queen Victoria. For Stephens' future plans, California must be American! The election was bitterly contested. Polk, getting only a 6,000 majority in New York, squeezed through with a majority of electoral votes and was elected president. Matters now moved with bewildering complexity; President Tyler as a last act of office, anticipating his successor in office, annexed Texas. And the Mexicans, as expected, broke off diplomatic relations. We now claimed Texas to extend to the left bank of the Río Grande. Polk, no sooner than his wife had rearranged the furniture in the White House, sent General Taylor with a detachment of troops to take up positions on the frontier; a young captain of the U. S. Engineers, John C. Frémont, was sent overland to California, ostensibly on an exploring expedition, but actually to be in California when action for its acquisition would be needed. Commodore Sloat, commanding the Pacific station, had secret orders to seize San Francisco the moment that he should "ascertain with certainty" that a state of war existed with Mexico. The pulse of the nation quickened. It stood on the edge of great events. The majority, it is true, did not want war with Mexico. Yet if war were necessary to satisfy the demon expansion, "let it come."

In upstate New York a conflict was already in progress, the "Helderberg War," as it was locally known. It had been in progress for some time. Ever since the death of the good patroon, Stephen Van Rensselaer, in 1839, a war had been waged between the much-landed gentry and their tenants of the upstate counties. "Nowhere in the America of the late eighteen-thirties," writes

Henry Christman in his excellent book *Tin Horns and Calico*,[7] "were the promises of the Declaration of Independence less fulfilled than in Albany. . . . Here was the seat of power of a landed aristocracy. . . . Under the patroon system, a few families, intricately intermarried, controlled the destinies of three hundred thousand people and ruled in almost kingly splendor over nearly two million acres of land." These lands were leased to tenants, seldom owned. Many tenants were in arrears in rent, and so long as Van Rensslaer lived, he ruled his domain with light, generous hands; but when he died and his sons found his tenants to be in arrears in rent to the sum of $400,000, they moved to foreclose.

That was the touchspring of revolt. There were mass meetings, tar barrels of fire, burning of writs, intimidations of sheriffs, and barn burnings, which led to the growth of a radical section of the Democratic party, the Barnburners. In sympathy, there sprang up antirent newspapers, antirent parties, and now, in the aftermath of the Helderberg War, a general conflagration—the antirent war. Sheriff Osman Steele was mortally wounded while trying to carry out a foreclosure procedure against the Barnburners, the governor called out the militia, the antirenters were arrested, and the trials which followed tore wide open the sectional jealousies, crossing party lines—Whig and Democrat. It became apparent that the laws of New York needed adjustment. A Constitutional Convention was called for June 1, 1846, to be held in Albany. Those elected from New York City were Charles O'Connor (famous as the lawyer of Jefferson Davis at his treason trial) and John L. Stephens. So popular was Stephens that he was selected to represent both Whig and Democratic parties.

Stephens took seat number twenty-seven in the great convention and was placed on the judiciary committee. One can follow his voting, almost always Jacksonian in outlook, in the huge *Journal of the Convention*. Although he had to go with the Democrats who cited the Bible to prove that the Negro was destined to occupy an inferior social position,[8] he sided with the antirenters in

[7] Henry Christman, *Tin Horns and Calico* (New York, 1945); quoted with the permission of the author.
[8] Stephens to George W. Randolph (MS letter in the possession of Albert Williams, Houston, Texas):

their demands for an elective judiciary to break the system of the domination of privileged men. Stephens' performance was remembered by James Starbuck, secretary to the Convention: "Aug. 6, 1846 . . . Mr. Stephens spoke . . . sensibly and well on the motion to consider the Loomis report." Out of the clash of interests and of equivocal ambitions, Stephens assisted in procuring an anti-renters victory; the Convention approved an elective judiciary.

The war with Mexico was already in its third month when Stephens returned in October, 1846, from Albany. War had been inevitable from the beginning and, in many quarters, principally among New England intellectuals, it was violently opposed. But Polk had presented the Congress with a *fait accompli*. General Taylor, in setting up his blockade of Matamoras, had stung a crop of Mexican dragoons into action. There had been bloodshed. Polk gave before Congress on the eleventh of May, 1846, his famous war message beginning: ". . . the cup of Forbearance has been exhausted." Polk expected an easy victory. There was talk, in the flush of the first victories, of annexing Yucatán.

Frederick Catherwood, in the interim, had returned from England, after the publication of his *Views of Ancient Monuments*, his head filled with new plans. There was even some talk of an expedition to South America. "Stephens tells me," Prescott wrote to him, "you have talked of a trip to Peru. This is my ground, but

Convention Chambers
Albany   June 11, 1846.

George W. Randolph, Esq.
      Dear Sir,
           I hasten to acknowledge the receipt of your long and interesting communication on the subject of abolitionism for which I return you my warmest thanks. You may rest assured I shall endeavor to make the best possible use of it, and it will give you pleasure to learn, in this early stage of our proceedings, that so far as I understand public sentiment here, it is most decidedly against negro suffrage in any shape. I feel confident that our actions in this matter will [*one word illegible*] our state at least has this right feeling towards the South.
    Should I make any remarks I shall not fail to send them to you.
    Again returning you my thanks, and begging you will convey my acknowledgments to Mrs. Randolph.
           I am
           Very Respectfully
           Your Obedient Servant
           John L. Stephens

I suppose it will not be the worse for your mousing into the architectural antiquities, and I wish I could see the fruits of such a voyage in your beautiful illustrations." For Prescott, following the success of the *Conquest of Mexico*, had started the writing of the *Conquest of Peru*; as he wrote to Lord Morpeth: "I have been carrying on the Conquest of Peru while the Government has been making the Conquest of Mexico. But mine is the best of the two since it costs only the shedding of ink instead of blood and if I get ever so little fame by it that is better than the dirty superfluous acres which we shall get by the other Conquest."

But Catherwood did not get to Peru; instead, he returned to his profession of architect, designed residences for wealthy New Yorkers in the romantic Gothic style, a fountain for Gramercy Park, and entered a competition for a memorial to George Washington. Stephens, too, was involved in other matters. He became a founder member of the famous Century Club[9] in New York; the American Philosophical Society of Philadelphia recognized his great contributions by elevating him to a fellowship; he, with Catherwood, became founder members of the American Ethnological Society. Yet by the time that society had printed their second volume of proceedings in 1847, Catherwood and Stephens were no longer carried as "active members." Catherwood was building a railroad in the miasmic swamps of British Guiana, and Stephens was opening a steamship route to Europe.

The American armies, following the path of conquest of Hernán Cortés, were midway between Vera Cruz and Mexico City when the S. S. *Washington*, making oceanic history, sailed on June 1, 1847; on board, as vice-president–director of the line, was John Lloyd Stephens. His interest in steam navigation was helping to create one more link to bind the continents, for although not

[9] In 1846 John G. Chapman suggested a club, limited to one hundred members—hence the name "Century"—to be composed of artists and literary men only. Proposal letters were sent to the hundred selected, and to these, most responded. They met, on January 13, 1847, in the rotunda of the New York Gallery of Fine Arts in City Hall Park. The committee of management was composed of John L. Stephens, Gulian C. Verplanck, Asher B. Durand, David C. Colden, William Bryant, Gouverneur Kemble, John G. Chapman, and Charles M. Leupp. —*Memorial History of the City of New York*, III, 429.

one of the original incorporators of the Ocean Steam Navigating Company, Stephens had followed its development closely and invested some of his book profits in it. Now, on its maiden voyage, he was its representative.

As advertised, the S. S. *Washington* sailed on June 1 to Bremen, with its 120 passengers, first and second class, and its three special passengers, Major Hobbie of the Post Office Department who would attempt to make postal agreements with the Hansa free states and with England, Herr Schmidt, the son of Burgomeister Schmidt of Bremen, and John Lloyd Stephens, the representative of the *Washington*. Unfortunately for the *Washington's* reputation, it was beaten by the British steamer *Brittania*, which had left Boston two days after it had sailed. Major Hobbie, who represented "competition" to the Cunard liners, was coolly received in Southampton. The *London Times* called the *Washington*, even though $390,000 was spent upon her, "about as ugly a specimen of steamship building as ever went through this anchorage."

The reception was very different at Bremerhaven, however. The whole harbor was in a gala mood, banners flying from the ships, American and German flags flying side by side, giving color to the historic moment. An official dinner was given at the Hunter's Club, Burgomeister Schmidt presiding. The enthusiasm of the moment was so contagious that the orchestra leader composed on the spot "the Washington Polka." Major Hobbie, who had prepared for this moment by learning German, began haltingly in it and then changed to English, to which the good-natured gathering, glowing in the historical moment, paid a thumping tribute.[10] There was a succession of dancing and fireworks, Captain Hewlett of the *Washington* was introduced, and Herr Oelrichs, resident officer of the line, presented a model of the ship to the city. It was then announced that the next ship would be called the *Hermann* in honor of the German who delivered the Alemani from the Romans. Then, with great solemnity, Burgomeister Schmidt introduced "Herr Stephens, the great American Traveler, who opened New Worlds and Old." And as almost everyone present had read a summary of the German translation of his

[10] Frank C. Bowen, *A Century of Atlantic Travel* (London, 1936).

Yucatán book, which was eventually to be published in book form,[11] they welcomed Stephens with a standing ovation.

After the reception Stephens left for Berlin. "There was but one object in it," he wrote of his quick trip to the German capital, ". . . to see . . . Humboldt. I might visit Berlin again," he said, "the other monuments of the city would remain but Humboldt might pass away."

Stephens had called upon Mr. Charles Donaldson, the American minister, to see if he might arrange an introduction to Humboldt, but there he learned much to his regret that the great man, in feeble health, was with the king at Potsdam and unable to receive visitors. When he called upon Baron von Ronne, formerly Prussian minister to Washington, he expressed his disappointment at not being able to visit the famous explorer. "He stopped me abruptly and, with friendly earnestness, said that I must not leave Berlin without seeing Baron Humboldt, at the same time looking at his watch, calling up my servant, telling him that the cars for Potsdam started at twelve; and hastily writing a line of introduction, without allowing me time for acknowledgements, he hurried me off to my carriage. A brisk ride brought me to the depot, just in time for the cars; three quarters of an hour carried us to Potsdam and almost before I had recovered from my surprise I was at Baron Humboldt's residence.

"Ascending to the door of his apartment I was disappointed anew by positive word from the servant in attendance, that the Baron would *not* receive any visitors that day. With very little hope of success, I left my letter and card, with an intimation that I would call again at two o'clock. On my return the expression on the servant's face as he opened the door relieved me of all apprehension."

Stephens had encountered that tyrant of servants, the celebrated "Seifert," a rotund, square-headed man of fifty, who had served Humboldt most of his adult life and now in his twilight years lorded over his debility. He showed Stephens into an adjoining apartment. Baron Humboldt came toward him with the flattering greeting "that no letter of introduction was necessary."

As if in a dream Stephens had come face to face with "the

greatest man since Aristotle." All his life Stephens had heard the name "Humboldt." At Columbia College he had read in the original Humboldt's *Voyage Aux Regions Équinoxiales*[12] and had followed the great traveler, wide-eyed, through his ascent of the Orinoco. He had seen, on booksellers' shelves, locked behind glass, the beautiful hand-colored aquatints that illustrated the archaeological phases of his universal interests. "Humboldt" had been on the lips of Americans as long as the names of Washington, Franklin, or Jefferson.

It seemed hardly possible to believe that the man who had made more contributions to positive sciences than any other before him was also, in the same breath, a diplomat, a geographer, an archaeologist, and above all a friend of America. Col. John C. Frémont, not many years before, had sprinkled the name "Humboldt" on rivers, mountains, and cities until it was famous throughout the American earth. Time was riding fast now for the celebrated Humboldt, for, born in 1769, he was, at the time of Stephen's visit, seventy-eight years of age. Even then he was to outlive the discoverer of the Maya by seven years, and to die ten years short of a century of existence.

"I was entirely mistaken," Stephens wrote, "in the idea I had formed of his personal appearance, and was surprised at not finding him bowed down and bent by age. Nearly half a century ago, he had filled the first place in the world of letters, sitting as it were, upon a throne, lighting up the pathway of science to the philosopher, and teaching the schoolboy at his desk. He was recorded in the annals of a long generation. Indeed, his reign had been so long and his fame went back so far, that until I saw him bodily I had almost regarded him as a part of history, and belonging to the past; even then, alone and in the stillness of the palace, I could hardly keep from looking at him as something monumental, receiving the tribute of posthumous fame.

"The ruined cities of America being the means of bringing me

[11] John Lloyd Stephens, *Begebenheiten auf einer Reise in Yucatán*, Deutsch von Dr. N. N. W. Meissner (Leipzig, 1853), *xviii*, 438 pp., plates, maps, plans.

[12] See Victor Wolfgang von Hagen, *South America Called Them* (New York, 1945).

to his acquaintance, were, of course, the first subject referred to, but learning my connection with the line of steamers to Bremen was the immediate object which had brought me to Germany, he expressed his satisfaction that I was identified with an enterprise at that moment interesting to Germany. He considered the action of our government in establishing the line, wise and statesmanlike, as for a commercial people like ours, it must be the means of opening relations and a wide field for the enterprise of our citizens. He himself felt a lively interest in its success, believing that the Germans of all classes were desirous of direct intercourse with us; that they had a great variety of manufactures which might be exchanged to advantage for the large amount of our staples now consumed in that country, when more frequent intercourse should give a better knowledge of each other's wants and resources; as between the United States and Germany there never could be any feeling of rivalry, or any cause of collision, and the closer we could be drawn together, the better it would be for both countries.

"Outside of Europe, Mexico seemed to be the country which interested him most; perhaps from the connection with those countries which had brought me to his acquaintance, or, more probably because it was the foundation of his own early fame. He spoke of Mr. Prescott's History of the Conquest [of Mexico] and said that I might, when the opportunity offered, to say to that gentleman, as from himself, that there was no historian of the age, in England or Germany, equal to him.

"I had occupied, without any interruption, more than an hour of Baron Humboldt's time, when Seifert entered to summon him to dinner with the king . . . he urged me to remain a few days for the purpose of making certain acquaintances at Berlin, and pressed as he was, insisted upon giving me a line to a distinguished gentleman of Berlin, without seeing whom he said, I ought not to leave. Circumstances did not permit me to deliver the letter; but I had the satisfaction of bringing it home with me, written in German, in a strong firm hand an autograph of *Humboldt*.[13]

13 John Lloyd Stephens, "An Hour with Humboldt," Littel's *Living Age Magazine*, Vol. XV (1847), 151 ff.

Chapter xxi ○○ ○○ Two months after James Wilson Marshall (in that famous January of 1848) found gold in California, John Lloyd Stephens disappeared from New York. He was no longer seen in his usual haunts—sipping ice-brandy at Delmonico's, thumbing through the latest books at Bartlett and Welford's in the Astor House, or talking politics with William Cullen Bryant at the office of the *Evening Post*. His father, the Honorable Benjamin Stephens, bent with age, met all inquiries for him at their splendid 13 Leroy Place residence with polite misinformation. Stephens had been seen in Washington dining with Senator Tom Benton and the tempest in crinolines, his daughter Jessie Benton Frémont, and his friends knew that he had taken dinner with President Polk, along with a few other gentlemen of business and politics, including the handsome William H. Aspinwall, owner of the Pacific Mail Steamship Company.[1] After that, he disappeared from the American scene.

Then suddenly, in November, 1848, and without explanations, Stephens was back again in New York. Charming as usual, with his flow of anecdotes, Stephens used conversation to hide his thoughts. The only hint of his activities, given more by his company than his conversation, was his close intimacy with the elegantly bearded Mr. Baldwin. Obviously the mystery was not connected with the literary; James Baldwin was a well-known railroad surveyor.

After the 1848 election, Stephens settled in Washington. Polk, worn out by the four vigorous years of "Manifest Destiny," refused to try again for the presidency, passing on his baton to Lewis Cass (who many years ago had reviewed Stephens' *Arabia Pe-*

[1] "I gave a Cabinet dinner to-day at which were present all members of the cabinet . . . Senators . . . Dr. Foltz of the Navy, Mr. Aspenwall [*sic*] . . . and Stevens [Stephens] of N. York, the latter the traveller.—Polk's *Diary*, December 14, 1848, Vol. IV, 235.

traea), an ardent expansionist who received the Democratic nomination. It was not enough. There was a split Democratic ticket; Martin Van Buren, running for the presidency on the Barnburners' radical Democratic ticket, exerted enough diversion to split the vote and usher in the Whigs once again. "Old Rough and Ready" Zachary Taylor, the hero of Buena Vista, was elected president.

Stephens, at least in this election, was above partisan politics. He hardly had time for it. In Washington through November as the election returns kept pouring in, he was closeted in the home of Senator Tom Benton ("we pronounce it Bane-ton, Sir"), the senior senator from Missouri. An ardent Jacksonian, Benton had entered the Senate in 1820 and had since been a commanding figure on the floor—his surging periods of eloquence drowning out all Whiggish opposition by his roaring, with deep-seated conviction: "Nobody opposes Benton, Sir . . . Benton and the people are one, synonymous terms, Sir, synonymous terms." Now in the fatal year 1848, Thomas Hart Benton, feeling his sixty-five years (but with fight still in the timbre of his voice), and inwardly shaken by the events leading to his son-in-law's court-martial, prepared to wage a great Senatorial fight for North America's first great extra-territorial project—the Panama Railroad. Thoroughly familiar with the eloquent tricks of Senate memorials, Benton checked Stephens' drafts, and then, when he was fully satisfied, it was submitted to both houses on December 1, 1848. The mystery of Stephens' six months' disappearance was solved on December 11, when to both houses of Congress there was read:

Memorial
of
Wm. H. Aspinwall, John L. Stephens and Henry Chauncey
in reference
To the construction of a Railroad across the Isthmus of Panama[2]

Stephens was to realize the dream of the centuries: the connection of the two oceans with a practical means of transport—a railroad was to lead, inevitably, to the Canal.

[2] 30 Cong., 2 sess., *Senate Misc. Doc. No. 1*, Memorial, December 11, 1848.

The Congressional piece, although couched in the stuffy language of a Congressional memorial, was still the prose of Stephens. It is instructive to listen to a portion of it again: "That the acquisition of California and the settlement of our boundary line in Oregon have opened a new era in the history of this country . . . the mildness of the climate, the richness of the soil, the great promise of mineral wealth and above all, the long coast with the magnificent harbors of the Pacific. . . . At this moment, hundreds of young men full of enterprise, from our Eastern States, are buffeting the storms of Cape Horn, while, with the coming spring, the hardy pioneers of the west will be moving by thousands over the desolate prairies, or climbing the rugged steeps of the Rocky Mountains . . . no means of returning or of personal intercourse with friends at home except by the stormiest passage ever known at sea, or the most toilsome journey ever made by land.

"In view of this condition of things, and, to hold out some encouragement to emigrants that they might not be virtually expatriated when upon their own soil . . . there was established a monthly mail steamer from New York to Chagres [Panama], on the Atlantic . . . and on the Pacific side, to California and Oregon.

"The Isthmus of Panama is about fifty miles in breadth—less than on any part of the continent of America; and from the falling off of the great range of Cordilleras, running from the Rocky Mountains to the Andes, it has always been considered as the region in which, if ever, an easy communication would be effected, either by canal or road, between the two seas. . . . The route over it is probably worse now than in the early days of Spanish dominion . . . no wheel carriage has ever attempted to cross it in the present mode. . . .

"The Pacific Mail Company, charged with the transportation of the mail from Panama to California and Oregon, comprising your memorialists [i.e., Aspinwall, Stephens, and Chauncey] . . . saw the necessity, for their own interest, of improving the road across the isthmus. . . . One of their associates [John Lloyd Stephens], to whom the execution of this work [an exploration of the Isthmus for a railroad] was intrusted . . . passed the winter on the isthmus, attended by two engineers [James Baldwin and Colonel

G. W. Totten] of high standing, who, besides making general observations upon the face of the country, commenced a regular survey at high water mark on the shore of the Pacific, and carried it across the Cordilleras down to the first stream that empties into the Atlantic. . . .

"Impressed with the importance . . . involving the prosperity of California and Oregon and the welfare of all who are in any way connected with our citizens in those territories; and regarding it as vitally affecting the best interests of our government, in a political and pecuniary point of view and having under their control the maps, drawings and other information procured by the Pacific Mail Company, your memorialists have secured to themselves an exclusive grant . . . for ninety-nine years from the republic of New Granada [Colombia], for constructing a railroad across the isthmus of Panama, and they, the memorialists, have come before your honorable body to ask the co-operation and aid necessary for carrying out this great American work."

There had been, in the past, a plethora of talk; and the public, as was to be expected, was apathetic, not because a communication across the Isthmus was not desired, but because they had heard without cease, ever since the troubled times of Simón Bolívar, about the connection of the two oceans by canal or rail. Every year new companies were formed to break the back of the Andes, and, like the eternal melting of the winter's snows, investors lost their money, and the ill-conditioned Isthmian explorers left their bloated corpses in the amoral embrace of the jungle. There was a difference, howover, with this, the latest project; John Lloyd Stephens, the eminent traveler, was connected with it—and he, as they soon learned, provided the wellsprings of action. On December 28, 1848, seventeen days after the "Memorial" was read in Congress, Stephens made his appearance before General Pedro Alcántara Herrán, minister plenipotentiary for the Republic of New Granada in Washington, and turned over to him in specie 600,000 francs ($120,000), and the Isthmian grant was in operation, even though General Herrán had the sum placed in the vaults of the New York Life Insurance Company pending ratification of

274

the treaty with his government. The vacillation of a half-century was at an end. The speed of Stephens' negotiations was bewildering: he had within six months made with Baldwin and Totten a survey of the Isthmian situation, he had presented his memorial to Congress with strong Senatorial backing from Thomas Benton and T. Butler King, and the 600,000 francs—as the *deus ex machina* of the Colombian contract—had been paid. Stephens' good fortune held up to the very end, and a concatenation of events made possible the Isthmian railroad, the great project that was to transform America into a world power.

General Pedro Alcántara Herrán had come to Washington, in the autumn of 1848, to campaign quietly for the passage of the reciprocal treaty between New Granada and the United States in connection with the Isthmus. In 1846, after the acquisition of California, the representatives of the two countries signed a treaty, subject to ratification in their respective legislative bodies, in which, for certain commercial concessions, the United States guaranteed (may the ghosts of broken promises rest in peace) New Granada's sovereignty over the Isthmus. Ratified by the New Granadian Senate after a short violent debate in May, 1847, the treaty provided for reciprocal commercial arrangements in peace and war, guaranteeing "the right of way or transit across the isthmus of Panama upon any modes of communication that now [in 1846] exist, or that may be hereafter constructed, shall be open and free to the Government and citizens of the United States and for the transportation of any articles . . . of lawful commerce, belonging to the citizens of the United States."

There had been much international interest in an Isthmian canal. The French, English, Spanish, Dutch, and the Americans had essayed adventures that had made Granada very uneasy over her nominal sovereignty of the Isthmian route. The treaty with America was not, as interpreted, "a favored nation treaty" but a prototype of treaty which Granada hoped to develop with other interested powers. But President Polk, directing the expansion ogre—the Mexican War, California, Texas, Oregon—showed nothing of his usual impatience for ratification. Thus General Herrán, envoy sufficiently extraordinary, arrived in Washington to try, through conferences with Senatorial "whips," to get the treaty to the floor for ratification. This he accomplished in June, 1848. His presence in Washington was providential, for his position as envoy allowed him in the name of the government to sign the contract with Stephens and associates, sealed with the security of 600,000 gold francs. For at that precise moment, the French concession, held by Augustin Salomon et Compagnie since 1838, had terminated due to the failure of their agent, M. Mateo Klein, to put up the 600,000 francs demanded as security. June 6, 1848, was the deadline. A day later the treaty confession was forfeit. America, or rather, an American, that is, John Lloyd Stephens, seized the initiative.

Stephens did not dream the Isthmian dream; he gave it substance. Ever since the blood-drenched days of the *quattrocento*, man had though of finding a strait to Cathay and the spiceries. That had been the impulse that had sent Columbus to the West— not in search of new worlds, but an entrance to the old.

In 1833, the Republic of New Granada opened negotiations with several world powers—Great Britain, France, Spain, The Netherlands, and the United States—for financial assistance to build the canal. And that, too, came to nothing. Then the New Granadian Congress authorized its government to conclude a contract with any group—be they individual or organization—to scoop out a canal, or, failing that, to construct through the seemingly bottomless miasmas a rail line or a macadamized road.

Now the French seized the initiative. Baron Charles de Thierry, London born of a French *émigré* family, with a Cambridge education, arrived in the United States in a penurious state. Finding that there one must work for a living, he departed for the West Indies. At Guadeloupe he met a Jewish merchant capitalist, Augustin Salomon,[3] to whom he expatiated upon the advantages to be derived from an Isthmian canal as a shorter route to his holdings in New Zealand. He managed to convince M. Salomon. They formed a syndicate, *Augustin Salomon et Compagnie*, and for the

[3] Gerstle Mack, *The Land Divided: A History of the Panama Canal and Other Isthmian Canal Projects* (New York, 1944), wherein is summarized from the literature the historical connections of Augustin Salomon and the Panama Canal, pp. 126–27.

next ten years it held a monopoly on all Isthmian projects. After years of comic-opera projects, the climax came when their engineer, the great Napoleon Garella, famous for his engineering works in the Alps, wanted to tunnel the Isthmus so as to allow ships to pass through it. The idea of the canal once again fell into its place in the museum of ideas—yet a railroad seemed practical, even though Garella's survey could locate no pass lower than 675 feet.

The canal—definitely beyond the technics of the time—gave way to the idea of a rail line. In 1846, the government of New Granada signed with M. Mateo Klein, an emissary of Salomon et Compagnie,[4] an exclusive contract to build (and to operate for ninety-nine years) "an iron railroad across the Isthmus of Panama." On paper, at least, the organization called "The Panama Company" appeared as a financial power, with a British banker, William Henry Bainbridge, and Sir John Campbell, an official of the Oriental Steam Company, named in the directorate. Had this organization been able to carry through this project, the "passage" would have been in the hands of a non-American power—contrary, at least in an American interpretation, to the Monroe Doctrine. Eventually it would have stifled the passage to California and Oregon, and the whole American structure of an ocean-to-ocean nation endangered. Providentially for the United States, France was suddenly precipitated into another revolution and its pyramided financial speculations fell with the closing of the Bourse. Augustin Salomon fell with it. He was unable in July, 1846, to comply with Article IV of the contract—"The company shall give as security for the fulfillment of the obligations—six hundred thousand francs." The whole contract was forfeit. America was given one more opportunity to control its destiny.

And now enters the discoverer of the Maya.

John Lloyd Stephens had long been aware of the necessity of

[4] A member of the French Consulate at Panama was irate at this contract and, hinting at Salomon's Semitic origin, wrote: "The Keys of the world are here [at Panama]: but the name of Señor Salomon does not seem to me sufficiently Christian to qualify him for the role of their guardian, St. Peter."—Adolphe Denain, *Ensayo sobre los intereses politicos i commerciales del istmo de Panamá* (Panama City, 1844), 2.

North America's controlling the passage to the Pacific. That interest had made him take, on his own initiative and at his own expense, a troubled and dangerous expedition in Nicaragua in 1840, while he alternately searched for governments and Maya ruins. His secret report to John Forsyth of the possibilities of the "Nicaraguan Passage" was the most accurate that the United States possessed. But in the tangled jungles of Nicaragua "the scales," as he wrote, "fell from my eyes"; for he knew that the Nicaragua canal project was of a complicated nature. Yet he challenged the New York bankers in print to undertake it.

When the Panama project slipped into the hands of the French syndicate, Stephens' chagrin was tempered by the knowledge of an important, much overlooked fact: the terrain. He knew that any project carried elements of disaster if those involved approached that tropical terrain in ignorance. His Panama agent kept an eye on the progress of the French organization. And the "canal idea" was a subject of conversation between Stephens and Humboldt when they met at Potsdam. Even at that time Stephens apparently believed that the French syndicate could not carry through their project. He watched for the break in negotiations. Humboldt had always desired to see the Americans build their own canal, and he read Stephens a passage from the *Conversations with Eckermann:* "Humboldt," wrote the aged Goethe from Weimar in 1827, "with his thorough knowledge of the problem, has indicated several places. . . . But I ask myself whether the United States will let this opportunity slip through their fingers. It may be foreseen that this young state, with its decided predilection to the West will, in thirty or forty years, have occupied . . . the land . . . beyond the Rocky Mountains. . . . It is absolutely indispensable for the United States to effect a passage from the Mexican Gulf to the Pacific Ocean; and I am certain that they will do it. Would that I might live to see it!"

It was John Lloyd Stephens who gave substance to Goethe's dream. He was the motivating force behind the formation of the triumvirate of the Panama Railroad Company—Aspinwall, Stephens, and Chauncey—and they were dependent on his knowledge, his enthusiasm, and his energy. But it was a clever combination. William H. Aspinwall already had hold of the southern flank, so to speak; he owned the Pacific Mail Steamship Company which maintained communications on the Pacific side from Panama to Oregon. A Columbia College graduate, Aspinwall was a young man with a Midas touch. He had joined the mercantile-shipping firm of his uncles, G. C. and Samuel Howland, and by 1832, at the age of twenty-five, he was a member of the firm which operated clipper ships to the West Indies, to China, and to England. In April, 1848, he incorporated the Pacific Mail Steamship Company and put into operation the steam-driven vessels *California*, *Oregon*, and *Panama*, investing a considerable portion of his half-million in the California project. Yet business alone did not absorb him. He collected paintings (he opened his private museum to the public once a week), and was the first vice-president of the organization which became the Metropolitan Museum. His interest in literature, while that of a collector and patron, was not wholly sterile, as a director of the Astor-Lenox Library he helped form the policies that eventuated in the great New York Public Library.

The third member of the triumvirate was Henry Chauncey, a quiet, unassuming capitalist worth, in 1848, the not insignificant sum of $200,000. He had been born on April 3, 1795, in Middletown, Connecticut, a descendant of the Reverend Charles Chauncey, the second president of Harvard College. Early in his life, through family connections, he entered business in New York. His interests were far flung: crockery, mining, and railroads. He had, besides, investments in a copper mine in Valparaiso, Chile, and this attracted him to the Panama project.

These three men, Stephens, Aspinwall, and Chauncey, raised the initial $120,000 necessary to secure the contract. In April, 1849, they incorporated the Panama Railroad Company in Albany with a capital stock of $1,000,000 (with liberty to increase to $5,000,000).[5]

[5] The incorporators were: William Aspinwall, John L. Stephens, Henry Chauncey, James Brown, Cornelius W. Lawrence, Gouverneur Kemble, Thomas W. Ludlow, David Thompson, Joseph B. Varnum, Samuel S. Howland, Prosper M. Wetmore, Edwin Bartlett, and Horatio Allen.

Speed was a factor in the building of the road; even though the contract called for eight years, Stephens wanted it done in three. The reasons were obvious. The British, out to checkmate "Manifest Destiny," had seized the Mosquito Coast—including the mouth of the San Juan river which led to the interior Nicaraguan lakes. Lord Palmerston, who had returned to power in the Foreign Office, was not going to allow America to have a monopoly on the passage to the South Sea. There had already been clashes between American and British ships at Greytown in Nicaragua, an ugly international situation that only ended in the consummation of the Clayton-Bulwer Treaty. As speed was important, Stephens and associates asked for an annual government subsidy of $250,-000. The chairman of the House Naval Committee, Thomas Butler King of Georgia, a vigorous advocate of governmental subsidies for incipient monopolies, reported favorably to the House on the Panama Railroad; his argument: ". . . that without efficient aid from government, the memorialists [i.e., Stephens, Aspinwall, and Chauncey] will probably be compelled, as all others, who have moved in this matter hitherto have been, to abandon the undertaking." Moreover, King, as few others, was impressed with Stephens' vision that the railroad treaty would be "but a simple advertisement to all the world that . . . we will, with the permission of New Granada, cross the isthmus of Panama and you must not interfere."[6] Thus the Naval Affairs Committee recommended it without reservation as did Jefferson Davis, chairman, Committee of Military Affairs. There were powerful voices in the Senate, too, although Senator Tom Benton had lost much of his value since his break with President Polk over the court-martial of his son-in-law, Colonel Frémont.

Polk did not like the sponsors of the Panama Railroad Bill, and he raised his voice against it. As he says in his diary: "*Tuesday, 30th January 1849*— . . . some of the Cabinet engaged in a conversation in which Mr. Buchanan led, about the practicability of making a road across the Istmus [*sic*] or at some other point, and seemed to treat the subject as though it was within the constitu-

[6] *House Report No. 26*, January 16, 1849: *Railroad Across the Isthmus of Panama.*

tional competency of the Government of the U. S. to apply public money in the form of a contract with a company to make the road. I listened to the conversation for some time, when I arrested it by expressing a decided opinion that no such power existed. And in relation to the Bill [30th Cong. 2 sess., 382, on the "Panama Railway"] now before Congress which proposed to pay to Aspinwall, Stephens and others $250,000 per annum for 20 years, to enable them to construct a road across the Istmus [sic], I informed the Cabinet that if it passed I should veto it. I consider that the Government possesses no constitutional power to apply the public money either within or without the U. S. for any such purpose. I stated that I considered the proposition of that Bill as but little better than a proposition to plunder the Treasury, & that it should never pass with my approval."

The Panama Railroad project went on, without government aid. Aspinwall tightened his hold on the Pacific side of the communications, while in the Atlantic—in effective monopoly—"Live-Oak" George Law threw new vessels into the traffic between New York and Panama. A self-made man, Irish-born George Law was as ruthless, as soulless, as a corporation head could be. His face brick red from an excess of drink—which never seemed to becloud his cold calculations—George Law was, over and above being the president of the Dry Dock Bank, an owner of railroads and canals. He operated the Atlantic connection to the Isthmus, and when stock was offered by the Panama Railroad company, he became, through many proxies, one of its principal and most influential stockholders.

Stephens had not been idle. He managed to have assigned to the railroad a group of engineers directed by Lieutenant Colonel George W. Hughes of the United States Topographical Corps, and they, accompanied by Stephens and James Baldwin, left for the Isthmus in April, 1849, to make a final survey. The previous year Stephens had discovered a pass through the divide at 337 feet elevation (the lowest heretofore known had been 625 feet), and this knowledge was the topographical secret that made possible the railroad, for steam engines could pull a pay load up that grade.

This time, the engineering expedition found even a lower gap (at 275 feet above the level of the sea). Of his survey Colonel Hughes made a detailed report to the Secretary of State; he confirmed Stephens' contention that the rail line was practicable. After that, it was again in the hands of the Panama Railroad, or more properly, those of John Lloyd Stephens.

Stephens had found, very fortunately, two American engineers with tropical experience, the hard-bitten John Cresson Trautwine and George M. Totten. They had both finished a battle of climate by digging the Canal del Dique, an artificial waterway that linked Río Magdalena—the fluvial highway of Colombia—with its chief port, Cartagena. They arrived rich with experience. Trautwine, still in his thirties, already bore on his full-bearded face the scars of the enervating climate of the tropics. He had been born in Philadelphia in 1810, had studied engineering with William Strickland, and became an early railroad pioneer as chief engineer for the Wilmington and Baltimore Railroad. In addition to his work on the Canal del Dique and the Panama Railroad, he was to survey the Inter-Ocean Railroad in Honduras and build a portion of it. He is still remembered for *Trautwine's Civil Engineer's Pocket Book*.

George Totten, as amiable as Trautwine was ferocious, was a Norwich University graduate who attained his engineering majority in constructing the Canal del Dique. He was as much a diplomat as he was an engineer. He had to be. Out of the tropical potpourri of swamp, malaria, physical corrosion, lethargic Panameños, ill-mannered, hustling Americans, gold fever and Chagres fever; out of a jumbled chaos of nationalities—Chinese, Colombians, Jamaican Negroes, Irishmen, and Germans—Totten was to build the railroad, and, moreover, to remain as its chief engineer until 1875, when the great Ferdinand de Lesseps was to name him *chef de corps* of his scandal-ridden Panama Canal project.

Under Stephens' leadership—he had been made vice-president of the railway—the materials of the great project were gathered, ships chartered, and the whole complex paper plan put into movement for the building of the first transcontinental railroad. Anyone who had experience building railroads in the tropics—and persons of this stripe were almost nonexistent—were asked to submit suggestions. Curiously enough the most valued opinions came from Catherwood—Frederick Catherwood, C.E. (Civil Engineer, no longer Arch^t); for since 1845 Catherwood had been bogged down in British Guiana building the first railroad in South America. Self-taught in engineering, although he knew surveying through his training as an architect, Catherwood had taken, even as Stephens, a profound interest in railroads.

In 1845 the sugar planters of British Guiana had proposed a railroad along its miasmic coast to connect the outlying sugar plantations on the Demerara River with Georgetown, the colony's capital. Catherwood, having submitted his qualifications to the London Committee, was chosen engineer-in-chief of the proposed railroad, and proceeded in his usual taciturn, workmanlike manner to make a survey of railroads in America and Jamaica. He arrived in British Guiana in December, 1845, to make the final surveys, and on August 17, 1847, the first railway in South America began its slow progress down the coast. There were, as was to be expected, violent disagreements—Catherwood had become increasingly querulous—costs were higher than anticipated, and there were unexpected developments, such as the necessity of establishing company-sponsored *bordellos* to release the energies of the imported workmen. The pitch-pine ties that Catherwood brought from Savannah were only a toothsome morsel to the termites, and these had to be replaced with lignum vitae, hard as iron and as difficult to shape. Catherwood did not help the difficulties by fighting with His Excellency the Governor over the ceremonies of turning over the first sod of the first South American railway.[7] In May, 1849, several thousand pounds and eight miles of rail line

[7] These details of Catherwood's construction of a railroad in South America were taken from reports discovered by the author in Georgetown, British Guiana, and were typed for him from the originals:

1. "Report of the London Committee, April 15, 1847, by Frederick Catherwood, esq., C.E."
2. "Report of Mr. F. Catherwood C.E. on the Construction of a Railway from Georgetown to Mahaica."
3. Sydney H. Bayley, "Railways in British Guiana."
These will be used more completely in the book, *Frederick Catherwood, Arch^t.*

later, Catherwood's agreement was terminated "for reasons of economy." He left for Panama.

In a drenching rain, on the verdure-engulfed embankment of Gorgona overlooking the Río Chagres, Stephens and Catherwood embraced. With the specter of death peering over their shoulders, for they were both infected with malaria, they were to work together for the last time. Now they were to open not an old world but a new one. And Catherwood agreed to take over temporarily the administration, while Stephens, with high purpose, left for South America.

It was only the "great enterprise" that would have sent Stephens eight thousand feet high to sign the agreements with the Republic of New Granada at Bogotá. It was, however, something like old times—the odor of vanilla and banana, the ardent hues of the bougainvillea that covered the dwellings in Cartagena—the great lichen-covered walls of the fortress—the amiable chatter of the Latin Americans. He crossed the swampy delta of the Río Magdalena, took passage on an ancient side-wheeler up New Granada's main artery of trade and communication, the Río Magdalena. At Honda, the end of navigation, he mounted a small mule and climbed the side of the Andes to heaven-high Bogotá. Riding the edge of precipitous slopes offered nothing exciting to one who had traveled through three thousand miles of revolution and jungles in Central America, or the length and breadth of Russia. But this time there was an accident. Stephens' mule, half way to Bogotá, startled by falling earth, bolted and unseated him. Stephens was thrown violently to the ground, striking the small of his back on a rock, chipping the vertebra. It paralyzed his lower extremities.

In writhing agony he directed the natives to build him a palanquin and on it he was carried to Santa Fé de Bogotá. He allowed himself several days of rest, then made his visit to the American Embassy carried on a pillowed stretcher, his twisted spine encased in bandages. He allowed nothing to stem his activity. In the protracted negotiations he had the active assistance of the American Embassy, as we know from a letter written by Thomas M. Foote, chargé d'affaires at Bogotá, to the Secretary of State:

"Mr. John L. Stephens, Vice-President of the Panama Railway Company, has just concluded [June 21, 1850] in behalf of that Company a new and advantageous contract with the Government here. As the undertaking in which he is engaged is highly honorable to American enterprise, and promises, when completed, to be eminently useful to the commercial world and especially to the United States, I felt it my duty to promote as far as I could properly the objects of his visit to this capital."

Carried to the Presidential Palace on his bed, Stephens, on June 20, 1850, signed with Victoriano de Diego Paredes, the foreign minister of New Granada, a new contract for the building of the Panama Railway, "the exclusive right of building a railroad between the two oceans across the Isthmus of Panama." In the sixty-one articles that constituted the contract "to bridge the oceans," Stephens was laying down—and knowingly—the means by which one day America would build a canal which would fulfill four centuries of dreams. How many men had left their swollen carcasses in the jungle, how many ships had been sunk, how much of the royal fifth of usurped Inca gold had been lost, how many cities had been destroyed into archaeological heaps before John L. Stephens, New Yorker, completed the final contractional arrangements to link the oceans? Goethe, who envisioned the link, had long since died, but in the royal palace at Potsdam, the aging, gray-thatched Humboldt nodded his head in approval.

In June, 1850, still carried on his litter, Stephens made a Zarathustra-like descent from the Colombian Andes to the Río Magdalena. At Cartagena he met engineer George Totten, who had come to drum up workers for the Panama road. The sea voyage to Jamaica seemed to give Stephens new strength (physically he seemed to have suffered more than he realized). Yet the pallor did not leave his face. He walked with a slight limp, his left shoulder drooped, deep laughter caused a spasm of pain in his chest. He no longer smoked the interminable black stogies.

The vessel paused at the Isle of Jamaica; and Stephens, feeling the exhilaration of that halcyon tropic background, made a rapid tour, filling his notebook in the hope of writing a book on Jamaica. It never materialized. When he arrived in New York, he found that in his absence he had been elected president of the Panama Railway Company.

Then there came a strange light in his eyes. Did he know that an infection was making headway in his wasted body? He made elaborate jests about it. But he seemed to sense that he was soon to die. One day when in Washington Stephens was at the Benton residence. Over a third cup of tea he leaned toward Jessie Benton Frémont and in a light tone said: "You must be very good to me, for some day soon perhaps, I'll be sent to the Isthmus to die." Yet he gave no evidence of a decline. He was indefatigable, as usual. When he returned to Panama, in August, 1850, actual work on the railroad had already started.

Like the disjointed neck of a garroted turkey, the twisting Panama land lies between the seventh and ninth latitudes north, a jungle-choked nexus of land that held the mastery of the world. Assailed by winds of the *chubasco* on its Caribbean side, Panama is deluged between April and December by an annual rainfall of 150 inches. Nurtured by these rains, the earth's warm and luscious body throws out an exuberant wealth of vegetation. Trees crowd closely upon one another, with delicately flowered parasites hanging on their branches, great aerophytes holding up spined leaves to catch the ever present moisture and wrist-thick lianas, rooted somewhere in the humid earth, twist from tree to tree until whole sections of forest are woven into a single element. So humid the atmosphere, so moisture laden the air, so luxurious the warm embrace of the jungle that earth is not a requisite for growth; a year unattended and man's work is smothered by a bewildering complexity of growing plants. The whole of Panama's 430 long miles of twisting earth is covered, from sea-battered shore to jagged antillean peak, with insistent verdure. Indian cultures came to terms with this environment and developed high civilizations, which left in the ordered disarray of their graves beautiful, fantastically cast gold ornaments encrusted with green emeralds, or placques of hammered *repoussé* gold, representations of ancient Coclé gods. These profusions of golden ornaments Columbus saw, and he called the whole mystically defined area "Golden Castille."

The first shanty built off the coast above the Río Chagres.

Woodcut from *Harper's Monthly Magazine*, January, 1859

Stephens' cottage on the Río Chagres.

Woodcut from *Harper's Monthly Magazine*, January, 1859

Terminus of the Panama Railway below Panama City. *This was the rally ing point of the Californians, the gold miners, and the adventurers of three continents.*

Woodcut from *Harper's Monthly Magazine*, January, 1859

Stephens' tree.

Woodcut from *Harper's Monthly Magazine*,
January, 1859

The Stephens residence at 13 Leroy Place, Greenwich Village. *From a drawing by Andrew J. Davis, engraved by Dick.*

Courtesy The New-York Historical Society, New York City

Broadway. *The Astor House, at No. 7, is the Astor House Bookshop of Bartlett and Welford.*

Courtesy Old Print Shop, Inc.

John Lloyd Stephens at the age of forty. *From a woodcut made at the time he was president of the Panama Railway Company.*

From *Harper's Monthly Magazine*, January, 1859

White man, unwilling to submit to the inexorable laws of this nature (by making himself an integrated part of the forest), came in 1509 with liquid excitement in his eyes. He assaulted this jungle fortress for centuries. He came in the person of Balboa, and crossed in clanking armor the dread Isthmus to discover the Pacific. Later, in 1519, man spilled across to build *Ciudad Panamá*, haughty and brave men in black velvet doublets collared with starched white ruffs. But they did not come to terms with the jungle, as did the Indian who had lived with it for centuries; white man opposed it. It was not the nocturnal jaguar that emptied his ranks, nor the herds of peccaries with their knife-sharp hoofs, nor the Indian whose ranks were quickly thinned with the harquebus and steel-tipped *partisans*. His enemies were smaller, each in itself insignificant, yet in the myriads in which they abounded in the jungle habitat, they, in the end, overwhelmed white man. The enemy were the antennaed insects; the large, the small, the buzzing, the crawling, the droning, flying, swimming, ubiquitous insecta; they govern the green world. There was the black-haired tarantula, as large as one's hand, that hunted in the dark interstices of the jungle; four-inch-long praying mantes, folding from their delicate waists their death scythes in an attitude of prayer. And the large yellow-bellied wasps. And huge scorpions that carried their exposed stings overhead. And ants, all forms of ants—harvesting ants, weaver ants, solitary ants, umbrella ants—and the terrible-mandibled *ecitons*, the army ants that move in solid black columns through the jungle, putting everything to flight. These were the insects that were to be seen and to be felt. There were others which one never saw, the cryptobiotic termites, working within all wooded things, night and day, day and night cutting with their serrated mandibles the very stuff which man regarded as solid. And the death-watch beetles. Panama was an entomological Elysium.

Yet it was the things that man did not see in Panama that killed him. In all the hours of his tropical day and night, there were insects to plague him; a mosquito of midday—the *Aëdes aegypti*—sucked his blood, and in terrible reciprocity introduced into his blood stream the yellow-fever scourge, the *vómito*, the Spaniards called it, since in one's last life-consuming fever there was painful retching, convulsive vomiting, until one's very entrails were wrenched loose and one died drowning in mucus and blood. And at dusk, came the thin whine of the *Anopheles* flying in from the stagnant pools where it had pupated from an aquatic form into an insatiable blood-sucking mosquito, the bearer of the malaria. It introduced into the blood stream terrible microscopic armies of flagellated protozoa. A dull pain in the back, a fierce headache, then the victim paled sheet-white, the finger nails turned blue, the body cold, the eyes bloodshot, and the infected one's teeth chattered as if he had just been fished from Arctic waters. Then, without prelude, heat, fever, an inferno raging, sweat pouring from every open pore until the very flesh seemed rendered. After that—death. And if not malaria, or *vómito*, then typhoid, dysentery, typhus, sprue, bubonic plague, filariasis, or encephalitis.

All these feverish plagues the American lumped into one generic name—the *Chagres fever*.

The Río Chagres flowed in twisting caprice for one hundred miles through the Isthmus, beginning as a tinkling rill near the Pacific and gathering hundreds of streams into its darkly sedimented body, brawling its way through the heavy parapets of the jungle until, many leagues later, in a surging flood of dark water, it poured into the Caribbean. Since the Chagres was the one navigable stream into Panama's interior, it had been used since the beginning of Spanish occupation. The Spaniards had built a fort at its Caribbean mouth to guard it, a huge, solid pile, meant to be impregnable. Now, in the memorable year of 1850, when the Isthmus was to undergo its final siege—the assault of Big Business—the fortress stood gaunt and blackened on its Chagres hill, strangled by the grey roots of the *matopalo* and smothered by the smooth green leaves of wild heliconias.

This was the Panama, which Stephens and his men were to defy; this was the Panama which was to hold the rails of the first transcontinental railway; this was the Panama which was, in effect, to be Stephens' deathbed.

No ceremony marked the beginning. On May 2, 1850, laborers, faces masked in netting, waded ashore, and under the direction of engineer James Baldwin fell to cutting the vegetation that covered the Isle of Manzanillo. Work on the railroad had begun. The Atlantic terminus of the railroad was to be located in Limon Bay on the mile-wide island right offshore. The island, fringed with mangrove which grew out of a noisome slime that emitted the odors of an undrained cesspool, was separated from the mainland by a narrow firth; this was to be trestled. Living quarters for the workmen were at first in the condemned hull of the old sidewheeler *Telegraph* anchored off the Río Chagres.

By August, the Manzanillo had been cleared and bridged with the mainland; by September's end, the project had lost half of its workers to Chagres fever. Others to replace them—Irish, Germans, and Negroes—in response to the posters which advertised "money, adventure, women," piled in on the Isthmus—and another station, Gatun (now the site of the Gatun Dam of the Panama Canal), seven miles inland was started. As Gatun was situated on the banks of the Río Chagres, vessels of small draft could move up the river and there dump the needed machinery, stores, and building material. The work of grading was carried on toward Limon Bay from here.

At the same time another engineer, James Young, was sent around the Horn with several vessels of equipment. He was to begin the rail line from the Pacific side, so that both sections, Atlantic and Pacific, would work toward each other. By October, 1851, the railroad was running eight miles between the terminus and Gatun, but it had drained the company's resources. Thus far the line had cost $350,000 a mile. On Wall Street the stock was beaten down far below its par value; and many men, including George Law, were selling their holdings as fast as they could unload. They looked to Stephens. And Stephens refused to let go. The company was refinanced, Aspinwall, Stephens, and Chauncey investing more of their own money when the market would absorb no more shares. They had to combat the terrible propaganda of the workers, for death had eaten huge holes in their ranks. There were so many dead that there was no longer any room on the small island for burial, for although Stephens, with unvarying Jacksonian principles, thought of the conditions of the workers, he was unable to stem the fearful mortalities of the Chagres fever. It appeared then that the Panama Railway would enter the lists of four centuries of failure.

Then gold! Gold fever was to change the destiny of the railroad, and with it, America. Gold fever was to overcome the disadvantages of the Chagres fever.

James Marshall's discovery of gold at Sutter's Mill did not bring, at least in the East, any immediate migration to the gold fields. The eastern newspapers printed the fantastic news without fanfare, merely as news items: "Oh this California," said the writer in the *Herald*, "this gold fever! it is turning the Californian country upside down, people are leaving their wives and daughters and laughing at an offer of ten dollars per day." Some in the East thought the "gold strike" an effort by President Polk to populate quickly his latest acquisition. But letters from California were being printed with precipitous editorial fervor: ". . . the immense quantity of gold daily gathered by the people . . . exceed in romance and riches the ancient stories of *El Dorado*."

The gold rush gained momentum. By autumn, 1849, the fever was in full spate. Vessels first were chartered to carry their passengers around Cape Horn, but this voyage was both dangerous and slow. Soon The Harnden Express Company was making arrangements to get people to the gold fields of California via Panama for two hundred dollars. Hotels sprang up on the sand bars below Chagres fortress; express companies, using natives as polers, were there like tropical leeches to bleed the gold seeker. When the builders of the Panama Railroad needed labor most, their workmen caught the gold fever, for men catch thoughts from one another as they take disease. Soon the whole Río Chagres was flooded with people California bound, men in red-checkered shirts, high cowhide boots, belts studded with bowie knives and revolvers. Women came, too, with their children; bankers, clergymen, and firemen joined the parade. *Ho! for California*. And the builders of the railroad merely suffered the gold seekers, for they impeded the work. Thousands continued to pour down upon the Isthmus. In vain did the editors of the *New York Herald* tell them: "Hurry out of the village of Chagres, which is pestilential. . . .

avoid the sun, do not sleep out of your boat, bear the heat, bear the mosquitoes, do anything rather than expose yourself to the night air. Take from two to four grains of quinine every morning." And yet they came on in streams singing a ditty called "Oh, Susanna."[8]

By autumn of 1851 so many dead lay on the Chagres trail that the coleopterous beetles had to work over time.

In November, 1851, two New York vessels, the *Georgia* and the *Philadelphia*, filled with more than one thousand California-bound passengers, arrived at Chagres, but the *chubasco*, whipping up huge waves, prevented the vessels from landing the passengers. The captains put into the wharfs at Limon Bay. There the railroad had erected a small hotel, a stone church, and workshops for the maintenance of its engines that ran the seven miles of line to Gatun, on the Río Chagres. The emigrants clamorously demanded that the railroad transport them these seven miles into the interior. Colonel Totten protested in vain. The road was not yet built for passengers; they had no accommodations for passengers, only flat work cars; rates had not been established. But to rid themselves of the frenetic gold seekers, they named an impossible sum, seven dollars for the seven miles. With loud huzzahs, the thousands of passengers flashed their rolls and were transported to Gatun. They had been saved the misery of a trip on the Chagres, and the railroad had been saved from the Panamanian limbo. For at a dollar a mile, and fifty cents a cubic foot freight, the rail line's seven miles began to make money. The passengers rode in open flat cars, crossed crazy trestles built of green lumber; some were scraped off by low hanging limbs, others tossed into the fetid waters. Still they came on.

[8] "I'll scrape the mountains, the
mountains clean, my boys,
I'll drain the rivers dry,
A pocket full of rocks bring home,
So brothers, don't you cry!
Oh, California!
That's the land for me,
I'm going to Sacramento,
With my washbowl on my knee."

Public confidence rose at once in the railroad. The stock soared. Credit was extended. The gold rush had saved the line. Henceforth people traveled the railroad rather than the Chagres route. It was little short of miraculous. By 1885 the line had earned $2,000,000 in rail fares alone and in its first ten years of operation $12,000,000—four million more than the entire cost of the road. Later it would earn a 24 per cent dividend. Ten years later it was considered the safest investment on Wall Street and by far the most successful enterprise ever attempted outside of the continental limits of the United States. After it had earned millions, the Panama Railroad was sold in 1877, to the French Panama Canal Company, for a cool $25,000,000.

With the financial crisis ended Stephens settled down midway between the two oceans to personally superintend the rail line. At Bujío Soldado (now submerged in the canal's waters), thirty miles up the Chagres, Stephens built a cottage. "It was here," runs a contemporary account, "that Mr. Stephens, whose fame as a traveler and writer is world-wide and whose later life was spent in developing this great railway enterprise, loved in his intervals of labor to rest in his hammock and enjoy the luxuriant beauties of the surrounding landscape."[9]

Yet these intervals of rest were growing increasingly long. Malaria, "his old enemy," was shaking him more and more frequently even though he daily consumed head-spinning doses of bitter quinine. In a moment of repose, he would suddenly be visited by a fierce headache and then the chills would come over him, shaking him until he was numbed with cold. At these moments, his dainty, dark-eyed housekeeper, who attended him in all matters, would take over the care of his fever-racked body.

Malaria had already driven Catherwood from Panama. In November, 1850, he turned a sickly green color after having had a perilous bout with black-water fever—the result of excessive quinine-taking and malarial fever—and Stephens insisted that he depart for a northern climate; he chose California. Stephens accompanied Catherwood, as he had so many times in their travels, in

[9] "The Panama Railroad," *Harpers New Monthly Magazine*, Vol. XVII, No. CIV (January, 1859), 159–61.

a palanquin to Panama City. There Catherwood was placed aboard the newly commissioned *Golden Gate*, a three-decked side-wheeler, built in New York for Aspinwall's Pacific Mail Steamship Company. On the ramparts of Panama they embraced each other for the last time. Stephens stood by, watching the *Golden Gate* until it was a thin ribbon of smoke on the tropical horizon. For the last time, for after a few years in California, surveying railroads and rubbing elbows with the argonauts of the gold rush, Catherwood returned to England. He was on his way back to California, in 1854, when he went down in the sinking S.S. *Arctic*.

Stephens worked with daimonic fury on the rail line, as if he wished to see it completed before he died. There was little doubt that he was very, very ill. The financial crisis solved by the revenues from the gold rush, he doubled the number of his employees; by 1851 the tracks were approaching Barbacoas, twenty-seven miles inland. The other section of the line—the Pacific side—was mushrooming at Panama City, the material supplied by ships from the Panama Mail Line that rounded the Horn, the plan—Stephens' plan—being that both sections of the line commence from the two oceans and meet midway in the Isthmus.

Panama now teemed with the sour breath of gold fever; people accustomed to the comparatively gentle life of the city left the United States to wander through the miasmas of Panama, clothed in coarse pants, red flannel shirts, their pants stuck into thick cowhide boots. In two years, twenty thousand people had flowed across the Isthmus, some coming up the Chagres, others by the rail line, and all, no matter in what conveyance they arrived, breathing the odor of riches and enveloped in the golden dreams of El Dorado. The *cimarrones* had reawakened under the impact. Lawless bushmen, half-Negro, half-Indian, they had lived in the jungle since the conquest, preying when opportunity offered on the mule trains of the Spanish colonists. Negro slaves brought from the black-belted Africa had escaped and had come to jungle terms with the Indian, mating in colored miscegenation. They became the dreaded *cimarrones*, feared only a fraction less than the dreaded *vómito*.

When commerce streamed to a mere trickle, they peacefully cultivated their manioc crops in the forested sections where they lived, but when it quickened under the impulse of railroad and gold, the *cimarrones* came to life again. They first began to appear on the "Cruces trail" at the small factor town (where in the period of Spanish occupation the wet-months' trail, the Chagres, met with the dry-months' trail, the road from Porto Bello). Las Cruces was the point of transshipment. Here in the cover of darkness, their bodies smeared with black pine-smudge, the *cimarrones* would waylay Americans, California bound. Travelers would just disappear. Then, weeks later, their bloated bodies, half-eaten by animals, feasted upon by burying beetles, would be discovered. The raiding soon reached serious proportions. Stephens protested to the Colombian authorities. They were unable to do anything to prevent the mounting crimes. Eventually the Panama Railroad brought down Ran Runnels, the famous Texas Ranger, "bestowing," said a Panama newspaper, "the liberal largess of four thousands a month upon Ran Runnels and his Ragged Regiment."

Gradually out of the chaos of the jungle, order, an American order, appeared. Hospitals were erected; quinine, discovered to be a specific against the Chagres fever, was placed upon dining tables for the workers. Dr. Chauncey Griswold was brought down from New York to organize the sanitation, and was put in charge of the main hospital, facing Stephens' cottage at Bujío Soldado. He found that the " 'ague' . . . with the judicious use of fifteen grains of quinine could be entirely removed, leaving patient, after one paroxysm, as well as he was before." Diarrhea and dysentery caused him more difficulties. Pneumonia was not infrequent. But malaria still remained the "curse" and until it was finally eliminated along with yellow fever by the American Canal Commission prior to the full construction of the canal, every enterprise disintegrated before it.

To Dr. Griswold—as well as to all medical science of that period—"*miasma* was the essential cause of the fevers." One avoided the evening air because of the "unhealthy exhalations which hover near the earth like smoke and fog." When Griswold arrived in Panama in April, 1851, for a six months' period, he gave one glance at Stephens and knew him to be infected with some virus. The two men saw a great deal of each other. Griswold, who later wrote a book which he dedicated to Stephens, *The Isthmus of Panama and What I Saw There*,[10] declared that "Mr. Stephens has been, emphatically, the pioneer in this enterprise, and the duties of his office could not have been placed in better hands, not only from his thorough knowledge of the country, and the habits of the people he had to deal with officially . . . but for his accurate judgment, liberal policy, and untiring devotion to the interests of the work."

But Stephens was paying for these "interests."

The intervals became less between the paroxysms of his malarial attacks. His body, which had held up so well from the trying days of his youthful travels in Arabia and the more terrifying Central American days, was falling apart. Yet he seemed to deem it an obligation on his part to assist travelers across the Isthmus. Many were personal friends. Jessie Benton Frémont, pale and outwardly delicate, came through the Isthmus with the personal assistance of Stephens, to join her husband in San Francisco. One of the most curious of meetings was the encounter with a small nervous German merchant—Heinrich Schliemann—bound for Sacramento to take charge of his brother Louis' estate in Sacramento.

---

[10] Published in New York in 1852 and dedicated to John Lloyd Stephens: ". . . Years ago, when I first read your books on Central America, I felt that I had made a new acquaintance, who introduced me to a better knowledge of a strange land, a peculiar people, with all that was known of a still more remarkable race which left but tottering monuments to tell us that they have existed.

"I little thought that it would ever be my privilege to know you, except as my instructor through your writings; and much less did I think it were possible that I should ever sit down with you beneath the shade of the Palm, in the same sunny clime, bordering on the field of your former investigations, and there listen while you taught me many things which I was so glad to learn.

"Since commencing the preparation of these pages for the press there is no name that has been more familiar in my thoughts that yours—not that we ever spoke one word together on the subject, for I had not the task in contemplation when I saw you last—but because I regard you more earnestly the author of works on facts, than of fiction; and as a slight tribute to one of the most useful among living writers, I crave the permission to dedicate this unpretending volume to you.

Chauncey D. Griswold

22 Warren Street
New York, December 1851"

Schliemann was then only twenty-eight years of age. The officers of the line were amazed that Herr Schliemann had come all the way from Russia, where he was a merchant, to claim the small inheritance left by his brother, who had died of the "typhoid" in Sacramento. They met, John Lloyd Stephens, discoverer of the lost world of the Mayas, and Heinrich Schliemann, who would, in the not too distant future—taking Homer at his word—discover the lost city of Troy and the golden treasures of Priam. Later the Frémonts returned, in the rainy season, when the streets of Panama were quagmires. And Jessie Benton Frémont remembered, in her later life, the visits of Stephens—"a beneficent gargoyle," she called him, "with his short squat body, unshapely head, long arms, beardless and wrinkled face." He had the Frémonts installed at Madame Acre's, a cousin of General Herrán, the Colombian ambassador in Washington, and there in the wet afternoon he would come over to visit them, murmuring in pallid whispers: "I have come to take my chill with you."[11]

Colonel Frémont, bound for Washington as a senator-elect from California, was bedridden with rheumatism, and Jessie, weakened by her ordeals, was physically unable to make the trans-Isthmian passage. John Stephens took charge. He found four of his best Indians, had them construct a palanquin, in which they were carried to the first train terminus. It was Stephens' last official act. That is, the next to last, for in February, 1852, it was decided to name the new city they had built in Limon Bay on the mangrove-bound islet of Manzanillo. Now there were wharfs where ships from New York and Europe debouched their cargo; hotels, whorehouses, and an Episcopal church, built of stone brought from Vermont. Stephens suggested that they call it "Aspinwall," after the name of one of the triumvirate of the Panama Railway, and Aspinwall it became, that is, to the Americans. But not to the Colombians. They insisted upon calling it "Colón" after the navigator who discovered America. They refused to accept any mail for the city named "Aspinwall." And the Americans refused to recognize a city called "Colón." The name remained a diplomatic

[11] Catherine Coffin Philips, *Jessie Benton Frémont: A Woman Who Made History* (San Francisco, 1935), 89, 100, 106, 169–70.

impasse for decades. There in 1855, on the completion of the rail-road, a monument was erected to the builders.

Days later, Stephens was found unconscious under a huge liana-draped ceiba tree[12] near Lion Hill beyond Gatun Station. The natives who found him at first thought him dead. No one had any idea how long he had lain, in a coma, under the giant ceiba. As they bore him away limp and unconscious to a vessel leaving for New York, rumor had it that he was dead.

For fifty years this tree was called "Stephens' Tree," for legend, more persistent than truth, had it that John Lloyd Stephens, finally succumbing to the tropical hydra, died under the ceiba tree.

[12] "The original lay-out of the road involved destruction this [ceiba] tree, but the admiration of Mr. Stephens for this Monarch of the woods was so great that he ordered a slight diversion of the line."—Donald Mitchell, *American Lands and Letters* (New York, 1899), 115–16.

Chapter XXII   In the end it was Stephens' "old enemy" that won. The malarial Plasmodia that had remained in his blood stream, that had descended upon him at intervals, chilling him and fevering him, had at last taken full possession of his body, but not as malaria. Stephens' liver had become infected. There was a general debilitation. Pains shot through his body. His brain was dull and confused. He had fallen into a lethargy. The disease, after considerable consultation, was diagnosed as hepatitis; the prognosis was death.

The hot summer days of New York's 1852 gave way to the first breathings of autumn. The sycamores outside 13 Leroy Place, russet with the first chilling whispers of fall, began to loose their foliage, the trefoil-shaped leaves glided slowly in the subtle air currents downward to the streets of Greenwich Village.

Propped up by the window, Stephens' eyes followed these leaves to the ground, watching them with those brilliant "great eyes" once so admired by young Herman Melville. His eyes were now the only elements of animation. He was slowly dessicating as if death were emptying all his vital juices. His ironical humor he tried to maintain to the end. In playing out the human comedy, he insisted with mock firmness to his doctors that they must have him up by the end of September so that he could be present at the launching of a ship that would bear his name. For his friend William H. Aspinwall could think of no greater honor than to name the new flag vessel of the Panama Mail Steamship Company, the magnificent side-wheeler, the 275-foot-long vessel destined for the California run, the S.S. *John L. Stephens.*

On September 22, 1852, the ship was launched from the yards of Smith and Dimon, the ceremonies attended by the Honorable Benjamin Stephens, "a retired merchant of wealth and probity" who represented his son. For many years this ship was John Lloyd

Stephens' only immortality. He had fallen into a coma the day the ship was launched, and he died on October 13, 1852, without regaining consciousness.

"The death of the celebrated traveller, John L. Stephens," wrote the *New York Daily Tribune*, "which took place on Tuesday evening at the residence of his father in this city, will cause a lively emotion of sorrow, not alone in the large circle of personal friends, to whom he was the object of distinguished pride and affection, but in the far wider sphere of intelligent persons who have been indebted to his admirable writings for rare and valuable information, as well as mental entertainment of the choicest character." Then Stephens was forgotten; he was buried in the wrong tomb, in Marble Cemetery,[1] in an unmarked grave. He and the civilizations he had discovered died with Manifest Destiny.

It was not until fifty years later, when North America had expanded to its optimum, that Americans again had leisure to turn their interests to the elements that make America America. In Stephens' footsteps, all inspired by his books and his discoveries, came the famous names of archaeology: Maudslay, Goodman, Brinton, Brendt, Schellas, Seler, Maler, Gordon, Thompson, Bandelier, Charnay, Gates, Spinden, Morley, Joyce, Tozzer, Gann, Kidder, Mason, Lothrop, Valliant, Blom, Eric Thompson, La Farge—and the ancient American map was unrolled. "I well remember," said Dr. Alfred M. Tozzer of Harvard, "how, forty years ago, I began my first lecture on Maya archaeology. . . . 'From the delightful descriptions of Stephens aided by the faithful pencil of Catherwood, we learn for the first time of the magnitude and the magnificence of the Maya civilization. . . . After one hundred years, these descriptions are still read and these drawings are still studied by archaeologists and by laymen interested in this part of our continent.' "

---

[1] Records of the New York City Marble Cemetery (Second Avenue between First and Second Avenues): "October 15, 1852. Interred (in Vault #240 standing in the name of Ferris Pell) J. S. Stephens . . . Sexton MacLain."

See Harvey E. Molé, "John L. Stephens, Traveler," *Proceedings* of the New Jersey Historical Society, Vol. LXI, No. 2 (April, 1943), 98–115.

Chronology 1805 Stephens born, November 28, Shrewsbury, Monmouth County, New Jersey.

1806   Stephens' family moves to New York, 185 Greenwich Street.

1812   Enters school of Mr. Boyle.

1815–17 Classical School of Joseph Nelson.

1818–22 Columbia College, A.B. (1828, M.A.).

1822–24 Tapping Reeve Law School, Litchfield, Connecticut.

1824   Tour of the Illinois prairies; floats down Mississippi to New Orleans.

1825–34 Law practice, 67 Wall Street; politics in New York. Home, 13 Leroy Place, Greenwich Village.

1834–35 Travels: England, France, Italy, Greece, Turkey, Russia, and Poland.

1835–36 Travels: Malta, Egypt, Arabia Petraea, Jerusalem, and the Levant.

1837   New York: publishes *Incidents of Travel in Egypt and Arabia Petraea.*

1838   Publishes *Incidents of Travel in Greece, Turkey, Russia, and Poland.*

1839   Archaeological expedition, with Frederick Catherwood, to Belize, Central America, Mexico, and Yucatán; returns, autumn, 1841.

1841   New York: publishes *Incidents of Travel in Central America;* leaves again for Yucatán, with Catherwood and Dr. Samuel Cabot; returns, summer, 1842.

1843   New York: publishes *Incidents of Travel in Yucatán.*

1846   Delegate, New York Constitutional Convention.

1847   Official, Ocean Steam Navigation Company; goes to Germany, meets Humboldt.

1847   Publishes "An Hour with Humboldt" in the *Living Age Magazine.*

301

1848   Secures with Aspinwall and Chauncey the option to build a railroad across the Isthmus of Panama.

1849–51 Involved in building railroad; president of the Panama Rail Road Company.

1852   Dies, October 5, in New York; buried in unmarked grave in Old Marble Cemetery.

Bibliography There is a strange paucity of materials on John Lloyd Stephens. Somewhere, unless they have been destroyed, are the personal letters, journals, and half-completed manuscripts which he willed to his father, Benjamin Stephens, in 1852, although extensive research has failed to reveal them. The published primary sources of Stephens' life are few, fragmentary, and in the main repetitious. These, in the order of their appearance, are:

New York Daily Tribune, editorial, October 14, 1852: "John Lloyd Stephens."

New York Times, obituary, October 14, 1852: "John Lloyd Stephens."

Hawks, Francis Lister. "The Later John L. Stephens," *Putnam's Monthly Magazine*, Vol. I (1853), 64–68.

Catherwood, Frederick (ed.). *Incidents of Travel in Central America*, by John Lloyd Stephens. London, 1854, 2 vols. "Biographical Notice," 2 pp., with engraving from daguerreotype.

Duyckinck, E. A., and G. L. "Stephens," in Vol. II of *Cyclopedia of American Literature*. 2 vols. Pp. 146–49, with portrait of Stephens, p. 147.

"Oran." "Stephens and the Panama Railroad," *Harper's New Monthly Magazine*, Vol. XVIII, No. CIV (January, 1859), 146–49. Portrait of Stephens, p. 147.

Carrillo y Ancona, Crescencio. "Mr. John Lloyd Stephens," in *Reseña Biografica*. Mérida, 1863.

Martínez Alomía, Gustavo. *Historiadores de Yucatán*. Campeche, 1906. Pp. 159–62.

Encyclopedia Brittanica, eleventh edition. 1910. "John Lloyd Stephens," Vol. XXV, 888.

Case, Henry. *Views on and of Yucatán*. Mérida, 1911. Pp. 43, 45, 88, 101, 228.

Spinden, Herbert J. "The Stephens Sculptures from Yucatán," *Natural History Magazine*, Vol. XX (1920), 379–89.

Kelemen, Pál. *Battlefield of the Gods*. London, 1937. Chapter entitled "Two American Law Graduates" (Prescott and Stephens).

Albion, Robert G. "John Lloyd Stephens," in the *Dictionary of American Biography*, Vol. XVII, 579–80.

Lizardi, Ramos Cesar. "*La Vida Heroica de Juan Lloyd Stephens*," *Revista de Revistas, Ano* XXVIII (February, 1938).

Dauterman, Carl C. "The Strange Story of the Stephens Stones," *Natural History Magazine*, Vol. XLIV (1939), 288–94.

Von Hagen, Victor W. *Jungle in the Clouds*. New York, 1940. "Stephens," pp. 162–223.

Rodríguez Beteta, Virgilio. "*Es Celebrado el Centenario del Viaje de Stephens a Centro America 1840–1940 Descubridor de la Cultura Maya*," Soc. de Geog. e Hist. de Guat. *Anales*, Vol. XVI (1941), 490–92.

"The Discoverer of a New World in the New World," Pan American Union *Bulletin*, Vol. LXXV (1941), 12–19.

"*El Centenario de un Libro que en Tres Meses Alcanzo Diez Ediciones el de* John L. Stephens 'Incidents of Travel in Central America, Chiapas, and Yucatán,'" Soc. de Geog. e Hist. de Guat. *Anales*, Vol. XVII (1941), 66–73.

Lizardi, Ramos Cesar. *Los Mayas Antiguos*. Mexico, 1941. A book of archaeological papers dedicated to the memory of Stephens and Catherwood. Of particular significance to Stephens are the following: "*Bibliografía de* John Lloyd Stephens," *por* Arthur E. Gropp (pp. 19–32); "Stephens and Prescott, Bancroft and others," by Dr. Alfred M. Tozzer (pp. 33–60); "*Cien Anos Después de* Stephens," *por* Enrique Juan Palacio (pp. 276–342).

Kelemen, Pál. "The Stephens Centenary," *El Palacio*, Vol. XLVIII (May, 1941), 97–110.

Molé, Harvey E. "John L. Stephens, Traveler," *Proceedings* of the New Jersey Historical Society, Vol. LXI, No. 2 (April, 1943), 98–114.

Von Hagen, Victor W. "Frederick Catherwood, Archt," *New York Historical Society Quarterly*, Vol. XXX (1946), 17–29.

———. "How the Lost Cities of the Maya Were Rediscovered," *Travel Magazine*, Vol. LXXXVI, No. 6 (April, 1946).

———. "Waldeck," *Natural History Magazine*, Vol. LV, No. 10 (December, 1946).

———. "Blazing the Trail for the Panama Canal," *Travel Magazine*, Vol. LXXXVIII, No. 2 (December, 1946).

———. "Mr. Catherwood is also Missing," *Natural History*, Vol. LVI, No. 1 (March, 1947).

I

To set the scene of Stephens' ancestry and birth, his life in New York, grammar schooling, college, the law school at Litchfield, and his first journeys to the Illinois country, I used, in one way or another, the following:

Beck, Henry C. *Fare to Midlands.* New York, 1939.

Branch, E. Douglas. *The Sentimental Years.* New York, 1934.

Brooks, Van Wyck. *The World of Washington Irving.* New York, 1944.

Burnaby, Andrew. *Travels Through the Middle Settlements.* New York, 1904.

Dayton, Abram C. *The Last Days of Knickerbocker Life.* New York, 1882.

Elliss, Franklin. *The History of Monmouth County.* Freehold, New Jersey, 1885.

Fish, Carl Russell. *The Rise of the Common Man.* New York, 1927.

Fisher, Samuel H. *The Litchfield Law School.* New Haven, 1933.

Fox, George. *The Journal of George Fox.* New York, 1924.

Haswell, Charles W. *Reminiscences of an Octogenarian of New York.* New York, 1897.

Hone, Philip. *Diary*, ed. by Bayard Tuckerman. New York, 1889, 2 vols.

———. *Diary of Philip Hone*, ed. by Allan Nevins. New York, 1927, 2 vols.

———. Diary, holograph, 28 vols. In possession of the New York Historical Society.

Horner, William S. *This Old Monmouth of Ours.* Freehold, New Jersey, 1932.

Lundin, Leonard. *New Jersey, Cockpit of the Revolution.* Princeton, 1944.

Mandeville, Ernest W. *The Story of Middletown.* Middletown, Conn., 1927.

Mansfield, E. D. *Personal Memories, Social, Political, and Literary.* Cincinnati, 1879.

Minnigerode, Meade. *The Fabulous Forties.* New York, 1924.

Salter, Edwin. *The History of Monmouth and Ocean Counties.* Bayonne, New Jersey, 1889.

Schlesinger, Arthur M., Jr. *The Age of Jackson.* New York, 1945.

Stillwell, John E. M. D. *Historical and Genealogical Miscellany.* New York, 1932, 5 vols.

Steen, James. *History of Christ Church, Shrewsbury.* Shrewsbury, New Jersey, n.d.

Stone, William L. *The Centennial History of New York City.* New York, 1876.

Vanderpoel, Emily Noyes. *Chronicles of a Pioneer School.* Cambridge, 1903.

———. *More Chronicles of a Pioneer School.* New York, 1927.

II

For the section that deals with Stephens' voyage to Europe, Greece, Egypt, Arabia Petra, the Holy Land, and his return to New York, where he published his first two books, I have used:

Allibone, S. Austin. *Critical Dictionary of English Literature.* Philadelphia, 1877.

Armstrong, Margaret. *Trelawney.* New York, 1840.

Bulwer-Lytton, H. *An Autumn in Greece.* London, 1826.

Burckhardt, John Lewis. *Arabic Proverbs, etc.* London, 1830.

———. *Travels in Arabia, etc.* London, 1829, 2 vols.

———. *Travels in Nubia.* London, 1819.

———. *Travels in Syria and the Holy Land.* London, 1822.

Dearden, Seton. *Burton of Arabia.* New York, 1937.

Denon, Vinant. *Travels in Upper and Lower Egypt.* London, 1803.

Dinsmoor, William. "Early Studies of Mediterranean Archaeology," *Proceedings,* American Philosophical Society, Vol. LXXXVII, No. 1. Philadelphia, 1943.

Dodwell, Henry. *A Study of Muhammad 'Ali, Founder of Modern Egypt.* Cambridge, 1931.

Doughty, Charles M. *Travels in Arabia Deserta.* New York, 1923, 2 vols.

Gliddon, George R. *The American in Egypt.* Philadelphia, 1842.

Guedella, Philip. *Palmerston.* London, 1927.

Harper, J. Henry. *The House of Harper.* New York, 1912.

Hemstreet, Charles. *Literary New York.* New York, 1903.

Howe, Samuel G. *An Historical Sketch of the Greek Revolution.* New York, 1828. 2nd edition.

Laborde, Léon de. *Voyage de l'Arabie Petrée, par Léon de Laborde et Linant.* Paris, 1830; English trans., London, 1838, 2nd edition.

Legh, Thomas. *Narrative of a Journey in Egypt and the Country Beyond the Cataracts* (in the year 1812). London, 1816.

——. *Travels in Egypt, Nubia, Holy Land, Mount Lebanon, and Cyprus* (in the year 1814). London, 1818.

——. "Excursion from Jerusalem to Wady Musa," in William Macmichael's *Journey from Moscow to Constantinople* (in the years 1817–18). Chap. IV, p. 185. London, 1819.

Loti, Pierre. *La Mort de Philae.* New York and Paris, 1900.

Ludwig, Emil. *The Nile.* New York, 1941.

Mabie, Hamilton W. *The Writers of Knickerbocker New York.* New York, 1912.

Nichols, Thomas Low. *Forty Years of American Life.* New York, 1937.

Robinson, George L. *The Sarcophagus of an Ancient Civilization, Petra, Edom and Edomites.* New York, 1930.

Steindorff, George. *Egypt,* with photographs by Hoyningen-Huene. New York, 1943.

Trent, W. P. *The Cambridge History of American Literature.* Part III, "National Literature." New York, 1918.

Trübner, Nicolas. *The Bibliographical Guide to American Literature.* London, 1859.

Turnbull, Archibald. *David Porter.* New York, 1929.

Waugh, A. *A Hundred Years of Publishing.* London, 1930.

Winwar, Frances. *The Romantic Rebels.* New York, 1935.

The reviews of Stephens' first book, *Incidents of Travel in . . . Arabia Petraea* (New York, 1837), are: Philip Hone's Diary, Vol. 13, pp. 141–59; *Princeton Review* (A. Alexander), Vol. X, No. 10 (1838), pp. 55 ff.; *North American Review* (Lewis Cass), Vol. XLVIII (1838), pp. 181–256; *New York Review* (Edgar Allan Poe), Vol. I (1837), pp. 351–67; *The American Monthly,* Vol. III (1837), p. 406 ff.; *Christian Examiner* (Henry Ware, Jr.), Vol. XXIV (1838), pp. 31–47; *American Quarterly Review,* Vol. XXI (1837), pp. 439–58; *Knickerbocker Magazine,* Vol. IX (1837), pp. 515–20.

Reviews of *Incidents of Travel in Greece, Turkey, Russia, and Poland* (New York, 1838): *Christian Review,* Vol. XIV (1838), pp. 162–80; *New York Review* (Edgar Allan Poe), Vol. III (1838), pp. 460–63; *Dublin University Magazine,* Vol. XIII (1839), pp. 338–49.

III

For the part of the book that concerns Stephens' first inquiry into ancient American civilizations and the history of Central America, I have consulted and used:

Bartlett, John Russell. *Journal of.* MS in the collections of the John Carter Brown Library.

Galindo, Juan, Col. "The Ruins of Copán in Central America," in *Proceedings* of the American Antiquarian Society, Vol. II, 543–50. Worcester, Mass., 1835.

García, Gregorio. *Origin de los Indios.* Madrid, 1729.

Godbey, Allen H. *The Lost Tribes, a Myth.* Durham, N. C., 1930.

Humboldt, Alexander von. *Vues des Cordillères, et Monuments de Peuples Indigènes de l'Amérique.* Paris, 1809.

Kingsborough, Lord. *Antiquities of Mexico.* London, 1831–48, 9 vols.

Manning, W. R. (ed.). *Diplomatic Correspondence of the United States: Inter-American Affairs (1831–1860), Central America.* Washington, 1932.

Martínez López, E. *Biografía del Gen. Francisco Morazán.* Tegucigalpa, 1941.

Mitchell, J. Leslie. *The Conquest of the Maya.* New York, 1935.

Reyes, R. *Vida de Morazán.* San Salvador, 1925.

Spence, Lewis. *The Problem of Atlantis.* New York, 1924.

Spinden, Herbert J. "Origin of Civilization in Central America and Mexico," in *The American Aborigines,* ed. by D. Jenness. Toronto, 1933.

IV

For Central America, its history and description:

Baily, John. *Central America, etc.* London, 1850. (Baily made the first accurate survey of the proposed Nicaraguan Canal, commissioned by General Francisco Morazán, when he was president. Baily turned over all his reports to Stephens, who used them in his book *Incidents of Travel in Central America.*

Bancroft, H. H. *History of Central America.* San Francisco, 1883.

Burdon, Major Sir John. *Brief Sketch of British Honduras.* London, 1937.

Dunlop, R. G. *Travels in Central America.* London, 1847.

Dunn, Henry. *Guatimala: or the United Provinces of Central America in 1827–28; Being Sketches and Memorandums Made During a Twelve Month Residence in That Republic.* New York, 1828.

Elliott-Joyce, L. E. *Central America.* London, 1925.

Gage, Thomas. *The English-American; a New Survey of the West Indies,* ed. by A. P. Newton. London, 1928.

Honduras Almanack, The. London, 1830.

Huxley, Aldous. *Beyond the Mexique Bay.* New York, 1934.

Juarros, Domingo. *Compendio de las Historia de la Ciudad de Guatemala.* Guatemala, 1808, 2 vols.; English translation by John Baily, 1823 (1825).

Lockhorst (M. van). *État de Guatémala.* 14 lithographic views, scenery, and towns. Paris, 1840.

Montgomery, G. W. *Narrative of a Journey to Guatemala.* New York, 1838.

Montúfar, Lorenzo. *Reseña Historica de Centro-America.* Guatemala, 1887, 8 vols. (Has a contemporary portrait of Francisco Morazán, Vol. II, p. 72.)

Morelet, Arthur. *Voyage dans l'Amérique Centrale, etc.* Paris, 1857, 2 vols.

Popenoe, Mrs. Dorothy. *Santiago de los Caballeros.* Cambridge, 1935.

Squier, E. G. *Nicaragua.* New York, 1852, 2 vols.

———. *Notes on Central America.* New York, 1855.

———. *The States of Central America.* New York, 1858.

Thompson, G. A. *An Official Visit to Guatemala.* London, 1829.

Wells, William V. *Explorations and Adventures in Honduras.* New York, 1857.

The list of books used in describing Stephens' expedition to the Mayas is in no sense a bibliography of the immense collection of literature on the Maya. Only those works used specifically for the explanation of Stephens' Maya journeys are given here.

Bancroft, H. H. *Antiquities,* Vol. IV of *The Native Races.* San Francisco, 1882, 5 vols.

Blom, Frans. *The Conquest of Yucatán.* Boston, 1936.

———, and La Farge, Oliver. *Tribes and Temples.* New Orleans, 1926–27, 2 vols.

Cabrera, Félix de. *Description of the Ruins of an Ancient City Discovered near Palenque.* London, 1822.

Caddy, John Herbert. "The City of Palenque." MS report. 1840. (Known only by the description given to this important, never published work by Marshall Saville in his "Bibliographic Notes on Palenque.")

Catherwood, Frederick. *Views of Ancient Monuments*. London, 1844.

Charnay, Désiré. *The Ancient Cities of the New World*, trans. by J. G. and H. S. Conant. New York, 1887.

Cogolludo, Diego López de. *Historia de Yucatán*. Mérida, 1867–68, 2 vols.

Dupaix, Guillelmo. *Antiquités Mexicaines*. Paris, 1834, 2 vols.

Fernández, Miguel A. "*El Tiemplo Num. 5 de Tulum*," in *Los Maya Antiguos (q.v.)*, pp. 157–80.

Friederichsthal, E. "*Les Monuments de l'Yucatán par M. le Chevalier Emmanuel de Friederichsthal*," in *Nouvelles Annales de Voyages*, Vol. XCII, pp. 291–314. Paris, 1841. (The first modern reference to Chichen Itzá.)

Gann, Thomas, and Thompson, Eric. *The History of the Maya*. New York, 1931.

Gordon, G. B. *Prehistoric Ruins of Copán, Honduras*. Cambridge, 1896.

———. *The Hieroglyphic Stairway, Ruins of Copán*. Cambridge, 1902.

Hall, J. Louis, Jr. *River of Ruins*. New York, 1941.

Holmes, William H. *Archaeological Studies Among the Ancient Cities of Mexico*. Chicago, 1895–97.

Jenness, Diamond (ed.). *The American Aborigines*. Toronto, 1933.

Joyce, T. A. *Maya and Mexican Art*. London, 1927.

Kelemen, Pál. *Medieval American Art*. New York, 1943, 2 vols.

Lothrop, S. K. *Tulum, an Archaeological Study of the East Coast of Yucatán*. Washington, 1924.

Lundell, C. L. "Phytogeography of the Yucatán Peninsula," in *Contributions to American Archaeology*, Vol. XI, No. 12, 255–321. Washington, 1934.

Maler, T. "*Yukatekische Forshungen*," *Globus*, Vols. LXXXIII, LXVIII. Braunschweig, 1902.

Martínez Alomía, Gustavo. *Historiadores de Yucatán*. Campeche, 1906.

Maudslay, Anne Cary, and A. P. *A Glimpse at Guatemala and Some Notes on the Ancient Monuments of Central America*. London, 1899.

Maudslay, A. P. (ed.). *Archaeology. Biología Centrali-Americana,* ed. by F. DuCane Godman and Osbert Salvin. London, 1889–1902, 4 vols.

Maya Antiguos, Los. Mexico, 1941.

Mitchell, J. Leslie. *The Conquest of the Maya.* New York, 1935.

Morley, Dr. S. G. *The Inscriptions at Copán.* Washington, 1920. (One of the finest studies of Copán, by the greatest of Maya scholars.)

——. *Guide Book to the Ruins of Quiriguá.* Washington, 1935.

——. *The Ancient Maya.* Palo Alto, 1946.

Morris, E. H., Charlot, Jean, and Morris, A. A. *The Temple of the Warriors at Chichen Itzá.* Washington, 1931.

Mumford, Lewis. *Technics and Civilization.* New York, 1939.

——. *Culture of Cities.* New York, 1941.

Norman, B. M. *Rambles in Yucatán.* New York, 1843.

Pollock, H. E. D. "Sources and Methods in the Study of Maya Architecture," in *The Maya and Their Neighbors,* pp. 179–201. New York, 1940.

Rau, Charles. *The Palenque Tablet in the U. S. National Museum.* Washington, 1876.

Roys, Ralph L. *The Indian Background of Colonial Yucatán.* Washington, 1943.

Saville, Marshall H. "Bibliographic Notes on Uxmal, Yucatán," *Indian Notes and Monographs,* Vol. IX, No. 2. New York, 1921.

Sauer, Carl O. "A Geographic Sketch of Early Man in America," *Geographical Review,* Vol. XXXIV, No. 4 (1944).

Seler, Eduard. *Die Ruinen von Uxmal.* Akademie der Wissenschaften No. 3. Berlin, 1917.

Spengler, Oswald. *The Decline of the West.* New York, 1932.

Spinden, H. J. *A Study of Maya Art.* Cambridge, 1913.

——. *Ancient Civilizations of Mexico and Central America.* New York, 1913. Revised edition.

——. "The Population of Ancient America," *Geographical Review,* Vol. XVIII, No. 4 (October, 1928), 641–60.

Standley, Paul C. *Flora of Yucatán.* Chicago, 1930.

Thompson, E. H. "The Ruins of Labna." MS in Peabody Museum, Harvard University. 1889.

Tozzer, Alfred M. *Landa's "Relación de las Cosas de Yucatán."* Cambridge, 1941.

Velásquez, Pedro. *Memoir of an Eventful Expedition in Central America . . . Described by John L. Stephens.* New York, 1850.

Von Hagen, Victor Wolfgang. *"Les Ruines de Copán, Metropole des Mayas,"* *l'Illustration* (Paris), July, 1939.
——. "Cities of the Mayas, Copán," *The Geographical Magazine,* Vol. VIII, No. 3 (January, 1939).
——. *The Aztec and Maya Papermakers.* New York, 1943.
Waldeck, Jean Frédéric. *Voyage Pittoresque et Archéologique dans la Province d'Yucatán.* Paris, 1838.
——, and Brasseur de Bourbourg, C. E. *Monuments Anciens du Mexique: Palenqué et Autres Ruines de l'Ancienne Civilisation du Mexique.* Paris, 1866.

V

For that section of this volume which concerns Stephens' books, the reviews of his *Central America* and *Yucatán*, as well as the details of his life between 1843–47, I have used the following:

Babcock, F. Lawrence. *Spanning the Atlantic.* New York, 1931.
Beach, Moses Yale (ed.). *Wealth and Pedigree of the Wealthy Citizens of New York City.* New York, 1842.
Bowen, Frank C. *A Century of Atlantic Travel.* London, 1927.
Christman, Henry. *Tin Horns and Calico.* New York, 1945.
Curry, Daniel. *New York, by a New Yorker.* New York, 1853.
Fish, Carl Russell. *History of the State of New York.* New York, 1934.
Francis, C. S. *A Picture of New York in 1848.* New York, 1848.
Journal of the Convention of the State of New York. Albany, 1846.
Lincoln, Charles Z. *Constitutional History of New York.* Rochester, 1906.
Merchants Magazine, The, Vol. XVII, No. 4 (October, 1847), 357–64.
Michaelis, Prof. A. *A Century of Archaeological Discoveries.* New York, 1908.
Morrison, John H. *History of American Steam Navigation.* New York, 1903.
Prescott, William H. *The Correspondence of William Hickling Prescott,* ed. by Roger Wolcott. Boston, 1925.
Priego de Arjona, Mireya. *Las Ediciones en Español de la Obra de John L. Stephens "Incidents of Travel in Yucatán."* Bib-Yucateca No. 7-3-6. Mérida, 1939.
Sabin, Joseph. *Biblioteca Americana.* New York, 1868–1937, 29 vols. "Stephens" in Vol. XXIII.
Schlesinger, Arthur M. *The Age of Jackson.* New York, 1945.

Scoville, J. A. *Old Merchants of New York City*. New York, 1862.

Stephens, John Lloyd. "An Hour with Humboldt," *Littell's Living Age Magazine*, Vol. XV (1847), 151 ff.

Villacorta C., J. Antonio. *"El Primer Centenario de un Libro"* (Stephens, 1841), Soc. de Geog. e Historia de Guatemala *Anales*, Vol. XVII (1941), pp. 62–65.

Villalobos, Angel. *Antiguos Poscedores del Continente Americano "Colmena"* (Vols. I and II). Mexico, 1842–43.

Wilson, J. G. *Memorial History of the City of New York*. New York, 1893, 4 vols.

The reviews given to Stephens' *Incidents of Travel in Central America, Chiapas, and Yucatán* (New York, 1841) were found in: *North American Review* (J. G. Palfrey) Vol. LIII (1841), pp. 479–506; *Edinburgh Review* Vol. LXXV (1842), pp. 397–421; *Chambers' Edinburgh Journal*, Vol. XLVIII, pp. 764 ff.; *Dublin University Magazine*, Vol. XII (1842), pp. 184 ff.; *Monthly Review* (London), Vol. CLVI (1841), pp. 30 ff.; *New Englander*, Vol. I, pp. 419–34; *New Quarterly Review* (London), Vol. III, pp. 416 ff.; *New York Review*, Vol. IX, pp. 225–42; *Quarterly Review* (London), Vol. LXIX (1841), pp. 52–91; *The Athenaeum* (London), 1841, pp. 575 ff.; *The North American Review*, Vol. LIII, pp. 479–506; *Graham's Magazine* (Edgar Allan Poe), August, 1841.

Reviews of Stephens' *Incidents of Travel in Yucatán* (New York, 1843, 2 vols.) are found in the following: *The New Englander*, Vol. I (1843), pp. 419–34; *The United States Magazine and Democratic Review* (Henry Ware, Jr.), Vol. XII (1843), pp. 491–501; *The Southern Literary Messenger*, Vol. IX, pp. 509–11; *Dublin University Magazine*, Vol. XXIII, pp. 204–22; *The Athenaeum* (London), 1843, pp. 203 ff.; Knickerbocker *Magazine*, Vol. XVI (June, 1843), pp. 364–67; *Christian Family Magazine*, Vol. II (1843), p. 196; *The New Quarterly Review* (London), Vol. III (1854), pp. 416 ff.; *Methodist Quarterly*, Vol. III (1843), pp. 288–302; *North American Review*, (J. Inman), Vol. LVII (1843), pp. 86–108; *Eclectic Museum* (London), Vol. II (1844), pp. 249–54.

VI

For the final part of Stephens' active life that deals with the building of the Panama railway, the gold rush, and all other allied events, and which leads to his death, I have used these books:

Anderson, C. L. G. *Old Panama and Castillo del Oro*. Boston, 1914.

Arciniegas, German. *Caribbean*. New York, 1946.

Bancroft, H. H. *History of California*. San Francisco, 1884.

Bishop, Farnham. *Panama, Past and Present*. New York, 1913.

Castillero, Ernest J. *El Ferrocarril de Panama y su Historia*. Panama, 1932.

Derienni; or Land Pirates of the Isthmus. Being a True and Graphic History of Robberies, Assassinations. Philadelphia, 1853.

Fabens, J. W. *A Story of the Isthmus*. New York, 1853.

Frémont, Jessie Benton. *Souvenirs of My Time*. Boston, 1887.

Gage, Thomas. *The English-American; a New Survey of the West Indies*, ed. by A. P. Newton. First published in 1648. London, 1928.

Griswold, Chauncey D. *The Isthmus of Panama, and What I Saw There*. New York, 1852.

Kemble, John Haskell. *The Panama Route, 1848–1869*. Berkeley, 1943.

Knower, Daniel. *The Adventures of a Forty-niner*. Albany, 1894.

Mack, Gerstle. *The Land Divided; a History of the Panama Canal and Other Isthmian Canal Projects*. New York, 1944.

Miner, Dwight C. *The Fight for the Panama Route*. New York, 1940.

Nevins, Allan (ed.). *The Diary of Polk (1845–49)*. New York, 1929.

"Oran." "Stephens and the Panama Railroad," *Harper's New Monthly Magazine*, Vol. XVIII, No. CIV (January, 1859), 145–69.

Otis, Fessenden N. *History of the Panama Railroad*. New York, 1867.

Panama Railroad Company. Collection, Miscellaneous material. MS Division, The New York Public Library. 58 items.

———. Incorporation. *Laws of New York*, 72nd Session, Chap. 284. Albany, 1849.

———. *Memorial . . . to the Congress of the United States*, 1849.

———. *Prospectus*. New York, 1849.

Stone, Irving. *Immortal Wife, a Biographical Novel of Jessie Benton Frémont*. New York, 1944.

Taylor, Bayard. *Eldorado, or Adventures in the Path of Empire*. New York, 1864.

Tomes, Robert. *Panama in 1855*. New York, 1855.

The end:

McKelway, St. Clair. "The Marble Cemeteries," *The New Yorker*, August 4, 1934.

New York Daily Tribune, October 14, 1852; October 16, 1854.

New York Times, October 14, 1852; October 13, 17, 1854.

Index

316

319

MAYA EXPLORER

HAS BEEN SET

IN THE ELEVEN POINT SIZE

OF LINOTYPE JANSON